Louisianians in the
Western Confederacy

Louisianians in the Western Confederacy

The Adams-Gibson Brigade in the Civil War

STUART SALLING

McFarland & Company, Inc., Publishers
Jefferson, North Carolina, and London

LIBRARY OF CONGRESS CATALOGUING-IN-PUBLICATION DATA

Salling, Stuart, 1973–
Louisianians in the western Confederacy : the Adams-Gibson brigade in the Civil War / Stuart Salling.
p. cm.
Includes bibliographical references and index.

ISBN 978-0-7864-4218-8
softcover : 50# alkaline paper ∞

1. Confederate States of America. Army. Adams-Gibson Brigade.
2. United States — History — Civil War, 1861–1865 — Regimental histories.
3. Louisiana — History — Civil War, 1861–1865 — Regimental histories.
4. United States — History — Civil War, 1861–1865 — Campaigns. I. Title.
E565.5.A33S25 2010   973.7'463 — dc22   2010011968

British Library cataloguing data are available

©2010 Stuart Salling. All rights reserved

No part of this book may be reproduced or transmitted in any form or by any means, electronic or mechanical, including photocopying or recording, or by any information storage and retrieval system, without permission in writing from the publisher.

Cover photograph: Attack on the Hornets Nest. Part of a cyclorama painted of the Battle of Shiloh in which Gibson's Brigade was included. In the background, cluster of horses, Gibson is depicted with his staff. In the foreground are parts of the 1st Arkansas (left) and 13th Louisiana (right). At the far left, the officer on horseback getting shot is Lieutenant Colonel Thompson of the 1st Arkansas (courtesy of the U.S. Army Military History Institute)

Manufactured in the United States of America

*McFarland & Company, Inc., Publishers
Box 611, Jefferson, North Carolina 28640
www.mcfarlandpub.com*

To the memory of those men from
Louisiana who sacrificed so much and
have received so little in return

Acknowledgments

I would like to first and foremost thank my Lord and Savior Jesus Christ in providing the ability and opportunity for this endeavor. Much appreciation to my family in their support and sacrifices they made in my undertaking this project. My wife, Stephanie, deserves most of my appreciation for her continual support in many capacities from helping in interpreting old letters, support in extensive research, and her literary suggestions and editing. She has made this project possible through her own sacrifices and her patience over the past 15 years.

I would like to thank the open and friendly support of Confederate Memorial Hall in New Orleans, its staff and Glen Cangelosi. Glen's generosity and assistance was equaled only by the assistance of Wayne Cosby and the staff of Camp Moore Museum. Camp Moore was an amazing asset in my research for primary sources. The staffs of the Shiloh, Perryville, Murfreesboro and Chickamauga-Chattanooga sites were always willing to assist in my research. Particular attention to Lee White of the Chickamauga-Chattanooga Battlefield Park who has assisted me for the past thirteen years on various topics with Louisiana units. A special thanks to Dr. Jane Johansson, of Rogers State University, who provided a vast number of sources, information and other items on Louisiana units and her work on Daniel W. Adams. Other individuals who provided invaluable assistance in research were Bruce Allardice, Ron Coddington, Greg Williams, Art Bergeron, Peter Reichard, Lanny Smith, Terry Scriber, and Greg Biggs and his vast knowledge of flags used in the Army of Tennessee that he graciously shared. Appreciation is extended to Edward Beniot for cartography consulting on map work; to Vincente Bullara, Brian Richard and Kip Hidalgo for sharing crucial insight and suggestions on my work. Thanks also to fellow Civil War enthusiast and researcher John Walsh, as well as Bryan Howertson, Bill Boggess, Beth Horner, and Mrs. Peggy "T." I thank Dr. Judith Gentry, of the University of Louisiana at Lafayette, who encouraged me to pursue this work more than ten years ago, and also the numerous individuals who supplied family histories, photographs or leads to other sources.

Repositories and archives that were extremely helpful and beneficial to this work were the staffs of Hill Memorial Library at Louisiana State University, Special Collections at Howard-Tilton Library at Tulane, Manuscripts Department of Wilson Library at the University of North Carolina, The Museum of the Confederacy, Kentucky Library & Museum at the University of Western Kentucky, Special Collections at Mississippi State University, the Mississippi State Archives, Louisiana State Archives, Alabama State Archives, Manuscript Archives and Rare books at Emory University, Special Collections at the University of Arkansas and the help of my local library and staff of Opelousas Public Library with interlibrary loan materials.

Contents

Acknowledgments vii
Preface 1

1. Off to War: April 1861–April 1862 3
2. The Shiloh Campaign: April 1862 17
3. The Louisiana Brigade Takes Shape: April–August 1862 37
4. The Kentucky Campaign: August–October 1862 62
5. Murfreesboro Campaign: November 1862–January 1863 79
6. Retreat, Politics and to Mississippi: January–August 1863 102
7. Chickamauga Campaign: September 1863 117
8. Chattanooga Campaign: September–December 1863 136
9. With Joe Johnston: December 1863–July 1864 155
10. Battles for Atlanta: July–September 1864 179
11. Tennessee Campaign: September–December 1864 200
12. End of the War: January–May 1865 220

Chapter Notes 237
Bibliography 249
Index 255

Preface

Enthusiasts of Louisiana's role in the Civil War are familiar with the exploits of that state's soldiers who fought in Virginia under Richard Taylor, Roberdeau Wheat, Harry Hays, Zebulon York, Charles Dreaux, Leroy Stafford and others. The exploits and turbulent career of Major Roberdeau Wheat's battalion brought early fame and nickname to his unit, and then eventually to all the Louisiana soldiers who served in the Army of Northern Virginia, the Louisiana Tigers. Under the command of Robert E. Lee this army and its two Louisiana brigades enjoyed many successes on the battlefield. As Lee became the embodiment of the Lost Cause after the war his fame grew in the postwar years as did that of his army and its veterans. Thus, what is left behind is a well documented history of the Army of Northern Virginia. Louisiana regiments that served with that army have received their due place in history.

After reading Terry Jones' excellent book, *Lee's Tigers*, on Louisianians in the Army of Northern Virginia I became curious as to the role of the Louisianians in the west. The Army of Tennessee had Louisianians in its ranks but who were these men, its leaders, the units involved and what battles did they fight? Unfortunately their history was blemished with continual defeats and instability in command that did not bring the postwar attraction as did Lee's Tigers. Research also revealed the Louisianians in the west served in several commands in what appeared no coherent and coordinated manner. Units served at Vicksburg and surrounding areas, garrisoned Mobile, and fought in the Army of Tennessee. The topic and scope was narrowed to that of the Louisiana Brigade of Daniel W. Adams and Randall L. Gibson. What I found was a very rich and scattered history that was largely untouched and unconnected.

During this time, the 1990s, publications about units and people in the brigade began to surface. Scholarly research had finally made its way from Virginia to Tennessee. Several articles by Art Bergeron appeared in periodicals in 1995 about the brigade at the Battles of Shiloh and Florence and the Siege of Jackson. Nathaniel Hughes put forth an excruciatingly detailed history of the 5th Company of Washington Artillery, *The Pride of the Confederate Artillery: The Washington Artillery in the Army of Tennessee*, in 1997. Other books to appear on units from the brigade were Thomas Richey's *Tirailleurs: A History of the 4th Louisiana and the Acadians of Company H* (2003) and Terry and Theresa Scriber's *The Fourth Louisiana Battalion in the Civil War: A History and Roster* (2008). Printed during this time was a much overdue and beautifully done biography on the main character of the Army of Tennessee's Louisiana Brigade, Randall L. Gibson, done by Mary Gorton McBride and Ann Mathison McLaurin titled *Randall Lee Gibson of Louisiana: Confederate General and New South Reformer* (2007). In previous works the disparaging remarks of Bragg after Shiloh and Gibson's removal from command after Murfreesboro have all been documented but poorly explored beyond that point. McBride was the first to tackle the history and depth of the Bragg-Gibson conflict in a scholarly publication.

The addition of these scholarly works with the multitude of small articles of personal experiences in various older publications provided an immense amount of information on Louisianians in the western army but there still lacked an overall unit history dedicated to the Adams-Gibson Louisiana Brigade as told entirely from their perspective. Pieces of the puzzle lay everywhere but had yet to be brought together for a comprehensive history of the brigade. It is the goal of this book to put forth such a history. Campaigns and battles are discussed in depth and from the perspective of the Louisianians themselves. Instead of the Louisiana Brigade simply being part of an overall narrative, it is now instead the focus of all campaigns. Personal accounts, battle reports and regimental-brigade reports are used to bring forth a firsthand account of the Louisianians.

The politics of command are covered from the recruitment of units with its politicking to the lobbying of promotions for social status and protection of honor. Randall Gibson was caught up in the mini–civil war of the Army of Tennessee due to conflict with the army's commander, Braxton Bragg. This turmoil is followed from the Battle of Shiloh, where Bragg began his criticism of Gibson, through the Battle of Chattanooga, when Bragg's career with the army ended. Promotion for Gibson came shortly thereafter. Conflict within the Army of Tennessee rose again under the tenure of John Bell Hood. Gibson avoided the conflict of this second round of inter-army fighting. Gibson became a supporter and good friend of John Bell Hood and avoided the postwar criticism of Hood.

Chapter 1

Off to War: April 1861–April 1862

"The whole country is evidently in arms, as every train that passes is crowded to overflowing, with brave, generous hearts, who are willing to sacrifice all, for their country's honor."
—Private John D. Austin, 4th Louisiana,
Co. E, 17 May 1861

The morning of 6 April 1862 slowly emerged onto the pages of history as the culmination of weeks of stressful scrambling by General Albert Sidney Johnston. Johnston and other officers stood next to a fire early that morning to warm themselves, just as Johnston stood on the verge of launching a major attack that would, hopefully, turn back those agonizing weeks of February through early April of 1862. Fighting began shortly after 5:00 a.m., and it spurred the general to the front. While riding to the sound of guns through large numbers of his men, Johnston spotted a familiar family face, that of Randall L. Gibson. Describing the encounter sixteen years later was Johnston's son, William Preston Johnston. Gibson was William's second cousin and very close friend, they having been roommates in college before the war. At a bark of an order, Gibson ordered his soldiers to salute their army commander. Johnston stopped and met Gibson by grabbing his hand. "Randall, I never see you but I think of William. I hope you may get through safely this day, but we must win a victory." Johnston turned his horse and rode off. It was the last time the two men would speak. Johnston was killed that afternoon, but for Gibson, the Battle of Shiloh marked the beginning of a heroic and troublesome military career.[1]

Randall Gibson was a young Louisianian with a promising career before him when war broke out in April 1861. He was born into a wealthy family from Terrebonne Parish on 10 September 1832 while his parents visited his grandfather's estate near Versailles, Kentucky. Young Gibson's parents sought for him a good education. Once old enough, Gibson attended Yale University, where he roomed with his cousin William P. Johnston. After graduating from Yale in 1853, Gibson studied law at the University of Louisiana in New Orleans. After receiving his law degree in 1855, Gibson began a three-year tour through Europe. He visited several countries and served as part of the United States Embassy in Madrid, Spain. When Gibson returned to Louisiana in 1858, he purchased his first sugar plantation, Lackland. Lackland was in Lafourche Parish, just north of Thibodaux close to old Colonel Braxton Bragg's plantation. Bragg himself had only recently bought his plantation in Lafourche Parish in 1856, after he retired from the U.S. Army. With unclear roots there emerged a less than friendly relationship between the neighboring planters that surfaced during the Civil War.[2]

For the next couple of years, Gibson practiced law. In the fall of 1859, he received a lieutenant colonel's appointment in the Louisiana militia from Governor Thomas O. Moore. When Louisiana left the Union in January of 1861, Governor Moore appointed Gibson as one of his aides-de-camp. When Moore abolished his military staff, Gibson received a commission in the 1st Louisiana Artillery, where he was joined by his brother Tobias. Gibson remained stationed with his unit below New Orleans at Fort Jackson until September. In that month he took leave and traveled to Camp Moore, north of New Orleans, and "politicked" for a position in a unit that was destined for duty in Kentucky or Virginia.[3]

Camp Moore was established in May of 1861 in Tangipahoa Parish along the Jackson and New Orleans railroad, about 75 miles north of New Orleans. The poor conditions at Camp Walker in New Orleans forced the creation of this camp. The area was picked because it was close to the railroad, had plenty of drinking water, and was well drained and short on mosquitoes. Camp Moore became the hub for companies formed across the state to be organized into battalions and regiments for service in the Confederate army. Eventually, nineteen infantry regiments and battalions would be formed at Camp Moore from May of 1861 to May of 1862. Although a better substitute for training than Camp Walker, Camp Moore did not receive flattering reports from some of the Louisianians who were camped there: "The suffering too, was as great to many, for many sickened and died at this miserable place.... The trees seemed to engender heat. The red sandy soil looked parched and baked."[4]

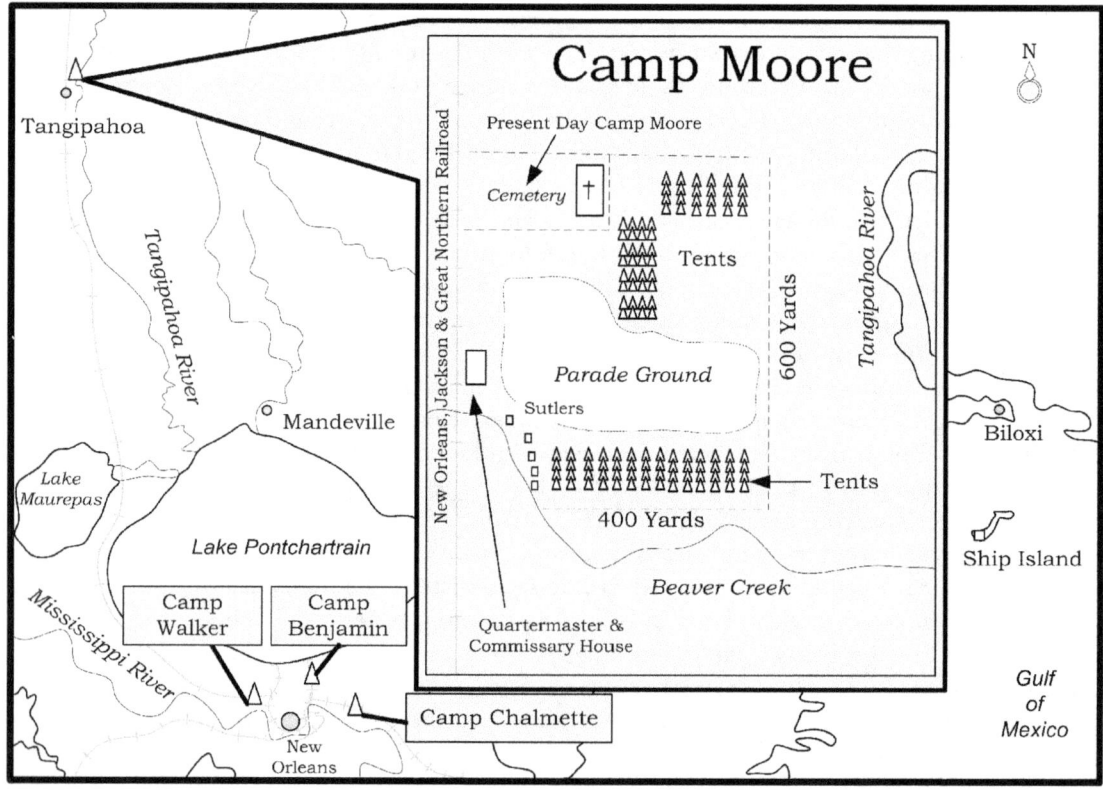

Eastern Louisiana, Military Camps, 1861.

Randall L. Gibson pictured early in the war while colonel of the newly formed 13th Louisiana Infantry (courtesy of the U.S. Army Military History Institute).

William H. Russell of the *London Times* visited Camp Moore in May of 1861 and provided a detailed account of what he saw. Russell's views were very perceptive and provided a viewpoint outside the flurry of patriotism. As he looked over the rows of tents and watched as groups drilled and marched in their multitude of different uniforms, Russell said the whole scene before his eyes was like "a holiday experiment of soldiering, rather than the dark shadow of forthcoming battle," and referred to the green volunteers as "ball stoppers." Russell attributed the circus to his front due to the lack of training in the Louisiana militia. "The militia of Louisiana has not been called out for many years, and its officers have no military experience and the men have no drill or discipline ... there is not I think, a single West Point officer in this whole command." Contributing to the whole chaos of things was the election of officers by the volunteers. Russell described the process: "The system of electing officers by ballot has made the camp as thoroughly a political arena as the poll districts in New Orleans before an election, and thus many heroes, seemingly ambitious of epaulettes, are in reality only laying pipes for the attainment of civil power or distinction after the war." This was the very process that young Randall partook in when he went to Camp Moore.[5]

A young, promising and connected Gibson would obviously profit from military service and an officer's commission equal to his social status. Gibson's visit to Camp Moore proved successful and was no accident; influence from a strong family helped get Gibson his promotion to colonel. On 6 September, Gibson tendered his resignation to the 1st Artillery and accepted his new position as colonel on 9 September with the newly created 13th Louisiana Infantry. The core of the new regiment were the six companies of Zouaves known as Avegno's Zouaves, or the Governor's Guards. The battalion's leaders were Lieutenant Colonel Aristide Gerard and Major Anatole Placide Avegno. Both men maintained their positions in the creation of the 13th Regiment. Anatole Placide Avegno was a native of New Orleans and a graduate of the Western Military Institute in Georgetown, Kentucky, and the law school of the University of Louisiana. When war broke out in 1861, Avegno was practicing law in New Orleans and put his energies and money into raising a unit for the war, the Governor's Guards. Despite Aristide Girard being made the commander, unit became known as Avegno's Zouaves.[6]

The battalion was an extremely diverse group of individuals made up of many immigrants from many backgrounds with laborers and draymen being the dominant professions of its men. It was said that the only sense of unity in this battalion was its colorful Zouave uniform with red caps, red trousers and gold braided blue jackets. Otherwise, the unit was comprised of "Frenchmen, Spaniards, Mexicans, Dagoes, Germans, Chinese, Irishmen, and, in fact, persons of every clime known to geographers or travelers of that day." Another observer called the regiment an "Irish Creole" unit, but a critic of that description had this to say: "You should know the regiment better ... should know enough not to call Creoles Irish, or Irish Creoles, and not to leave out the Americans, Germans, Dutch, Prussians and others ... it so truly represents the mixed character of the population of New Orleans." Frank Richardson, not of New Orleans, was not so impressed: "Most of the common soldiers ... are a very low set of men being composed of low Irish and the scum of creation." Despite being comprised of so many nationalities, the unit drilled in French, because it was the only language everyone understood. A humorous story from 1st Lieutenant John McGrath of Mike Brenigan, an Irishman of Company K, relates to the battalion using French as its language of drill and command: "Branagan [Brenigan], while somewhat more than half drunk, approached the writer, and, touching his kepi, said: 'Leftenant, I don't know what oi'll do. You want us to drill in English, and the divil a wurd I know but French.' Absurd as it may appear, he spoke the truth."[7]

In early September, the battalion was ordered up from its camp at Mandeville, Louisiana, to Camp Moore where it was joined with four independent companies. On 11 September 1861 the 13th Louisiana was mustered into Confederate service with 830 officers and men. Added to the Governor's Guards Battalion were the Southern Celts, Gladden Rifles, the Norton Guards and the St. Mary Volunteers. Of the four independent companies added, Captain James Murphy's St. Mary Volunteers (Company G) was the only non–New Orleans company in the entire regiment. The four independent companies, including the St. Mary Volunteers, were not dressed in the Zouave uniforms. This helped add to the mismatched, colorful display of the regiment's appearance. Richardson continued his criticism of Avegno's Zouaves by mockingly saying about their Zouave appearance, "They say they are not going to carry any knapsacks or haversacks as they will put everything in their britches legs."[8]

Despite the better living conditions at Camp Moore the camp became a milling ground for diseases. Thousands of men who converged on the camp were from rural areas and were not exposed to the diseases that men from the larger towns were exposed to. The result was sickness in a large number of men during Camp Moore's life and numerous deaths. Being mostly from New Orleans, the 13th Regiment escaped most of these incidents, but the same could not be said for Murphy's company. It escaped relatively light, losing one man to disease. Frank Richardson gave a vivid description of his experience at Camp Moore in several letters home (which was a recurring theme for many from rural units):

> A sick soldier is the most miserable animal on earth. I speak from experience for the last 3 or four days I have been one of those helpless pittyful no account animals and what makes my condition so much worse is that I have not a cent of that all needful thing money ... I have been laid up with diarrhea principally a very bad cold and sore throat, have had fever or chill since the day I was first taken which was a week ago.... How I wish the war was over. There aint a bit of fun in it. I wouldn't object to being at home again in the least.[9]

Richardson's spirits picked up with the arrival of a family slave from home, Allen, who began doing work for Richardson and members of the company (and began to record a nice little profit). Richardson's health also improved, and word came that the regiment was soon being shipped out of Camp Moore to Kentucky. The green soldier expressed his opinion to his father:

> You may believe I am glad to leave this place for I am most assuredly tired of it. This is the most boring place imaginably and very unhealthy.... A poor sick soldier is far from being a happy in creature in camp. I have had some experience in that myself and I know I felt as if I had nearly be willing to desert, and go home as not caring for the disgrace or honor.[10]

The regiment was shipped out of Camp Moore on 23 September, not to Kentucky but to Camp Chalmette on the east side of New Orleans. With nine out of its ten companies from New Orleans, it was a homecoming. The regiment was met by large crowds of people at the train station and during their march to camp. For the next two months, the regiment remained at Camp Chalmette training and parading for the visitors from New Orleans. Parades and visits from the public helped to maintain morale and sustain the enthusiasm of military life. Outside of these distractions the men continually turned to drinking in their off duty time. As at Mandeville and Camp Moore, whiskey remained a perpetual problem. When the Guards Battalion departed Mandeville for Camp Moore, a drunken brawl broke out in the company left behind to bring up the battalion's gear. It took all the officers, NCOs and the sober enlisted men to restore order. To get their hands on liquor at Camp Moore, men simply forged officers' signatures. This practice led to a severe brawl at Camp Moore that was recounted by Lieutenant Charles Johnson of the 11th Louisiana: "On the day before we left Camp Moore I was on duty at Tangipahoa and had a great deal of trouble with drunken soldiers; I put about a dozen in my guard house and they kept getting drunk coming with orders from their captains to purchase whiskey, until finally I called out my guard and shut every store in the place." That only intensified the situation with the Dillon Guards burning up the floors to their tents and their benches. Johnson was forced to call up companies with weapons loaded to quiet the situation down. An extreme case involving whiskey culminated while in New Orleans between two members of Company D of the 13th Louisiana. A "Frenchman ... who, crazed by drink," Francois Messier, shot and killed a German of his same company. Messier was arrested and found guilty of manslaughter and remanded to serve his sentence. This would not be the last time the thirsty men of the Thirteenth and whiskey were allowed by their officers to share troubled times.[11]

In November, Gibson's regiment was finally sent to the front. It was sent up the Mississippi River to join the command of Major General Leonidas Polk in Columbus, Kentucky. It was a reunion of sorts; Gibson's men were met by the 11th Louisiana and 5th Louisiana Battalion, both units being entirely from New Orleans. The 11th Louisiana was baptized in the Battle of Belmont about three weeks earlier, while the 5th Battalion stayed in Columbus. Frank Richardson expressed the emotion of the 13th Louisiana as they listened to the war stories of Belmont, which were probably bigger than the battle itself: "We felt grievously disappointed at not being there in time to take part in it.... We feared the war would end before we had a chance to take part in it." Richardson's time would come, but for the time being his regiment settled down to the glorious routine of camp life: drilling and boredom. It was also a reunion for Gibson as he was placed under command of his prewar friend, Polk.[12]

The western Confederacy, the area between the Mississippi River and the Appalachian Mountains, had been relatively quiet during the first months of the Civil War. The commander of Confederate forces in this area, Albert S. Johnston, was faced with a shortage of soldiers and was forced to draw up a defensive line through southern Kentucky. He spent the months of late 1861 and early 1862 trying to strengthen his weak line that stretched from Columbus on the Mississippi River to the Appalachian Mountains. With the exception of two minor battles, Confederate and Federal forces remained quiet, busying themselves with building their armies. In a bold move in early February of 1862, the war in the West came alive. Union brigadier general Ulysses S. Grant launched an attack on Johnston's defensive line at Forts Henry and Donelson, located on the Tennessee and Cumberland rivers, respectively. Grant's capture of these two forts put Johnston's entire line in jeopardy and eventually caused it to become untenable. Johnston was forced to retreat from his positions in Kentucky and fall back into Tennessee.[13]

The military situation in the West went from bad to worse when Johnston was forced to evacuate his river fortress at Columbus and Nashville, the state capital of Tennessee. Within a few weeks, the entire Mississippi Valley lay open to Federal invasion. Upon the fall of Fort Donelson, Johnston called on the Confederate government for immediate help. To stop the Federal penetration, a slow concentration was begun in northeast Mississippi at the small but strategically important town of Corinth where two major railroads

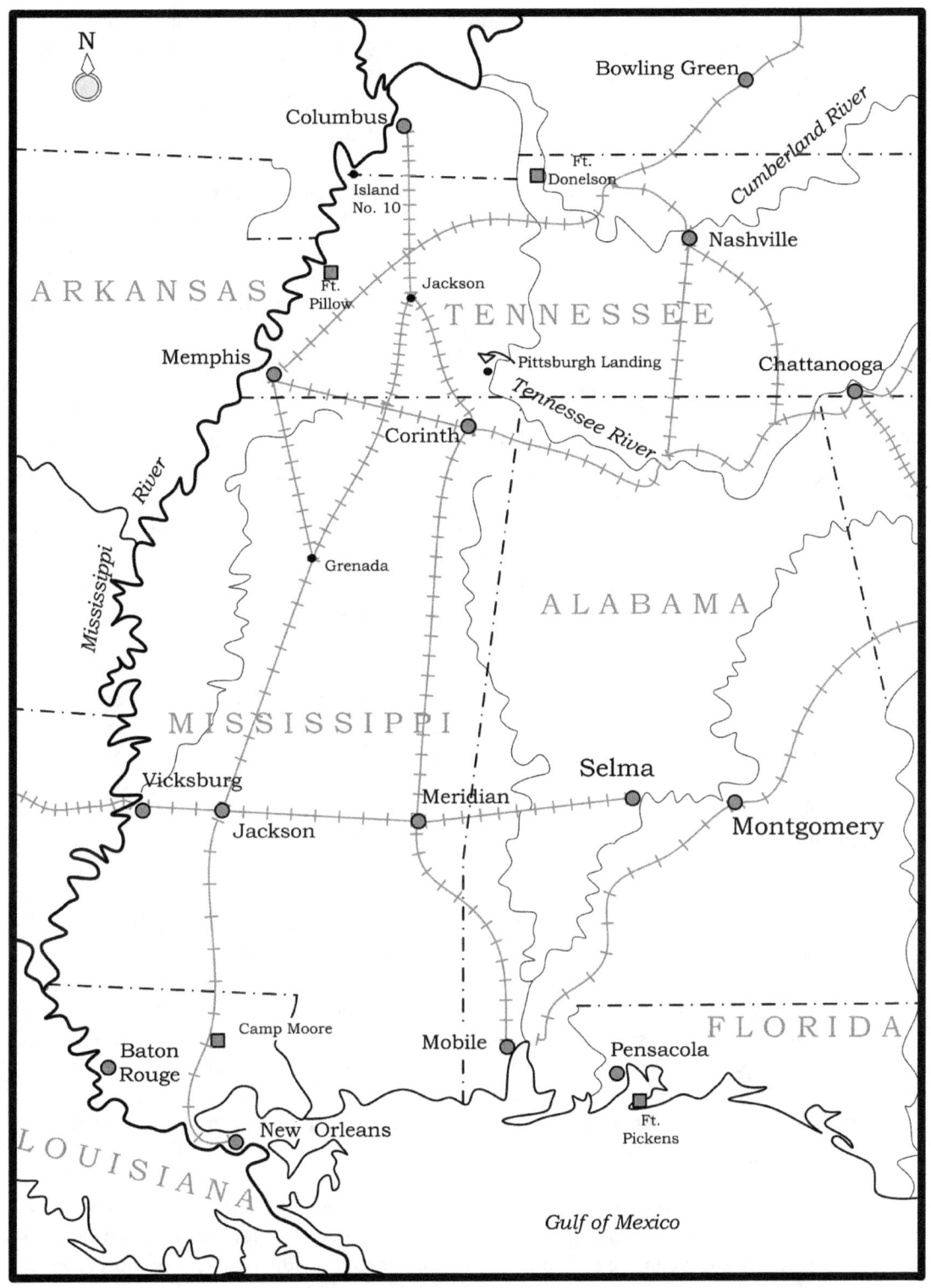

Western Theater, Early 1862.

intersected: the east-west railroad, the Memphis & Charleston, and a north-south line, the Mobile & Ohio. The Confederates in the West spent the latter part of February and March concentrating every available soldier at Corinth.[14]

The capture of Fort Donelson made Columbus untenable. The evacuation began in late February to the Humboldt and Jackson area. What could not be carried was packed onto steamers and sent south to Memphis; everything leftover was burned. The 13th Louisiana lost many materials this way, and the extra goods like blankets, clothing and cooking utensils that went by steamer never made it back to the regiment. Included in the burned items were the regiment's tents; this meant that the march through Kentucky and Tennessee would be done with no cover from the cold conditions. Symbolic of all things to come, the first day's march was done in a cold downpour of rain. When the regiment limped into Humboldt the next day, the men quickly found a way to warm themselves: whiskey. Access to liquor was not restricted, whether on purpose or not. The past two days of hard marching that the regiment was forced to endure was their first real taste of marching in the war. Whiskey was a common remedy to smooth things over for the cold and tired soldiers. Officers of the regiment became aware of their error while they were eating supper at the local hotel. The officers, in their haste to get out of the weather and taste a warm meal, left places with liquor unguarded. Suddenly their meal was violently disturbed. All liquored up, Private Mike Brenigan burst into the dining hall of the hotel where the officers were eating and went on a mad rampage. It took the former New Orleans police chief, Captain Stephen O'Leary of Company A, to smash Brenigan through the window to end the melee. With their lesson learned, the officers did not let the stores go unguarded again.[15]

The 13th Louisiana arrived outside of Corinth in late March where it met thousands of fellow Louisianians. "Louisiana was certainly well represented," said Captain McGrath. "I counted ten regiments of them, besides a great many independent battalions and ninety day organizations." McGrath was not exaggerating what he saw. In this concentration at Corinth, units from Johnston's forces in East Tennessee; the former garrison of Columbus; a large column from Pensacola, Florida, and Mobile, Alabama; and forces from New Orleans, Louisiana, converged on the town. In this massive buildup, Gibson's regiment met many of their fellow statesmen. From Major General Braxton Bragg's command in Pensacola came the 1st Louisiana Regulars, "the professionals ... a determined body of men," under Colonel Daniel Weisger Adams. Joining Gibson from the Columbus garrison was the 11th Louisiana. The 4th Louisiana Regiment came from various garrison posts around south Louisiana. From New Orleans came Colonel Augustus Reichard's German filled 20th Louisiana Regiment and Brigadier General Daniel Ruggles' Brigade consisting of the 16th, 17th, 18th and 19th Louisiana Regiments. Then there were ninety day organizations such as the Orleans Guards Battalion, the Crescent Regiment and the 5th Company of the Washington Artillery. Louisiana was well represented but made up only a fraction of the men assembled from all over the western theater. These forces, eventually numbering over 40,000 men, were organized into the Army of the Mississippi in late March, with Johnston as its commander.[16]

In this organization, Gibson found himself placed in the division of Major General Daniel Ruggles of Major General Braxton Bragg's II Corps. Ruggles had been stationed in New Orleans prior to coming to Tennessee. In answer to Johnston's plea for reinforcements, the War Department on 5 February ordered Major General Mansfield Lovell, whose department included Louisiana, to send 5,000 men to Johnston. The unit Lovell picked to send north was Ruggles' brigade. Ruggles was a man the Louisianians were not too fond of. "He [Ruggles] was an old brute. Being an old army officer and a New Englander, he had no conscience or mercy on any one," noted one of the Louisiana soldiers. On 12 February Ruggles was ordered to prepare his brigade, consisting of the 16th, 17th, 18th and 19th Louisiana Regiments, for a move to Tennessee. In the organization of the Army of the Mississippi, Ruggles was elevated to division commander and his old brigade was partially distributed within two new brigades that formed his command. Gibson was placed in command of one of Ruggles' brigades which included his regiment, one of Ruggles' regiments, the 19th Louisiana, and the 4th Louisiana and the 1st Arkansas.[17]

In direct contrast to Gibson's "cosmopolitan" group came was the 4th Louisiana made up of "young sugar planters and slave-owners ... wealthy, refined, gentlemanly fellows." The nucleus of the 4th Louisiana was five pre-war militia companies that were merged with five volunteer companies at Camp Walker in New Orleans on 25 May 1861. The majority of the 900-man unit was from the Florida Parishes of east Louisiana. Robert H. Barrow was elected colonel of the regiment, but his continued health problems forced his retirement from the service. Elevated in Barrow's position on 21 March 1862 was the regiment's fiery and colorful Lieutenant Colonel Henry Watkins Allen. Allen was a forty-one-year-old native of Virginia. He moved with family to Missouri at age 13 and at 15 he began attending college. Two years later he left home and found his way to south Mississippi where he became a tutor at a plantation and studied law at night. In 1841, Allen passed the bar in Mississippi but did not pursue law; instead he joined the Texas army in 1842 to help fight against Mexican aggression in that state. He returned to Mississippi that year, got married and then was elected to the Mississippi State House of Representatives.[18]

Colonel Henry Watkins Allen, 4th Louisiana Infantry (courtesy of Confederate Memorial Hall Museum, New Orleans).

After his wife's death in 1851, he moved to Louisiana and purchased a large plantation in West Baton Rouge Parish. After failing to get elected to a state senate seat, he journeyed to Europe to join the Italians in their wars to gain national unity. Failing to join forces with Italy's Risorgimento leader Giuseppe Garibaldi, Allen instead toured Europe and returned to Louisiana to be elected to the state House of Representatives in 1857. When hostilities erupted in December of 1860, Allen joined the Delta Rifles militia company from West Baton Rouge Parish. He took part in seizing the Federal arsenal in Baton Rouge in January of 1861. When the Delta Rifles were attached to the newly created 4th Louisiana in May, Allen was quickly recognized and elected lieutenant colonel.[19]

Once organized, the 4th Louisiana remained at Camp Walker for the next month. The newly formed 4th Louisiana remained in New Orleans for a few weeks before it was shipped north to Camp Moore. The Metairie Race Track, Camp Walker, proved a very unfavorable place; Robert Patrick described their desperate water situation: "The water we used was brought from the river in old pork barrels, and in addition to being warm and muddy, the old grease and salt that had been in the barrels previously gave it a very bad taste." The time spent at Camp Moore, however, seemed to make up for the misery of Camp Walker. Robert Patrick was more optimistic in his recordings about Camp Moore: "We had excellent water and plenty to eat." Private John Austen of Company E confirmed Patrick's enthusiasm about their new camp: "We have plenty of shade, so much so, that the companies, as they arrive, are compelled to clear the ground in order to pitch their tents. A large space also had to be cleared to secure an ample parade ground and drill ground.... We have a merry camp ground — fun, sparing matches, and good singing are the order day and night." What a stark contrast from the views of men in the 4th Regiment who were at Camp Moore from May through June to those of the 13th Louisiana in September.[20]

The rest of 1861 was spent doing what the volunteers of the regiment hated the most — performing garrison duty instead of fighting. For a time the regiment was sent to the Gulf Coast in Mississippi where companies of the regiment were detached to parts of Ship Island, Biloxi and other surrounding areas. The only positive remarks coming from the men were how much they enjoyed camping on the coastline and entertaining the local ladies. Physical work remained a nuisance for the well-to-do "gentlemen" of the regiment, and drill remained the daily routine. "Clearing off parade grounds drilling and standing guard on the gulf shore looking out for Old Abes Gun boats," is how Franklin Eady described life on the Mississippi coast to a friend. Garrison duty in Mississippi ended in early October. The regiment was sent back to New Orleans but did not stay in the city. Instead, the regiment was sent west to Brashear City.[21]

Brashear City sat at the mouth of the Atchafayla in south central Louisiana and at the end of the Opelousas & Great Western Railroad. It was founded in 1860 and was the midpoint of collection of cattle from Texas and the rich agriculture of southwest Louisiana's farms. Dr. William Brashear, a surgeon-politician turned sugar planter, was the city's namesake. Barely three hundred people in population, it was once described as a "miserable dirty village of a dozen houses," where "an old hotel was the most conspicuous feather of the hamlet." While stationed here and across the bay at Berwick City, the regiment spent its time manning the local forts, working on the forts and, for the most part, staying separated and detached defending the area. The men of the regiment grew tired of the "long days" at Berwick and the surrounding area. A frustrated soldier said, "It seemed distinctly inglorious to be condemned to the humdrum existence of a neglected post in Southern Louisiana. Stories of battles reached us from Tennessee and Virginia, and we yearned to be on the fighting line."[22]

Then on 13 February 1862 as if the answer to a prayer for action, the regiment received orders to prepare itself for a movement out of state. The regiment was ordered north as part of the Confederate concentration to stop Grant's quick thrust into Tennessee. Between February 20 and 22 the 4th Louisiana loaded up and headed out toward New Orleans for its long trip north, with many "aching heads" after "extensive jubilations" before leaving Berwick. On the twenty-sixth the regiment left New Orleans for Tennessee. One member of the regiment was reported to have a severe case of measles and would miss the upcoming battles in Tennessee. Men in the regiment easily found a remedy to his situation: whiskey, and a lot of it. "They decided that whiskey was the only medicine which would do him any good. Whiskey was accordingly administered to him in large quantities and at frequent intervals." The trip north was an experience Robert Patrick never forgot: "The weather was dreadful, for it was cold and the rain poured down in torrents." The regiment made its way through Grand Junction, Tennessee, and reached Jackson by March 1 "in the midst of a blizzard." Their stay in the Jackson area lasted about two weeks before they were ordered to Corinth. On their trip to Corinth they were forced to stop because of a train wreck. The Louisiana boys of the Fourth were forced to spend the night alongside the tracks without any sleeping or tenting gear. Exposure in such an alien climate took its toll on the regiment. The conditions convinced old Colonel Barrow it was time to quit field duty, and he resigned his commission. This was when Allen was made colonel, and Samuel Hunter was elected to lieutenant colonel. Of the original 900 men mustered into service, 575 were present in the ranks by late March and early April of 1862. Once the regiment reached Corinth, it was attached to Gibson's brigade.[23]

The other Louisiana unit attached to the brigade was the 19th Louisiana Regiment. The Nineteenth was another Camp Moore organized unit. As the future companies of the Nineteenth poured into Camp Moore in the late summer and early fall of 1861, there was much excitement and anxiety as to what unit they would be attached to and if they would reach the front in time for the war. Private John Marler of the Henry Marshall Guards (soon to be Company F of the Nineteenth) expressed the frustration with his wife by letter: "Some of the boys say if they were at home they would stay.... If I knew where we would be sent I would be perfectly satisfied. The Thirteenth regiment is made up yet and will leave in a few days for Kentucky. The fourteenth regiment leaves soon ... there is some talk of our joining that regiment." As Marler watched, the 13th Louisiana was formed in early September and quick on its heels two weeks later came the 16th and 17th Regiments. In October the 18th Regiment was partially filled out and shipped off to south Louisiana. The Nineteenth was not formed until 19 November and had only eight of the required ten companies. Those two companies were added on 11 December and brought the regiment's total number of men mustered into service to 873.[24]

Leaders elected for the unit were Benjamin L. Hodge for colonel, James M. Hollingsworth for lieutenant colonel and Wesley P. Winans for major. None of the three men were natives to Louisiana, which was a trend with a lot of Louisianians in this period and of the companies from north Louisiana. Thirty-six-year-old Benjamin Lewis Hodge, a native of Tennessee and a wealthy lawyer from Caddo Parrish, was elected colonel of the regiment. Hodge initially turned to politics in the new Confederate government but came up short for a position as a Confederate state senator. Denied power in politics, Hodge turned his talents to securing a position in the new army. He originally joined the Shreveport Grays and secured a lieutenant's position. Hodge's company was originally destined to be part of the 1st Louisiana Regulars but then became part of Dreaux's 1st Louisiana Battalion. The Grays went to Pensacola, then were shipped to Virginia and, for unknown reasons, Hodge resigned his commission. The lack of seeing action could not be a reason since his battalion was one of the first Louisiana units to be sent to Virginia. Major General Leonidas Polk requested for Hodge to serve as judge advocate in his command but the request was rejected by the secretary of war. Hodge made his way back to Shreveport where he joined the Keachi Warriors which eventually became Company I of the 19th Louisiana Regiment.[25]

Lieutenant Colonel Hollingsworth was a 31-year-old native of Alabama. At age 20 he entered the Western Military Institute in Kentucky. In Hollingsworth's four years at the institute, he proved himself to be a leader and possessed many skills. He was given highest honors in his class, was raised to the position of captain and graduated valedictorian in 1854. Upon graduation he moved back to Monroe County, Alabama, and managed his father's plantation. Three years later he purchased a plantation in De Soto Parish and became an adopted son of Louisiana. His holdings included sixteen slaves according to the 1861 Slave Owners Census. Hollingsworth brought with him to Camp Moore military training. This training was a culture shock to the farmers of North Louisiana. It's apparent that he pushed his men, for they began to call him "Old Double Quick," which suggests he liked to march and drill them at the double-quick pace.[26]

Colonel Benjamin Hodge, 19th Louisiana. (courtesy of Louisiana State University Archives, LSU Libraries, Baton Rouge, LA).

Major Wesley Winans was a thirty-six-year-old native of Mississippi. He and his family moved to Louisiana in 1838 when he was thirteen. His Methodist preaching father reared Wesley working in the cotton fields with the family slaves. At sixteen he was sent to school at Centenary where he graduated first in his class. From there he went on to pass the bar exam and was practicing law in Shreveport when the war broke out. Very little is known about the company that Winans joined or possibly helped organize, the Caddo 10th. Winans was made captain of the company and it made its way to Camp Moore where he was made major of the regiment, possibly from the assistance of Hodge.[27]

The regiment was composed of companies from north Louisiana, and this proved a problem healthwise as it did for the 4th Louisiana. Instead of battling "yankeys," the Nineteenth spent time in camp battling rumors and, more importantly, diseases. As talk whipped around camp about what regiment the men would be attached to or where their unit would be shipped John Marler admitted, "A private don't now one minute what he will do the next." Rumors weren't the only things being whipped around. The rural north Louisiana boys weren't exposed to as many diseases in their lives before, but at Camp Moore they were exposed to men from all over the state, especially New Orleans. A member of the 13th Louisiana noted, "The measles broke out among the members of the 19th and 17th Regiment encamped near us, and the mortality was very great." Richard Eddins of Company G, writing home to his wife from the camp hospital while suffering from the measles, wrote, "All the boys has the measles that never had them." The regiment left its mark on Camp

Moore by leaving ten of its members dead of disease in its cemetery.[28]

The 19th Louisiana moved to Camp Benjamin outside of New Orleans after it was mustered into Confederate service. The regiment remained there until it was ordered to proceed to Corinth, Mississippi, as part of Ruggles' brigade. Sergeant Thomas Davidson of Company F was not surprised by the order one bit. "Beauregard sees the immanent necessity for more troops he will call for us ... we will be soon sent to Ky." Davidson was right, for four days after he penned those words to his sister, his brigade was ordered north to Tennessee. Davidson spoke confidently for the rest of his company when he said, "I am quite anxious to go ... I do not wish to serve out my twelve months without being in a battle. I left home to fight." Davidson's wish would be met soon, but first his regiment had to survive the Tennessee–North Mississippi winter.[29]

The Cater brothers, Rufus (left) and Douglas (right), answered the call for volunteers. Douglas originally joined a Texas cavalry regiment before he transferred and joined his brother's unit, the 19th Louisiana (courtesy of the Cater Family).

The ride north was through cold and then snowy weather. Worse than the trip north was the regiment's first day in Tennessee: "Ground still covered in snow. The train with tents, luggage etc. of the Reg't caught on fire and was completely destroyed just as it was coming in behind us, so we weathered it till next day. The consequences of this exposure was fearful. The men became sick of pneumonia ... the death rate was tremendous." Sergeant John Anderson of Company A recorded that 36 men of his company died of disease at Corinth out of the 116 at time of muster. Private John Harris of Company D described the situation of his regiment in early March 1862: "We have a great deal of sickness in our regiment and very fatal, we have lost at least 50 men since we got here [Corinth].... We have about 20 men unfit for duty — sick with colds." Of the 873 men in the regiment in early December, only 300 were fit for duty in early April, only four months after mustering into service.[30]

The remaining unit of the brigade was the only non–Louisiana unit, the 1st Arkansas. The First was organized by a prominent politician and planter from Laconia, Arkansas, Thomas B. Flourney. Governor Henry Rector of Arkansas was requested by the new Confederate government in late April 1861 to raise a regiment for Confederate service. The aspiring Flourney quickly jumped at the opportunity. He quickly gathered companies arriving in Little Rock and notified Rector he had a unit ready but simply needed weapons to arm the new regiment. When the regiment was organized and elections held Flourney did not receive the position of colonel; all of his political goons were defeated.[31]

The man elected colonel of the 1st Arkansas was thirty-three-year-old James F. Fagan of Saline County. Fagan was born in Louisville, Kentucky, in 1828. In 1838 the Fagan family moved to the new state of Arkansas and settled in Little Rock. After his father died Fagan's mother married Samuel Adams, who was later elected governor of Arkansas. Fagan eventually took over the family farm in Saline County, dabbled in politics by serving a term in the state legislature and even enlisted in the army for the Mexican-American War where he reached the rank of lieutenant. When hostilities erupted in April of 1861 Fagan organized a company of volunteers and went to Little Rock to offer his services. There he was attached to Flourney's 1st Arkansas. No doubt his ties to his former father-in-law and his family ties by marriage to Governor Rector assisted in his company being attached to the first regiment heading to Virginia.

The 1st Arkansas was organized quickly and sent to Virginia per the request of the Confederate government. The regiment was actually accepted into Confederate service on its trip to northern Virginia at Lynchburg, Virginia, on 27 May 1861. Fagan's regiment was present at the 1st Battle of Manassas but not engaged. The regiment remained in Virginia until February of 1862. When the regiment reenlisted for the war it was furloughed and ordered to convene itself in Memphis, Tennessee, on 15 March 1862. When the regiment reformed itself in Memphis Grant was making his quick strike at Corinth. It was ordered to Corinth as part of the Confederate concentration to stop Grant. Once there it was attached to Gibson's Brigade.

Colonel James F. Fagan, 1st Arkansas (courtesy of the University of Ark., Little Rock).

Once the Army of the Mississippi completed organizing itself by late March Gibson's brigade was organized as follows:

Colonel Randall Gibson

1st Arkansas — Colonel James F. Fagan
4th Louisiana — Colonel Henry W. Allen
13th Louisiana — Major Aristide Avegno
19th Louisiana — Colonel Benjamin L. Hodge.[32]

CHAPTER 2

The Shiloh Campaign: April 1862

"The enemy reserved their fire untill we were within about twenty yards of them and then the whole line simultaneously with their battery loaded [us down marked through] with grape. opened on us again mowing us down at every volley we still pressed on until the undergrowth prevented us from going farther."
— Private Thomas Robertson, 4th Louisiana,
Co. C, 9 April 1862

With his motley army organized, Johnston pushed his army from Corinth to attack the Federals at Pittsburg Landing on the Tennessee River. On 31 March, Gibson's brigade took to the march in an east to northeast direction on the road to Monterey, Tennessee. One could mistake the Confederate advance to Shiloh for anything but a concentrated attack designed to deliver a killing blow to the enemy. It was a jumbled and confused march done at a leisurely rate, due in part to very confusing orders and bad weather. The first day's march was but a few miles followed by four to five miles the next day which brought them into Monterey. The pace of advance didn't increase but the horrible weather conditions did. From the time the brigade broke camp and headed north it was done through muddy roads. A private in the 1st Arkansas said, "The constant rains had made the roads so bad that we had to pull the cannon by hand as the horses mired in the mud." The brigade finally limped into position at 5 P.M. on 5 April where it stacked arms and rested for the next day's battle.[1]

This was not the plan Johnston had imagined. After a horribly disorganized march toward Pittsburg Landing, Johnston was ready to launch his attack on the morning of 5 April, or so he thought. Trailing far to the rear were two divisions, one of Polk's and one of Bragg's. An irritated Johnston found Ruggles' division sitting along the Monterey Road, blocked by wagons and artillery. Lieutenant Donelson Jenkins of the 4th Louisiana relates his experience those preciously spent days before Shiloh: "Road blocked up with trains stopped.... Raining hard no tents or protection of any kind.... Called up at three o'clock by a false alarm still raining.... A miserable looking set we are." It was not until late afternoon that his army was ready for the attack. Johnston postponed the attack to the next morning. Disorganization plagued Johnston's march to Pittsburg Landing and carried over into the Battle of Shiloh, April 6 and 7. Johnston deployed his four corps into four parallel lines: Bragg's and Major General William Hardee's corps formed the first two lines of the attack with their brigades deployed in single lines. Polk's and Major General John C. Breckinridge's corps, behind Hardee and Bragg, were deployed in a column of brigades. The positioning of corps behind each other, rather than side by side, spread units across the entire battlefield the next morning. The result was the disruption of the command structure of the army. Brigades found themselves separated from their divisions and taking orders from corps commanders, other division commanders, or from Johnston himself. This disorganization of command would affect Gibson in the upcoming battle.[2]

The clumsy Confederate advance on Pittsburg Landing, surprisingly, was unnoticed by the Federals. The Louisianans even discharged their rifles, to clean them out due to the weather, before they ate breakfast just a few miles from Grant's army. When Johnston's men began their advance before dawn on 6 April, most of Grant's army was preparing breakfast or still asleep. When fighting began early that morning, the Federals were totally caught off guard. Although able to offer stiff resistance in certain spots, the front of the Federal line gave way under the sudden attack.[3]

The morning of 6 April found Gibson and his brigade deployed in the center of the second line of the Confederate attack formation. Gibson was posted on Ruggles' right, with his own right resting across the Pittsburg-Corinth Road. Deployed in front of Gibson, in the first line, were the brigades of Brigadier General S.A.M. Wood and Colonel R.G. Shaver. When the attack began at about daylight, 6:30 A.M., Ruggles followed behind the first line, keeping his division to the west of the Corinth Road. Bragg pulled Gibson away from Ruggles and ordered him to march to the right, to support Wood's and Shaver's brigades. Per orders, the brigade kept up a slow but steady pace in order to remain in supporting distance of the first line.[4]

The advance of Shaver and Wood brought them into contact with Colonel Everett Peabody's brigade of Brigadier General Benjamin Prentiss' division. Gibson followed the advance which brought him into the southern tip of Rhea Field. This is where the brigade came under enemy fire for the first time. Captain Allen Waterhouse's 1st Illinois Light Artillery of Brigadier General William T. Sherman's division was posted on the north end of Rhea Field and caught Gibson's brigade sitting in Rhea Field while Shaver and Wood struggled to dislodge Peabody. The 4th Louisiana, being on the left of the brigade, suffered the most from Waterhouse's shots, while the 19th Louisiana, being the only regiment in the cover of woods on the brigade's right, suffered only two wounded. After a nerve-racking thirty minutes, Waterhouse was forced to turn his guns on other advancing brigades. Peabody was forced back to the division's campsite by 8:30 A.M. With support to their right, Wood and Shaver attacked Prentiss' camp site. The battle for Prentiss' camp lasted about half an hour, and by 9:00 A.M., he was forced to retire north through Barnes' Field. After the capture of Prentiss' camps the brigades of Wood, Shaver and Major General Alexander P. Stewart, who was following behind Wood and Gibson, were directed to change the line of advance to the left oblique. This change of direction was directed by Johnston himself, and by doing so, put Gibson on the front line.

As the brigade passed through the camps of Prentiss' division, the men did not hesitate to help themselves to the food, clothing and weapons left behind. Private William Bevens of the 1st Arkansas described the scene as they passed through Prentiss' camp: "We drove the officers from their hot coffee and out of their tents, capturing their camp and tents. Captain Shoup and John Loftin and Clay Lowe each got a sword. In the quartermaster's tent we found thousands of dollars in crisp, new bills, for they had been paying off the Yankee soldiers." Members of the 13th Louisiana took the time to exchange some of their inferior rifles for Belgian Rifles left behind by Prentiss' men. The quick pillaging was inter-

2. The Shiloh Campaign: April 1862

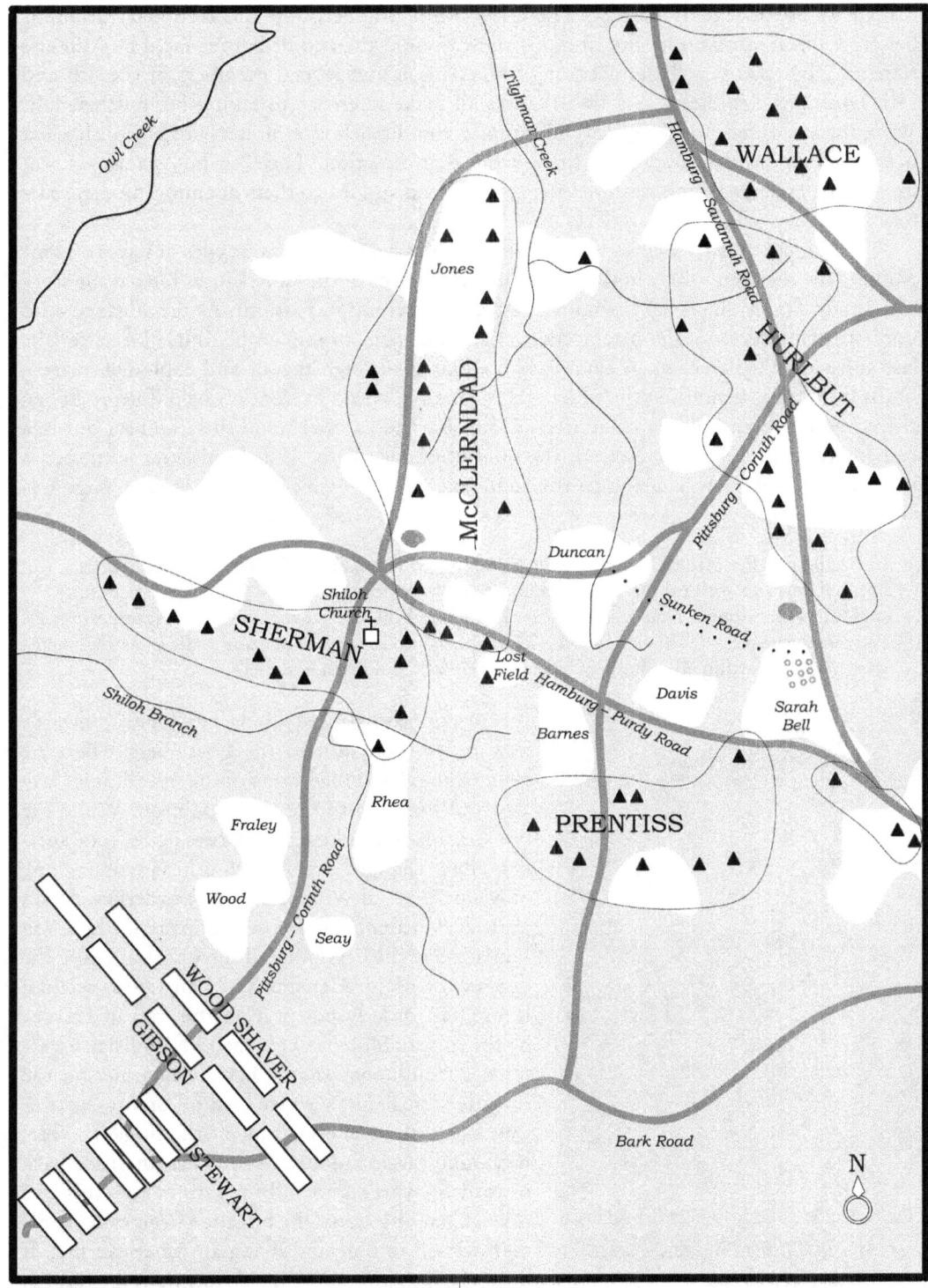

Battle of Shiloh, dispositions on the morning of 6 April 1862. Single names that are italicized show fields pertinent to Gibson's brigade. The only Confederate brigades labeled are those directly involved with the Louisiana Brigade on 6 April.

rupted by fire an enemy battery. There are conflicting accounts but secondary accounts believe Gibson came under fire from his right front at the end of Barnes Field by Munch's retreating battery. First hand accounts from Gibson and several members of the 4th and 13th Louisiana Regiments and 1st Arkansas all make reference to taking fire on their left. With three Confederate brigades obliquing across his left it is difficult to establish what battery could have possibly been firing from that direction. The 13th Louisiana was sent forward in a charge which scattered the artillerymen and led to them abandoning their battery flag.[5]

Documented fairly well by the brigade were a couple of humorous tales of slaves accompanying the regiments early in the battle. Private Bevens of the 1st Arkansas related the story of Captain Scales' slave, Sam, who refused to stay behind in Corinth. As the advance onto the battlefield began Scales attempted to convince Sam to remain behind. "Just after the last appeal the fight began. A cannon ball whizzed through the air and exploded, tearing limbs from trees, wounding the soldiers. One man fell dead in front of the old negro. Then there was a yell, and old Sam shouted, 'Golly, Marster, I can't stand this,' and set out in a run for Corinth." William Paxton, the quartermaster for the 19th Louisiana, witnessed a familiar scene as he was racing to the front to catch up to his regiment with a wagon of ammunition:

> Upon the first fire came a dozen niggers belonging to the camp, who had been detailed as a hospital corps to pick up the wounded and bear them from the field — The Darkies couldn't stand fire — I stopped them with my guard and asked them what they meant by scampering away in that style — "Why bless God, Capn. them Yankees was a shooting right at us and them wing shells a busting all around us — Blest God! We couldn't stay there!"[6]

Private William Bevens, 1st Arkansas. *Reminiscences of a Private, Company "G," First Arkansas Infantry, May 1861 to 1865* (Newport, Ark: N. ub., 1914), 2.

As Gibson paused in Barnes Field, Stewart's new route took him to the Lost Field where he reached the abandoned camp of the 4th Illinois Cavalry and lined up to the left of Gibson. While the two brigades sat in Lost and Barnes fields, they accidentally exchanged fire on each other involving one of Major General William Hardee's orderlies, Aaron Vertner. Vertner belonged to Company C of the 4th Louisiana at the beginning of the war, but being the nephew of Major General Earl Van Dorn, secured himself an orderly position on the staff of Hardee by the time of Shiloh. Once the 13th Louisiana scattered an unknown enemy battery hammering the brigade's left flank, Vertner sped off on his horse to investigate the scene in front of the brigade. Vertner found the abandoned Federal flag and rode back toward Stewart's and Gibson's lines to show the prize. Charging across the brigade's front came a soldier dressed in blue and flying an American flag. It drew the attention of Vertner's former unit, the 4th Louisiana, and several companies opened fired and killed the young aide. When the Fourth fired at Vertner, several of its shots hit the rear of one of Stew-

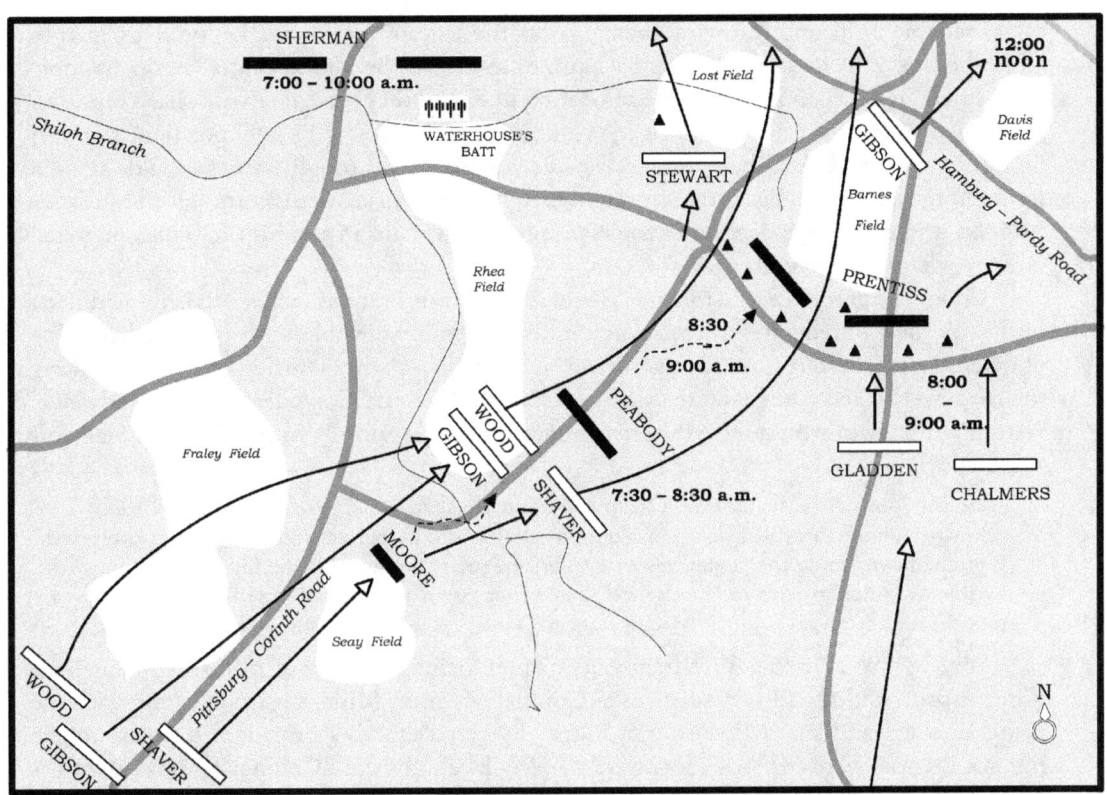

Advance to the Hornets Nest, 6:30 a.m.–Noon. Early morning hours Gibson trailed the advance of Woods and Shaver. Above map shows the crushing of Peabody's brigade and then Prentiss' division. Once Wood, Shaver and Stewart obliqued to the left Gibson found himself on the front line in Barnes Field.

art's regiments, the 13th Arkansas. The Arkansas troops, confused and in shock of an attack from the rear, immediately turned and returned fire. Before order was restored, the Fourth lost at least twenty-seven men to Stewart's fire. The rattled brigade lost 105 men in the brief exchange and succeeded in wounding Gibson's horse. Throughout the madness and chaos of the upcoming fighting Allen said that this firefight between friendly units unnerved his men the most that day. There is confusion as to who the 4th Louisiana got into a firefight with. Allen believed it to be a Tennessee regiment "immediately in our rear." This would be the 4th Tennessee Regiment which got separated from Stewart in his left oblique change of direction per Johnston. The 4th was lagging behind the rest of the brigade and was in fact the right regiment in Stewart's alignment. No one from the 4th Tennessee, however, reported a friendly firefight. Major James Mcneely of the 13th Arkansas does confirm the firefight in his report on Shiloh.[7]

From about 10:30 to 11:30 Gibson sat in Barnes Field while the fighting raged to his left across the Hamburg-Purdy road. The Federal left had been swept away from its positions around Shiloh Church but attacks on the middle were beginning to run into tough resistance. By 10:30 the middle of the Federal army began to pull together and form a defense stretching from behind Duncan Field to Sarah Bell's field and peach orchard to the southeast. General Bragg arrived on the left center of the line and immediately began grabbing available units and throwing them against the Union line. As the Union left began to be pushed back, it naturally brought its aim of attack to the Union center. Bragg haphazardly threw individual units into the reforming line, and they were met with sharp repulses. He turned to the next available brigade to knock loose the new Federal position; the unit he ran up on was Gibson's. Gibson advanced his brigade through Barnes's Field, aligned from left to right as follows: 4th Louisiana, 13th Louisiana, 1st Arkansas and 19th Louisiana. At noon, the green brigade crossed the Hamburg Road. Gibson and his 1,800 plus men had no idea what they were up against.[8]

Under the guidance of Brigadier General Benjamin Prentiss, whose division had been routed by the Confederates' surprise attack, the Federals were able to throw together a line of defense along an old sunken wagon road situated on a slight elevation. A rail fence along the road overlooked a huge dense thicket, through which the Confederates had to advance. A Louisianian who would taste the effectiveness of the position Prentiss picked to make his stand wrote:

> They were posted on the crest of a steep hill in an old road which by frequent travel has been worn about three feet deep consequently they could lie perfectly concealed and protected [written above] while they could see everything [regular] besides this the hill was covered with the thickest undergrowth of "black jack" that I ever saw it was almost impossible for a man to walk through it under ordinary circumstances.[9]

Prentiss was able to gather fragments of men belonging to four of his regiments: the 18th Missouri and the 18th Wisconsin of Colonel Madison Miller's brigade, along with the 12th Michigan and 21st Missouri of Colonel Everett Peabody's brigade. Deployed to the right of Prentiss were two brigades of W.H.L. Wallace's division, Colonel Thomas Sweeny's and Colonel James Tuttle's brigades. Supporting Prentiss on the left was Brigadier General Stephen Hulbert's division, with Brigadier General Jacob Lauman's brigade deployed next to the left of Prentiss. This line stretched from the Pittsburg-Corinth Road, along the sunken road, across the Eastern Corinth Road to the Hamburg-Savannah Road. Directly behind Prentiss and Tuttle were four batteries of artillery. Completely masked by the massive thicket to their front and lying on their bellies, Prentiss' line held its fire as Gibson's lone brigade advanced into the coming storm.[10]

Once across the Hamburg Road, the brigade ran into an "impenetrable thicket," and across the front of most of the 4th and 13th Louisiana was a large ravine. Descending into and climbing out of the muddy, heavily wooded ravine, the regiments attempted to reform themselves but were met by a "deadly fire" and a "murderous fire of grape and canister" from the combined fire of Tuttle, Prentiss, Lauman and three batteries. The brigade stopped in its tracks as "the surprise ... was complete and overwhelming." John McGrath of the 13th Louisiana remembered the sudden shock of enemy fire: "Strange to say we all fell over backwards, but most of us got up next moment unhurt, and returned fire." "Hail has nothing on that rain of lead," an Arkansas private said bluntly. The 4th and 13th Louisiana Regiments and the 1st Arkansas attempted to exchange volleys through the thicket. "Cant see the enemy. Our men falling thick and fast but shooting well," said Lieutenant Donelson Jenkins. So confusing was the firefight that the 4th Louisiana and 1st Arkansas were somehow exchanging fire with each other when the 13th Louisiana was in line between them! It took the direct intervention of Colonel Fagan to rectify the situation. Gibson, advancing with the 4th and 13th, attempted to stabilize the line and exchange fire. "Some of the weak hearted give way Col Allen and all the officers try in vain to rally them. The order is to fall back." The concentrated fire of the batteries behind Prentiss forced the regiments back into and behind the ravine they had just climbed out of. Allen rallied his men along the brow of the small hill, yelling and waving his sword in the air: "Form on this line!" Even though present at Manassas, the 1st Arkansas had yet to see such intensity in battle. Scenes such as Captain Jesse McMahan having the left side of his face shot off and seeing part of his jaw, some teeth and his tongue go with the face were enough to unnerve even the strongest man.[11]

The 19th Louisiana fared a little better. Hodge's regiment advanced across the Davis' wheat field and was spared the thicket-filled ravine. Once the regiment reached Davis' log cabin, about halfway across the field, they were hit by Federal fire at about 200 yards distance. Hodge quickly sent his men forward to take cover behind the fence on the north side of the wheat field. He was but a mere 100 yards from Prentiss' line and proceeded to exchange volleys with the remnants of Prentiss' and Lauman's brigades. Frustrated by the situation, Hodge ordered his men to fix bayonets, and they plunged into the thicket on the other side of the fence. The Nineteenth now faced the problem of its sister regiments: the dense thicket in front of the Sunken Road. Colonel Quin Morton of the 23rd Missouri reported that Hodge's and Fagan's advance came to within 25 or 30 yards of his line in the Sunken Road. One of Fagan's men said, "I could see the buttons on their coats." The 19th Louisiana came to within ten yards of Colonel Charles Cruft's 31st Indiana, which was on the right of Lauman's brigade next to the 23rd Missouri. "The slaughter among the enemy in its front was terrible," Cruft reported. Hodge was absorbing the fire of three regiments with their artillery support and was forced to extract his regiment, losing a sixth of his men in the attack.[12]

While Gibson and his officers rallied their men, he sent his civilian adjutant, Robert Pugh, to request artillery support from Bragg. Bragg refused Gibson's request and ordered the brigade forward again. When Colonel Hodge received orders to renew the assault, he also requested artillery support. After the battle Hodge reported, "I thought it impossible to force the enemy from this strong position by a charge from the front, but that with a light battery playing on one flank and a simultaneous charge of infantry on the other the position could be carried with but small loss." Hodge's plea to Bragg was ignored. Thus began the second attack at about 12:30. As somewhat symbolic of what to expect Captain Samuel Shoup of Company G, 1st Arkansas sensed the uneasiness of his men and stepped forward waving his sword to push them forward. Shoup's encouraging words had hardly left his mouth when he was abruptly interrupted by his sword being shot to pieces. The brigade advanced again getting slammed by batteries to its front and especially on its left flank by Munch's battery posted behind Tuttle's right. With no other targets coming their way, the combined batteries posted behind Prentiss were able to concentrate their fire on Gibson. For thirty minutes, Gibson held his ground while the 4th Louisiana got blasted with its left being exposed in Duncan's Field, the 13th Louisiana was pinned down in the ravine in front of Tuttle, the 19th Louisiana was pinned behind the north fence line of Davis' Field, and Fagan's poor Arkansas boys were pushing their way through the thickets with no cover. Riding up and down the line pushing his men forward, Colonel Allen was shot in the mouth with the ball entering one cheek and exiting his mouth through the other cheek. Allen fixed the wound by grabbing a swab of cloth and shoving it in the hole and then wrapping his handkerchief around his head to dress the wound.[13]

The Sunken Road line proved too much for the brigade, and Gibson extracted his men from the slaughter under a semi-orderly retreat. "With the enemy in front and on the flank, the regiment endured a murderous fire until endurance ceased to be a virtue," was how Fagan described the struggle of his 1st Arkansas. One of Fagan's men described the conditions his

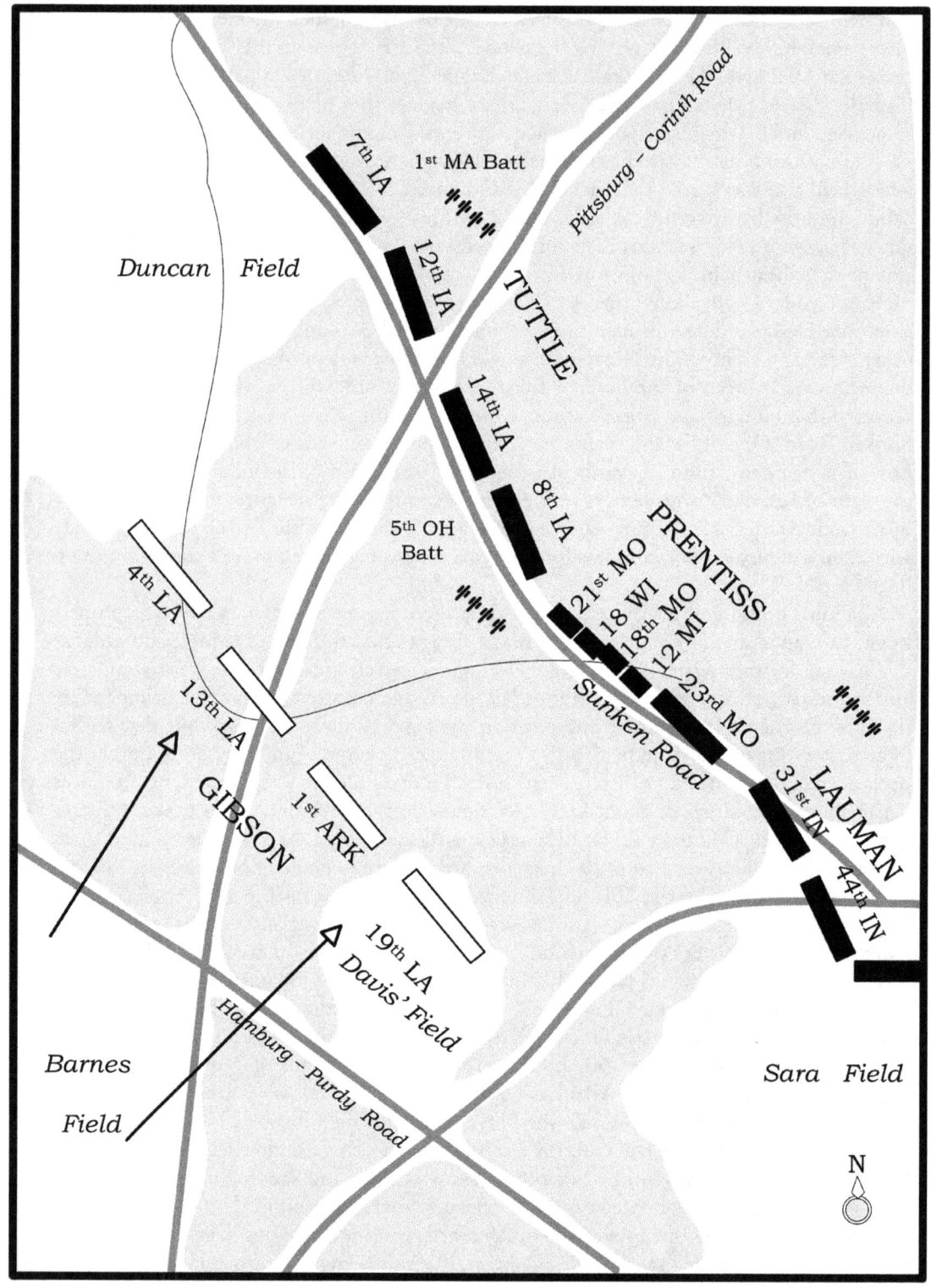

Attack on the Hornets Nest, Noon–2:30 P.M.

regiment faced: "The roar of musketry was incessant, and the cannonading fairly shook the ground." The second attack was intense and pushed the Sunken Road defenses the hardest yet. It took almost all the ammunition from the cartridge boxes of the 31st Indiana to repulse Hodge's second attack on his position, which Cruft described as an attack with "increased fury."[14]

The harrowing experience of Lieutenant Jenkins of the 4th Louisiana exemplified the intensity of the fight the Louisianians faced. In the first attack, he took fire at about 20 paces and actually had a piece of grapeshot slam into his side: "Fortunately its force had been spent before it got to me only knocking me down and making a pretty severe bruise." He limped back to the 4th Regiment, rejoined the ranks and joined in on the second attack. On the second go around, Jenkins had a part of a cannon ball graze his head, "cutting off the button of the left of my cap tearing my cap and cutting out a handful of my hair. This knocked me senseless for a time." When the beat up lieutenant finally made back to the brigade, his bumps and bruises were all remedied when he was given a shot of brandy, which "made me feel nearly all right again."[15]

The second attack had proved to be just as difficult as the first. Gibson gave command of the 13th Louisiana to Allen and went to see about the right of the brigade. For the next attack, Gibson rode over to Fagan and his 1st Arkansas to assist them in their advance. In doing so he left Avegno and the 13th Louisiana under Allen to coordinate their movements. While Gibson was making this adjustment, Braxton Bragg interjected himself onto the scene. According to Bragg in his official report, he and his staff were active in pushing Gibson's brigade into action. He described his role as several hours of "severe exertion." According to Colonel Allen, whom Bragg's staff officer soon approached, it was the first time all day he was approached by Bragg or his staff. What is known, though, is that Bragg was under the impression that the enemy in the Sunken Road was going to counterattack. He sent orders for Allen to take the 4th and 13th Regiments and "ambush them" and "serve them as they had served me [Allen]." In order to "ambush" them like Bragg suggested, it would be assumed he meant to use the brow of a small hill in front of the ravine as cover.[16]

As Bragg watched the brigade fall back from its second attack he sent Captain Samuel H. Lockett of his staff to rally a retreating regiment. The regiment that Lockett rode up to was none other than Allen's 4th Louisiana. Lockett ran up to the color sergeant of the Fourth and grabbed the colors from him. "The flag must not go back again, General Bragg says these colors must not go to the rear." At that moment, the color bearer from whom Lockett took the flag was shot down and dropped to the ground. To Lockett's amazement, the Louisianians didn't pay him any attention, and before he realized it, he sat alone between the Hornets Nest and the retreating Louisianians. Lockett was then approached by a very angry, bloodied Allen. "What are you doing with my colors, sir?" Lockett quickly defended his actions, "I am obeying General Bragg's orders, sir, to hold them where they are." Twice so far this day Bragg had insulted the honor of Allen and his regiment. "If any man but my color-bearer carries these colors, I am the man. Tell General Bragg I will see that these colors are in the right place." Allen reiterated his earlier demand for help by telling Lockett to tell Bragg, "He must attack this position in flank; we can never carry it alone from the front." Lockett sped off the rear to give Bragg Allen's message and Allen once again rallied his men for yet one more advance.[17]

It's at this time that Bragg interjected and ordered Allen to prepare for the counterattack. Bragg next ordered Allen to push his regiment forward again for another attack. Allen reaffirmed his request for artillery. The colonel's firm request for artillery support was met

Attack on the Hornets Nest. Part of the cyclorama painted of the Battle of Shiloh in which Gibson's brigade was included. In the background cluster of horses is depicted Gibson with his staff. In the foreground are parts of the 1st Arkansas (left) and 13th Louisiana (right). At far left, the officer on horseback getting shot is Lieutenant Colonel Thompson of the 1st Arkansas (courtesy of the U.S. Army Military History Institute).

with a quick reply from Bragg: "Colonel Allen, I want no faltering now." Instead of relying on sound doctrine of artillery support, Bragg instead leveled accusations of cowardliness. Allen, offended and disgusted, led his men forward again. "Here boys," yelled Allen to his jaded and disorganized regiment, "is as a good a place as any on this battlefield to meet death!" At once the batteries in the Hornets Nest "opened a powerful battery" on the Louisianians. As the guns in the Hornets Nest welcomed the 4th Louisiana back, Allen disgustedly watched as "General Bragg, staff, and body guard retired to a ravine" to seek cover from the fire.[18]

At 1:00 the Fourth moved forward into a severe fire; all the while Colonel Allen was screaming his men forward. A member of the regiment claimed the regiment pushed to within fifty feet of the Sunken Road before they had to jump to the ground to avoid the heavy fire. Allen was able to get his men up and begin advancing again when all heart was swept from his men. As Captain H.M. Favrot of Company F and another soldier jumped up to begin the last leg of the charge, a cannon ball swept through and took off half of the private's head. As Favrot swept the splattering of blood off of himself with his sleeve, the partially decapitated private managed to walk a couple more steps, flinging his arms in the air, before his body fell to the ground. "A sickening shudder ran through the ranks" and it managed to take the remaining wind out of the regiment. The Fourth Louisiana was finished, the attack being "as useless and ineffectual" as the others.[19]

Further down the line Gibson, with Fagan and the 1st Arkansas, pushed forward in the third and bloodier attack. At the commencement of this charge, Prentiss had ordered forward the guns of Captain Andrew Hickenlooper's 5th Ohio Battery in front of the 8th Iowa. Colonel James L. Geddes of the 8th Iowa reported that the guns in his front, Hickenlooper's, "made great havoc in the advancing columns of the enemy. It therefore became an object of great importance to them to gain possession of the guns." Geddes was right; Gibson geared the 1st Arkansas and 13th Louisiana toward the guns, and in "a struggle ... of terrific character," Gibson's regiments actually took Hickenlooper's battery and forced back the supporting 14th Iowa and 8th Iowa. Members of the 13th Louisiana and 1st Arkansas were able to make a slight dent in the Sunken Road. Smoke from the blazing lines now filled the thicket with a heavy fog which showed the intensity of the firefight. The 1st Arkansas was eventually forced to withdraw because it ran out of ammunition. The 8th Iowa was able to reform itself and push forward to retake Hickenlooper's guns but at the cost of 100 men killed and wounded, including a wounded Colonel Geddes. The combined fire of Sweeney, Prentiss and Lauman on the brigade's flanks finally forced it to crumble under the pressure.[20]

The losses in the brigade were not only rising in the rank and file but also with officers. Five captains and seven lieutenants alone in the 1st Arkansas had become casualties, four being wounded and killed. The 4th Louisiana had lost three captains with one being killed and Colonel Allen being wounded. In the 13th Louisiana, there were three captains wounded, and Major Avegno was forced to turn over command to Captain O'Leary, who was also slightly wounded. Avegno was unable to lead the regiment anymore because he lost his voice and could no longer communicate orders. The highest ranking officer lost that day was Lieutenant Colonel James Thompson of the 1st Arkansas, who was riddled with seven bullets. April 6 was his twenty-eighth birthday and he would die two days later from his wound. Thompson had written his father the night of April 5 almost eerily predicting his death: "My dear father, I write by the light of our bivouac fire. We expect, by God's help, a glorious victory tomorrow. If I should not see you again, take assurance that I trust in

God to be prepared for all. Day after tomorrow is my birthday. Love to all. Your devoted son, John B. Thompson." Besides Thompson, the 1st Arkansas lost four of its captains: one killed and three wounded. Two were mortally wounded and died from their wounds following the battle.[21]

The brigade was completely spent. For the past two and a half hours it was forced to make three unsupported attacks on the Hornets Nest, which resulted in its getting decimated. Captain Hickenlooper of the 5th Ohio Battery described the battle scene in front of him at the Hornets Nest as he contested Gibson's repeated attacks: "'Double canister' was delivered with such rapidity that the separate discharges blended into one continuous roar. Then the supporting infantry, rising from their recumbent position, sent forth a sheet of flame and leaden hail that elicited curses, shrieks, groans and shouts, all blended into an appalling cry.... Again and again, through long and trying hours, this dance of death went on." A 4th Louisiana veteran wrote in his diary about the attack on the Hornets Nest, "How I escaped unhurt is a mystery." One part of the Hornets Nest actually caught fire near the 19th Louisiana and, in the process, burned many of the dead and wounded. "The musketry had set fire to the dry leaves and grass covering the ground. The fire had burned all the clothes off from bodies.... The flesh had been burned from their set teeth, giving them a horrible grin."[22]

Despite all of the factors facing Gibson, Bragg blamed him for the repulse. In his official report of the battle you can read the animosity Bragg feels for Gibson. Gibson had been ordered to follow behind the front line and remain in support; not so according to Bragg. "I moved farther to the right, and brought up the First Brigade (Gibson) of Ruggles' Division, which was in rear of its true position." Bragg reported that Gibson's men "fell back in considerable disorder" after a "short conflict." He next laid claim that he and his staff had to rally the command and force it back into action two more times and then laid the complete failure on his lone brigade to carry the Sunken Road by saying, "This result was due entirely to want of proper handling." Gibson protested Bragg's report by requesting a court of inquiry from the secretary of war, but his request went unanswered. This issue was to be brought back in the future, however, and everyone Gibson solicited reports from all readily responded to support Gibson's case against Bragg.[23]

Another example of how Bragg slighted Gibson in his report, besides saying he was lagging behind his proper spot in line and he was a poor commander, is the comparison of Bragg's description of the attacks of Brigadier General Thomas Hindman's attack and Gibson's attack on the "same point" of the Sunken Road defense. Bragg reported that Hindman's brigade, which made only one charge, attacked a position that was "strongly posted, with infantry and artillery, on an eminence immediately behind a dense thicket." The attack was "gallantly led" and Hindman was forced to fall back "under a murderous fire." Gibson, Bragg reported, was "driven back by the enemy's sharpshooters occupying the thick cover," and the brigade fell back in "considerable disorder."[24]

Bragg was more openly hostile toward Gibson in a letter to his wife. As almost comparing Gibson to a skulker, Bragg wrote his wife, "I had not been able to force him into battle up to 12 o'clock. At last he was put in a hot place and at once retreated with his whole force." Bragg continued his sharp criticism of Gibson and his brigade: "They were demoralized and nothing would induce them to go. A want of confidence in their leader Gibson destroyed them. He [Gibson] is an *arrant coward*." Bragg even took the time to boast to his wife, and perhaps attempting to impress her, that he ran up to one of Gibson's regiments and "took their flag and led them in." After decimating Gibson's brigade, he claimed, he left the "crowd under Gibson to hold its ground" and moved on to the right of the army.[25]

During the morning and early afternoon, the Confederate left continually pushed back the Federals. With Grant's right wing in retreat, the Confederates were able to hit the right flank of the Hornets Nest. The left flank of the Hornets Nest was also exposed when other Federal units retreated. Leading his men forward on the Confederate right, opposite the Hornets Nest, A.S. Johnston was wounded, and General P.G.T. Beauregard assumed command of the army. As the Hornets Nest was being outflanked to the left and right, the Confederates brought together several batteries and shelled Prentiss's line. Eventually, Prentiss's position was taken, but this assault cost the Confederates several precious hours. Colonel Hodge, who had been ignored by Bragg earlier when he suggested that artillery be brought up and the Federal line be flanked, did not hesitate to make note of how the Hornets Nest was taken: "I may be permitted to add, sir, that this formidable position of the enemy, after having withstood the repeated attacks of various regiments, was only carried at last by a charge upon the right flank, supported by a battery on the left." The Confederate attack eventually lost momentum after taking the Hornets Nest and allowed Grant to regroup his army around Pittsburg Landing.[26]

Following the surrender of Prentiss, Gibson's movements are a little sketchy. According to Gibson, he was ordered by a member of Bragg's staff "to develop to the right ... I was ordered to hold a position slightly to our rear." He moved there with the 1st Arkansas and 19th Louisiana and waited "for a short while" until word came that Bragg had ridden to the far right upon receiving the word of Johnston's death. Gibson reunited his four regiments and moved toward the Tennessee River where he ran into Ruggles. Ruggles, under orders from Beauregard, ordered his troops to fall back. At dusk the brigade began its retreat from the river, under fire from Union gunboats, in "considerable disorder." Frank Richardson of the 13th Louisiana said his unit dodged the shells of the enemy ships "from tree to tree" as they passed over head "like shafts of lightning, cutting through the forest."[27]

The 19th Louisiana became separated from the brigade in the night. Hodge attempted to find the brigade throughout the night but resigned himself that it was impossible and bedded his men down for the night in captured enemy camps to the right of Anderson's brigade. The location of where Gibson and Anderson camped is not exact; neither one gives us a specific location except that Anderson says he camped near Bragg's headquarters. The tent that Bragg and Beauregard used that night as their headquarters was none other than Sherman's abandoned tent near Shiloh Church. This put Gibson near the crossroads of the Hamburg-Purdy and Corinth-Pittsburg Landing roads. The captured tents of Sherman's division provided the men with shelter from the downpour of rain that hit the area at midnight. "We retired to rest in yankee tents and under yankee blankets, but not before we supped sumptuously on yankee provisions. You cannot imagine how comfortably they were fixed up."[28]

At dawn the next morning, 7 April, reinforced by elements of the Army of the Ohio, Grant counterattacked the Army of the Mississippi. The majority of the Confederate army had pulled back a considerable distance, per Beauregard's orders, out of the range of the enemy gunboats. One unit, however, did not receive orders to retire in the rain soaked night, Ruggles' Third Brigade under Colonel Preston Pond. Pond's small brigade sat isolated in Jones' Field while the remainder of the army sat comfortably to the rear some 1 or 2 miles away. Sparring with enemy skirmishers started at about sunrise and soon escalated when an enemy battery was unlimbered at the north end of Jones' Field. Once contact was made,

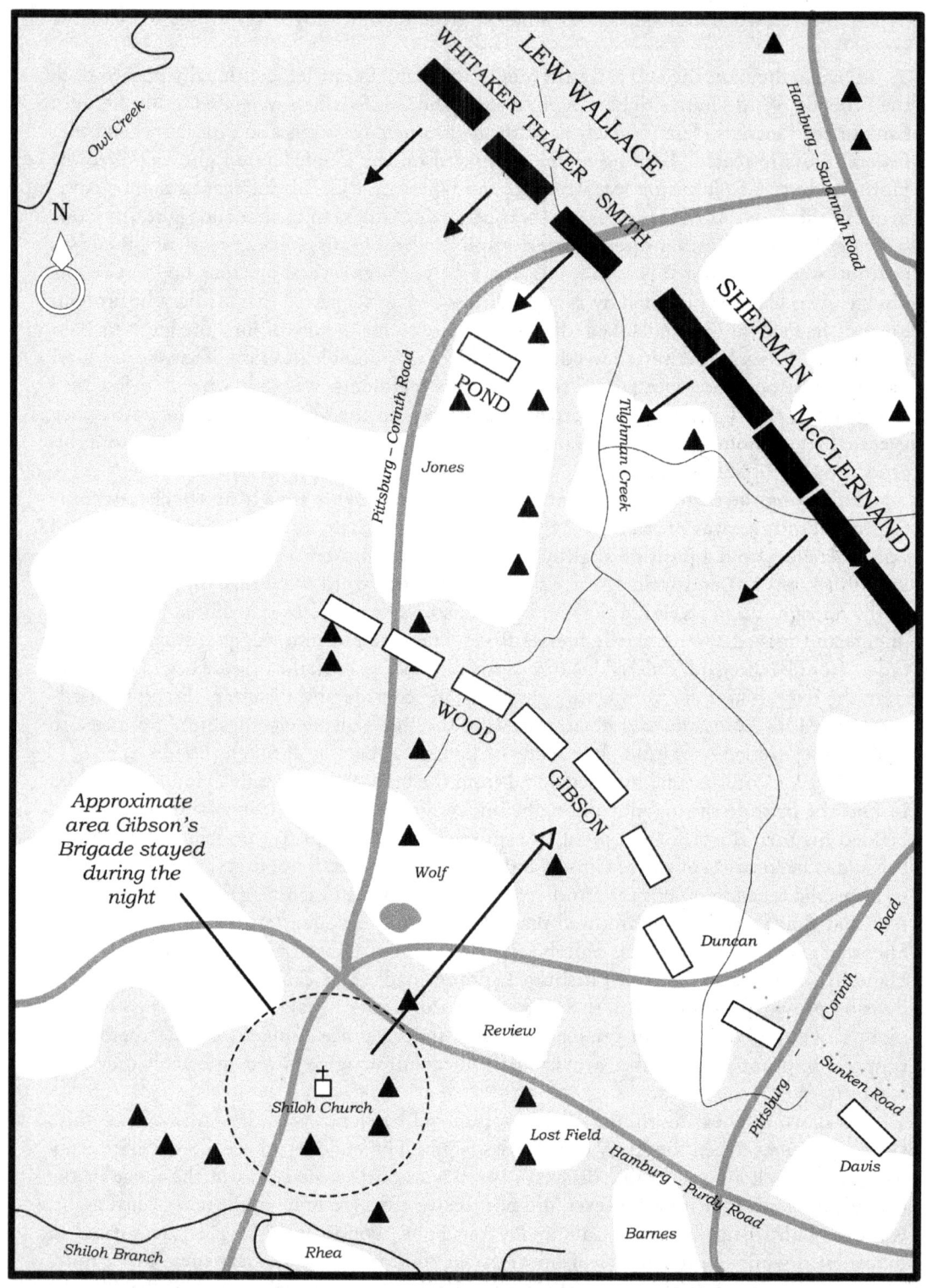

Shiloh, Morning of 7 April

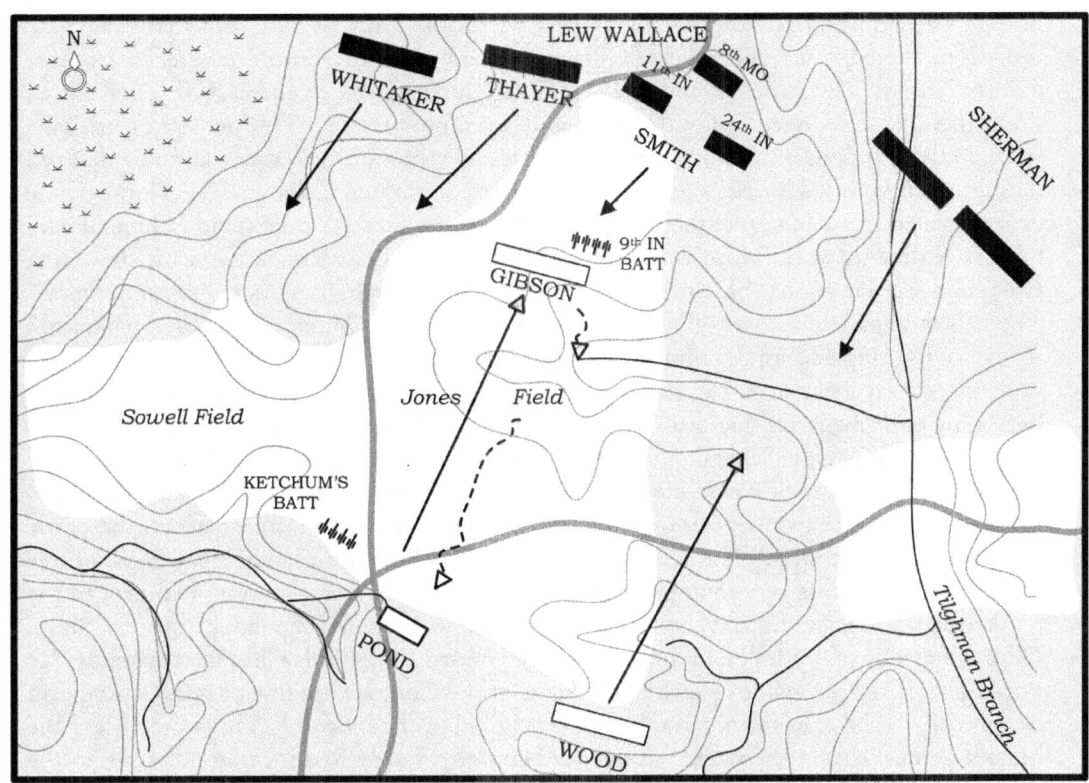

Shiloh, Jones Field, 7 April, 9:30 A.M.–10:30 A.M.

Pond called on Ruggles for assistance. At 6:00 A.M., Ruggles grabbed Gibson's command and ordered his regiments to "fall in to face the enemy again." The costly attacks on the Hornets Nest, "after an almost sleepless night" due to the rainstorm and periodic shelling of the enemy boats along with the accidental separation of the 19th Louisiana, must have left Gibson's brigade a skeleton of its former self when it stepped into line to support Pond on the morning of the 7th.[29]

As Gibson was forming his much depleted brigade in the woods at the southwest corner of Jones' Field, S.A.M. Wood's brigade filed into line on Gibson's right a short distance away. The force that pushed Pond from Jones' Field was that of Major General Lew Wallace's division. Wallace's First Brigade under Colonel Morgan L. Smith was formed on the north end of the field supporting the menacing guns of Lieutenant Charles Thurber's Battery I of the 1st Missouri Light Artillery and Captain N.S. Thompson's 9th Indiana Battery. Wallace had pushed Thompson's guns onto a small hill vacated by Pond and his battery just minutes before. Having fired all his rounds, Thompson was allowed to pull his guns back as Thurber rolled his battery into line, with "scarcely an intermission in the fire."[30]

Gibson was ordered to silence the guns pounding Jones' Field and soon his men were charging across the field. "Our brigade was soon pushed forward and ordered to charge a battery which was playing with terrible effect on our lines." The right of Gibson's brigade, the 1st Arkansas, managed to capture one of the guns and scare off Thurber's Missourians. Being master of the guns did not last long, as Captain E. M. Dubroca of the 13th Louisiana reported: "It was not our good fortune to hold them long." With the Missouri gunners out of their way, Smith's two front units, the 11th and 24th Indiana Regiments, let loose a "brisk fire" from the edge of Jones' Field. Gibson withdrew his men into a ravine, in front of Thurber's guns, that ran east and west from Tilghman Creek to the east of Jones' Field. From there he exchanged fire with Smith and attempted to turn Thurber's guns on Wallace's advancing division. Wallace was not impressed with Gibson's attack and downplayed its success in taking Thurber's guns: "The infantry attempted a charge. The First Brigade easily repelled them." Despite the minute detail given to Gibson's brief stand in Jones' Field, Smith's regiments were forced to go toe to toe with the Louisianians for a bit, in which Colonel Alvin Hovey of the 24th Indiana described the firefight as "a stubborn conflict." The 11th Indiana was actually given the order to fix bayonets which reflects the preparation for heavy fighting and an attempt to dislodge Gibson from the ravine.[31]

Gibson sat isolated in the north end of the field. Wallace's other two brigades were beginning to flank Jones' Field to the left. On Gibson's right, Wood's brigade was beginning to retire as Major General William T. Sherman's division was advancing to the east of the field. Ruggles quickly extracted Gibson from the coming disaster: "I was ordered to proceed in all haste to the position assigned to me in the morning, near which the battle was now hotly contested." The Federal advance was not limited to Jones' Field. Buell's three fresh divisions, at this very moment, had pushed into the Sara Bell cotton field next to the Sunken Road, not far from where Gibson's brigade was mauled the day before. By 10:30, Gibson was out of Jones' Field and sent south toward the Shiloh Church crossroads. It's not known if Gibson made it back to the right of the Confederate line or not. Gibson said he was ordered back to the position he had occupied in the morning. This would place the brigade somewhere in the woods across the Hamburg-Purdy Road facing north to northeast and north of Review Field. Colonel Fagan states that from the time they retreated from Jones' Field to the time they were engaged again it was "an hour or so later." This time span would roughly be around 10:30 to noon that the brigade was not engaged. What was the brigade doing that whole time? The men were "considerably jaded and scattered in the rapid march" from Jones' Field back to the Shiloh Church area.[32]

This time span corresponds with the counterattack led by Major General Frank Cheatham and the remnant of his division, in which Gibson participated. Cheatham was pulled back on the night of the sixth to the rear of Shiloh Church. By the time Cheatham was able to scrape together scattered units, get them organized and advance into the fight, it was close to noon. His division slammed into the advancing divisions of Sherman and McClenard to the right of the Pittsburg-Corinth Road where it crossed the Hamburg-Purdy Road. So severe and intense was Cheatham's attack that it stalled Grant's counterattack in its tracks. Following Fagan's time line, Gibson's command would have been thrown into the fray with Cheatham around this time. Cheatham simply reports, "During the engagement here I was re-enforced by Colonel Gibson, with a Louisiana brigade," and Gibson and his regimental commanders give no times either.[33]

"It was impossible to preserve much order in this movement ... the regiments were somewhat mixed," and the brigade was thrown into action somewhere near the Pittsburg-Corinth Road in front of Shiloh Church. Men of the brigade describe their position as the spot they occupied in the morning. This would put the brigade near the crossroads north of Shiloh Church. The brigade was met by General Beauregard as they pulled into line. "Men the day is ours, you are fighting a whipped army, fire low and be deliberate." Encouraged by words from the commanding general and forming up to the tune of "Dixie" being played on a flute, men who were "sinking with fatigue or wounds rallied again and reentered the lines." "Now we are on them," wrote Jenkins of the 4th Louisiana, "They fall back we shout and advance." The brigade joined in Cheatham's attack and pushed forward. This was the last charge for Jenkins, for he was shot in the knee, and when the brigade was forced back under increased enemy pressure, he was left behind and eventually captured. As his comrades finished out the Battle of Shiloh and eventually retreated, he was brought behind enemy lines and left to lie in the open rain and become a spectacle to jeering enemy soldiers.[34]

The fighting on this part of the field remains sketchy from both Union and Confederate reports. Kendall of the 4th Louisiana described the scene of fighting around the Shiloh Church area the best: "My recollection supplies me with no special incident connected with this seesaw of battle." The stand along the Hamburg-Purdy Road front shows that the Louisianians made at least two charges on the Federals. The first major push with Cheatham stopped the enemy in their tracks, but then the "seesaw battle" began. Toward the end of this fight, close to 2:00 P.M., Captain Dubroca, now commanding the 13th Louisiana for the wounded O'Leary, said there was one last push with about 200 men from the various regiments. Major Avegno, even though giving up command, was present in this last charge. He was unable to command due to his loss of voice, but he was still able to fight. In the last charge of the day, he was severely wounded in his leg and was borne off the field. Avegno's wound was so severe that his leg was amputated and he was soon sent to New Orleans from Corinth to recuperate. Avegno made it only as far as Camp Moore before he died from his wound.[35]

From roughly noon to 2:00 the Army of the Mississippi withstood the Federal attack by mainly being posted in the Hamburg-Purdy Road. By 2:00 to 2:30, the fresh numbers of Buell's army were too much for a depleted and worn out Confederate army. At Beauregard's order, the army began to pull off the field of Shiloh. In the retreat, Gibson's command lined up in front of Shiloh Church as part of the rear guard with the 13th Louisiana forming the nucleus. "It was gratifying to see so many officers and men of the brigade formed in line ready to meet the enemy," a proud Gibson said after the battle. Colonel Allen was also instrumental in helping to form the rear guard. On the evening of the sixth, he turned command of the 4th Louisiana over to Lieutenant Colonel Samuel Hunter and he went to the hospital near Shiloh Church. A "stampede of wagons, ambulances, and men" caught the attention of a resting Allen in one of the tents. He immediately began rallying men and units to form a line in front of the church to protect the retreating army. A witness to Allen's rallying men for a last stand was described as such:

> There was Allen, his face tied up in a bloody handkerchief, with a bit of raw cotton sticking on his cheek — which certainly did not improve his beauty — one minute entreating, praying, weeping, tears streaming as he implored the men to stand; the next moment, swearing, raging at them, abusing them, berating them, giving them every angry epithet he could think of; then addressing them in the most affectionate words. But he succeeded in gathering together not only his own men but a number of stragglers from other regiments, whom he coaxed or abused back into the ranks. The last I saw of him he was off with them like a whirlwind into the thick of the battle.

The worn out enemy was in no hurry to pursue the retreating Confederates.[36]

Throughout April 7, the 19th Louisiana remained separated from the brigade. Hodge had camped his regiment the night before to the right of Anderson's brigade, and in the morning he attempted to find the brigade again but was stopped short of doing so. Brigadier General Jones Withers stopped Hodge and ordered him to the right of the army. Hodge was given orders to turn the regiment over to Lieutenant Colonel Hollingsworth, and With-

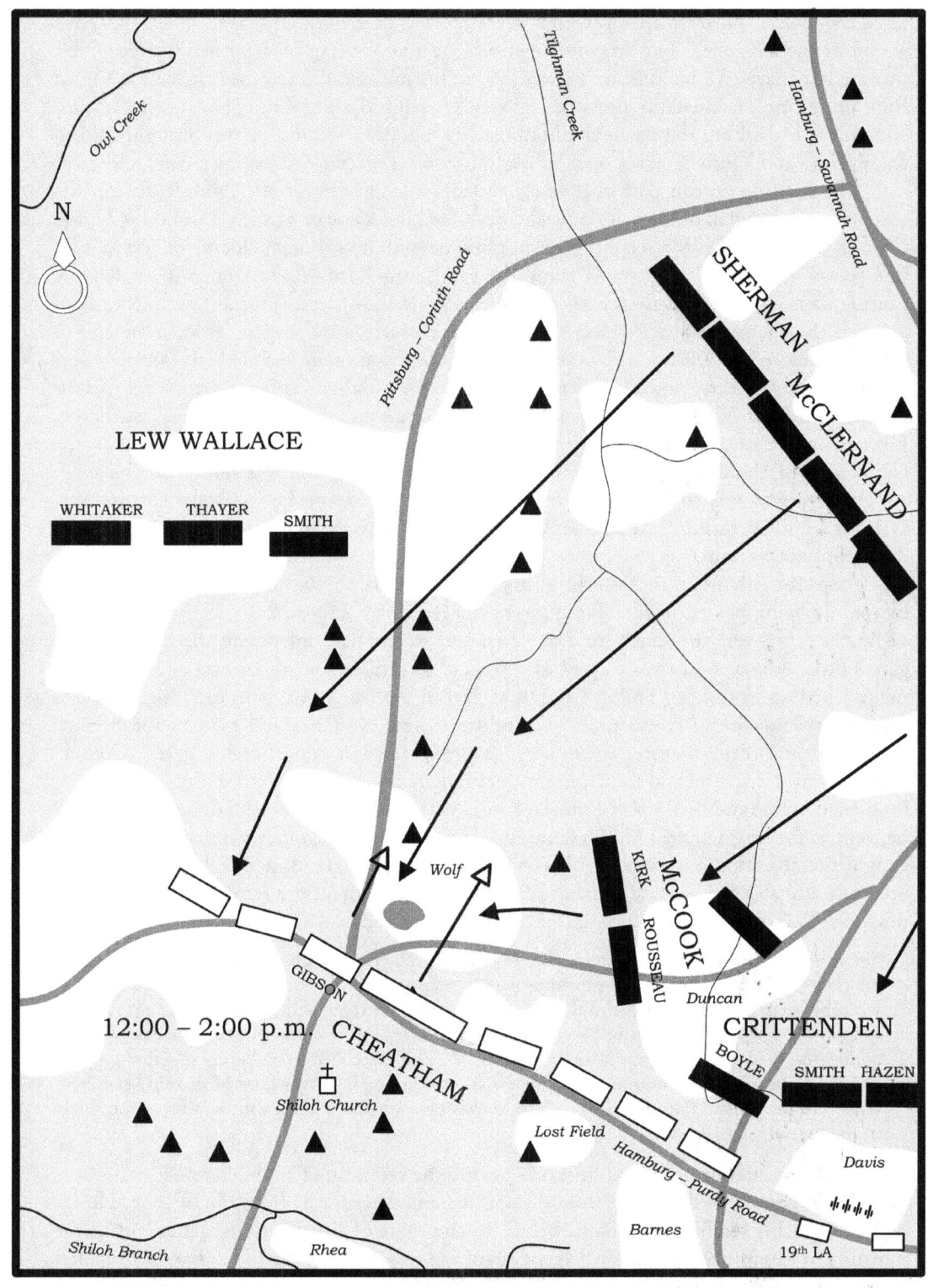

Shiloh, 7 April, Noon–2:30 P.M.

ers put him in charge of a small demi-brigade by putting him in command over the 24th Louisiana and Captain Washington Hodgson's 5th Company of Washington Artillery, along with his own regiment. Hodge took his new command and proceeded to the right of the army to support Brigadier General James Chalmers' brigade.[37]

Hodge and his command deployed to the left of Chalmers, and of all places the 5th Company could have stopped to deploy its guns it was none other than Davis' Field. Hodge and his men battled over this very field the day before and were not excited to see it again. The exact role of the 19th Louisiana on that part of the field is sketchy. It is suggested that the regiment deployed to the right of the 5th Company, and in the midst of the heavy cannon firing Hodge was thrown from his horse and had to be removed from the field. Hollingsworth's report was never found, and thus the Nineteenth's movements remain unknown. The regiment was engaged at Davis' Field, but there is no mention of the 19th Louisiana from any surrounding units. It did, however, rejoin the brigade that evening in Monterey.

That evening the brigade camped at Monterey in the field where it had camped two days before while heading to Shiloh. The retreat from Shiloh was a torturous experience. Having experienced the nightmare of a lifetime by having endured the largest and bloodiest battle to this point in the war, and of their life to this point, the march back to Corinth brought no comfort to the men. The terrain was soaked from the rain on the night of the sixth and it began to rain again that afternoon. The retreat was done so "amidst a terrible storm of rain and sleet." John Kendall said, "Soon a tremendous rainstorm set in.... The ground was soaked.... But I was too weary to mind that. Flinging myself down in the mud and rain, I slept the dreamless sleep that only comes to soldiers when they are dead tired." Gibson closed his report to army headquarters about the Battle of Shiloh by describing the condition of the brigade when it limped into Corinth: "The loss of so many brave officers and true men, together with the hardships endured in falling back to this point, had at first a depressing effect on the command, but it is rallying very fast." Captain Asa Morgan of the 1st Arkansas backed Gibson's description—"I have just this moment arrived from the field 16 miles; tired, hungry, wet and dirty"—but Morgan ended optimistically as Gibson did in his report: "We are far from being whipped."[38]

If the brigade didn't take a whipping at Shiloh it was the closest thing they had seen as of yet. Gibson lost one-third of his command at Shiloh: 682 were killed, wounded or captured. The 4th Louisiana lost a staggering 209 out of 575 men, including half of its captains with two being killed and three wounded. The 1st Arkansas lost a total of 277 men (46 killed, 214 wounded and 20 captured) of its 800. What testifies to the intensity of the fighting at the Hornets Nest is that of those 277 men lost in Fagan's regiment, 240 were lost on the first day with the vast majority being at the Nest. No detailed losses were given for the 13th and 19th Regiments; by subtracting the losses of the other two regiments, then these regiments' combined losses were 196 men. Of that number about two-thirds were losses from the 13th Regiment.[39]

Shiloh was a wake up call to the reality of war. The heroic, chivalrous notion of coming home as heroes was replaced with the grim fact that many men were either dead or maimed for life. The men reached the conclusion that army life was not all it was cracked up to be. Shiloh left an empty and angry feeling. There was no crushing victory like Bull Run like in the east. Major Wesley Winans of the 19th Louisiana put full blame on Beauregard for their failure at Shiloh: "And what did he ever do. Happy fortunate child of luck. Manassas according to his own report gained itself.... Johnston planned Shiloh, and Beauregard's order to fall back instead of to advance Sunday evening, lost us the chance of victory." There were many factors that necessitated the withdrawal Sunday night, but explaining that to the men who bled on that field did not reach the most sympathetic ears. The pre–Shiloh enthusiasm was replaced soon afterwards with boring trench warfare of a miserable Corinth.[40]

CHAPTER 3

The Louisiana Brigade Takes Shape: April–August 1862

"Our Brigade now consists of the 11th, 13th, 16th, 20th, and 25th Louisiana Regiments, and the 5th Company of Washington Artillery—all from Louisiana and many from New Orleans. We will be called 'Adam's Louisiana Brigade.'"

—W. L. Trask, adjutant, Austin's battalion,
22 August 1862

After Shiloh, as the army was licking its wounds in Corinth, the Army of the Mississippi underwent several reorganizations. Changes were pretty widespread in Braxton Bragg's II Corps. As early as 9 April, Bragg demanded reports from commanders and lists of casualties so as to "further and complete the reorganization of the Second Corps." Bragg created a track record throughout the war of removing, transferring or court-martialing officers he did not deem qualified to lead. The Battle of Shiloh was a glaring slap in the face to Bragg showing the need to restructure his command, even though he neglected to see his own faults in reference to the Hornets Nest. In this reorganization of his corps he didn't hesitate to stifle or restrict Gibson's ability to command a brigade. There are no written words left by Bragg explaining his actions regarding Gibson and his regiment following Shiloh but one must look at the facts and Bragg's unforgivable personality toward what he deemed unqualified officers. To discipline Gibson for what he perceived as a lack of military leadership it looks as though Bragg sought to deny him command of anything above his regiment. After Shiloh Gibson and his 13th Louisiana were transferred to the Third Brigade, which was under the command of Brigadier General Lucius M. Walker. Being outranked, Gibson resumed command of his regiment and relinquished command of his brigade.[1]

Gibson was actually swapped for Colonel Preston Pond's 16th Louisiana Regiment. Pond commanded the Third Brigade but with his resignation after Shiloh command was assigned to Walker. Being outranked, Gibson reverted to regimental command. This was something that would not have bothered Bragg much since he did not hold Gibson in high esteem as a commander. Meanwhile, the officer designated to replace Gibson in command of his old brigade was newly promoted Brigadier General Alfred Mouton, the former commander of the 18th Louisiana. At the time of the promotion and appointment to the brigade, Mouton was recovering in New Orleans from a wound he received at Shiloh. Mouton would never return to the Army of the Mississippi. Instead, he obtained a transfer to the Department of Western Louisiana. With Mouton absent from the army, Colonel Daniel Gober, Colonel Pond's successor, of the 16th Louisiana, took command of Gibson's old brigade by 28 April. As Gibson sat in exile his old brigade began to rapidly change over the next few months with the addition of new units and the transfer of old ones.²

The 16th Louisiana joined the brigade as the most diversified regiment in terms of the geography of its companies: It was composed of companies from Caddo and Bienville in the northwest corner of the state, three companies from central Louisiana (two from Rapides and one from Avoyelles), three from the Florida Parishes (St. Helena, Livingston and St. Tammany), and it was rounded out with two companies from Cajun country out of St. Tammany and St. Landry parishes. Perhaps the only unifying factor in these varying cultures was their rural and small town backgrounds. The regiment was thrown together on 29 September 1861 at Camp Moore. Thirty-six-year-old Vermont born Preston Pond, Jr., of East Feliciana Parish was elected the regiment's colonel with Enoch Mason as its lieutenant colonel (of the Caddo Fencibles, Co. C) and Captain Daniel Gober (of the Big Cane Rifles, Co. K) was promoted to major. Pond, a northerner by birth, was an attorney serving as a colonel in the Louisiana militia. When Louisiana seceded he was appointed inspector general of the Third Division of the state militia. With the formation of the 16th Louisiana he was politically connected and qualified to fill the commanding position.³

Colonel Preston Pond, 16th Louisiana (courtesy of Camp Moore Historical Association).

The 16th Louisiana was another regiment made up of rural boys that suffered heavily from disease. Fannie Pittman visited her brother of the Castor Guards, Company I, while they were in New Orleans in February 1862. When Mrs. Pittman arrived, she found her brother Terrel Bryan sick. Mrs. Pittman headed home after spending a week in camp nursing her brother back to health. "I have been quite uneasy about him ever since [leaving New Orleans] as there has been such a great deal of rain and it is such a muddy place where they are." The exposure to new diseases, poor living conditions and inadequate medical attention proved a serious challenge to the Sixteenth Regiment. Even though conditions improved for the regiment at Camp Moore, the brief stay there took the life of at least twenty men, five being from Company K alone.⁴

Louis Stagg of the Big Cane Rifles, Company K, reaffirmed the situation very descriptively in a letter to his wife: "I had an attack of diarrhea that nearly killed me.... There is always a great deal of sickness in the camp ... all those who fall seriously ill die from exposure and poor medical care, especially those who catch the measles; almost none of them recover." The Big Cane Rifles were from rural St. Landry Parish along the Atchafayla Basin, and their exposure to outside diseases was limited. James Pittman of Company I pointed out measles as the culprit in his company; in mid–November there were "some thirty that is down" and unfit for duty. Worse than all of the above listed conditions was the scarcity of good and consistent food. In mid–October, several hundred members of the regiment stormed the quartermaster's tent and ransacked the regimental stores in order to find food.

The assistance of other units allowed the officers of the regiment to restore order and finally get food to the men. Despite a supposed improvement in food a homesick Louis Stagg penned to his wife what probably summed up the feelings of his company: "I would give anything to be home eating a good gumbo."[5]

Despite the boredom of camp life, inconsistent food provisions, rampant disease running through the companies and the reality of military life setting in, the Sixteenth was quickly turned into a cohesive unit. An admiring private from the 17th Louisiana wrote home describing the Sixteenth Regiment while at Camp Moore: "The 16th Regt is well drilled, much better than ours. The 16th. has had the best drilled officers in the State." Pond broke the routine of camp life with five hours of drill spread out during each day from 4:00 A.M. to 9:00 P.M.; the results obviously paid off from the affectionate words from the 17th Louisiana.[6]

Organized, drilled and equipped, the regiment was transferred to New Orleans in late November or early December. As typical with units stationed around New Orleans, the Sixteenth performed garrison duty at various points. The regiment was sent to Camp Chalmette then to Camp Benjamin and then back to Chalmette during the months of December through February. The regiment was sent north with Ruggles as part of Johnston's concentration to meet Grant's advance on Corinth. When Pond's regiment reached the Corinth area in March, it was exposed to the same conditions of other Louisiana units, including very cold conditions not seen by the country boys of Louisiana. Already hit hard by disease from their exposure at Camp Moore the regiment could ill afford more men absent from duty due to sickness, but that is precisely what happened. Of the original 851 mustered into service about six months before, the Sixteenth would have 330 men in line when it marched onto the fields of Shiloh in April of 1862. Abraham Nesom of Company F described his company's experience at Corinth:

Colonel Daniel Gober, 16th Louisiana. Postwar photograph (courtesy of Peggy T.).

Waters was up and I had to wade a good deal ... and it snowed on us some and the wind blew very cold and in a few days we had to start back to Corrinth again and we started late in the evening and dark overtaken us and we could hardly see the road we got in the mud and water up to our knees and I have had a very bad cold every since.... The boys is very ner all sick out of about 95 privates about 25 or 30 answers to the roll call.[7]

Ruggles' brigade was dispersed to several brigades in the creation of the Army of the Mississippi and the 16th Louisiana was placed in the Third Brigade of Ruggles' division where it joined fellow Louisianians from the 18th and Crescent Regiments and the 38th Tennessee. Pond, due to seniority of rank, was placed in command of the brigade. At Shiloh the regiment lost 27 percent of its strength, a total of 90 men. Included in the wounded was Pond. By the time the 16th Louisiana joined the brigade, its high command had been shaken up. Under the Conscription Act, the regiment reorganized in May and elected its officers. Pond was not retained and headed back to Louisiana where he served in the Opelousas area for some time before he removed himself to Clinton, Louisiana. Pond attempted to reenter Confederate service through communication with the governor of Louisiana in 1864 but he died that summer at the age of 40. Enoch Mason was not reelected by the men, due to "physical disabilities," and command fell onto the shoulders of Major Gober. In the reorganization he was elevated to colonel and with a shadow of his former regiment he took command of Gibson's old brigade.[8]

Daniel Gober, son of a Virginian Revolutionary War veteran, was native to Georgia. Gober and his twin sister were born in 1828 in DeKalb County, Georgia. Young Daniel made his way to Tennessee and Kentucky and got married. In 1852 he graduated from the University of Louisville in medicine. Soon after, Daniel opened a practice in Memphis, Tennessee. At the insistence of his twin sister, Daniel moved to the small community of Ville Platte in rural St. Landry Parish. Gober was a practicing physician in this town when the war broke out in April of 1861. Gober was elected captain of the Big Cane Rifles which eventually became Company K of the Sixteenth Regiment.[9]

Other changes were made that affected the shape of Gibson's old brigade. General Order No. 23, dated April 28, reported the organization of the II Corps of the Army of the Mississippi. Perhaps in some form of disgrace, Gibson's (now Gober's) brigade was redesignated the Second Brigade of Ruggles' division instead of the First. Replacing Gober's as the First Brigade was Brigadier General Patton Anderson's brigade, formerly the Second. Anderson was one of Bragg's Pensacola Boys and remained a personal favorite of Bragg's throughout the war. In Bragg's report on Shiloh, he had nothing but positive reporting on Anderson's role in the battle. Bragg broke up Gibson's former command and dispersed the regiments to other brigades. By 28 April Gibson's old brigade, by then under Gober, contained only one of its original regiments from Shiloh, the 19th Louisiana. The 13th Louisiana had been transferred to Walker's brigade. The 1st Arkansas was part of a new Fourth Brigade in Ruggles' division, under Colonel J.C. Moore. The 4th Louisiana was transferred to Anderson, and eventually to another department.[10]

Colonel Fagan of the 1st Arkansas soon fell victim to Bragg's disfavor when Fagan was on outpost duty outside of Farmington near Corinth. Bragg claimed Fagan's command "stampeded," when "not even a picket of the enemy from there here and no sign of any force having been on the road." Bragg suspended Fagan from command of his brigade for this action. This eventually led Fagan to transfer back to Arkansas where he fought for the remainder of the war. Fagan ascertained the rank of major general before the war ended and commanded the District of Arkansas at the close of the war. Following the war, he returned to his home in Arkansas but got caught up in the Brooks-Baxter War in 1874. In the election for governor, there was a dispute as to who the real winner was, and it ended up with the two candidates, Joseph Brooks and Elisha Baxter, calling on armed supporters to back their claims. There was an armed showdown in Arkansas, and in this showdown Fagan allied himself with the Brooks side, the liberal Republican. He was later appointed as a federal marshal by President Grant, and he served for two years before taking a position in the Land Office. He worked at this position until 1890 and eventually died in 1893. He was buried in Little Rock, Arkansas. As for the 1st Arkansas it continued to serve with the same army as the Louisiana Brigade. It would eventually become part of the Arkansas Brigade of Major General Patrick Cleburne's famed, tough fighting division. It fought through all of the major battles of the army with the Louisiana Brigade, and it eventually surrendered in 1865 in North Carolina.[11]

Two units, the 11th and 18th Louisiana Regiments, were added to Gober's brigade to complete its roster. The 11th Louisiana, under Colonel Samuel Marks, was transferred from Colonel Robert Russell's Tennessee Brigade to Gober's brigade on 26 April. The 11th was a veteran unit, not only from the Battle of Shiloh, but also from the Battle of Belmont in November of 1861. The 11th had been part of Polk's garrison of Columbus, Kentucky, but when that town was evacuated, the 11th was ordered to Island No. 10. From there, the regiment became part of the Fort Pillow garrison along the Mississippi River. Just prior to Shiloh, the 11th was ordered to Corinth, and in the organization of the Army of the Mississippi, it was attached to Russell's Tennessee Brigade of Clark's division. Neither regiment would remain long in the brigade. The 18th Regiment, temporarily commanded by Captain E. Camille Mire, was transferred from Walker's brigade. The 18th Louisiana was originally mustered at Camp Moore in October of 1861 under Colonel Alfred Mouton. When Ruggles was sent north to Corinth, Mouton's regiment was part of his brigade. When the Army of the Mississippi was organized Mouton was assigned to Pond's brigade and fought with that brigade at Shiloh. The regiment suffered 211 losses at Shiloh with Mouton being one of the wounded.[12]

Private Daniel Blue, 16th Louisiana. Blue was one of many Louisianians who died from the disease of war (courtesy of Camp Moore Historical Association).

Gober's command spent most of its time after Shiloh, during April and May, manning the works surrounding Corinth. "We have bin laying at the works nearly all the time day and night" was how one Louisiana private described it to his sister. Besides boredom, the poor conditions around Corinth continued to take their toll on the Louisianians. "We have a great deal of sickness in Camp — scarcely a man fit for duty," wrote Private William Paxton of the 19th Louisiana. Paxton would continue to say, "Our regiment will not soon be in a condition to render much service." Paxton attributed most sickness to diarrhea: "The water here is very bad. It produces flux and dissentery." Silas Grisamore of the 18th Louisiana described the water as "the most abominable stuff that was ever forced down men's throats ... was of a bluish color and greasy taste." Private Daniel Blue of the 16th Louisiana wrote his young wife, "I told you in the outset that I was sick. I am but dangerously sick. My stomach has been very bilious, today I have vomited a great deal of bile and now I am much better. I think I shall be fit for duty in a few days." To the contrary, young Private Blue would die that year from his disease leaving behind his wife and two young daughters.[13]

Besides digging and working on the trenches, picket duty remained the major activity for the brigade. The Louisiana volunteers seemed to be frustrated with the labor that accompanied military life. There were numerous slave owners, or gentlemen, in the units and they complained that they were being treated like slaves or performing work not of gentlemen. Take the case of the 4th Louisiana, filled with many well to-do young men. When building trenches outside Corinth, a member of the regiment said, "It was very hard work for us, who had little knowledge of the use of either an ax or a spade.... We could not dig. We said we were gentlemen, and such work was not for people of that stamp. We offered to hire Negroes to do it." Colonel Allen appealed to his corps commander at the time, Bragg, and his reply was to simply get more axes and spades and see to it they dug "as fast and as frequently as possible." Disliked and misunderstood, Bragg was intolerant of the volunteer-civilian outlook on military life and understood how to whip an army into shape. Soldier life was a wake up call for many, and a member of the 13th Louisiana echoed one of Allen's regiment: "The life of a common soldier is a most hard and rough one it is a great deal worse than that of a common field negro.... Most of the common soldiers have to be treated as negroes or they will not obey."[14]

It was a natural inclination on the part of the men to relegate hard, dirty labor to slaves or negroes. It was the culture and way of life of the time for a good portion of the Louisianians. Besides the lower-end white farmer, field hands, or laborers from New Orleans a rough, hard working lifestyle was expected. Many of the gentlemen brought slaves with them early in the war, and as seen from the Battle of Shiloh, many were on the field with the units. Colonel Allen of the 4th Louisiana took time to point out to his servant, Hyppolyte, where to find his body if he were to fall in the Hornets Nest. Allen was forced to wrestle himself from a very emotional and weeping Hyppolyte so he could begin his advance. It became common for slaves to be a part of camp life and make a nice living from doing so. Several continued service with their masters throughout a long period of the war, serving in a variety of positions. William Kennedy, formally of the 11th Louisiana and soon to be part of the 13th Louisiana, wrote home to his wife concerning himself and his slave, Josh: "I send you my uniforms ... Negro Josh sends his uniform. He wants you to send them out the first chance." John Harris of the 19th Louisiana, even though he did not bring a slave with him to the front, took time in a letter to his wife to say, "Tell all the black folks howdy for me." The warm relationship was not always the case. Private Lufoy Auguste of Company K of the 16th Louisiana was found out to be a mulatto and was obviously very light skinned. Upon discovering that he was a "colored man," he was dropped from the regimental rolls and discharged, after having served over a year. Maintaining the social barrier was a cornerstone of society for rural Big Cane, Louisiana. This was not the case for the 13th Louisiana from the multicultural city of New Orleans. As noted, the 13th Louisiana had blacks that did serve in the regiment, and there is no record of treatment like Auguste.[15]

Another example of this close relationship between master and slave is exemplified in the 19th Louisiana of the Vickers brothers and their slave, Dick, who "was strongly attached to his young masters, and in turn they confided in him." First Sergeant John Vickers left his and his brother's money with Dick as they entered the Battle of Shiloh. Following the battle it was learned that John was thought to be killed and left behind, and Dick could not be found. Dick had been to the rear with the wagon train and, upon his return, not only did he have the Vickers' money but the two brothers could not induce Dick to enter Union lines to look for John's body. Dick could have left with a lot of money on hand and had opportunities to enter Union lines to be freed but instead stayed with his masters.[16]

An article published many months later in the *Mobile Register* by a member of the Louisiana Brigade described the black servants of officers. It is not a fond piece that reflects the bond seen in several of the Louisiana units. Instead, it is very candid, descriptive and reflective of the period. The article's author, only known as "I.G." and possibly a member of the 19th Louisiana, gave a very descriptive impression of what the volunteer saw, in contemporary language:

> A peculiar institution of our army here is the "colored wing"—the military niggers—I mean the officers' servants. They dress well, ride thousand dollar horses, smoke two-bit cigars, live on the fat of the land, get up five dollar dancing parties, put on airs over the country niggers, break the wenches' hearts, and lay over the army and mankind in general. So far as ease, comfort and pleasure go, they seem to be the finest gentlemen in the army. They observe keenly the distinctions of rank; a General's nigger won't associate with the Colonel's or Captain's nigger if he can help it; and they look upon the white foot soldiers as the wretchedest of mankind. Very often a tired and dusty volunteer, trudging along the road with his gun and knapsack, hears a clatter behind him, steps aside, and a dandy nigger gallops by without turning his head, stiff and dignified as a Major General. The soldier looks as if he would rather make a target of the saucy black rascal; but as he happens to be quite as rich a man as the nigger's master, and has pet niggers of his own at home, he doesn't do it.[17]

The only major action that Gober's men took part in came in early May when Beauregard decided to take advantage of the Federal snail-paced advance toward Corinth and strike one of its advanced units at the small town of Farmington. On 8 May Ruggles' division was moved from its trenches to the east of Corinth and prepared for an attack on the Federal vanguard at Farmington. The force Beauregard was attempting to destroy was that of Major General John Pope's Army of the Mississippi. Pope's army joined Hallack's concentration of forces after the capture of New Madrid and Island No. 10 along the Mississippi River. Pope's army held the left flank of the advance on Corinth and had captured Farmington on May 3. Beauregard realized that this flank of the Union advance was exposed and planned to converge four divisions onto Farmington to crush Pope.

Ruggles' division filed out of the works around Corinth and deployed between the trenches and Bridge Creek. Walker's brigade, with Anderson's brigade in support, deployed just north of the Memphis & Charleston Railroad. Gober's brigade was posted to their left across the Corinth-Farmington Road behind Bridge Creek. Gober's regiments were deployed in columns as they prepared to cross the creek and advance. Near Farmington was the brigade of Brigadier General J.B. Plummer under the command of Colonel John Loomis of the 26th Illinois. Loomis occupied Farmington on the eighth but with no rations left in their haversacks, Loomis' brigade was ordered to retire behind Farmington for the night and be prepared to retire in the morning once it was relieved. Only a small skirmish line manned by the 8th Wisconsin stood guard for Loomis' unsuspecting brigade.[18]

Farmington was quickly taken on the morning of 9 May and Ruggles quickly deployed his division on the other side of town with Gober's brigade, with the 11th, 16th and 18th Louisiana Regiments forming the left of the line. Soon forming into line on the left of Gober was Brigadier General Trapier's Division of Polk's Corps. J.H. Loomis was heavily outnumbered and was reinforced by Brigadier General John Palmer's brigade. What ensued was a fighting retreat for the two brigades when it was realized how large the Confederate force was in front. Gober's brigade mainly encountered skirmishers and pursued them until the artillery of Trapier's division prevented Gober's regiments from advancing any further. Gober "participated to a small extent in the action and behaved in a spirited manner, advancing with the line, without, however, encountering any great force of the enemy." The hour or so long skirmish with Pope's retreating outpost cost Gober's command 41 causalities. By that evening the brigade was back in the safety of the Corinth trenches where it remained for the next three weeks. The grand attack planned for 9 May became a grand maneuver instead. Units that were supposed to be the flanking part of the attack, and the key to the attack, were late to arrive. The attack that was planned to destroy part of the advancing enemy army never happened.[19]

Another change in the brigade occurred in late May, when on the twenty-seventh, the 20th Louisiana, under Colonel Augustus Reichard, was transferred from Walker's brigade. This transfer put Reichard in command of the brigade over Gober due to the seniority in date of rank. Reichard was described by a superior officer as "untiring energy and careful attention not life to the details of official business, than to the drill, efficiency and general well being of his command, he has shown himself an excelling tactician, a good disciplinarian and an accomplished officer." Reichard was born 9 April 1820 in Munden, Hanover. He immigrated to the United States in the early 1840s and settled in New Orleans. The young Reichard became a successful broker in cotton and sugar while serving as a consul to the embassies of Hanover and Prussia in the Crescent City.[20]

When the war started, Reichard was in command of the 2nd Brigade of Louisiana Militia. He attempted to unite the German companies of the city into its own unit. It looks as though his goal was to ascertain a general's rank in this adventure. Helping this goal, no doubt, was the fact that his business partner was the brother-in-law of none other than the secretary of war, Judah Benjamin. Four German companies, the Turner Guards, Steuben Guards, Reichard Rifles and the Louisiana Volunteers, were organized into the 6th Louisiana Battalion at Camp Lewis, outside of New Orleans, in September 1861 with 315 men. Reichard's battalion then became the nucleus of the 20th Louisiana Infantry Regiment. The regiment was formed on 3 January 1862 by the merging of six independent companies to the 6th Louisiana Battalion. This brought the regiment's numbers up to 879 men. Reichard was made the colonel of the new regiment, Samuel Boyd was made lieutenant colonel, and Leon von Zinken became major. Von Zinken was another German immigrant from Prussia. The 34-year-old Prussian came from a history of military training, himself having served in the Prussian army and his father having been a Prussian general. The pre-war builder was made the major of the 6th Battalion, bringing with him much needed training.[21]

The regiment was sent to Camp Benjamin the day after being organized, and several of its companies were detached to posts across south Louisiana. When the regiment was ordered to Corinth as part of the buildup to face Grant, it left New Orleans with only eight of its ten companies. Companies B and E were left behind on garrison duty at Berwick City and New Orleans. Captain Charles Assenheimer's Company B was sent to Fort St. Phillip where it fought for New Orleans and surrendered. The eventual outcome of Company E is speculative; it probably was in New Orleans at the time of that city's surrender and disbanded. Once in Corinth the regiment was attached to Anderson's brigade of Ruggles' division. The regiment would not be brought up to the full status of ten companies until 19 August 1862: the Noel Guards of the 21st Louisiana was attached on July 28 to form a new Company B, and Company I of the 11th Louisiana was attached on August 19 to form a new Company E.[22]

For the Battle of Shiloh, the regiment was part of Anderson's Second Brigade of Ruggles' division. The regiment was short 372 men from its original 879 when it was mustered into service just three months before. Subtract the two detached companies and the small number of sick and unfit and the regiment's numbers stabilized at 507 for the fight at Shiloh. The regiment took part in the breaking of Sherman's division around Shiloh Church and then took part in the attacks on the Hornets Nest through Duncan's Field. Reichard was complimented by Anderson who said Reichard "deserves the highest commendation and praise for his indefatigable valor in leading his command wherever the foe was strongest." The regiment's German colonel was in the thick of fighting throughout and had his horse shot out from under him. The regiment lost 131 men or about 26 percent (16 killed, 83 wounded and 56 captured, of which 24 were already wounded).[23]

Following Shiloh, the Twentieth Regiment was moved to Walker's brigade. Reichard was in command of the brigade for barely two days before orders were received to prepare to evacuate Corinth. On the night of 29–30 May, the Army of the Mississippi began a silent retreat forty miles south into Mississippi to the town of Tupelo. Although the Army of the Mississippi was able to make a swift retreat without much loss, the Louisiana troops, who had grown accustomed to their camps, lost a lot of their personal belongings. Many soldiers had to discard extra clothing and other belongings, while those sick in the hos-

Colonel Augustus Reichard, 20th Louisiana (courtesy of Peter Reichard).

pitals lost almost all of their holdings. "Only a tithe of our property saved. Great waste and destruction. Vast piles of every kind of valuable clothing, beds, bed clothing, blankets, camp stools, book, chairs ... ready for the torch after we leave tonight." Silas Grisamore of the 18th Louisiana said the men of his unit got rid of their pots and used the opportunity to trash their greasy kettles. The retreat that night was about as organized and neatly conducted as the army's advance on Shiloh almost two months before. The brigade did not get moving until midnight, after standing in line for several hours, and marched through the night. At dawn the marching was halted. The brigade managed to march a very unimpressive six miles.[24]

Desertions were on the rise the longer the siege continued. During the last week of the siege six men from the 20th Louisiana deserted while on picket duty on the night of 24 May, and on the night of 27 May three Irish of the 13th Louisiana deserted. Desertions peaked on the night of 29 May when the army retreated. The confusion of the retreat allowed for those who had decided they had seen enough of war to find a way to desert or slip into enemy lines and surrender. The 20th Louisiana suffered a wave of desertion losing 57 men that night. Of that number, 15 men deserted Company A's effective total of 38 men. In contrast, the 19th Louisiana lost just five deserters.[25]

The brigade marched south through Baldwin and camped for about a week at Clear Creek, about 25 miles south of Corinth. On 7 June the retreat was continued south until the brigade reached its destination on the evening of 8 June, Tupelo. For all of June, the Louisianians were camped at Tupelo, enjoying the fresh atmosphere and better water that the town had to offer. Despite the improved conditions, diarrhea remained a serious problem. It was such a problem that the colonel of the 19th Louisiana issued orders that any soldier who broke ranks during drill and spent too much time answering the call of nature would be punished. Louis Stagg of the 16th Louisiana said that at Tupelo they were able to dig "wells which supply us with good water, very fresh; but still, incredibly, almost all those who are sick die after three or four days of illness." Wesley Winans of the 19th Louisiana said it bluntly in his journal while describing the condition of his regiment at Tupelo: "Dysentery very bad." "It is regrettable," one soldier wrote, that "a great many have Diorhear, and they have to suffer — some do their business occasionally in their clothes ... let loose goose fashion in their clothes." Being hit by the bug himself, John Harris had to slip out of his tent in the middle of the night to relieve himself in a thicket about two hundred yards off. Being mistaken for a deserter, Harris was arrested while attending to his business. Brought before his company commander, Harris' *shitting* case" was dismissed. Soldiers of the 16th Louisiana did not trust their regimental doctor because he was from Ohio. Louis Stagg said there was "distrust in the regiment.... There is not one poor soldier who does not protest at being sent to his hospital."[26]

In the months following Shiloh, the Louisiana units in the army underwent major organizational reshuffling due to two reasons. First, Shiloh and the hardships of Corinth destroyed the fairy-tale glorious life of soldiering, and this led to a realization that military life, and the war, was long and tough. Second, the Conscription Act of 1862, passed on 16 April, required all males from 18 to 35 to serve in the military. This cemented the realization that the war was not going to be over and also provided an out for those outside the age limits. These two conditions led to a way out of the army for many men who were too old, felt they were too unfit, or were disenchanted with army life. Thomas Davidson of the 19th Louisiana shared his frustration with some in the army: "There are many and one in our army who would rather Lincoln would conquer, than that the war would last six months longer ... thus you see how necessary the conscript act was." The reality that beset Davidson was not so much a lack of patriotism to the Confederate cause as it was, as he said, "too much of the weak effeminate spirit engendered by ease and a long period of peace." A lot of men who were over thirty-five took advantage of the law and retired back home once their initial enlistment was up. For the rank and file, their only perk was the ability to reorganize themselves and elect their officers under the Conscription Act. The numerous vacancies and obvious inept social-political leaders were soon filled and replaced. Another Louisianian expressed his concern over the Conscription Act to his brother and echoed Davidson's impression of some in the service: "It will take seventy conscripts to fill our company ... I wish they was here & wanted to see them for what kind of fellows they will be. I want them to be niese [nice] men not those free negros from the southern portions of the state for I am tired of being in a company of loafers."[27]

Homesickness had taken strong root by early and mid–1862. Most men hoped to be home for the spring or have a furlough for that time. Instead, the passage of the Conscription Act killed those hopes. W.E. Paxton of the 19th Louisiana planned full well to take advantage of the age limit and return home. "As soon as the reorganization of the Regiment takes place (at the end of the 12 months Service) I will consider the circumstances that

2nd Lt. Henry Stengel, 4th Louisiana. The ability for officers to resign their commissions and head home was often very appealing to homesick Louisianians. Lieutenant Stengel, here pictured with his wife, was one of many officers that took that route in the post–Shiloh months in 1862 (courtesy of Confederate Memorial Hall Museum, New Orleans).

surround us — and if I can consistently with my honor & duty — I will leave the service — as I am not affected by the Conscript Law — and make the best of my way home ... I shed many bitter tears at the cruel separation." Major Wesley Winans of the same regiment was willing to turn down promotion because General Bragg "refused my request for a four weeks' leave of absence to attend to my private affairs ... I would serve for the war, but if my request was refused I should be forced to claim exemption from the conscript law on account of my overage." Eventually, Winans got his furlough and he accepted his elected

Leon Campbell (brother of Eloy; see page 184), 16th Louisiana, discharged in June 1862 (courtesy of Camp Moore Historical Association).

promotion. Homesickness was a major cause, but finding a way to return home and do so with honor during war was something most men could not conquer. T.H. Wimberly told his brother he wanted a furlough: "I would like to get one this summer and spend summer at home but if I should get one it will be more than I expect now from the fact they don't care any more for a volunteer than we doe for a dog at home." The realities of war and its hardships worked on Wimberly. When he told his brother, "I wish peace would be made some way," he spoke for many of the Louisianians.[28]

E. John Ellis of the 16th Louisiana was able to express his feelings to his sister in late 1862 about being away from home and his words were an umbrella to the morale of Louisiana soldiers facing the realities of war: "If the worst comes to the worst I will resign and join one of the Regiments in Louisiana as a Private—I don't care a straw for myself—I can get along anyway, put up with anything, sleep in the mud and feed and grow fat upon hatred for the infernal Yankee nation, but I cant bear for a moment to entertain the idea of seeing my home desolated." The capture of New Orleans in April and the growth of Yankee occupation symbolized the growing concerns of the men serving in northern Mississippi.[29]

Regardless of the varying reasons that played into disillusioning the soldiers, the majority of the men patriotically reenlisted for three years or the war. To retain honor men wanted to reenlist rather than be known as conscripts who were forced to fight. In accordance with the Conscription Act, the regiments were allowed to reorganize themselves and elect their officers. The result was a significant change in leadership in Louisiana units in the post–Shiloh months.

All three of the brigade's Louisiana units at Shiloh saw these changes take place. On 2 May the 4th Louisiana was transferred to Edwards Station, Mississippi, to recruit its lost numbers and to reorganize. Under the Conscription Act, the regiment was allowed to reorganize itself and elect its officers. The men quickly voted out unqualified or unpopular officers and promoted efficient or popular individuals. Company F of the 4th Louisiana exemplifies the change in leadership that commonly occurred at this time at the company level. When the company reorganized itself, there was not one original officer left in the company: the 2nd junior lieutenant had retired in October of 1861; the captain and 1st lieutenant were both lost at Shiloh and the 2nd lieutenant had been promoted and transferred out of the regiment. The ranking officer was the new 2nd junior lieutenant, J.K. Womack, who was then elected Company F's new captain. After reorganization was complete, it was without its original officers from the start of the war. This was typical in several companies through many of the Louisiana regiments during the reorganization process following Shiloh. There was a wholesale shuffling not only in Company F but in the entire regiment. Allen was retained as the colonel, Hunter as lieutenant colonel, and Major Thomas Vick was dropped for Captain William Pennington of Company C. Of the original ten captains when the regiment was mustered a year ago, only one remained in that position; that person was Thomas Vick, who was voted out as major and took back his company. During this time period, Captain James Wingfield's Company G was transferred out of the regiment. Wingfield was able to secure a command in East Louisiana by organizing a battalion of partisan rangers to operate there. His company, from St. Helena Parish in East Louisiana, became the company upon which the battalion would be built around. A new company was added under Captain George H. Packwood's Packwood Rifles, which was recently organized at Camp Moore.[30]

With the transfer and reorganization, the 4th Louisiana spent the next two years in the Department of Alabama, Mississippi and East Louisiana. The regiment bounced around in the department from Mobile to Vicksburg and from Camp Moore to Port Hudson. In this time period, it participated in the defenses of Vicksburg and Port Hudson, the Battle of Baton Rouge and the Siege of Jackson. At the Battle of Baton Rouge Colonel Allen was wounded while charging an enemy battery. While recovering from that wound, he was promoted to brigadier general, transferred to the Trans-Mississippi Department and eventually elected governor of Louisiana in 1864. He served in that position until the end of the war. In fear of reprisals at the close of hostilities he removed himself to Mexico where he died in 1866.[31]

The major obstacle of the 13th Louisiana in its reorganization was not a wholesale changing of officers at the company level. Instead, it was command issues involving the positions of major and lieutenant colonel. The regiment had two captains and five lieutenants resign or get dropped in this period and thus did not present a major change. Major Anatole Avegno's death left the position of major open, which was filled by the promotion of Captain Stephen O'Leary. O'Leary's promotion, though, was directly affected by the problems presented with the wounding of Lieutenant Colonel Aristide Gerard at the Battle of Farmington. In Gibson's absence, Gerard led the 13th Regiment at Farmington in which he was wounded in the thigh. This was the last Gerard served with the 13th Louisiana.

He was soon appointed to command the post of Okolana, Mississippi. He was there until November 1862 when he was ordered to Major General John Magruder in Texas. Later, he was assigned to duty under Major General Richard Taylor. He was given command of Fort DeRussy near Alexandria and was eventually court-martialed for not following orders to evacuate and blow up the fort. He was released from arrest in July of 1863 and was actually promoted to colonel in January of 1864. From there, though, he was eventually dropped by a review board designed to "relieve the army of incompetent, disabled and disqualified officers." The 13th Louisiana operated from mid–1862 to early 1864 with no lieutenant colonel and at times without a colonel. The regiment's duties in 1862 continually fell on the shoulders of its new major, O'Leary.[32]

Private John R. McAuley, Lake Providence Cadets, 4th Louisiana Regiment. McAuley's company was originally Company B of the 4th Regiment but after its reorganization following Shiloh it became the "New Company C." Eventually, McAuley's company was detached from the regiment and served with the garrison defending Port Hudson. Including the Cadets, almost 100 men from the 4th Louisiana were captured at Port Hudson (Dave Lewis Collection).

The 19th Louisiana faced more serious changes from the top. Lieutenant Colonel James Hollingsworth resigned in May, "on account of failing health." In July he was followed by Colonel Benjamin Hodge. Hodge's first love was politics, and after serving a year in the field with his regiment, it looks as though his eyes began looking that way again. He was elected to the Confederate House of Representatives and served in that position until his death while visiting Shreveport in 1864. Hollingsworth retired to De Soto Parish and eventually Caddo Parish, dabbling in planting and business until his death. The departure of these two officers left a void in leadership. Major Winans, once his furlough was approved, accepted his election as colonel of the regiment. Captain Richard W. Turner of Company A was elected lieutenant colonel. Turner was a thirty-two-year-old Georgian who had moved to Bossier Parish in 1857, settling in Bellevue. Turner became an important figure in his community. Not only a lawyer by trade he was also the editor of the Bossier *Banner* and a member of the local militia. When the war began he became captain of the Vance Guards from Bossier Parish, which eventually became Co. A of the 19th Louisiana. Turner temporarily filled the void of major until his election as lieutenant colonel. To fill the new position of major was Loudon Butler of Company B, also of Bossier Parish. Like the rest of the leadership of the 19th Regiment, Loudon was not native to Louisiana but instead came from South Carolina. Born in 1833 in Edgefield, South Carolina, he graduated from South Carolina College in 1855 and by 1860, at age 27, he was a lieutenant colonel in the South Carolina militia.[33]

At the company level the 19th Louisiana lost a lot of officers from Shiloh into the summer. In that period the regiment lost five captains: one retired immediately after Shiloh, one retired in the summer due to health reasons, and three were forced out at the reorganization of the regiment on 8 May. Ten lieutenants were dropped in the reorganization while two more were lost in early in April due to death by disease and retiring. Such a huge change in officers reflects the desire of the men to elevate to command men they observed as being leaders and who had their best care in mind. R.F. Eddins wrote his sister, "Capt. Bridges [Captain of Company G, J.P. Bridges] resined and will start home tomorrow. 1st Lt. C. Flurnoy was unanymosly elected in his sted." Flournoy was not elected due to popularity but due to his ability to command and lead. He eventually rose to major in the 19th Louisiana and served the regiment throughout the entire war.[34]

Other units affected, whose history was intertwined with the Louisiana Brigade, faced the same changes. Lieutenant Colonel Samuel Boyd resigned from the 20th Louisiana and went to Louisiana to become the commanding officer of the 9th Louisiana Battalion. He was wounded at Baton Rouge and resigned his commission due to that wound. Replacing Boyd as lieutenant colonel was Major Leon von Zinken, and filling von Zinken's spot was Charles Guillet. The 16th Louisiana's command structure change was discussed earlier with Colonel Pond and Lieutenant Colonel Mason being dropped. They were replaced with Gober and William Walker, respectively. Walker was the captain of Company D and Robert H. Lindsay, captain of Company C, filled the major's position vacated by Gober. Walker, a doctor, and Lindsay, a pharmacist involved in the cotton trade, were both instrumental in organizing their companies in 1861. Walker's tour with the regiment would be over by the year's end but Lindsay, the 29-year-old Scottish immigrant, emerged as a leader in the regiment and brigade before the war's end. At the company level the 16th Louisiana had four lieutenants and five captains step down during this period. Three of the captains were dropped at the regiment's reorganization. The youngest and newest regiment of the bunch, the 25th Louisiana, escaped the post–Shiloh changes with only one captain resigning. The

18th Louisiana had to replace the newly promoted Mouton. The regiment did so by promoting its lieutenant colonel and major to fill the positions above them and elected a lieutenant from Company E as their new major. In regards to the position of captain, the 18th Louisiana elected seven new men. The 11th Louisiana survived with only three captains resigning, but a much bigger reorganization awaited this regiment with the coming months. The overall result of these changes is that many more competent men were elected to positions of leadership. This would pay off in the coming months.[35]

The Louisianians were not the only ones affected by a change in leadership. The army went through a leadership change as well. Beauregard had proven to be unfit to command the army and was widely criticized for losing Shiloh because of the order to pull back during the night of the sixth. On 17 June Braxton Bragg was promoted to commander of the Army of the Mississippi. Obviously, the decision to promote Bragg was not a good sign for Randall Gibson, whom Bragg disliked. With him came more discipline and an old army attitude that wasn't the most popular with his volunteer army. Opinions, with what few sources are available about Bragg are mixed. Private Douglas Cater of Company I, 19th Louisiana, remained critical of his commanding general: "We were at Tupelo several weeks and time was spent in drilling. The men needed rest and better food. The drill could not give this, but if Gen. Bragg ever did anything right, I never heard of it." A somber T.H. Wimberly told his brother a little over a week after Bragg took command, "They have commenced drilling us tite again have very strict discipline." William Kennedy of the 11th Louisiana backed up Wimberly's experience: "I'll tell you that they are mighty strict on soldiers now."[36]

In the latter part of June, Bragg planned on moving the Army of the Mississippi to East Tennessee. Bragg's intention was to protect that region from a Federal move from Corinth. Buell's Army of the Ohio had begun a march across North Alabama toward Chattanooga, the rail hub located in the southeast corner of Tennessee. The loss of Chattanooga would mean the loss of East Tennessee and one of the Confederacy's two main railroad connections with the East.

The Army of the Mississippi would have to take a long, circular route from Tupelo, south to Mobile, north from Mobile to Montgomery, east to Atlanta and northwest to Chattanooga. On 3 August, Reichard's brigade began the week-long trip to Chattanooga. Half of the brigade left that morning, and the remainder began its trip the next day. The ride from Tupelo to Chattanooga was one of excitement for the Louisiana troops. "All along at the depots crowds were collected to see the soldiers off," wrote a member of the 16th Louisiana. Ladies threw all sorts of foodstuffs to the troops as they passed through their towns and "those who had nothing to eat gave us their smiles." On the way to Mobile, a serious accident occurred at Citronelle Station. On the morning of 4 August, the train carrying the 18th Louisiana had stopped to reload wood in a bend of the railroad. When the 18th's train began to leave, the train carrying the 19th Louisiana came speeding around the corner and slammed into its rear. Several soldiers were wounded or killed, most in the 18th Louisiana. In the 19th Regiment, "three men were killed outright, crushed, mangled, cut in two. 2 are crushed to helplessness and will soon die. Can't live many hours. One poor fellow had both legs broken, and they have been amputate." It was a shock to the two regiments, and after some confusion, the men unloaded their gear and hoofed it up the railroad until another train from Mobile arrived to carry them the distance.[37]

It was during the transfer from Tupelo that the concentration of Louisiana regiments into a single Louisiana Brigade began to take shape. Prior to leaving Tupelo, the 18th and

3. The Louisiana Brigade Takes Shape: April–August 1862

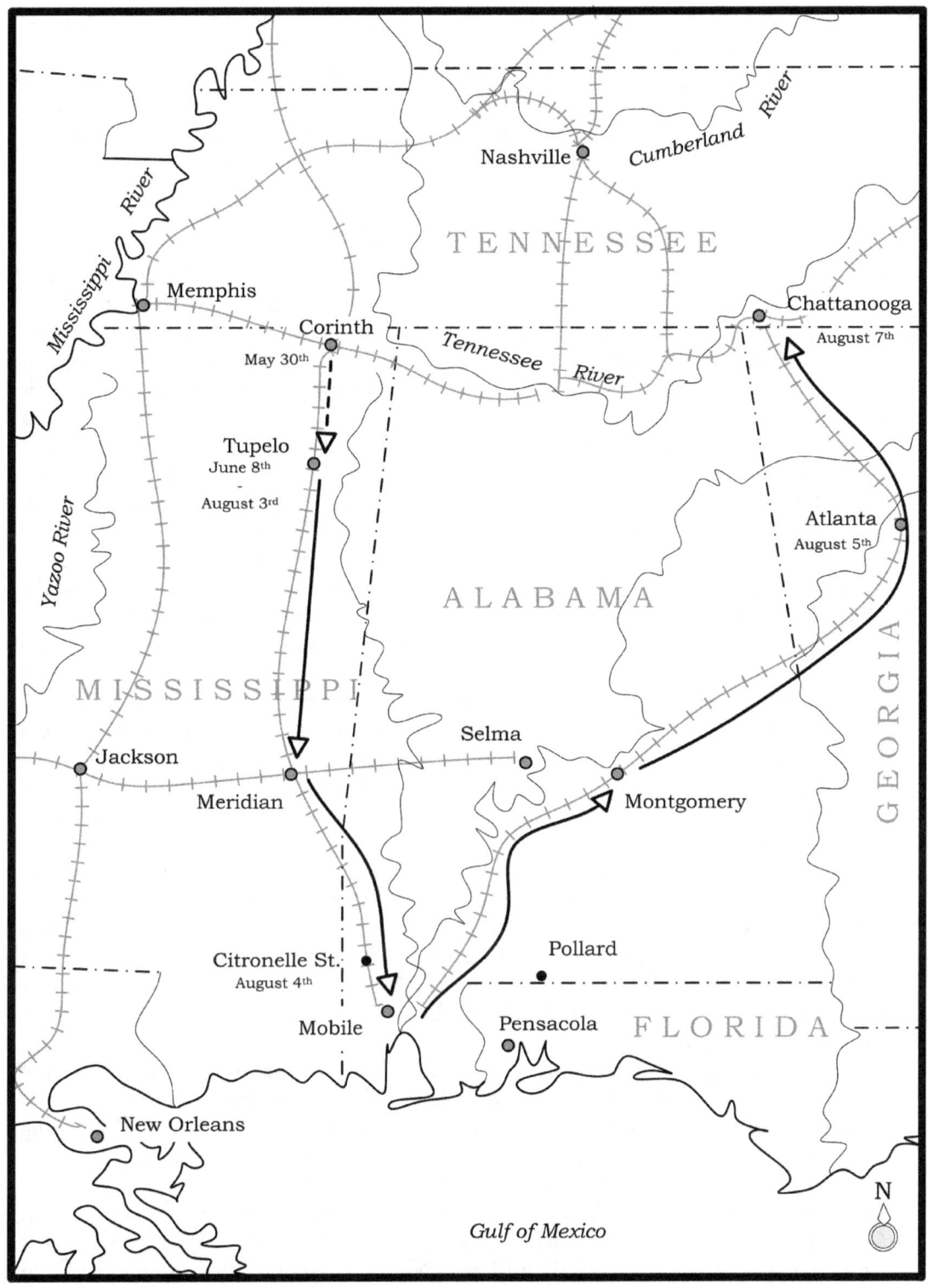

Movements of the Louisiana Brigade, May 1862 to August 1862.

19th Regiments were given orders to be detached from the brigade and join the garrison at Mobile, Alabama. Several regiments from the Mobile garrison had been ordered to East Tennessee to meet Buell's threat, and regiments from the Army of Mississippi were ordered to replace their departure. When Reichard's trains reached Mobile, the two regiments were detached and soon went into camp at Pollard, Alabama, "thrown out to the woods on the frontier." The 18th Louisiana was later transferred back to Louisiana where it would fight the rest of the war. The 19th Louisiana remained part of the Mobile garrison until the spring of 1863 when it was shipped north to Tennessee where it was reunited with the brigade.[38]

Once Reichard's brigade began to arrive in Chattanooga, other changes were soon made. On 13 August Brigadier General Daniel Weisiger Adams replaced Reichard in command of the brigade, and Reichard reverted to command of his regiment. A native Kentuckian, Adams claimed Mississippi as his home state. Born in 1821, Adams was the son of the prominent Federal judge George Adams. At the age of 22, young Daniel confronted James Hagen, the editor of the *Vicksburg Sentinel and Expositor*, for having attacked his father in several editorials. Hagen was known as an editor who "delighted in satire and ridicule, and in both of these he was most potential [sic]." Hagen did not stand down to Adams, and the two men began a "knock-down drag-out fight on the streets of Vicksburg" which resulted in Adams shooting and killing Hagen. In a strange turn of events, in 1885, Daniel's brother, Wirt Adams (who had also been a Confederate general), was killed in a street encounter with John Martin, the editor of the Jackson newspaper.[39]

By 1861, Adams was practicing law in New Orleans. When Louisiana seceded from the Union, Governor Moore appointed Adams to a three-man committee to ready the state for war. Soon afterwards, Adams was appointed lieutenant colonel of the 1st Louisiana Regulars. In the summer of 1861, this regiment was sent to Pensacola, Florida, to reinforce Bragg's force facing Fort Pulaski. During garrison duty at Pensacola, the 1st Regiment's colonel, Adley Gladden, was promoted to brigadier general, and Adams was promoted to colonel. At the Battle of Shiloh, Adams was wounded while leading his men in a charge and holding the unit's regimental colors. A bullet pierced Adams' right eye, causing the loss of it. Following Shiloh, Adams, at the suggestion of Bragg, was promoted to brigadier general on 23 May. From May to early August, Adams commanded the post at Columbus, Mississippi.[40]

Just two days after Adams became commander of the brigade, Bragg reorganized the army. He created two wings, under Major Generals William Hardee and Leonidas Polk, consisting of two divisions each. Jones was replaced in command of the division by Anderson. Anderson's division became part of Hardee's wing. It was during this reorganization that a single Louisiana Brigade was created. The 25th Louisiana from Anderson's former brigade was transferred to Adams. Also joining Adams, or rejoining, was the 13th Regiment from Walker's brigade.[41]

The 25th Regiment was organized on 26 March 1862 at New Orleans with a total of 1,018 men. The regiment was organized with Stuart W. Fisk as its colonel, Joseph C. Lewis as its lieutenant colonel and Frank C. Zacharie as its major, the group of new officers being described as "a good set of officers." Fisk was a forty-two-year-old Mississippian who graduated from Yale and Harvard Law School and was practicing law before the war. Three days after the firing on Fort Sumter, Fisk joined Dreaux's 1st Louisiana Battalion as a captain of Company B. He traveled with the battalion to Pensacola and then to Virginia where he was baptized under fire on 5 July in a skirmish near Newport, Virginia. Toward the end of 1861 Fisk petitioned the War Department for permission to raise a regiment of volunteers. His request was met in December by the secretary of war, Judah Benjamin, and Fisk was given authorization to muster companies into Confederate service "for the war" as fast as they could be mustered. Arms, clothing and equipment would be forthcoming after its mustering, but Fisk did not wait for the War Department to equip his new regiment. He petitioned the assistance of Major General Leonidas Polk, who was commanding the post of Columbus, Kentucky. Fisk personally outfitted the new regiment from his own pocket to the sum of $19,157.95. Included in this bill were blankets, 86 tents, 34 cases of shoes, the material and labor to make uniforms for 800 men and everything else, besides guns, needed to outfit a unit.[42]

Lewis was a native of South Carolina who moved to New Orleans in the 1850s. At the outbreak of the war he was working as a commission merchant and cotton factor. It is unclear what role Lewis played, if any, in the military prior to his appointment to the 25th Regiment and exactly how he attained his rank. Frank Zacharie was the son of a wealthy and politically connected Louisiana merchant.

Colonel Stuart Fisk, 25th Louisiana Infantry (courtesy of Confederate Memorial Hall Museum, New Orleans).

When Louisiana seceded young Zacharie started his career as a non-commissioned officer in the Confederate State Infantry in Mansfield Lovell's department. He was promoted to 1st lieutenant and was appointed adjutant to Coppen's Zouave Battalion when it was formed in March of 1861. In December 1861, Zacharie was temporarily assigned to Company E of the 9th Louisiana while at Camp Carondelet in Virginia. He was relieved in January of 1862 and ordered to report to Lovell. Once back in Louisiana Zacharie was appointed a major of the newly formed 25th Louisiana Regiment.[43]

The 25th Louisiana was made up of companies entirely from north Louisiana from the parishes of Caddo, Franklin, Concordia, Morehouse, Claiborne and Catahoula. Even though being mobilized fairly late in the war, the war bug was still very active in the new companies. All ten companies were organized in March from as far as Shreveport and Vidalia, Mississippi, and converged on New Orleans for mustering into service. "Companies are forming heare [New Orleans] every day and being sent off to all parts of the Confederacy.... All I want is now to be sent off as soon as our Regiment is formed. I am tired of staying here," expressed an anxious Carter Johnson of the Caddo Guards. Johnson's desire for transfer to the front was quick in coming. The regiment was organized to meet Grant's push through Tennessee toward Pittsburg Landing. It was ordered by Beauregard to proceed to Memphis and then to Corinth as part of Johnston's massive buildup to crush Grant's invasion. The first part of the regiment, seven companies with 651 men, arrived in Memphis on 2 April with just 80 muskets between them all. The remaining three companies arrived between the next five to six days. As the Battle of Shiloh was being fought, the 25th

Regiment was collecting itself and arming itself in Memphis. It was not until 11 April that the regiment rolled into Corinth.[44]

The 25th Louisiana was attached to Patton Anderson's First Brigade once in Corinth and it was with this organization that it saw the elephant at the Battle of Farmington on 9 May 1862. Anderson praised Fisk and his regiment: "The Twenty-fifth Louisiana Regiment, though recently raised and arrived since the battle of Shiloh, behaved like veterans, maintaining their line unbroken, and always moving forward with spirit and alacrity whenever ordered to do so. Great credit for this state of things in a new regiment is due to the discipline as well as the gallantry displayed by the officers of the regiment, both field and company." It was during the Siege of Corinth that the regiment got to enjoy the reality of war. Picket duty, drilling and performing camp duties and fighting disease became the daily life of the green regiment. "If I ever do get to come home," said a member of the regiment who was met with the drudgery of army life, "if I do not enjoy the pleasures of home and I will know how to appreciate it." During the April to August time span the regiment's strength is estimated to have dropped about 510 men, or around 50 percent of its original strength. The regiment's only battle losses were at Farmington, and that amounted to only 29 men. Being a rural based regiment, the Twenty-Fifth's losses were due to diseases that the men were exposed to. The regiment remained in Anderson's brigade until it was transferred to Adams in August.[45]

A detailed account of the 25th Regiment's experience at Corinth was left behind by Captain Samuel Scott of Company C. One of Scott's company, Private John F. Gibson, died of disease on 13 May. Scott had the unfortunate duty to write Gibson's sister to inform her of her brother's death. A veteran of the Mexican-American War, Scott was accustomed to campaigning, and death in service was not new to him. The remorse for Gibson's death, though, flowed through Scott's letter as he tried to explain the conditions his company faced:

> ... your brother was well attended during his last illness, but as you truly remark, he met the usual fate of the soldier in our army, the poverty of our Government, the scarcity of the proper medicines, and the want of nurses, has been the cause of the death of many of our Gallant Men.... You must not think that the privates are the only men who suffer, far from it. Except in the higher grades, we are all on the same level. You will excuse this long letter, but I am aware that the relatives of soldiers in the field, sometimes think that Company Commanders could do more for the health of their Command than they do, but I assure you that in this Army we are powerless.[46]

Captain Scott claimed that out of 950 men present for duty in the regiment in April only 180 were present for duty by early July. He accredited the demise in strength of his regiment due to facing constant action during the siege—"...28 days we were on Out Post duty 24 under fire of the Enemy"—and that the majority of this time the men were "...without cover at night, even without blankets, spending night after night in the cold dew." Besides the conditions, Scott accredited the "...filthy water and corrupt atmosphere of that foul place called Corinth," that "poisoned" his regiment. A testament to Scott's own loss was his own brother-in-law. He was left behind during the retreat because he was wounded and sick. "He stayed on the platform that whole day and night, he with many others of the sick were thus left, many of them died from the exposure and I regret to say he also died from the same cause...."[47]

Over a year of war had depleted the strength of many of the Louisiana units due to battle and health reasons. In theory, companies consisted of 100 men and each regiment

3. The Louisiana Brigade Takes Shape: April–August 1862

April 6, 1862

Ruggles' Division

First Brigade Gibson
- 1st Arkansas
- 4th Louisiana
- 13th Louisiana
- 19th Louisiana

Second Brigade Anderson
- 1st Florida Bn.
- 17th Louisiana
- 20th Louisiana
- 12th Louisiana Bn.
- 9th Texas

Third Brigade Pond
- 16th Louisiana
- 18th Louisiana
- 24th Louisiana
- 38th Tennessee

April 28, 1862

Ruggles' Division

First Brigade Anderson
- 1st Florida Bn.
- 4th Louisiana — *To Vicksburg*
- 17th Louisiana — *To Vicksburg*
- 25th Louisiana

Second Brigade Gober
- 11th Louisiana
- 16th Louisiana
- 18th Louisiana
- 19th Louisiana

Third Brigade Walker
- 13th Louisiana
- 20th Louisiana
- 24th Louisiana
- 38th Tennessee

Fourth Brigade Moore
- 1st Arkansas
- 2nd Texas
- 51st Tennessee
- 12th Louisiana Bn. — *Merged with 1st Florida Bn, Ordered to Louisiana*

June 30, 1862

Jones' Corps

First Brigade Anderson
- 25th Louisiana
- 30th Mississippi
- 37th Mississippi
- 41st Mississippi

Second Brigade Reichard
- 45th Alabama
- 11th Louisiana — *Disbanded*
- 16th Louisiana
- 18th Louisiana — *To Pollard, Ala.*
- 19th Louisiana — *To Pollard, Ala.*
- 20th Louisiana

Third Brigade Walker
- 1st Arkansas
- 13th Louisiana
- 21st Louisiana — *Disbanded*
- 24th Louisiana — *Disbanded, Reorganized in Louisiana*
- 38th Tennessee

August 15, 1862

Anderson's Division

First Brigade Brown
- 1st Florida
- 3rd Florida
- 41st Mississippi

Second Brigade Adams
- 13th Louisiana
- 16th Louisiana
- 20th Louisiana
- 25th Louisiana
- Austin's Bn.

Third Brigade Powell
- 1st Arkansas
- 29th Tennessee
- 24th Mississippi
- 45th Alabama

Fourth Brigade Jones
- 27th Mississippi
- 30th Mississippi
- 37th Mississippi

The Transformation of Gibson's Brigade to the Louisiana Brigade from April to August of 1862. On 18 May, Ruggles was transferred from the army and Major General Samuel Jones took command. The transferring of John C. Breckinridge's Reserve Corps to Vicksburg forced a reorganization of the Army of Mississippi. The Second Division of the II Corps became the reserve corps while Jones's division was simply renamed a corps. All four corps of the army were simply one division corps, each having only four brigades. The 5th Company of Washington Artillery, not shown on this chart, was part of Anderson's brigade from the creation of the Army of Mississippi to August when it was attached to Adams' brigade. Compiled from *OR*, vol. 10, pt. 1, 382, 787–88, 811 and pt. 2, 461, 528 and vol. 16, pt. 2, 733; and Bergeron, *Guide to Louisiana Confederate Military Units*, 70, 78, 99, 104, 113, 116, 121, 123, 125, 133, 167.

consisted of ten companies. So, the standard strength for a regiment was 1,000 men. Most of the Louisiana regiments serving in the Army of the Mississippi never totaled 1,000 men when they were organized. Considering both disease and battle losses, several of the Louisiana units were severely depleted by August of 1862. To strengthen regiments, some units were either disbanded or combined. To solidify the strength of the Louisiana units, Bragg ordered the 11th and 21st Louisiana Regiments to disband. When the 21st Louisiana was disbanded, on 23 July, Company C was transferred to the 20th Louisiana to become the new Company B, and it became the nucleus for other members of the regiment to transfer to. The original Company B of the 20th Regiment had been detached in early 1862 to Berwick Bay, Louisiana. When the 20th left for Corinth, the company was left behind and was eventually captured by the Federals during the seizure of New Orleans. Between 64 and 73 men from Kennedy's regiment went to the 20th Louisiana, with the bulk forming Captain Alexander Dresel's new Company B. The remainder of the 21st Regiment was disbanded, with the vast majority of the men transferring to the 1st Louisiana Regulars. Incomplete company roster or service files make it impossible to track the exact number of men that transferred to the 1st Regulars but it is documented that at least 99 men were transferred into that regiment.[48]

No official reason was submitted as to why Bragg wanted the 21st Regiment disbanded. In April, the regiment was recorded as being in good condition in terms of appearance, instruction and clothing and its discipline as "very good." In November of 1862, the War Department ordered the regiment reorganized and the reinstatement of the regiment's colonel, J.B.G. Kennedy. Bragg protested immediately to Samuel Cooper, calling it a "great evil." Cooper also received a letter of disapproval from a C.C. Miller, who was formerly associated with Kennedy in the militia. In 1861, Kennedy went to Columbus with the 1st Battalion of the Jackson Regiment of Louisiana militia, while the regiment's colonel, C.C. Miller, remained with the balance of the regiment in Louisiana. While at Columbus, Leonidas Polk organized these companies into the 5th Louisiana Battalion, with Kennedy as its commander. In early 1862, companies were added to the battalion to form the 21st Regiment. Miller was not made colonel of the regiment, "notified of appointment but failed to obtain commission," and instead Kennedy was made its colonel. Obviously, this must have left a bad taste in the mouth of Miller. Upon hearing that Kennedy was ordered to reform the 21st Louisiana, Miller wrote Samuel Cooper and said the following: "Now this same Kennedy is a notorious *thief* an imposter of the [illegible word] kind, void of all principal, honor and integrity." Miller went on to say, "Genl Bragg displaced him knowing his bad character" and that Kennedy's reinstatement was a "shame and disgrace." In contrast came a letter in 1863 from Leonidas Polk himself, under whom Kennedy served at Columbus and Island No. 10. In his letter Polk full-heartedly supported Kennedy's reinstatement back into Confederate service.[49]

The "great evil" Bragg speaks of leaves circumstances up to speculation. Regarding Bragg's professional army career and his disdain for, and hard discipline to dissuade, desertion then it is easy to see why Bragg would not be a fan of the 21st Louisiana. The regiment was plagued by massive desertion; whether or not this lies in the fact that the Louisiana militia units were converted for Confederate service is not known. When looking at the rosters of Companies A through F, the companies that made up the 5th Battalion, there are at least 154 men who enlisted in and deserted their commands before leaving New Orleans for Kentucky. After leaving New Orleans to their disbanding in July of 1862 there were at least an additional 24 men who deserted. During the retreat from Corinth, Company E got separated from the regiment and was clobbered by part of the pursuing enemy cavalry. At least eight men were captured and most of them, once in enemy hands, took the Oath of Allegiance. In fact, there was a high percentage of the men who were transferred to the 1st Regulars and 20th Louisiana that deserted and took the oath once captured or once captured in battle took the oath, and there were several that joined the United States Navy to avoid prison time. The 5th Battalion–21st Louisiana was a unit with less than an honorable career as a whole. Combine the desertion plagued regiment with an officer that supposedly Bragg knew was dishonorable and it leads to a determined Bragg, in the post–Shiloh months wishing to put the army into shape, targeting this unit as a symptom of the army's problems.[50]

Likewise, the disbanding of the 11th Louisiana, on 19 August, raises several questions. "The peculiar circumstances of the regiment renders this step necessary" was the reason Bragg gave. The commander of the 11th Louisiana, Colonel Samuel F. Marks, argued against the order by stating that Bragg disbanded the regiment by "an illegal and arbitrary" order and went on to state that, with 515 officers and men present for duty, the regiment did not lack the numbers to require it to disband. The exact reason why the regiment was ordered to disband is unknown. "The peculiar circumstances of the regiment" has never been elaborated on. The adjutant and inspector general, Samuel Cooper, in late September of 1862, ordered Bragg to reorganize the 11th and 21st Regiments. Bragg replied in November by contesting Cooper's command and saying that gathering the men, after they had been scattered throughout several regiments, and appointing new or old officers would present "almost insuperable" problems. Bragg never explained why he disbanded the regiments but did say: "It seems to me, under all the aspects of the case, that we are endeavoring to overcome almost insuperable difficulties in order to accomplish a great evil." The matter was finally settled in March of 1863 when the government rescinded its order to reorganize the two units. Perhaps foreshadowing problems in the 11th Louisiana was Charles Johnson when he wrote home as far back in August of 1861. He was frustrated with the lack of attention his officers gave the regiment and talked about transferring to another regiment "which have some show of order, discipline and organization and whose officers are of value, have sense & don't get drunk." Johnson took time to criticize and point out Colonel Marks was guilty of this offense more than once.[51]

On 21 August, when the 11th Regiment was disbanding, Adams gave orders for Captain John E. Austin of Company D to raise a battalion of sharpshooters by picking two hundred men from the disbanding regiment and organizing them into two companies. John Edwards "Ned" Austin was the son of Dr. William Austin from Yazoo County, Mississippi. Ned Austin was born in 1840 in either Yazoo County or Bayou Sara, Louisiana. After moving to Louisiana in the early 1840s, Dr. Austin befriended Samuel F. Marks, future colonel of the 11th Louisiana, and eventually became neighbors with Marks when Dr. Austin moved the family to New Orleans in the mid–1840s. Ned Austin was a clerk in a Carondelet Street office when war broke out in 1861. Because of his strong social ties, Austin secured a position in the prestigious Orleans Cadets which became Company A of Lieutenant Colonel Charles Dreaux's 1st Louisiana Battalion. Despite Governor Moore promoting him to 2nd lieutenant in the Orleans Cadets, Austin resigned that position and instead took a position of the same rank in Company K of the 1st Louisiana Regiment. Austin served in this position from mid–April to the end of July when he resigned his position to accept the commission of captain for Company D of the 11th Louisiana, whose colonel was none other than his father's close friend, Samuel F. Marks.[52]

Despite having family connections to help secure his commissions, Ned Austin quickly showed at age 22 that he was a qualified leader and soldier. When the 11th Louisiana's major was killed at the Battle of Belmont in November of 1861, he was nominated to replace him. With the regiment disbanded, Austin was the obvious choice: It would have been a disgrace for Colonel Marks or Lieutenant Colonel Robert H. Barrow to take a reduction in rank, and Major E.G.W. Butler, who had been wounded at Shiloh, was absent recovering from his wound. Also, Austin's father, Dr. William Austin, was a personal friend of Governor Moore; so, perhaps political influence was also a factor in securing Austin command of the battalion.

Austin's battalion consisted of two companies. Command of Company A was given to Captain Thomas W. Peyton, formerly the 1st lieutenant of Company C of the 11th Regiment. Command of Company B was given to Captain James Lingan, Austin's former 2nd lieutenant in Company D of the 11th Regiment. Austin hand picked the men from the disbanding 11th Regiment for his new unit. In looking at the roster of 150 of the men picked Companies D, E and F provided the largest number of men with 31, 20 and 38 respectively. The remainder of the companies provided a sprinkling of men to fill out the roster.[53]

What men who did not become part of Austin's command were dispersed to the 13th and 20th Louisiana Regiments. The 11th Regiment was dispersed as follows: Companies C, D, E, F and G were assigned to the 13th Louisiana and Companies A, B, H, I and K to the 20th Louisiana. These men were absorbed into the 13th and 20th Regiments and lost their company identities. The 20th Louisiana received around 213 men from the 11th Louisiana, 66 of which were part of the building of the new Company E. Captain Albert Lipscomb of the 11th's Company L became the captain of the new Company E. The same was of Company L's 1st and 2nd lieutenants, R.C. Vass and John Dunn. Edward Baines, a member of the Rosedale Guards (formerly Company I of the 11th Regiment), was not happy with the situation. His company was consolidated with the 20th Louisiana and eventually would be merged with the 13th Louisiana. "The few Rosedale Guards that are left are in the 13th Regt.... There are only eleven of them they [Rosedale Guards] are very much dissatisfied.... The 13th is composed principally of duch & the lowest kind the officers commanding the company that the RG [Rosedale Guards] are in are duch & the lowest kind. I feel sorry for the poor fellows, they are a fine set of young men. They are trying to get a transfer from the Regt but I am afraid they will not." Banes' solution was to try and get a transfer to the 4th Louisiana, which was filled with men more of his caliber.[54]

A new battery was also attached to the brigade. The 5th Company of Washington Artillery, under Captain Cuthbert H. Slocomb, was transferred from Anderson's old brigade to Adams'. The Washington Artillery was a prewar militia unit from New Orleans. In May of 1861, the Washington Artillery offered its services to the Confederate government, and on 13 May it was accepted into service for the duration of the war. The unit was so big that it was divided into four companies. When the unit left for Richmond in late May, Lieutenant Washington I. Hodgson and eighty-one men were left in New Orleans to raise a reserve force for the departing battalion. In two weeks Hodgson had raised a fifth company and was elected captain.[55]

After the fall of Fort Donelson, Hodgson's battery accepted Beauregard's call for ninety-day volunteers. On 7 March the battery was sworn into Confederate service, and on 8 March it departed from New Orleans for Johnston's army. When Confederate forces were concentrated at Corinth, Hodgson's battery was attached to Ruggles' division, Anderson's brigade. The battery fought with Anderson at Shiloh and remained a part of his brigade until the reorganization of the Army of the Mississippi on 15 August, when it was attached to Adams' brigade. Command of the battery, however, changed during the reorganization of the army. Hodgson resigned his position on 2 June but immediately appealed to the War Department for reinstatement. Hodgson's request was given to Bragg, who turned the issue over to the battery. In a vote as to whether to keep Hodgson or require his departure, the battery voted him out and elected Slocomb.[56]

Slocomb had served in the 2nd Company of the Washington Artillery as 1st lieutenant. In November 1861, Slocomb resigned his commission and returned to New Orleans where he joined the 5th Company in March of 1862. He was appointed 1st lieutenant of the company and was wounded at the Battle of Shiloh. On 13 August, when Hodgson was voted out of the unit, Slocomb's appointment to command of the battery was approved by the 5th Company.[57]

After the reorganization of the army, Adams' brigade was organized as follows:

3. The Louisiana Brigade Takes Shape: April–August 1862

13th Louisiana — Colonel Randall L. Gibson
16th Louisiana — Colonel Daniel Gober
20th Louisiana — Colonel Augustus Reichard
25th Louisiana — Colonel Stuart W. Fisk
Austin's Battalion — Major John E. Austin
5th Company of Washington Artillery — Captain Cuthbert Slocomb.

The Louisiana Brigade of the west was born. From this point on the Army of the Mississippi, soon to be renamed the Army of Tennessee, would maintain a single Louisiana brigade. There remained only one other Louisiana unit loose within the army, the 1st Regulars, but all others were combined under Adams. The period from April to August of 1862 was a weeding out process of Louisiana units that resulted in Adams' command.

CHAPTER 4

The Kentucky Campaign: August–October 1862

"The eyes of the whole country are turned toward this army and great results are anticipated in which, let us firmly hope, this brigade will play a conspicuous part."
— Colonel Augustus Reichard, 20th Louisiana,
Speech to the Louisiana Brigade, 12 August 1862

Once Bragg's army reached Chattanooga, he and Major General Edmund Kirby Smith, commander of the Department of East Tennessee, planned a joint offensive from Chattanooga and Knoxville into Middle Tennessee and Kentucky. When Bragg was reorganizing the Army of the Mississippi in mid–August, Smith left Knoxville with his small army for Kentucky. Due to the fact that the supply wagons for Bragg's army moved slowly across North Alabama from Tupelo to Chattanooga, the Army of the Mississippi had to delay its advance across Tennessee for two weeks after Smith began the campaign. On 28 August, Bragg began moving his forces from their camps around Chattanooga.[1]

On 29 August at 4:00 A.M., Adams' men broke camp and crossed the Tennessee River. The brigade spent the next day crossing over Walden's Ridge before arriving outside the small town of Dunlap at 4:00 P.M. on the thirtieth. Although it was completed in a short amount of time, the march over Walden's Ridge to Dunlap was one of the most exhaustive for the Louisianians, who were accustomed to the flat terrain in their home state. A member of the 20th Regiment said, "The roads were very mountainous and fatigued our men very much, which was the cause of straggling." W.L. Trask of Austin's Sharpshooter Battalion summed up the march over the ridge:

> The road up the mountain side was narrow and tortuous, besides being blockaded by a continuous line of wagons, all the way up. We were obliged to make our way around and through them and sometimes over them, thus rendering our ascent the more difficult, slow, and tiresome. There was no water and we suffered intensely from the lack of it.... Haven't seen a drop of water since leaving the foot of the Ridge.... *August thirtieth*— Moved at 6 A.M. At sunrise not a soul out of our entire Brigade was stirring — all were fast asleep.[2]

For the next few days, the army rested around Dunlap before restarting the march on 3 September. Passing through Pikeville, the brigade reached Sparta on the sixth. After a two-day rest, the march continued toward the Cumberland River. After leaving Sparta, Bragg sent Polk's wing to cross the Cumberland at Gainsborough and Hardee's wing to cross at Carthage. The Louisianians marched through Milledgeville and Pekin and crossed the Cumberland River on the ninth at Carthage.[3]

Once Bragg's army was across the Cumberland, it became a race between Buell and Bragg for Louisville, Kentucky. Bragg's quick advance into Middle Tennessee had forced Buell to abandon North Alabama and march north to protect Nashville. With Bragg marching into Kentucky, Buell had to continue his march north to protect Louisville. Bragg originally planned to combine his two wings at Tompkinsville, Kentucky, but he had Polk's wing move ahead and block the Louisville & Nashville Railroad by seizing the town of Glasgow. Buell grew desperate and quickened his pace to catch up with Bragg.[4]

From Carthage, the Louisiana Brigade continued its march through Pleasant Shade and rested just short of the Kentucky state line on the evening of 11 September. The brigade broke camp at daybreak on the twelfth and marched north. Around noon, the brigade crossed the Kentucky line and orders were received to stop marching. The brigade was formed into a hollow square with the units facing each other. From the middle of the square, Adams addressed his Louisianians to read news of a Confederate victory at Richmond, Kentucky, and of Robert E. Lee's victory in Virginia at the Battle of 2nd Manassas. With news of two great Confederate victories, Adams gave his men a great pep talk that their time would come and said he "hoped we would continue to deport ourselves as Louisianians had always done, and that, when the time of trial in battle should come, we would not be found wanting." News of the victories and a rousing speech from their brigade commander sent roars of cheers from the men for the next several miles until the summer heat drowned out their energies to cheer.[5]

The march continued through Tompkinsville, to Scragg's Creek halfway to Glasgow on the thirteenth and to Glasgow, Kentucky, on 14 September. From Glasgow, the Army of the Mississippi moved north and captured the Federal garrison at the town of Munfordville, a small town where the Louisville & Nashville Railroad crossed the Green River. Southern Kentucky was sympathetic to the Southern cause, and the people showered the men with what gifts they could. Unfortunately, one of the items that "flowed freely around the camps" was whiskey. The 13th Louisiana had a history of incidents with whiskey and this would prove no different. Only the worst were condemned for their actions. It led to thirteen men from just one company of the 13th Regiment being bucked and gagged. On the fifteenth, Adams' men left their camp at Scragg's Creek at about 2:30 P.M. and marched through Glasgow and arrived outside of Munfordville at 3:00 A.M. on the sixteenth "with less than half of our command, the remainder having straggled along the road." The next day, the Louisianians were present to witness the surrender of the garrison. For the next few days, the men were allowed to rest while Bragg awaited Buell's advance from Nashville. Coming on the heels of Richmond and 2nd Manassas, the surrender of Munfordville must have filled the Louisianians with a sense of invincibility in anticipation of the upcoming showdown with Buell's pursuing army.[6]

When Buell failed to attack Bragg in his position behind Green River, Bragg became nervous and worried about supply levels for his army. Finally, on 19 September, he ordered a withdrawal from Munfordville. Bragg withdrew into the interior of Kentucky to unite with Smith's forces around Lexington and Frankfort. Bragg hoped that moving into the interior of the state would allow his army to be better supplied. Buell was allowed to march freely into Louisville where he reequipped and resupplied his worn-down army. Once Buell had reinforced his army and reorganized it, he went on the offensive against Bragg and Smith.[7]

On the evening of the twentieth, Adams left Munfordville, marching north along the railroad toward Hodgensville, which he reached on the twenty-first. The next day, the army

Kentucky Campaign, August through October 1862.

crossed the Muldraugh Hills and camped at New Haven. On the twenty-third, Adams entered Bardstown and set up camp. The Louisianians would remain encamped at Bardstown for the next week and earn a much-deserved rest. "It has been very severe on the poor men," wrote Adams to his wife. "Many of them have been marching barefooted from choice as their feet became so sore they could not wear shoes." Despite the continuous march from Chattanooga over "rough mountainous country," the Louisianians were "generally cheerful, confident & happy." While at Bardstown, Polk was in temporary command of the army, while Bragg rode to Frankfort to oversee the installation of a Confederate state government for Kentucky. Bragg's preoccupation with political, rather than military, matters caused great confusion on the Confederate side in the coming week.[8]

On 1 October, Buell began advancing from Louisville with his objective being Polk's army at Bardstown. Bragg, thinking that Buell's objective was Frankfort and Lexington, ordered Polk to move the Army of the Mississippi in Smith's direction in order to strike Buell in the flank. When Buell entered the town of Taylorsville, he had almost divided Smith and Polk from each other. Under pressure from Buell's advance, Polk decided to retreat into the interior of the state. Confusion in the march allowed Buell to catch up to the Confederate rear. The pressure was so great on Hardee, that Polk ordered him to halt at Perryville, along the Chaplin River, to force the Federals to show their strength. Polk believed he faced a large force but not Buell's entire army. On the evening of 6 October, Anderson's division almost reached Harrodsburg. At 3:00 A.M. on the seventh, Anderson's division reversed its course and marched back to Perryville to join the rest of Hardee's wing. Around 3:30 in the afternoon of the seventh, Anderson reached Perryville. Adams' brigade was deployed directly behind Perryville, his right on the Danville Pike.[9]

Early in the morning of 8 October, the Battle of Perryville began. Bragg, who had ridden to Perryville to see the situation for himself, was unprepared for the fight at hand. Thinking that he faced only a portion of Buell's army, Bragg ordered what forces he had available, only 16,000 men, to attack. Bragg's plan called for an attack on the Federal left, north of the Mackville Pike. Unaware of the huge numbers that he faced, Bragg prepared his three divisions for battle. Facing Bragg were all three of Buell's corps. Buell's I Corps was the first to reach the Perryville area from the town of Mackville. Marching directly upon Perryville from the west, from the town of Springfield, was Buell's II Corps. From the town of Lebanon, Buell's III Corps advanced on Perryville from the southwest. Due to the I Corps arriving first, Bragg might have been fooled into believing that this was the only Federal force he faced.[10]

Just before noon, the Louisianians started across the Chaplin River. Anderson placed his division just west of Perryville. Two of Anderson's brigades, Colonel Tom Jones' and Brigadier General John C. Brown's, were moved north of the Mackville Pike to take part in Bragg's attack. Adams was posted between the Mackville and Springfield pikes. Supporting Adams was Anderson's Fourth Brigade under Colonel Samuel Powell. Powell's brigade was posted on Adams's left, across the Springfield Pike. Once Adams and Powell were deployed, Anderson moved them forward towards Bull Run Creek with orders to march at the right oblique so that they could support the attack across Chaplin Creek. The remainder of Bragg's force was deployed behind the Chaplin River and between the Chaplin River and Doctor's Creek, north of the Mackville Pike.[11]

At about 1:30 P.M., Adams reached Bottom Hill along Bull Run, where the house of Sam Bottom was situated. Slocomb deployed his battery on top of the hill just south of the Mackville Pike. At 2:00, Bragg began his attack against Major General Alexander McCook's corps on the Federal left. Attacking in echelon from right to left, Bragg engaged his units in a counterclockwise swinging door motion. At about 2:30, Hardee moved Major General Simon Buckner's division and Anderson's two remaining brigades from Chatham Hill and engaged the enemy across Doctor's Creek. Once Brigadier General Bushrod Johnson's Tennessee Brigade on Adams' right was engaged, Buckner rode over from Chatham Hill and ordered Adams to join in on the attack.[12]

Johnson's advance toward the enemy line was immediately wrecked with last minute orders that led to a confusing mess and disorganized attack. Buckner changed the line of advance of Johnson's regiments. Not all the regiments received these orders and it resulted in mass confusion. Adding to a now jumbled advance, Buckner, fearing his left was becoming exposed, detached a regiment from Johnson and a section of artillery to watch the Federal menace atop Peter's Hill to the southwest. What Buckner did not know was that Adams was advancing along his left in the exact area where he was dispatching part of Johnson's brigade. Through his last minute change in the path of advance, Buckner inadvertently threw Colonel John Fulton's 44th Tennessee into Adams' path.[13]

So, how did Buckner not know that the Louisiana Brigade was not to his left? Adams was actually under orders to proceed slowly as to allow Powell's brigade to dress on his left and thus provide security toward Peter's Hill, the very area Bucker was concerned about. Those orders also called for Adams to stop and wait for Powell if necessary. Adams did just that. "In obedience to this order I halted the brigade several times and moved very slowly" while waiting on Powell. The eager Adams also dispatched several messengers to Powell "to move up as rapidly as possible," but they brought no results to his painfully slow advance. When he finally came into position opposite Doctor's Creek, south of the Mackville Pike, Adams deployed Slocomb's guns and prepared for action. Still hesitant to break orders and thus expose his brigade to disaster, Adams dispatched his aide-de-camp, Lieutenant E. M. Scott, to personally hurry Powell forward so Adams could push the Louisianians forward. Still, no reply from Powell came, because Scott never returned and was, thus, assumed to have been captured. "Receiving no answer, and as it was then getting late in the day, I ordered the artillery to open fire" were the words of Adams on how he began his attack at Perryville.[14]

As if Johnson's luck could not get worse, when he finally was able to arrange his remaining four regiments in a coherent attack, what success he tasted in crossing Doctor's Creek was thrown to a standstill because of Slocomb! The enemy that the Washington Artillery was pounding was Johnson's poor Tennesseans. The error wasn't corrected until the wayward 44th Tennessee came crashing into Adams' right flank. As Fulton's regiment marched forward, he received "enfilading fire coming from the enemy on our right and a battery upon our left," but the problematic "enemy battery" on his left was Slocomb. "Obliquing to the left," per orders from Buckner, the 44th Tennessee "suffered terribly from the fire of the batteries right and left," because he was now totally exposing his flank to Loomis' guns atop Bottom Hill and skirmishers of the 3rd Ohio in the Bottom Orchard between the creek and the Bottom farm. Resolved to take out the nearest problem, Fulton ordered his men to fix bayonets to "silence and take the battery on our left," and to his total surprise he ran into fellow Confederates. The shocked colonel immediately passed word to the Louisianians that they were mowing down their own men at the front. With the problem rectified, Slocomb trained his guns on the Doctor's Creek — Bottom Farm area and then to Loomis' guns. The 44th Tennessee and then the 25th Tennessee regiments were detained by Adams to remain near Slocomb's battery as he began to slowly push his men in a westernly-northwesternly path toward Lytle.[15]

The Louisiana Brigade's push into action at Perryville began at 2:35 P.M. Leading the Louisianian's path was Austin's battalion. Since its creation back in August in Chattanooga this was the first time Austin was able to test out his crack two company unit of sharpshooters. They wasted no time in putting their skills to work. Below Adams' position ran Bull Run which emptied into Doctor's Creek. Posted opposite the creek from Adams and Johnson was Colonel William H. Lytle's brigade of General Lovell Rousseau's division. Rousseau had advanced this brigade to take command of a large hill upon which sat the H. Bottom Farm. In pushing Lytle's brigade forward, Rousseau was given the impression, by faulty communications and the wild movements on the Confederate side of the creek, that the enemy to his front was actually in retreat: "Everything indicated that the enemy had retired and it was so believed." Lytle's lead regiment, Colonel James Jones' 42nd Indiana, was given the gracious orders to stack arms and get what water they could from the drought-stricken Doctor's Creek and Bull Run. The lounging and thirst-quenched 42nd sat completely exposed and isolated in what Major James Shanklin of that regiment described as a "terrible position."[16]

When Johnson's Tennesseans and Austin's battalion hit Doctor's Creek they caught the Hoosiers off guard. Austin's men were about 100 yards from the creek bed when they began taking shots at the Yanks, against the orders of Adams. Either Adams was unsure of his path or was aware of the confused nature of Johnson's advance and had forewarned Austin not to fire on men in his front in order to avoid friendly fire. Austin's first wave of fire dropped five men from Jones' right wing. The 42nd Indiana quickly recovered and blasted a volley into the sharpshooters. Adams, who was only a couple of hundred yards to the rear helping with the placement of Slocomb's guns, felt the whiz of bullets by him. The order not to open fire was quickly countered with an excited and surprised Adams to say, "By God! They are Yankees — Fire!"[17]

Major Shanklin of the 42nd Indiana described his situation at the point Slocomb began searching for his men: "In front a concealed enemy firing volley after volley; on our right a battery throwing grape, with little accuracy, it is true, but all the time getting nearer the range; behind, a steep precipice, up which the men must climb, exposed to the fire of sharpshooters." A member of Austin's battalion remembered the effect of Slocomb's roar a little bit differently: "Slocomb opened up on them in great effect." Despite the accuracy of Slocomb's shells the 42nd Indiana could not stand in its exposed position. To make matters worse, part of Austin's men were now finding their way around the right flank of Jones' right wing. Jones was forced to extract his unit as best he could, and the scampering Yanks were exposed to deadly fire as they fought up the other side of Doctor's Creek to escape Austin's and Slocomb's punishing fire. Behind, in the creek, were up to 80 men from the 42nd Illinois with about 21 of them being prisoners.[18]

Austin's men were pulled back from the skirmish line and placed on the right of the brigade as the Washington Artillery began to pound the opposite bank. Sitting across Doctor's Creek, "on top of a sloping hill beyond a long line of battle could be plainly seen," was the rest of Lytle's brigade at the Bottom Farm. Lytle had the 3rd Ohio and 15th Kentucky deployed at the farm; his 10th Ohio was placed north of the farm, and Mackville Pike was on the right flank of Colonel Leonard Harris' brigade. The 3rd Ohio was placed uphill from the Bottom House behind a rail fence with his left resting on the Mackville Road and his right extending past the hay-filled barn of the Bottoms. Supporting the 3rd Ohio to its rear was the 15th Kentucky. Supporting Lytle were parts of two batteries, the 5th Indiana Light Artillery of Harris' brigade commanded by Captain Peter Simonson and

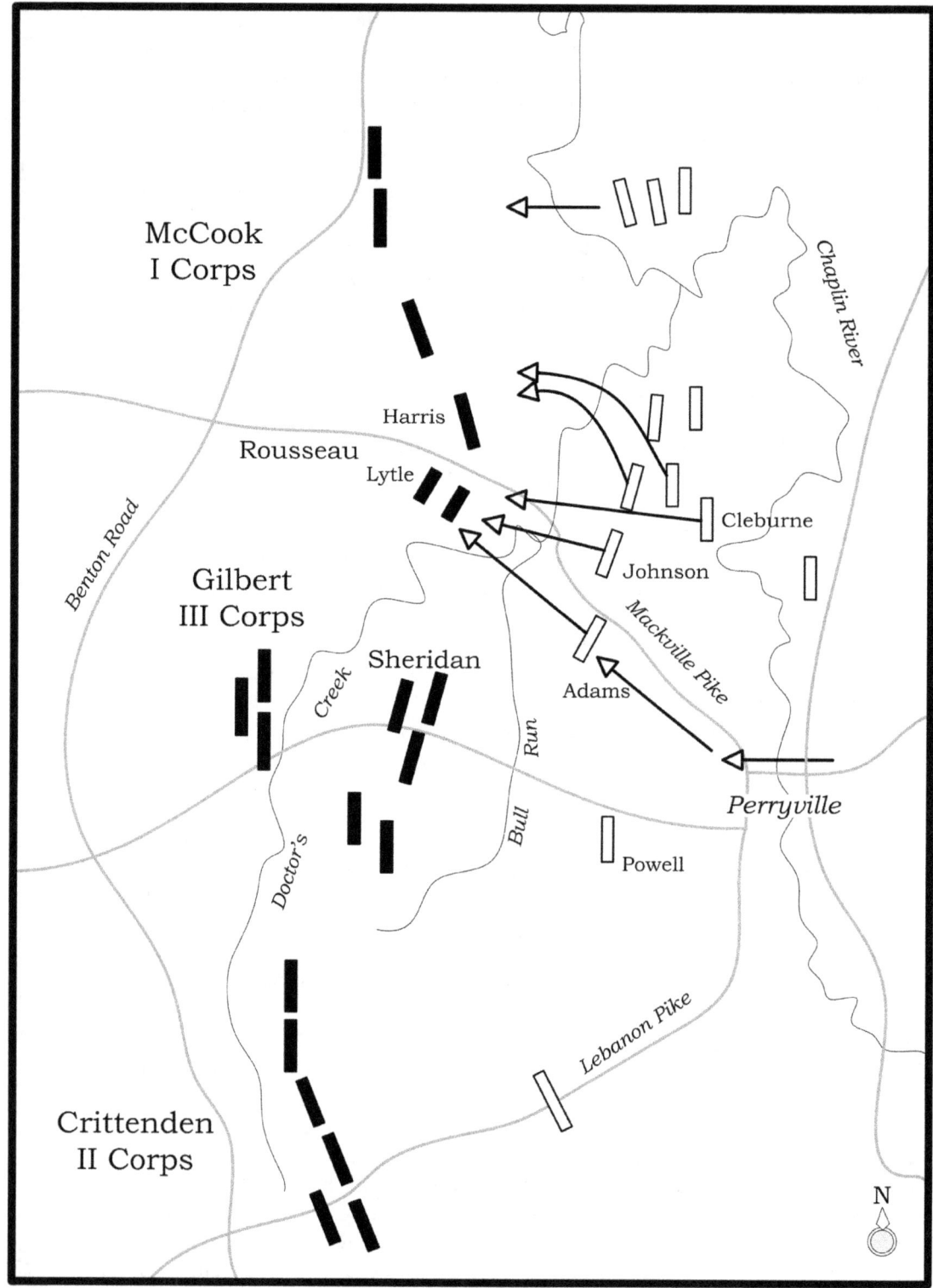

Battle of Perryville, 8 October 1862.

Lytle's own 1st Battery of Michigan Light Artillery led by Captain Cyrus Loomis. Simonson sat north of the Mackville Pike at the outset of the battle, and Loomis was situated near the Bottom Farm.[19]

Loomis and Simonson were exchanging fire with Confederate batteries across the river the whole while Adams was making his slow advance to the front and during the quick skirmish at Doctor's Creek with the 42nd Illinois. This changed when Slocomb moved his guns into position south of the pike. By 2:35, when Adams gave Slocomb the go ahead to open fire, Loomis had already withdrawn farther back behind the Russell House. There he provided support, and this left Simonson to bear the brunt of artillery support in Lytle's area. "Our firing up to this time," reported Simonson, "was directed principally against the two batteries in our front, up to which time we had suffered but little," but that changed after the Washington Artillery put his battery in a crossfire. "About 3 o'clock the fire of the battery on our right began to tell on us." Colonel John Beatty of the 3rd Ohio said of Slocomb's bombardment, "A well-handled battery playing upon us ... with destructive effect." To

Captain "Ned" Austin, postwar. Austin was a rising officer in the 11th Louisiana when that regiment disbanded. Recognized for his ability as a zealous officer, he was given authorization to organize a sharpshooter battalion (courtesy of Confederate Memorial Hall Museum, New Orleans).

protect his men from the barrage, Beatty had the 3rd Ohio lie down behind their fence.[20]

As Johnson moved forward against Lytle, Buckner became aware of the Louisiana Brigade's presence in the woods to his left. Buckner ordered Adams to advance his men in order to take advantage of the enemy's open right flank. It was obvious to all of the Confederates atop their position that Lytle was exposed. As John Headly was advancing with Austin's battalion, he described the picture before the Louisiana Brigade: "We were now getting close enough to see that the Federal line extended away to the right with a gap to the left." This gap "to the left" was dangerously close to another corps of Buell's army sitting atop Peter's Hill. Initially this body was about 700 to 800 yards away from Adams, but as "Old Pelican" began his advance it got as close as 400 yards. Incompetent leadership on the Federal side and great terrain shielded Adams from annihilation with his left flank hanging in the air.[21]

The Louisiana Brigade's advance threw them across Doctor's Creek at about 300 yards off the right flank of the struggling 3rd Ohio. Leading Adams' advance again were Austin's men. Once back in Doctor's Creek, Austin used the cover of the creek and its stone walls to march his men quickly upstream and right wheel into place. This put him facing the Bottom barn and on the flank of the 3rd Ohio. With a kick of his horse and a loud "Charge!" Austin pushed his two companies uphill. Beatty's Buckeyes easily brushed aside the miniature charge of Austin's small battalion. The battalion made it only halfway up before things became "too hot." Austin's five minutes of terror below the Bottom barn ended with the Louisianians scampering back to the creek. Once there they fell into line with the rest of the brigade as it reached the creek. It is at this time that rounds from Slocomb's guns avenged Austin's repulse. Rounds from the Washington Artillery slammed into the Bottom Farm and immediately ignited the hay filled barn into a blazing inferno. "Heat became so intense," said Beatty, "that my right was compelled to fall back." The barn fire was the last straw for the 3rd Ohio. They had lasted a couple of hours, bearing the brunt of the attack on the Bottom Farm. Of that regiment's 500 or so men present for battle, Beatty left behind 175 men along the wooden rail fence atop the Bottom Hill; included in that total were six color bearers shot. As Beatty fell back by filing to the left toward the pike, Lytle's reserve regiment, Colonel Curran Pope's 15th Kentucky, marched forward from the west side of Bottom Hill to hold its crest.[22]

For the first time the entire Louisiana Brigade was now pushing forward and engaging the enemy. It was the poor 15th Kentucky that was immediately threatened by the appearance of Adams from below the hill, to his right rear, into an orchard south of Bottom Hill. To cover such an exposure three companies of the 3rd Ohio were rushed back to the front and two companies of the 15th Kentucky were swung facing south. These five companies formed a perpendicular line facing south toward the Louisianians. It was too little too late; the Louisianians far outweighed this small force and were pushing fast. Either due to the pressure and intensity of the fight or to the angle of advance or the closeness of Adams, Lytle's refused right flank failed to put aimed shots into the Louisiana regiments. A member of the 16th Louisiana wrote home describing the scene: "They would fire away into our battalions at-no-more than 100 yards and often closer, the balls would plow up the earth, before, behind and cut air above and leave us unscathed." Farther down the line W.L. Trask of Austin's unit seconded the sloppy firing from the hill: "Thousands of their bullets would strike the ground in front of our line throwing the dirt up, several feet in the air. Our men were so close to them that they fired too low to do much harm." When Adams described the 15th Kentucky's and 3rd Ohio's stand against his front as a "short but spirited contest" he was not exaggerating.[23]

The 15th Kentucky was in a serious crunch. Its refused right flank was giving way fast; a fresh brigade, commanded by Brigadier General Patrick Cleburne, now entered the fray to its front. Cleburne managed to position himself as to lay down flanking fire on the Kentuckians' left. Taking advantage of the lack of artillery support near the Bottom House, Slocomb advanced his guns closer. Part of his battery moved farther up the Mackville Pike near Bull Run Creek with parts of other batteries, while the rest of it was moved a little to the west-southwest down Bull Run Creek. There he was able to hit the 3rd Ohio and then the 15th Kentucky with an almost enfilading fire. Reflecting on the dire situation was the quick loss of nine color bearers by the 15th Kentucky. Pope relinquished Bottom Hill and fell back down the hill on the heels of the 3rd Ohio.[24]

Bottom Hill was now in the hands of the Confederates. Adams and Cleburne now began to push forward to finish breaking Rousseau's right flank. The left regiment of Lytle's brigade, the 10th Ohio, sat north of the Mackville Pike along a small ridge with Harris' brigade. At the time, Lytle's other regiments were breaking. Lytle had ordered this regiment to lie down to avoid fire, and then he rode off to tend to his right flank. This put the

Opposite: **Captain Cuthbert Slocomb, 5th Company, Washington Artillery (courtesy of Confederate Memorial Hall Museum, New Orleans).**

4. The Kentucky Campaign: August–October 1862

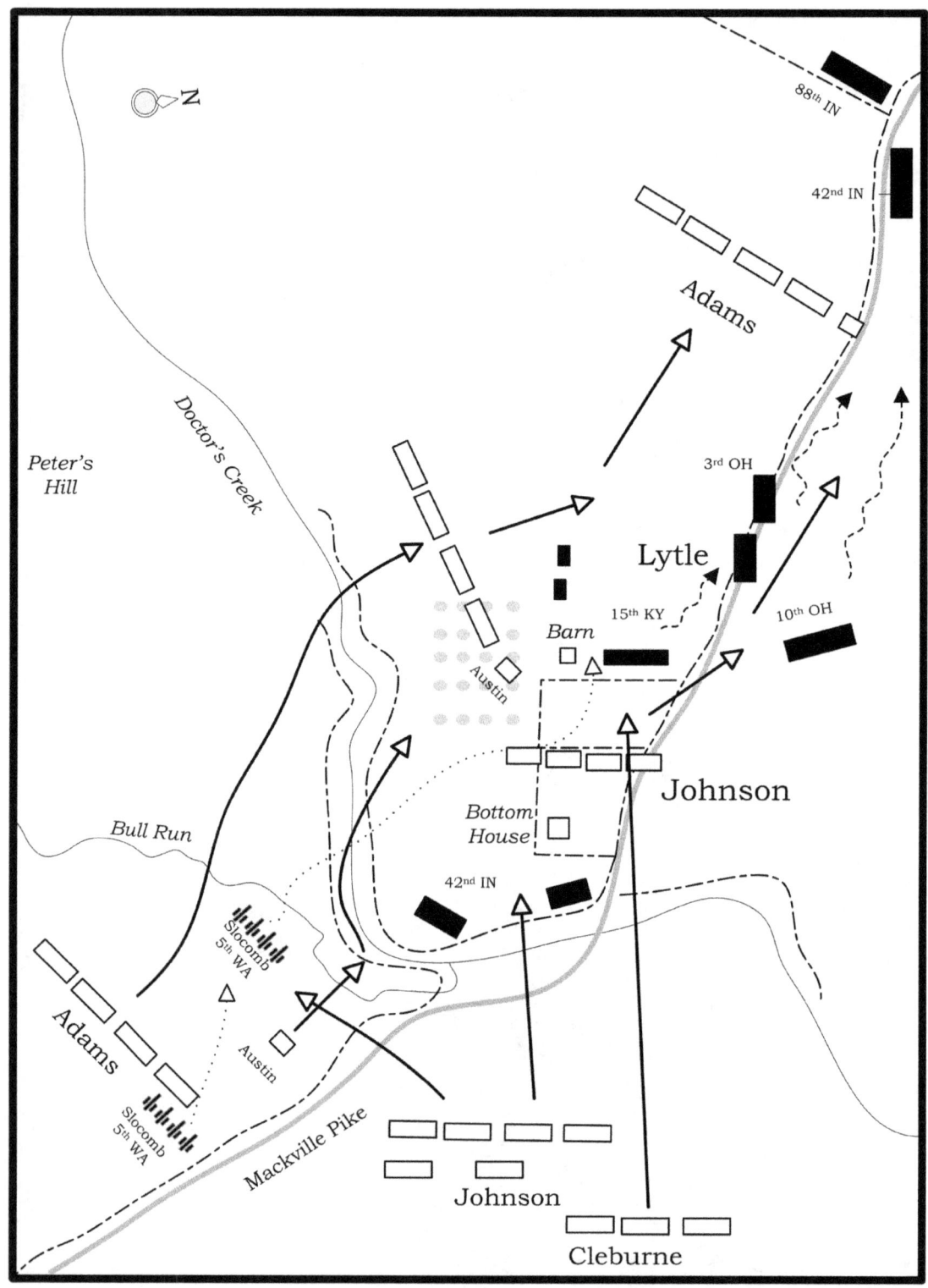

Adams' Attack, 8 October 1862, 2:00 P.M.–4:00 P.M.

10th Ohio in a bind, and combined with the topography, actually blinded the regiment from seeing Cleburne flank Bottom Hill. When Bottom Hill fell, Lytle's only option to protect the 10th from destruction was to reform the 3rd Ohio and 15th Kentucky along the Mackville Pike in a perpendicular line to the 10th Ohio. Things were not pretty for Lytle: the 10th Ohio and the remainder of Harris' brigade covering Lytle's left were either on their last rounds of ammunition pulled from the dead and wounded or were out of ammunition completely. Harris' units began to peel back under pressure to their front.[25]

All three of Lytle's regiments were shaky from a long, hard-fought day, and now appeared Adams' Louisianians over Bottom Hill "veering right" to Lytle's reformed line. The Louisianians gave little account to Lytle's last stand, as did other Confederates involved in the battle; considering the state of affairs in Lytle's brigade, it is no wonder. Colonel Beatty of the 3rd Ohio stated in his report that he and the 15th Kentucky reformed to face Adams, but he did not go into depth about the stand. Rather, the next sentence of his report says, "The fire of the enemy's battery, combined with that of his infantry, was so deadly that these men were again ordered to retire." Adams, in fact, simply described the scene to his front when taking Bottom Hill as, "They fled in great disorder, panic and confusion, throwing away their arms and equipment as they fled." He gave no account of

A soldier of the 5th Company Washington Artillery. Although this soldier's identity is unknown, his unit's presence never went unnoticed. From Shiloh through Missionary Ridge, opponents of the 5th Company attested to their destructive fire in combat. Daniel Adams praised Slocomb's Battery for their role at Perryville by saying: "The Washington Artillery did most essential and valuable service and deserve particular notice of praise, and I would especially recommend that they be allowed to have Perryville inscribed on their banner" (Dave Lewis Collection).

any last stand along the pike. "The Yankees were whipped at every point and driven back," bragged a proud member of the 16th Louisiana. In the desperate last stand to rally his regiments, Lytle was actually wounded. In the route of his brigade, he was captured by Austin's battalion as it advanced on the Mackville Pike.[26]

At this junction of the battle, Adams and Cleburne prepared their brigades for an advance west along the Mackville Pike. Their aiming point would be the Russell House near the Mackville and Benton crossroads, where Rousseau was rallying his regiments. The Bottom Hill was now a concentration for Confederate artillery. Slocomb's battery was moved to the cornfield on the hill along with two of Captain P. Darden's and Captain W.W. Carne's batteries. Placed under the eye of Johnson, and supported by his resupplied regiments, these batteries began to wreak havoc on the Russell House area. Before Harris' brigade crumbled under the pressure of Cleburne, Adams, Jones and Brown, Harris' battery, Simonson's, was retired to the rear and placed on the south side of the Mackville Pike. Simonson's position sat between the Bottom Hill and the woods surrounding the Russell House to the rear where the Mackville and Benton roads crossed. From this spot Simonson tried to lay fire into Adams and held his position from about 3:30 to 4:00, at about the time of Adams' advance up the Mackville Pike. The Washington Artillery upset Simonson's new position. When one of Slocomb's shells hit a limber chest in Simonson's battery it put on a huge fireworks spectacle. This was the cue for Simonson to join in the retreat of the infantry to his front.[27]

Adams pushed his Louisianians west up the pike and in doing so became an easy target for preying enemy batteries. To his front Loomis and Simonson were reorganizing and throwing their shells into Adams' ranks. From the left oblique came rounds from Captain William Hotchkiss' 2nd Battery of Minnesota Artillery. To the front of the Louisiana Brigade, in the woods surrounding the Russell House, were the reforming regiments from Harris and Lytle. Rousseau spent most of the morning on his left flank and, upon his return to his right found it in shambles. He rode among his men, rallying them and piecing together what units he could to allow the remainder to reload and return to the fight. Bracing the attack of the Louisianians were the 42nd and 88th Indiana Regiments, with Loomis' battery about 150 yards behind the Russell House. The 88th Indiana was marching forward from near Loomis' guns and through the woods around the Russell House to the fence line separating the cornfield in which the Louisianians advanced. Along the fence on the north side of the Mackville Pike was the 42nd Indiana which Austin's men had run from Doctor's Creek about 3 hours earlier in the day. The reason the 42nd Indiana's flank was not torn to pieces by Cleburne was that it was posted at a slight angle; they were lying down, and Cleburne was actually trailing behind Adams.[28]

For the first time today, Adams ran into concentrated fire on his brigade. His Louisiana regiments were able to flank Lytle and crush his rally attempt but with most of the enemy's attention being to their front. The advance toward the Russell House, as Adams described it, was "under a heavy and rapid fire." Headly of Austin's battalion said the scene "was a perfect storm, the sound of musketry never ceasing and the roar of cannon rolling without a break." Loomis' and Simonson's batteries were pouring canister into the Louisiana regiments at the direction of Rousseau. Rousseau said Loomis' guns raked Adams' line with "fearful effect upon the ranks of the enemy."[29]

What happened next seems to be one of those moments where witness accounts dramatically differ. From Union sources, Adams' brigade was decimated by the firefight and was sent rushing to the rear by a bayonet charge of the 42nd Indiana. These sources on the charge come only from the 42nd Indiana. There is no mention of such an attack by the neighboring 88th Indiana, Rousseau or any other Federal participants at this part of the battle. Colonel George Humphrey of the 88th Indiana described the attack of Adams, and there was no mention of a mad attack into the enemy: "I ordered an advance to a position behind a fence and poured in about 20 rounds of ammunition upon the advancing enemy, which drove them back in about thirty minutes." Likewise, neither Adams nor any other Louisiana soldier sources mention such an event. Instead, they all describe an intense firefight in which Adams was forced to fall back. W.L. Trask of Austin's battalion said that from Bottom Hill "we followed them as they ran until they made a stand where we engaged in a musketry duel about two hundred yards apart, for a while." Adams makes brief reference to the firefight from opposing units to his front and thus no mention of a violent counterattack on his right. In contrast, Spillard Horrall of the 42nd Indiana said the enemy to his front advanced to within 75 yards of the Hoosiers' line. What Horrall and Ellis of the 16th Louisiana did agree about was the procession in which the Louisiana Brigade advanced. Horrall said in admiration, "They moved on steadily; apparently, as if on drill in camp," and Ellis bragged, "The men stood right straight up on the open field (there were no woods) loaded and fired, charged and fell back as deliberately as if on drill." Judging from Ellis' memory, falling back "deliberately as if on drill" contrasts to being slammed into by a counterattack. If the 42nd Indiana's counterattack did in fact hit Adams' brigade, then this would suggest that the 13th Louisiana was posted on the right of the brigade near Austin's battalion which advanced up the Mackville Pike itself. Ideally, the Thirteenth would have been deployed on the right of the line. In Adams' General Order 6 issued while in Chattanooga, Adams set out marching and order of battle alignments for the regiments. From right to left and from front to rear while marching, 13th, 20th, 25th, and then the 16th Regiments were to be deployed. Both primary sources available from Austin's unit from Perryville both make no mention of the attack. The 42nd Indiana did make some sort of advance but from the Louisiana perspective it was not as grandiose as the Hoosiers remembered.[30]

During Adams' advance, the exposed left flank of Bragg's attack was now being realized. Earlier in the battle it was the biggest fear of the high command and was the reason for detaching units of Johnson's brigade and the tardiness of Adams getting into line earlier in the day. Adams was so exposed in the field between Bottom and Russell that he now became the target of artillery from Peter's Hill, and thus was now taking enfilading and, worse, rear fire. Discerning the situation and "using my glass," Adams was able to see at 600 to 800 yards away Brigadier General Charles C. Gilbert's I Corps, some 22,000 men, massing in that region. Adams withdrew his men in a fashion that backed up Ellis of the 16th Louisiana: "Deeming this position untenable I ordered the brigade to fall back, which they did in perfect order."[31]

The Louisiana Brigade fell back to Bottom Hill and behind the improvised collection of batteries. Their withdrawal was partially covered by two of Johnson's Tennessee regiments, the 25th and 44th Regiments, who were some 250 yards in front of the burning Bottom barn. Cleared of the retreating Louisianians, Slocomb and his sister batteries kept up a serious artillery duel and bombardment of the Russell House area until about 7:30 P.M. The battle continued while Adams' thirsty and tired men tried to collect themselves, rest and get some food and drink in their bodies. Men took the opportunity to get coffee and newspapers from enemy haversacks, care for the wounded and inspect the devastation around them at the Bottom Farm. Trask of Austin's battalion described the scene very vividly:

> Many of us visited portions of the battle field ... first going to a farm house in front of where the enemy's battery had fought so long and stubbornly.... The sight I witnessed around this house was horrifying. In the yard several of the enemy's dead were lying — in the smoke house near by several more lay dead, having crawled there during the fight to breathe their last. Several more were still groaning in the last agonies of death.... We then turned out attention to the main building. It had been used for a hospital by the enemy early in the fight, and it was afterwards badly torn by our shot and shell.... The Surgeons had left in a hurry, their tables and instruments were scattered around in confusion. A dozen dead and wounded still remained there some groaning piteously.[32]

"A little after nightfall the firing ceased as if by mutual consent." The Battle of Perryville was a short lived but "very *warm* place" for Adams' brigade, but the situation for the Confederate army was deteriorating fast. Even though the Louisiana boys got to enjoy the trail end of the battle out of the main line of fire, Gilbert's corps finally made a serious push toward Perryville. This move from Peter's Hill threatened the very capture of Perryville and cut Bragg's line of retreat. Members of McCook's corps were very critical after the disaster at Perryville of the neighboring corps. The advance of Adams, throughout the entire engagement, lay totally open to Gilbert's front and could have prevented the rolling up of Harris' and Lytle's brigades. Rousseau made sure to point out in his report when he reached the 15th Kentucky on Bottom Hill the unfolding disaster he saw could have been avoided: "It [Adams' brigade] was moving steadily up, in full view of where General Gilbert's army corps had been during the day, the left flank of which was not more than 400 yards from it."[33]

At the forefront of Gilbert's push was Brigadier General Phil Sheridan's division. Sheridan had been itching for most of the day to make a push, and when it finally came, his division crushed Powell's brigade. Powell was the only sizeable force between Gilbert and Perryville, and thus Bragg's left and rear were now completely open. One of the forefront regiments of Sheridan's advance was the 38th Illinois regiment. At around 4:00 P.M., when the Louisiana Brigade was engaged outside the Russell House, the 38th Illinois pushed to the western-northern outskirts of Perryville. In doing so this regiment dealt a major blow to the Louisiana Brigade by placing itself in the path of the brigade attempting to resupply itself. Lieutenant Philip Sayne was captured with 12 to 15 men and about a dozen wagons full of guns and ammunition. Also, Lieutenant Thomas Blair of the Washington Artillery was captured with 14 men and 2 caissons full of ammunition just pulled from the rear.[34]

Thanks to the incompetence of the Union high command, the history of the Louisiana Brigade does not end at the Battle of Perryville. Despite pushing hard into Perryville, Gilbert withdrew his men and thus gave Bragg the breathing room required to extract his men from disaster. Bragg realized that a retreat was necessary. During the night of the eighth, Bragg began withdrawing his units across the Chaplin River. Buckner withdrew his division around 2:00 A.M. but gave orders to Adams to bring up the rear of the division. By 3:30, preceded by Slocomb's guns, Adams was across the Chaplin River. This was the last unit of Bragg's army to leave Perryville. Trask spoke to the frustration of the Louisiana Brigade when he said, "We found ourselves back at the position we had left in the morning [heights east of Perryville across the Chaplin River] and were ordered to stack arms again. It was now 4 A.M. nearly daybreak — so ended the "Battle of Perryville"— a decided victory to our arms but like many others previously fought, a completely barren one."[35]

Obviously he was referring to the brigade's only two major battles, Shiloh and Perryville. In both battles the brigade had shown its ability to conduct itself well under fire. On both occasions, the brigade had hurled itself at enemy positions, and at the of both of those days (referring to 6 April, the first day of Shiloh) it had ended favorably for their side. In the end, however, their army was retreating. One stark contrast from Shiloh was that the brigade had escaped with relatively light losses. Adams' brigade escaped the battle with a mere 152 casualties: 6 killed, 78 wounded and 68 missing. One member of the 16th Louisiana went as far to say that his regiment "never fired a shot" during the battle. If this claim is true, it would suggest that the 16th was on Adams' left, the farthest away from any fighting, but it would have been subjected to serious artillery fire when advancing on the Russell House.[36]

The retreat was continued to Harrodsburg, where Bragg and Smith finally united. From Harrodsburg, the retreat continued east to Bryantsville where the army arrived at Camp Dick Robinson on 11 October. It was here that Bragg contemplated making a stand with his and Smith's armies. Everyone in the army expected a battle on the morning of the thirteenth. A member of Austin's battalion wrote on 12 October, "Four days rations were cooked, ammunition distributed and everything indicated a fight," but the same soldier recorded the next day: "Up at three o'clock this morning. Expected to go out and fight the enemy at daylight." To the Louisianan's surprise, they were not marching to engage Buell's army but instead retreating to Tennessee. "I thought we were going towards Lexington to concentrate all our force near there and fight ... convinced we were running out of Kentucky towards Cumberland Gap."[37]

The march across Tennessee and Kentucky was grueling enough on the Louisianians but what lay ahead in the next week dwarfed their marathon of the past two months. General Adams foreshadowed the conditions when he wrote his wife before the brigade left Camp Dick Robinson, "The weather now is quite cold and disagreeable & will I fear cause much suffering amongst the men." On the thirteenth, the grim march through barren, mountainous Eastern Kentucky began. The Louisianians marched "without resting, that too on half rations." The tough marching conditions resulted in the capture of many

Captain Samuel Scott, 25th Louisiana. The Perryville Campaign subjected the Louisiana Brigade to its first serious test of extended and forced marches. The strenuous campaign and the elements of the harsh retreat led to many casualties. Captain Scott was one of these losses. He died of disease, while on the retreat to Tennessee, on 15 October 1862 (courtesy of the U.S. Army Military History Institute).

men who were scattered across the state due to straggling or sickness. When the brigade crossed back into Tennessee on the eighteenth through Cumberland Gap there was no resounding speech from Adams or news of great victories. The landscape of the Cumberland Area was symbolic of their return to Tennessee; it was "the most desolate looking countries it is possible to imagine." Eight days and a grueling 157 miles later, Adams' men reached Morristown, Tennessee, on the East Tennessee & Virginia Railroad, on the evening of October 22. "The army was now in deplorable condition — ragged, barefooted and without tents — many sick and crippled." Marching by foot ended, and the men were loaded into cars to finish their retreat to Knoxville. "Such a shout as our men gave when they first heard the locomotive whistle!" A tired Louisianian complained to his mother, "We have arrived here ... weary and dispirited ... [we] have done enough to kill anybody." Fred Airey of the 20th Louisiana recalled the Battle of Perryville and the retreat from that field oddly very optimistic despite defeat and horrible conditions on the retreat: "We reached Perryville, where we gave them a regular fight and a splendid thrashing. We then took up the march for Tennessee."[38]

The Kentucky Campaign left a bitter feeling with the Louisianians. "It was reported that 32 regiments were organized in that state for the Confederate Service. We found instead

32 men who were willing to be Colonels, 32 willing to serve as Lieut Colonels and Majors, any quantity ready to tack on their collars the bars of a Captain or Lieutenant but few, very few willing to serve in the ranks. *Kentucky is subjugated.*" "The feeling against Bragg was great," remembered a member of the Washington Artillery. Whether justified or not, the quick retreat back to Tennessee was not understood by many men. "Our 'skedaddle' from Kentucky was as sudden as it was unexpected.... Many blame Gen. Bragg," recorded Ezekiel Ellis of the 16th Louisiana. Colonel Gibson, when speaking about the campaign, wrote: "I incline to think that the Kentucky Campaign was a failure from want of brains — it was a tiresome march through a land of plenty.... The Army — I deeply regret to say it — is without confidence in Genl. Bragg." The handling of the Kentucky Campaign sowed the seeds of discontent in the Army of the Mississippi.[39]

Chapter 5

Murfreesboro Campaign: November 1862–January 1863

"I was engaged in urging the men forward to charge a battery I had been directed to take—It proved a desperate undertaking and the enemys fire from artillery and small arms was terrible—The scene was bloodier and fiercer than any part of the battle of Shiloh."
— Brigadier General Daniel Adams, letter written to his wife, 19 January 1863

The stay in East Tennessee did not last long. The day that the army marched into Morristown, Bragg sent a message to Cooper informing him of his intentions to move the army into Middle Tennessee. President Davis, however, called Bragg to Richmond to discuss the failure of the Kentucky Campaign. Bragg placed Polk in temporary command of the army and ordered, on 23 October, just two days after ending the retreat from Kentucky, that he take the army into Middle Tennessee, to Murfreesboro, just below Nashville. Polk loaded the army into cars and began shipping them to Chattanooga along the East Tennessee Railroad. From Chattanooga, the army traveled west to Bridgeport, Alabama, over the Tennessee River and into lower Middle Tennessee. Within the week, the army was encamped at Tullahoma, Tennessee. During this transfer, Adams took leave and made a trip to Richmond, returning to his brigade on 12 November. During Adams' absence, Gibson, the senior regimental commander, took command of the brigade. Slocomb's battery did not enjoy as easy a ride as the Louisiana infantry. The artillery of the army had to make the trip from east Tennessee to middle Tennessee by road. Leaving Kingston, the battery went south and traveled through Pikeville, Dunlap and Jasper. From Jasper, the battery marched to Allisonia, on the Nashville & Chattanooga Railroad, just below Tullahoma, on 18 November.[1]

On 20 November, Bragg, having returned from Richmond, set up his headquarters in Murfreesboro and deployed his army across Middle Tennessee. In the deployment, Adams marched to Shelbyville on the Duck River. While settling into winter quarters, Bragg reorganized the army again. The term corps replaced the term wing. Anderson's division was broken up on 22 November, and his regiments were dispersed among the army. Of the four brigades in Anderson's division, only Adams' brigade remained intact. Bragg attached Adams to a newly organized division under the command of Major General John C. Breckinridge. Breckinridge filled Anderson's vacant spot in Hardee's corps. The army was also given a new name, the Army of Tennessee.[2]

There were also regimental changes within the brigade. On 30 November, after the

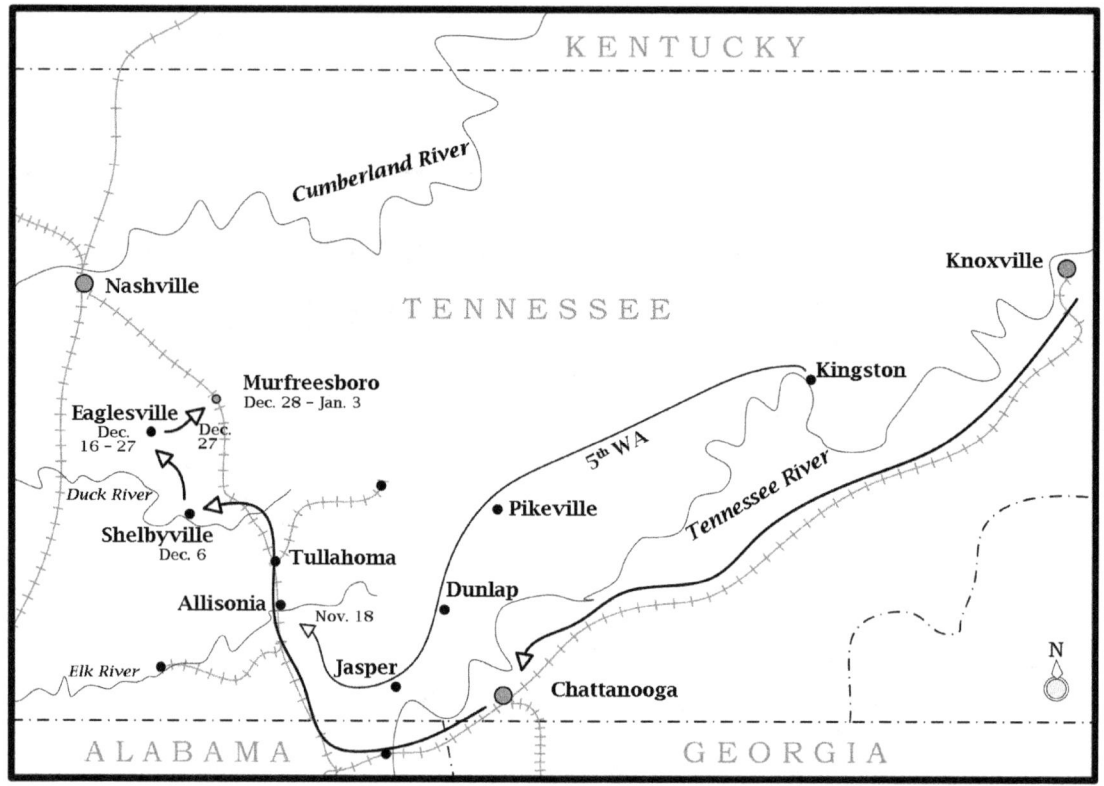

Movements of the Louisiana Brigade, October through December 1862.

brigade reached Shelbyville, Bragg ordered the 13th and 20th Regiments to be consolidated into one regiment and the 16th and 25th Regiments to be consolidated into another. Before the army had left East Tennessee, Polk reported to the secretary of war, George Randolph, that "many regiments" within the army "are reduced below 100 men. They are from the States south and west of this. What is the course to be pursued to get these regiments filled?" It does not seem likely that Polk was speaking directly of Adams' regiments, because when the four regiments were consolidated into two, they formed aggregate strengths of 1,075 and 1,078 men. These large aggregate numbers did not represent the effective strength of the regiments, or the number of men and officers effective for duty at that moment. The effective strength of these two regiments by late December was only 452 for the 13th & 20th Louisiana and 457 for the 16th & 25th Louisiana. What this reflects is that the months of October through December were not kind to the Louisiana Brigade. The 13th and 20th Regiments, even though not consolidated for the Battle of Perryville, were listed with a total strength of 688 men. The 16th and 25th Regiments fielded 932 men. These are large drops in men, especially in the 16th and 25th Regiments where we see a drop of almost 500 men.[3]

Under General Order 14, dated 30 November, the four regiments were all consolidated into five companies, each to form half of the new consolidated regiments. The 13th Regiment formed Companies B, C, E, I and K of the new 13th & 20th Consolidated, while the 20th Regiment formed Companies A, D, F, G, and H. The command structure was also mixed between the two regiments: Colonel Gibson from the 13th, Lieutenant Colonel Leon Von Zinken of the 20th Louisiana, and Major Charles Guillet from the 20th. Guillet filled the void left by the resignation of Major O'Leary from the 13th Louisiana. The command problems facing the 13th Louisiana, alluded to before, fell on the shoulders of O'Leary, and it was more than he wished for. "The Lt Col of the Regt was absent — the Major had been killed and the Col was often in command of the brigade. This officer was in consequence of this state of facts; assigned to duty as Major. It was more contrary to my wishes but it appeared unavoidable." Claiming to be unwell and unfit for duty because of the Kentucky Campaign, O'Leary resigned his position. One can only guess Gibson's temperament when he submitted O'Leary's resignation in which he bluntly stated, "This officer is not competence to discharge the duties of a field officer to which he was raised due to seniority or rank." General Hardee did not let this issue fall by the wayside after it went through the hands of Gibson, the brigade commander and the division commander, Patton Anderson. He demanded to know how "the promotion of an incompetent officer was permitted." An answer to Hardee's question is not known.[4]

Likewise, changes were also made in the new 16th & 25th Consolidated Regiment. The 16th Regiment's companies were combined to form Companies A, C, F, G, H and I, while the 25th Regiment formed Companies G, D, E, and K. Command of the regiment was similar to the 13th & 20th: Colonel Fisk of the 25th, described as "a miserable old granny" by one of his troops, commanded and the lieutenant colonel spot was filled by William Walker of the 16th Regiment. Shortly after the consolidation of the regiment Lieutenant Colonel Walker died. Major Robert H. Lindsay, of the 16th Regiment, was promoted to fill Walker's position. The problem with Lindsay's promotion is that the consolidated regiment already had a lieutenant colonel, Joseph C. Lewis. Why Lewis was not made the consolidated regiment's lieutenant colonel is unclear but it is known that at the time of the consolidation both Lindsay and Lewis were detached and away from the regiment.[5]

A new regiment was also attached to the brigade, the 32nd Alabama. The Thirty-Second Alabama was organized in April of 1862, with Colonel Alexander McKinstry and Lieutenant Colonel Henry Maury in command. McKinstry had Georgia roots but moved to live in Mobile

Colonel McKinstry, 32nd Alabama (courtesy of Alabama Department of Archives and History, Montgomery).

when orphaned at age 14. He worked in a drugstore, studied to become a lawyer and practiced law in Mobile, with Supreme Court justice John Campbell being his mentor. In 1847 he was elected colonel to the Alabama state militia. He served in that capacity until 1850, where he served as a judge until 1860. He resigned his position in that year to begin practicing law again. McKinstry decided to take his skills to the field by accepting the position of colonel in the new 32nd Alabama one month shy of his 40th birthday. His lieutenant colonel also brought with him military experience and also had roots in being a lawyer. Henry Maury moved to Mobile in 1848 and went into the shipping business. He became a lawyer in the early to mid–1850s and was elected to his first political position in 1855 as marshal of the City of Mobile. Maury was considered a "man's man" and brought with him military experience to the 32nd Alabama. Before the war, he took part in Walker's last attempt to take over Nicaragua. At the outbreak of hostilities, he was present with the troops that forced the surrender of Fort Morgan in 1861. He was commissioned colonel of the 2nd Alabama Infantry and was transferred to Fort Pillow, Tennessee, for duty. When that regiment disbanded in early 1862 he returned to Mobile in time to be commissioned the second-in-command of the 32nd Alabama.[6]

Half of the 32nd Regiment's companies were organized in the Mobile area from Mobile and Baldwin Counties. Following organization the regiment remained in the Mobile area performing guard duty. As their future brigade was being mauled to pieces the regiment spent its time garrisoning the coast and Fort Gaines. About the only things the regiment fought during its time garrisoning the area, April to July, were sicknesses and diseases. It was a new unit and thus had to undergo the growing pains of war. Private Stephen Burrell of Company A, while complaining of his own health, expressed his frustration to his wife while at Fort Gains: "Our men are all dissatisfied here. We have seen aufall cold weather here and winds enough to kill the devil." Private Burrell would himself succumb to measles less than a month after telling his wife of their condition. In July the unit's boredom of garrison duty and picketing beaches ended when it was ordered to Chattanooga, Tennessee, at the time the Army of the Mississippi was moving to meet Buell's advance. When the regiment reached Chattanooga, it was attached to Withers' division, but it did not participate in the Kentucky Campaign. Instead, the regiment was placed under the command of Brigadier General Samuel Maxey and left behind to help protect Chattanooga. On the day that Adams' brigade was crossing the Tennessee River to begin its march for Kentucky, the Thirty-Second was farther upriver opposite Bridgeport, Alabama.[7]

On the morning of 27 August Maxey pushed a small force across the river, as a diversion to Bragg's main crossing across the Tennessee River to Bridgeport. The 32nd Alabama had barely crossed the river when "clouds of dust in the roads" alerted the command that the Federals were approaching. Colonel Leonard Harris, commander of a Federal fort at the mouth of Battle Creek, sent the 4th Ohio Cavalry to contest Maxey's crossing at Bridgeport. Three times the 4th Ohio charged McKinstry's line and was repulsed each time. The Federals made a brisk retreat to Harris' fort. Although only a skirmish, with the regiment losing only two men wounded out of 330 men, Bridgeport was the 32nd's first test under fire. Maxey stated in his official report of the battle that McKinstry's men "did nobly, fighting like veterans."[8]

Following Bridgeport, the 32nd took part in an attack on Stevenson, Alabama, on 31 August. After the small Federal garrison there was ejected, the 32nd went on picket duty at the Water and Nickojack railroad bridges. On 21 September, the regiment was ordered to board the railroad cars at Bridgeport for Tullahoma, Tennessee. Maury's orders were to protect the Nashville & Chattanooga Railroad and to present an impression to the Federals that a large force was advancing on Nashville. At the beginning of October, the regiment received orders from Major General Sam Jones, commander of the Chattanooga post, to proceed to Murfreesboro and to harass Federal outposts in the area.[9]

While performing its assigned duty, the regiment was surprised at La Vergne, Tennessee, on 7 October by two Federal columns. The commander of the Nashville post, Brigadier General James Negley, was aware of a Confederate force at La Vergne. He feared that this force was going to attack Nashville, and he decided to disperse the Confederates. Negley sent General John Palmer with 400 infantry and 400 cavalry along the Murfreesboro Road toward La Vergne and sent Colonel John Miller with 1,800 infantry to the south of La Vergne. In a brief engagement, Brigadier General Samuel R. Anderson, commanding the Confederate force at La Vergne, realized that he was outnumbered and ordered a hasty retreat. The regiment was overpowered, and Lieutenant Colonel Maury and a portion of the unit were captured. The 32nd lost 2 men killed, 10 men wounded, about 60 prisoners, and even the regiment's band "lost everything."[10]

Following La Vergne, the 32nd moved back to Murfreesboro. At the end of October, Major General John C. Breckinridge arrived at Murfreesboro and organized all of the troops into a small division under his command. The 32nd Regiment was assigned to Colonel J.B. Palmer's brigade. When Anderson's division was broken up, the 32nd Alabama was transferred from Palmer's to Adams' brigade. The 32nd was the only non–Louisiana unit to serve with the brigade from its creation in August of 1862 until the end of the war. Absent from the regiment for the time of the Battle of Murfreesboro was Colonel McKinstry. The exact reason for his absence is not known, and he did not return to command the regiment. He does show up in 1863, though, as part of General Bragg's staff as provost marshal. During 1864 he was attached to Nathan Bedford Forrest's command and remained so until the end of the war.[11]

From Shelbyville, Adams was detached from Breckinridge's division and ordered to proceed to Eagleville, where Cleburne's division was posted. Bragg detached Breckinridge from Hardee and sent him with Polk's corps to Murfreesboro. As the brigade prepared for winter quarters, their planned hibernation was interrupted by the advance of the Federals from Nashville. On Christmas Day, Major General William Rosecrans, commander of the Army of the Cumberland, left his base at Nashville and marched on Bragg's position at Murfreesboro. Bragg hurriedly concentrated his army at Murfreesboro and prepared to meet the Federal advance. On the morning of 28 December, Breckinridge's division was deployed north of Murfreesboro from Stones River to across the Lebanon Pike. Breckinridge had Adams' brigade posted toward the right of the line next to the Lebanon Pike. The brigade remained in this position until the thirtieth, when it was moved farther to Breckinridge's left, next to Stones River and behind Wayne's Hill.[12]

As Rosecrans' army moved closer to the Army of Tennessee, skirmishing and fighting increased on the west side of the river. The only movement for the brigade during the next two days was when it was moved farther to Breckinridge's left, next to Stones River and behind Wayne's Hill. As the encounters increased and began to include artillery duels the Louisiana Brigade sat idle across the river. Arms were stacked and the men awaited orders. Men of the 13th Louisiana were "as gay and as unconcerned as if nothing unusual was going on." Captain John McGrath watched his men chase down a rabbit and then took part in their victorious feast that night, courtesy of the captured rabbit. The next day, however, proved to be a completely different set of circumstances and one that McGrath's unit would remember.[13]

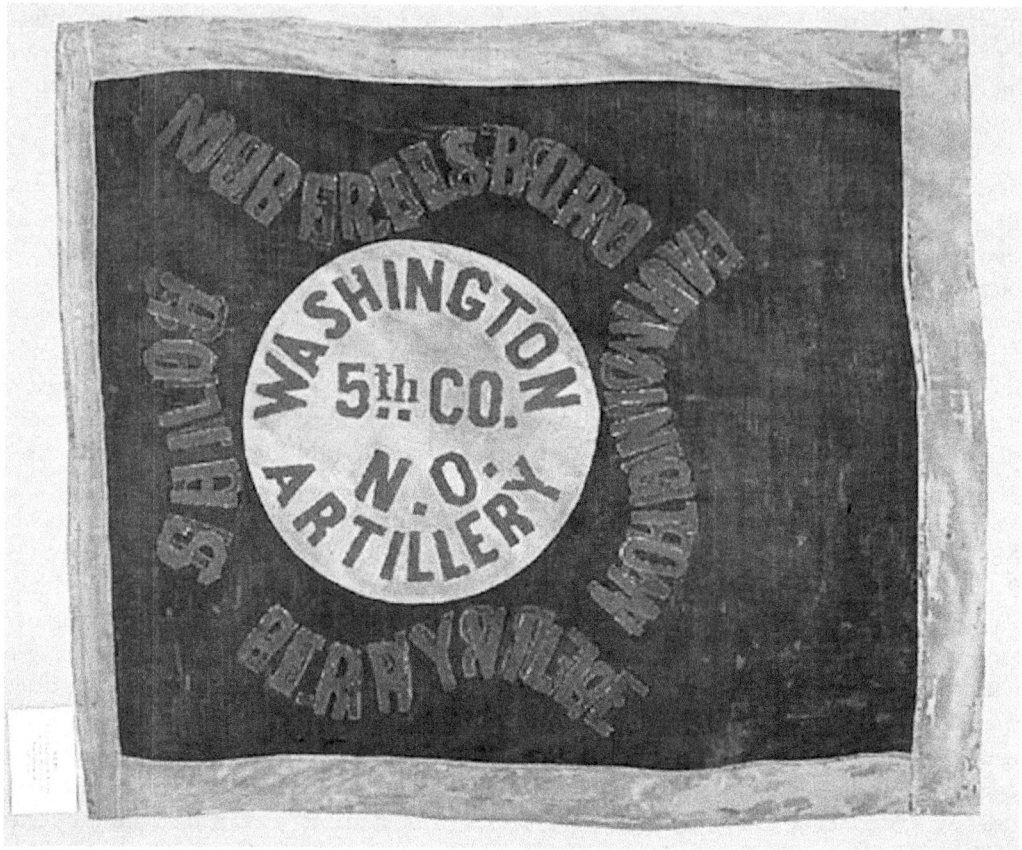

5th Company Washington Artillery's Hardee Pattern Flag (courtesy of Confederate Memorial Hall Museum, New Orleans).

For the Battle of Murfreesboro Adams' brigade was organized as follows:

13th & 20th Louisiana — Colonel Randall Gibson (457 men)
16th & 25th Louisiana — Colonel Stuart W. Fisk (452 men)
32d Alabama — Lieutenant Colonel Henry Maury (280 men)
Austin's battalion — Major John E. Austin
5th Company of Washington Artillery — 1st Lieutenant William Vaught[14]

At 6:00 A.M. on 31 December, Bragg opened the Battle of Murfreesboro (Stones River) with an attack on the right flank of the Federal army. Just as at Perryville, Bragg's plan called for his army to swing like a giant door and push the Federals off the field. For four hours, the Army of Tennessee enjoyed great success, capturing thousands of prisoners and several cannons. The entire left and center of the Federal army was in total rout. Not until the early afternoon were the Federals able to form a stabilized line. Adams' brigade, posted on the east side of the river, sat out of the battle until early afternoon when Bragg ordered Breckinridge to reinforce the faltering attack on the west side of the river. Breckinridge prepared Adams' and Brigadier General John K. Jackson's brigades to cross the river.

Initially, Bragg had called for help from Breckinridge at 10:00 A.M., but then countermanded his order when Breckinridge informed him of an enemy advance east of the river.

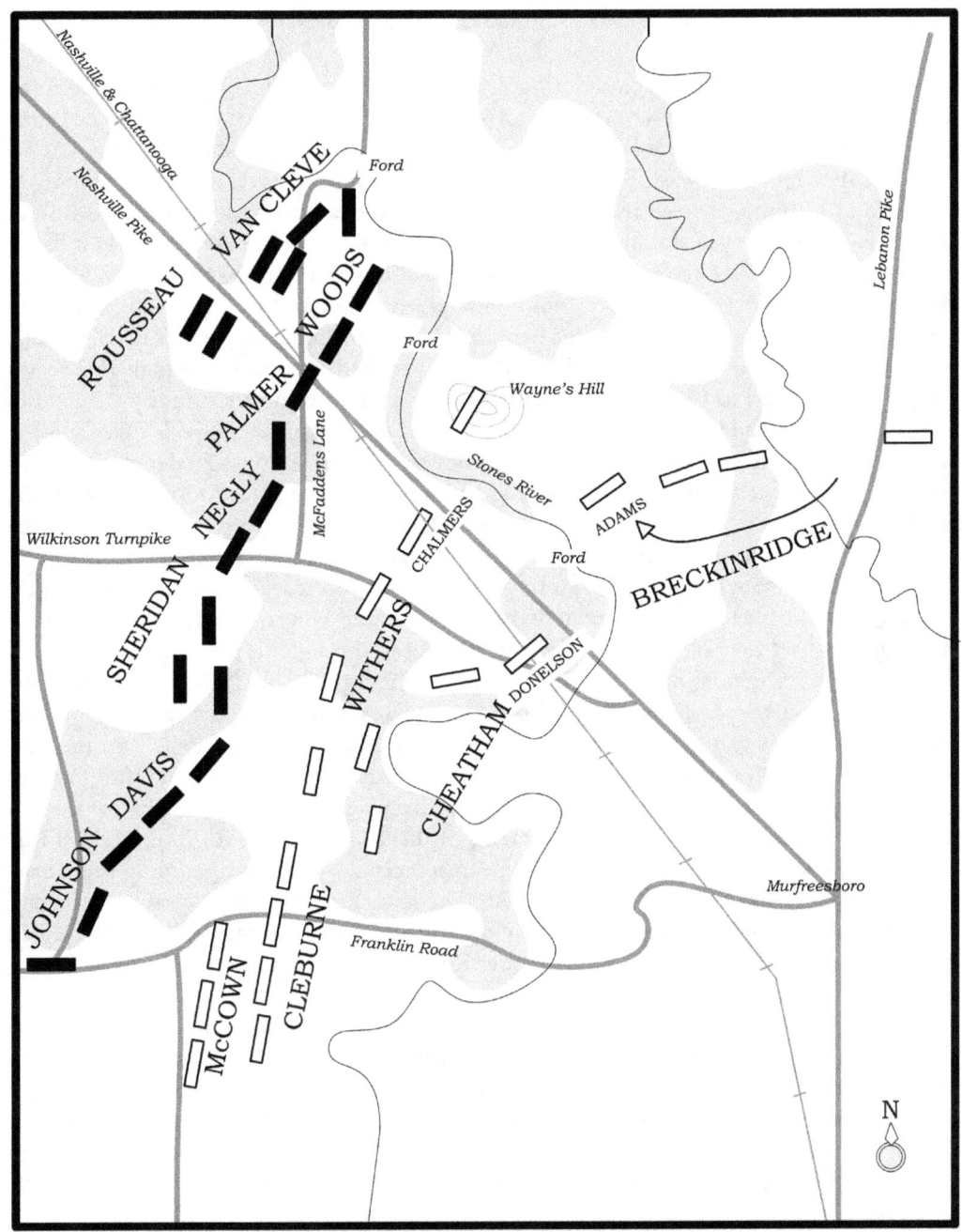

Battle of Murfreesboro, 31 December 1862, 6:30 A.M.

Bragg next ordered Breckinridge to attack any Federal units that had crossed the river and threatened his position. At 11:30, while Breckinridge was advancing his division for the attack, he received another order from Bragg to fall back and send help immediately to Polk. Only minutes later Breckinridge received another message for him to halt moving any brigades west of the river and to confirm if there was a sizeable enemy force threatening the Confederate right. Finally, when reports trickled in to Breckinridge that an enemy attack east of the river had proved false, Bragg ordered Breckinridge, at 1:00 P.M., to send Adams and Jackson to Polk's assistance. Nearing 2:00 P.M., the Louisianians splashed across the icy river. Polk directed Adams to lead his men toward an enemy battery posted on an "eminence" between the Nashville Pike and Stones River, about 800 yards distance.[15]

The spot that Polk was pointing to was the left wing of Rosecrans' army which was anchored at a clump of trees and rock cropping. This area became known as the Round Forest. There was a lot of shuffling of Union units in this sector, but defense of their flank, from the Nashville Pike to Stones River area, fell mainly on the three brigades of Colonel William Hazen of Brigadier General John Palmer's division and Colonel George Wagner and Brigadier General Milo Hascall of Brigadier General Thomas J. Wood's division. The collapse of their right flank farther down the line resulted in a lot of units in this sector being moved around to counter attacks from the south-southwest direction. By the 2:00 to 2:30 P.M. range, when the Louisiana Brigade began its march up the Nashville Pike, another brigade was thrown into the Round Forest to bolster Hazen. Colonel Frederick Schaefer's brigade of Brigadier General Phil Sheridan's division had been forced to retreat from the Federal right and north across the Nashville Pike. Once it had resupplied and rested itself, the brigade was moved to the Round Forest. Despite the almost chaotic situation that existed in the moving and removing of so many units in the Round Forest sector, its lines were solid.[16]

Hazen's brigade had the luxury of manning the Round Forest, studded with limestone outcroppings, and the railroad embankment, which ran through his position. The hinge to the Union left emerged to be Hazen's 9th Indiana. This regiment was posted along the railroad looking southwest. To the right of the 9th Indiana, and across the railroad, was the 58th Indiana. This regiment was posted at somewhat of an angle with its left on the railroad and its right near the pike facing in a south to southeasterly direction. With parts of Hazen's brigade to the rear resupplying, Schaefer's brigade was placed to the left of the 9th Indiana along the railroad. The four regiments of this brigade, the 44th Illinois, 73rd Illinois, 2nd Missouri and 15th Missouri, had been subjected to serious fighting in the morning, and its numbers were seriously depleted. The first three regiments were posted along the railroad with the 9th Indiana, and the 15th Missouri was deployed farther to the left in the field between the Round Forest and Stones River. Without detailed reports from Schaefer's commanders, it is difficult to determine an exact deployment.[17]

Regiments posted farther to the rear and to the left were Buell's 100th Illinois, then Hazen's 110th Illinois and finally Wagner's 57th Indiana and 15th Indiana regiments. The 100th and 110th Illinois were posted along the edge of the Round Forest line with their right near the 9th Indiana by the railroad. Wagner's two regiments were posted a little more to the left with the 15th Indiana's left being near Stones River. Behind this line were several regiments of not only these brigades but also of other brigades either resupplying or acting as reserves.[18]

Supporting this solid force were three batteries. Company F of the 1st Ohio Artillery under Lieutenant Norval Osburn manned a position between the pike and railroad for most of the day and had performed destructive duty. Once this unit was resupplied and refitted it was pulled back into action. Its position was "in a corn-field to the left of the railroad, supported by the Nineteenth Brigade [Hazen] on our left, and the Tenth Brigade, Colonel Grose commanding, on our right. Posted to their front were the 6th Kentucky and 58th Indiana Regiments." Another battery that was pulled into action against the Louisianians was the 8th Indiana Battery under Lieutenant George Estep. Like Cox, his battery was resupplying when the charge began but was pulled into line on the left behind the 110th Illinois and 57th Indiana.

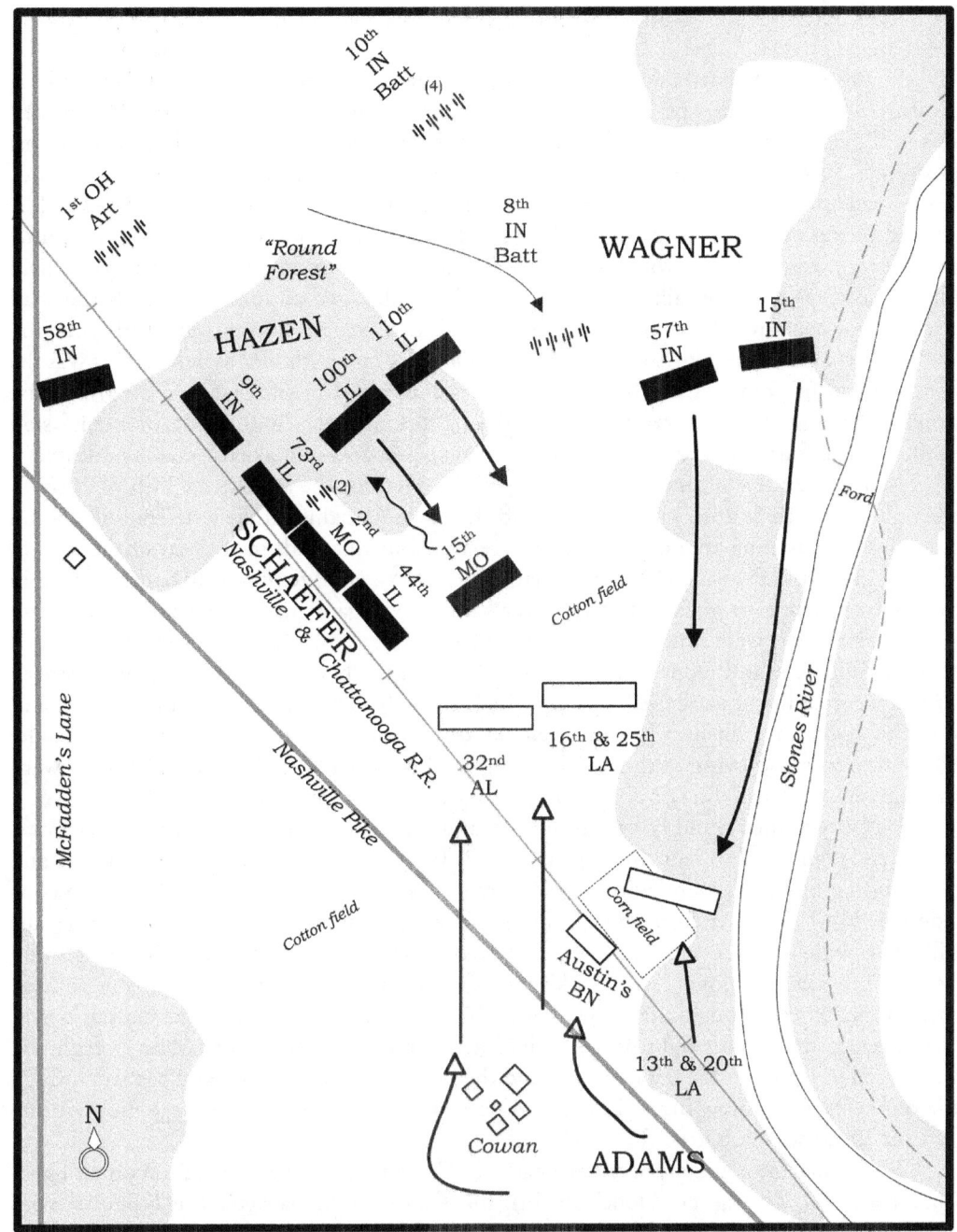

Adams' Attack on the Round Forest, 31 December 1862, 2:00 P.M.–3:00 P.M.

The only battery visible at the start of the attack for Polk to point to was that of Captain Jerome Cox's 10th Indiana Battery. One section of Cox's battery was posted next to the railroad near the 9th Indiana. The other two sections were placed atop a hill 200 yards north of this section, behind the Round Forest. Posted to the front of Cox were Wagner's regiments. Since Polk made Cox's two sections on top of the hill the target of the attack, Adams' advance was not head-on against the Round Forest. Instead, his advance was at more of an angle, heading more northern and to the right of the Round Forest.[19]

Facing a well manned and defended position and supported by artillery, Adams had the pleasure of attacking this position over unfavorable terrain. Earlier in the morning, Hazen was in the field that he was now defending against. He described the ground in front of his position as "utterly untenable ... being commanded by ground in all directions with cover of wood, embankment, and palisading at good musket range in front, right, and left." The ground between the Cowan house and the Round Forest was an old cotton field. To the southeast corner, close to where Stones River and the railroad almost met, sat a fenced in cornfield on the north side of the railroad. It was over this wide open cotton field that Hazen had already repulsed part of the attack by James Chalmers' brigade and was currently mauling the remains of Daniel Donelson's brigade. Both attacks met with bloody repulses. It was the commitment of Donelson to the battle, the last unengaged brigade west of the river, that prompted Bragg to call for reinforcements from Breckinridge at 10:00 A.M. After confusion at the top and four hours later the Louisiana Brigade prepared to make its "march of death."[20]

At about 2:00 P.M., the Louisiana Brigade formed for the attack: the 13th & 20th on the right, the 16th & 25th in the center, and the 32nd Alabama on the left. Trailing behind the brigade, Austin's battalion was put in reserve about 100 yards in the rear of the 16th & 25th Regiment. Adams ordered Lieutenant W.C.D. Vaught, temporarily commanding in Slocomb's absence, to remain near the river when the brigade made the charge. In front of Adams' men, there were almost 800 yards of open ground upon which the dead and wounded men of Chalmers' and Donelson's brigades lay. From the beginning, the brigade advanced "under a severe fire of artillery." The first shell to hit the brigade slammed into a private of the 16th Louisiana, cut him in half, then exploded and killed another soldier by his side. This was a foreshadowing of the hell awaiting the Louisiana Brigade as it marched forward into the most intense thirty minutes of fighting it would face in the entire war.[21]

Halfway to the Round Forest sat the Cowan farm, which "presented such serious obstacles" that Adams had to halt the brigade. To his front was the Cowans' burning home and surrounding buildings along with their fences that sat on terrain that "swelled into a considerable hill." To the right of the Cowen home was the railroad cut that went through the hill upon which the Cowen home sat, and to the right of it was the rocky, rough ground near Stones River. Colonel Stuart Fisk's 16th & 25th was thrown into columns of companies and marched through after Gibson was able to file his men through the Cowan obstacles and reform with his right near the river. Lieutenant Colonel Henry Maury's regiment was forced to march to the left to get around the Cowans'. With Gibson and Maury through the obstacles, Fisk threw his regiment into line, and Adams ordered a charge on their target, the 10th Indiana Battery.[22]

To Adams' immediate front, once past the Cowan house, were Donelson's men fighting for survival. The right of Donelson's brigade, Colonel John Savage's 16th Tennessee with a few companies of the 51st Tennessee, was fighting near the turnpike and railroad area. This small group was pushed into the open field where it had to stop due to the intense fire; it was facing a serious flanking maneuver by units of Colonel Hazen's brigade. The 39th North Carolina was sent to its aid but did not last long under the intense pressure; it collapsed under the fire, dropped its flag on the field and fell back. When the Louisianians passed the Cowan Farm, Savage's small band took the opportunity to pull back and reorganize. Savage and his Tennesseans pulled out the way for the Louisianians to take a shot.[23]

Adams now became the only target between the Cowan house and the Round Forest. He caught the combined fire of Osburn, Cox and Estep, and was now in full range of Schaefer's, Hazen's and Wagner's regiments. Reports put the Louisianians at about 300 yards from the front line when they were hit by musketry. Adams, as were the 32nd Alabama and 16th & 25th Louisiana, was stunned by the sudden intensity of fire. "We were checked by a terrible fire from his artillery," but at Adams' "repeated command" to charge, he was able to push his men forward into the "shower of grape, shell and canister."[24]

The angle of Adams' advance outflanked the left of Schaefer's regiments. The regiments along the railroad were facing in a southwest direction, whereas Adams' advance, coming from the southeast up the railroad and pike, took a more northern approach. Thus, in the process of the advance, Adams' brigade began to expose its left flank to the Round Forest. Reports from Schaefer's brigade are sketchy or non-existent; Schaefer was killed during Adams' advance and thus did not provide any details on his brigade. His successor, Colonel Bernard Laibolt, did say that the 15th Missouri was pulled back, and "being in danger of being outflanked, retreated toward the position of the brigade." The question at hand is where and what exactly was the position of the brigade? To remain in line along the railroad while you watched a large body of soldiers march past your left flank would be grossly negligent at best. It is known that the 73rd Illinois, in line next to the 9th Indiana, did pull back from the railroad to face Adams' attack and lay down in the field behind the tracks. This is supported by the report of Colonel William Blake of the 9th Indiana. As Adams' brigade continued its path past the flank of Blake's and Schaefer's regiments, Blake said this of the attack, "the enemy (re-enforced) again appeared on my left and rear. I again faced by the rear rank and opened obliquely to my left." Blake ordered his regiment to the about face and by doing so, its left oblique fire was actually to his right, facing Adams. For Blake to conduct such a measure through the ranks of several friendly units would not only be highly irresponsible but would also reflect incompetence. Captain John McGrath of the 13th & 20th Louisiana claimed his regiment came upon a full brigade of enemy troops lying in the field to their front. Naturally, with the 73rd Illinois turning to face Adams and the 15th Missouri falling back, then the 2nd Missouri and 44th Illinois would have pulled back also. Again, the lack of no report from the 44th Illinois and having a limited report from the 2nd Missouri blurs their actions at this time. Major Francis Ehrler of the 2nd Missouri said that, at the time that Schaefer was killed, during Adams' advance, his unit was posted behind the railroad embankment. Regardless of the sketchiness of the exact Union alignment, the Louisiana Brigade was absorbing "a very effective and steady fire" that was thinning their ranks by the step.[25]

Lieutenant Colonel Maury attempted to return fire once reformed past the Cowan house. He found that it was "not efficient on account of the excellent cover of the enemy," referring to the railroad embankment. Maury was described by one of his men as "a brave man and a soldier in every sense of the word," and he lived up to that description on New Year's Eve of 1862. Maury ordered the Alabamians to quit firing, grabbed the regiment's flag and threw his men into a charge. "Men were falling at every step," said Maury as he and his men pushed toward Cox's guns. The angle of Adams' brigade from the Cowans' farm exposed the left flank, the 32nd Alabama, to the flank fire from Schaefer's regiments, Cox's guns near the railroad and the 9th Indiana. Captain John Bell said that, when the regiment was within a quarter of a mile from the enemy cannons, two shots immediately hit the 32nd Alabama's line. One struck to the right of Bell and knocked down eight men, killing three outright. Immediately afterwards, another round "dropped" through the company to his left. "Within about one hundred and fifty yards," said Bell, "when they opened upon us with their small arms, and mowed us down like straw our boys stood up firmly and returned the fire with much energy.... Steadily the ranks were closed up and on we went." A green Alabamian said the fire from the Round Forest was "so terrible that its parallel is not Known in the history of warfare." Indeed, for a unit seeing its first major battle, it would appear as though hell on earth had indeed surfaced from the woods beyond. Colonel Laibolt of the 2nd Missouri described the fire of the brigade on Adams as "a galling and well-aimed fire." Adams concurred with the destructiveness of these regiments and batteries on his left a mere 200 yards away: "They [Adams' regiments] continued to advance until the enemy opened with a battery from a cedar thicket on my left." The guns Maury and Adams pinpointed must have been the section of Cox's battery near the railroad. Maury added that, in the midst of this beating, his regiment began to somehow take a "severe fire from the right." It was too much to withstand, and the Alabamians began to falter. Caught in this crossfire Maury was struck in his side by a minie ball.[26]

Fisk's 16th & 25th Regiment fared no better. The 16th & 25th Regiment was hit by the same intensity as the Thirty-Second. "We were met by a storm of missiles from small-arms," reported Major Zacharie. "Steadily the ranks were closed up and on we went. Shells, grape & canister were showered upon us and God's providence alone brought any of us out safe," wrote one Louisianian. A member of the 73rd Illinois described the scene before his regiment as the Louisianians closed in: "We lay down to wait the arrival of the Confederates within easy range of our pieces. They came steadily forward, until their heads began to show above the embankment; then we fired." Closing in on the Round Forest defenses, the 16th & 25th began to receive fire on its right rear. Fisk stopped the regiment and exchanged fire with the Federals with "great coolness." At this moment Fisk went down with a mortal wound, and command of the regiment passed to Major Zacharie (Lieutenant Colonel Robert Lindsay being detached at this time). Confusion swept Zacharie. Where was his support to the right, Gibson's 13th & 20th Louisiana? How was a "regiment of the enemy ... in our rear"? The impromptu regimental commander steadied his men in the firefight across the field and sent word to Adams' of the desperate situation.[27]

Absent from the bloody charge into the cotton field were Gibson's 13th & 20th Louisiana and Austin's battalion. As the brigade was clearing the Cowans' nightmarish terrain Gibson rode forward to reconnoiter the area ahead. He noticed a line of enemy units approaching down the river, at right angles to his flank. Riding forward up the railroad Gibson came upon enemy units, most likely Schaefer's, lining themselves along the railroad embankment "as a breastwork and to conceal them from our troops on the low ground to our left." Gibson was referring to the 32nd Alabama and 16th & 25th Louisiana as the troops on "the low ground on our left." Judging from Gibson's account, he was "ascending" the Cowan ridge when he saw the enemy movements and then referred to the other regiments in the brigade as "on the low ground." The 13th & 20th Louisiana was having a harder time keeping pace due to the terrain.[28]

Major Frank C. Zacharie, 25th Louisiana, postwar (courtesy of Confederate Memorial Hall Museum, New Orleans).

When the Louisianians made their advance

toward the cotton field, Colonel Wagner, posted on the very left of the Union line, saw an opportunity to flank the isolated incoming brigade. He had performed this very measure against the right of Donelson's brigade and he planned on carrying out his flanking maneuver again. Wagner could see Gibson's men about 300 yards out from his position and decided to push back rather than wait: "I preferred making the attack myself rather than waiting an assault from them." With that said, the 15th Indiana, with its left near the river, supported by the 57th Indiana in the cotton field, set forth on a crash course with Gibson's 13th & 20th Louisiana. Pushing forward also were the 100th and 110th Illinois regiments. These were both new, raw regiments tasting battle for the first time. The 100th Illinois moved forward with the 110th in support to show "what they were and make a reputation." They moved into the old cotton field and lay down to meet Adams' attack.[29]

Gibson rode across the railroad to inform General Adams of the prevailing flank attack before their eyes. It was too late for Adams to adjust, considering how far the remainder regiments were pushed into the fray. It was up to Gibson to stop Wagner's attack. The young colonel rode back to his regiment and prepared to meet the advancing enemy. The 13th & 20th Louisiana was ordered to the right flank at the double-quick, and with a loud yell, the Louisianians poured into the cornfield–cotton field area. Lying among the dead and dying from the units before them lay the flag of the 39th North Carolina, which was retrieved and brought to the rear. The unit Gibson saw and charged into was the 57th Indiana. James Jones of the 57th Indiana described the quick advance of Gibson: "The rebels made a charge on us ... they come rushing up double quick yelling like Indians." The 57th Indiana, though, was not alone. Captain John McGrath described what his Louisianians discovered: "We came up a brigade of Yankees laying down in a cornfield [the old cotton field sometimes referred to as a cornfield], who instantly raised up and poured a deadly volley into our surprised ranks we were knocked into confusion." For a few minutes the Louisianians attempted to exchanged shots, slug for slug, against overwhelming odds. "The firing began at once. Here the fire of small-arms was incessant and terrific," said the colonel of the 110th Illinois. Gibson was "determined to contest the field," but Wagner would have none of it. He ordered Lieutenant Colonel Gustavus Wood to have the Fifteenth fix bayonets and charge.[30]

The charge was "executed in a most brilliant style," in the words of Wood, and resulted in crushing the right flank of the 13th & 20th Louisiana. Louisianians threw down their guns in droves to escape certain death. The left wing of Gibson's regiment was able to pull back and use the fence of the cornfield to sustain a longer fight than the rest of the regiment. McGrath and company fell back to the fence where "we made a stand and fought against overwhelming odds for sometime." The combined fire of at least three regiments, possibly five, was too much to handle; "My gallant boys," said McGrath, "began falling pretty fast." James Jones of the Fifty-Seventh continued his description of the fight to his parents in a letter home: "They come up with a few rods of us wee give them Such heavy volleys of musketry and our batteries Just mowed them with grape and canister they turned & there course and went back about as fast as they come." Gibson defended his regiment, and rightly so, by saying, "It is difficult for troops to stand firm against great odds, under a heavy fire from the front and on the flank." "Hundreds of whom threw down their arms," gloated a member of the 57th Indiana. Wagner and his men estimated 170 to 200 men were captured in this charge alone. The charge of the 15th Indiana, though, took a severe toll and attested to the intensity of the fight of the 13th & 20th Consolidated. Of the 440 men who made the charge in the 15th Indiana, 130 ended up killed or wounded. Gibson had to hold on; Maury and Zacharie were engulfed in the field to the left and would have no way to escape; the brigade would be annihilated.[31]

Desperately, Gibson called on the only available reserves, Major Austin's battalion of sharpshooters. Austin joined just as it passed the Cowan house. The battalion had been on picket duty and was called in to join the brigade, but it had already left and crossed the river. Austin had his two companies "hoof" it to catch up with the brigade: "I accelerated my movements as much as possible." Austin caught up to the brigade as it was extracting itself from the maze of Cowan buildings. Adams directed Austin to follow behind the brigade at 100 yards and act as a reserve. This proved to be one the wisest moves on the field as far as the Louisiana Brigade was concerned.[32]

It's at this time that Zacharie's 16th & 25th began taking fire from the right flank and rear. "The enemy's fire from artillery and small arms was terrible," wrote Adams to his wife. "Under these circumstances ... I had reluctantly to give the command to fall back." "We completely broke up their lines and scattered them in great disorder over the field in front," said Captain Jerome Cox of the 10th Indiana Battery. Adams himself was wounded by the heavy fire. While leading his men forward, a shell fragment struck him on the outside of his left arm between his wrist and elbow.[33]

With orders to retreat, it did not take much for Maury to nudge his mauled unit from its exposed position. Maury claimed to have pulled his men back, "as far as I could see, [it] was done in good order." Considering the circumstances, "good order" could be a very flattering term for the chaos at hand. Morgan Smith of the 32nd Alabama escaped the slaughter with a bullet through his coat collar, one through the leg of his boot and another which hit his sword. Having so many close calls and having witnessed slaughter on a scale that his young regiment had never witnessed, Morgan was left with a very humbling experience: "Oh! It was during the heat of that severe contest, that I thought how insignificant we poor worms of the dust are, and upon what a slender, slender thread our lives are hanging. Men hardy and well like myself were cut down quick as thought, and their souls launched into the broad dark ocean of eternity." A hobbling Maury and his torn up Thirty-Second continued their retreat past the Cowan house before reforming. The retreat was not made in very good order and was done under enemy fire the entire way.[34]

Things did not go so smoothly for the 16th & 25th Regiment. Zacharie tried to extract his right four companies first. This part of the regiment was taking serious flank fire from Wagner's men. Having lost his horse to the rain of enemy fire, control of the regiment was difficult for Zacharie. A dangerous situation became precarious when his orders were confused with the company commanders, and before Zacharie knew it, the three left companies of the regiment "marched to the left," toward the 32nd Alabama. Confusion reigned, and in an instant, the regiment fell back "in disorder." The three center companies, however, kept their cool and were able to retreat off the field "in a very orderly and creditable manner," carrying the flag of the regiment with them. Zacharie attempted to rally his men who were trying to save themselves from possibly the worst experience of their life. All the horseless Zacharie could do was join his men on foot as they made for the Cowan house. E.J. Ellis didn't find time to blame his unit's poor situation on Zacharie, but rather described the scene at hand very vividly: "The 13th La got into confusion and finally retreat. The 32nd Ala Regt unable to stand the terrific fire, also gave way but the 16th stood firm and poored volley after volley into the enemy and finally retired but not until Gen Adams had ordered us to retreat."[35]

Meanwhile, Adams' sharpshooters were engaged in tough rearguard action. Austin swung his small command to the right and deployed his men parallel to the railroad behind the fence of the adjacent cornfield. From there, the sure shooting of his men made up for their disparity in numbers. Wood's 57th Indiana, standing in the open in the middle of the cotton field, was ordered to drop to the ground and exchange fire. Standing toe to toe with Austin's sharpshooters cost the Fifty-Seventh dearly. So intense was the fire of Austin's men that the 57th Indiana ended up losing all of its field officers. Lying in the cotton field, the regiment fired over a hundred rounds. A member of that regiment described the firefight: "Sometimes the Smoke was So thik Sometimes wee couldn't Shot to mutch certainity."[36]

Austin was able to allow the brigade to fall back and regroup itself, all with the loss of three wounded men. Assisting Austin, and shielding his retirement from the fence line, was the Confederate artillery. Wagner's men, along with the 100th and 110th Illinois who advanced out to assist Wagner, became easy targets for Confederate guns across Stones River on Wayne's Hill and at their main line 400 yards behind the Cowan house.

"Billy" Vaught, 5th Company Washington Artillery (courtesy of Confederate Memorial Hall Museum, New Orleans).

The 5th Company Washington Artillery soon joined in this fray. The battery was under the command of Lieutenant William Vaught and sat silent by the ford of the river, under orders from Adams to sit tight while the brigade made its attack. An odd order considering Adams needed all the support he could get. When Vaught saw men from the brigade falling back from the fight, he put the Washington Artillery into action. He moved the brigade to the southwest, atop a hill south of the Cowan house, and prepared his gunners for action. Once the Louisiana Brigade was behind the safety of Vaught's guns, the 5th Company began pounding the Round Forest area. Vaught didn't have all six guns of the battery with him. A section was left on Wayne's Hill, and to make up for it, a section was loaned to Vaught from Captain Semple's battery. Vaught's fire was effective in killing any attempt in pursuing after the brigade. The 15th Indiana "was withdrawn to escape the heavy raking fire which the enemy's batteries were pouring on us." Another member of the 15th Indiana described their dangerous situation after the repulse of Adams: "During our withdrawal it required the greatest exertion on the part of the officers and file-closers to preserve anything like order in the line. The continued fire of the rebel artillery ... cut down many of our men." Likewise, the 100th Illinois' brief show of support for Wagner ended with the men being ordered to the ground by its colonel to avoid the "perfect storm of shot, shell and grape" thrown on his men.[37]

The Louisiana Brigade did not leave an impression on the formidable line it attempted to attack. Instead, among the reports of Hascall, Hazen and Wagner, the consensus is that Confederate artillery was the reason for most of their casualties and was their biggest headache of the day. The exception to the rule were the regiments that entered the cotton field and engaged the Louisiana regiments up close, like the 15th and 57th Indiana regiments. Colonel Hazen spent little time in discussing the repulse of the attack at 2:30: "This assault was resisted much more easily than the previous ones, there being now a large force of our artillery bearing upon this point." Proof to Hazen's words are the reports of Osburn, Cox and Estep, in which massive amounts of ammunition were used. Osburn's 1st Ohio Artillery soon retired due to lack of ammunition; Cox ran out of ammo during the attack, and Estep, who showed up at the beginning of the attack, fired 66 rounds from his position on this part of the field. Hazen went on with his report on the attack: "The enemy also extended his lines much farther to the left, causing something of a diversion of our troops in that direction." A diversion ... so ended the longest hour of the war for the Louisiana Brigade.[38]

In what Adams would call a "desperate undertaking," his brigade suffered tremendously heavy casualties. "The scene was bloodier and fiercer than any part of the battle of Shiloh," was how Old Pelican began his description of the attack on 31 December. Of the 1,634 men brought into action that afternoon, 544 men became casualties: 7 officers and 75 men killed, 18 officers and 326 men wounded, and 118 men missing. The 16th & 25th Regiment lost 217 of its 457 men; Company K lost 28 men out of 55 who participated in the battle. Gibson's 13th & 20th suffered 187 of its 452 men, and the 32d Alabama suffered 126 casualties of its 280: 2 officers and 19 men killed, 4 officers and 80 men wounded, and 21 missing. Austin was able to escape the battle with just three men wounded. After the day's fighting subsided, a member of the 40th Indiana rode forward to "see the effect of our fire" in front of the Round Forest. The 40th Indiana had replaced the 58th Indiana in line around the time of the Louisiana Brigade's attack, so the ground he traveled included many wounded from the Louisiana regiments. "A prisoner," wrote the Hoosier, "we took said that the Louisiana regiment he had belonged to was almost exterminated; that one captain came out without a man left, and another had only ten."[39]

From the time he began his advance to the time he was repelled, Adams' attack lasted only one hour. Earlier in the day, Chalmers' attack had lasted only an hour, and Donelson's was able to last two hours. Bragg's failure to prepare a concentrated, organized attack against this position brought the inevitable: repulse after bloody repulse. Morgan Smith of the 32nd Alabama blamed their "mission of death" on Adams: "General Adams ... thinking that his brigade could 'move mountains and stop streams' sent word to Gen. Bragg ... that he would take the stronghold." Regardless if Smith's observation about Adams' boasting is true, such an attack made with small numbers against such a larger force brought the logical result of repulse and heavy casualties. Adams was a man who tended to avoid discussing too many military matters with his wife during his correspondence with her during the war. One of the few exceptions when he took time to divulge into military matters was the terrible repulse at the Round Forest: "How or why Genl. Polk who gave the order or Genl. Bragg who was standing by when it was given expected me to take it I cannot imagine," barked Adams to his wife after the battle. "I cannot help regarding the order as a very imprudent & unwise one — but *do not wish this mentioned or spoken of as it is not proper in me to speak publicky in terms of doubt or disrespect of my superior officers*— I have the consciousness of knowing that I did my entire duty — & that my men behaved very gallantly & bravely in attempting to execute the order." Adams pushed this point of view in his official report: "I was convinced it was more than any brigade could accomplish," and stressed that the only way the Round Forest could have been taken was, in his words, "full work for a division, well directed." It is no wonder the fight on 31 December left a bitter and confused taste in the mouth of the brigade. As the Louisianians pulled back to lick their wounds and reorganize their units, three more brigades were sent in against the Round Forest after Adams, in the same fashion, with the same results.[40]

That night the men slept west of the river in the woods near McFadden's Lane. E.J. Ellis of the 16th Louisiana described the battlefield that night as he looked for men of his company: "I was all over the battlefield. I took particular pains to go over it and notice what I saw. On the night of the 31st (the day of the hard fight) I was walking over the field till after 12 oclock, looking for my own men and assisting the wounded.... The earth was burdened with the Yankee dead. They were croped and piled over each other, nearly all of them lying upon their backs with their faces so ghastly turned up to the moon. Sleeping the last long sleep, Oh! it was horrible to look upon. God grant that I may never witness another such scene." John McGrath of the 13th & 20th Louisiana echoed the same feelings as Ellis. McGrath wrote his wife about two weeks following the Battle of Murfreesboro describing its aftermath. "Oh! Bernie my heart sickens when I think of the scenes of blood.... And in my sleep I see nightly the gastly upturned faces of the dead and hear the groaning of the mangled and dying, the hissing of the shot and shell, the shouts and curses of the victorious and the shrill whistles of the musket ball, as it wings its flight of death."[41]

Due to his wound, Adams was unable to take the field New Year's Day and turned command of the brigade over to Gibson. The first day of January was spent sitting in place west of the river with no major fighting taking place between the armies. Both armies used the day to reorganize and collect themselves. On the morning of 2 January Bragg received information that a sizeable body of enemy troops had forded Stones River opposite Breckinridge and taken a position on a large hill that overlooked McFadden's Ford. Bragg believed that this position would allow Federal artillery to enfilade Polk's position on the west side and decided to take the hill. Around noon, Bragg ordered Breckinridge to assault the Federals on the east side of the river with four of his brigades.[42]

Breckinridge argued with Bragg, asserting the impossibility of a successful attack against that position. Bragg refused to listen to Breckinridge and reiterated his command to attack. With the issue settled, Breckinridge committed himself, against his better judgment, to carry out the attack. The attack was to begin at 4:00 P.M., just one hour before sundown. In the intervening four hours, Breckinridge had to recall two of his brigades, Gibson's and Brigadier General William Preston's, from the west side to the east side of the river. Preston and Gibson were posted next to McFadden Lane, below the Cowan house, near a large cedar brake. It would take time for these two brigades to reach their appointed positions. Through a cold sleet, Gibson rushed his brigade across the waist-deep freezing river.[43]

Breckinridge formed his division into two lines of two brigades each for the attack. Brigadier General Roger Hanson's and Brigadier General Gideon Pillow's brigades formed the front wave, with Hanson on the left and Pillow on the right. Forming the second wave, 150 yards behind the first, were Gibson and Preston, with Gibson behind Hanson and Preston behind Pillow. Breckinridge ordered the batteries for each brigade to follow closely behind the attack and deploy once the hill was taken. Gibson formed Zacharie's 16th & 25th on his left and the 13th & 20th, now under the command of Major Charles Guillet, on his right. He placed the 32nd Alabama and Austin's battalion in reserve, with the 32nd Alabama behind the 16th & 25th and Austin behind the 13th & 20th. Vaught formed his guns to the right rear of Gibson's brigade, near Preston. "These dispositions had hardly been effected when the general advance began." With the sound of a single cannon, the division began the advance at 4:00 P.M.[44]

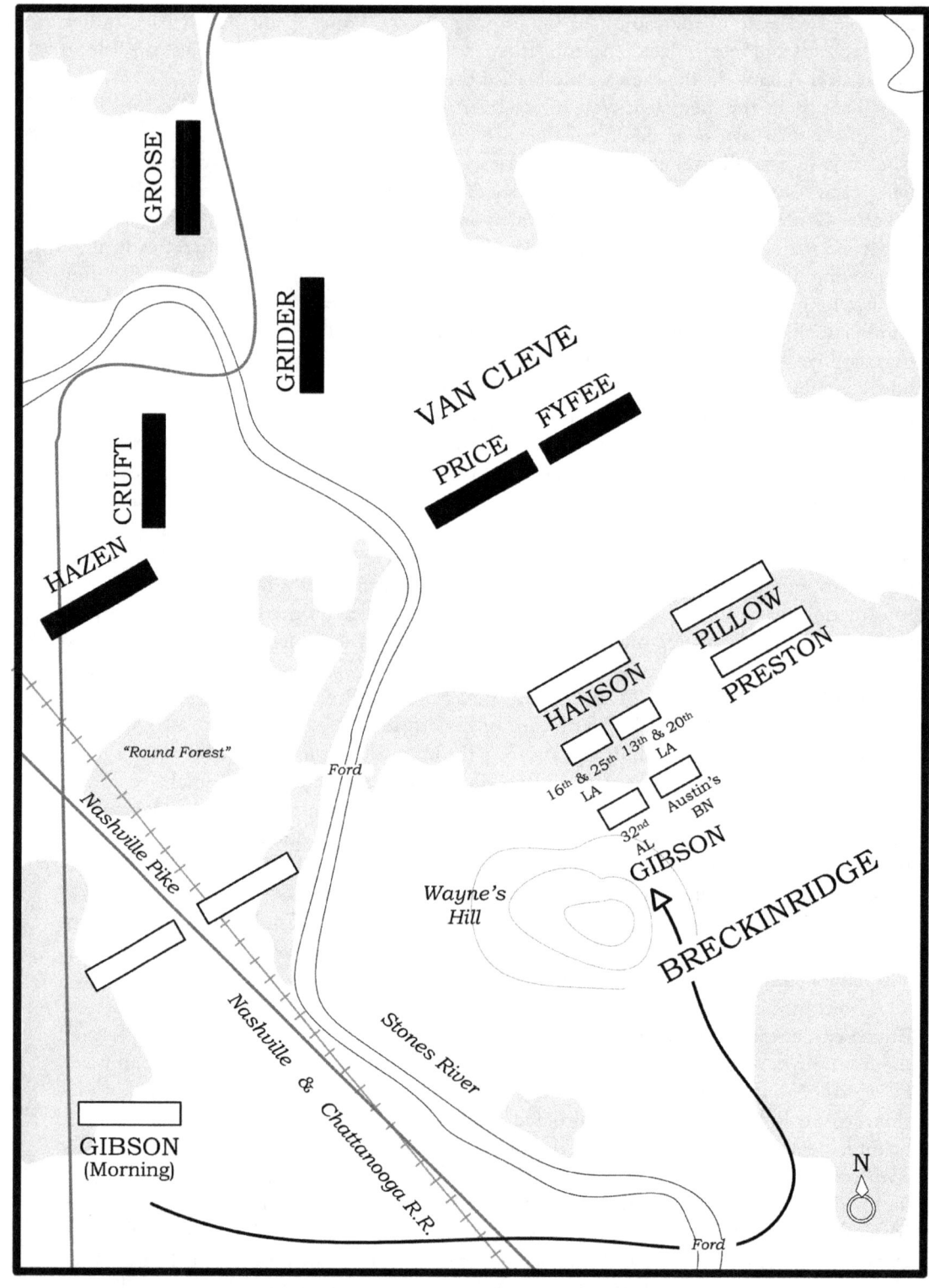

Breckinridge's Attack, 2 January 1863, 4:00 P.M.–5:00 P.M.

One thousand yards away, across the open field, lay the division of Brigadier General Horatio Van Cleve along a depression running perpendicular to Stones River. Colonel Samuel Price's brigade was posted next to the river, and to his left was Colonel James Fyffe's brigade. Directly behind Price was Colonel Benjamin Grider's brigade, with his right also resting against the river. Deployed farther back to the left, along McFadden's Lane, was Colonel William Grose's brigade of Palmer's division. Price's and Fyffe's regiments were posted behind a fence, and they worked feverishly to strengthen their line before an attack came. Supporting Van Cleve to the east of the river was only one battery of artillery. On the west side, though, sat several batteries deployed along McFadden's Lane.[45]

Once contact was made with Van Cleve's division, Gibson ordered his men to lie down to protect themselves from artillery fire. Van Cleve's men did not last long against the Confederates. Price's regiments quickly fell before Hanson, so quickly that Gibson thought it a mere skirmish line that Hanson had disposed of. Within moments, Fyffe's men broke before Pillow's Tennesseans. With Hanson mounting the hill before them, Gibson rode forward to confer with the Kentuckian. Just as Gibson rode up to Hanson, a shell fragment struck Hanson in the leg, dropping him to the ground. Unable to discuss the situation with the wounded Kentuckian, Gibson "determined not to engage" his brigade until the Kentuckians to his front showed signs of wavering. Gibson's wait did not take long: "General Hanson had hardly fallen, however, when his line began to show symptoms of yielding." Gibson immediately ordered his two regiments forward.[46]

Due to the angle of the river, Gibson ordered Major Guillet and the 13th & 20th "to oblique to the right" to avoid the river. With his horse disabled from enemy fire, Gibson dispatched Captain A.A. Lipscomb of the 13th & 20th Regiment to relay the same order to Zacharie. Gibson turned and personally led the 13th & 20th into the fight, proudly saying it "went into action in perfect order." Instead of staying with the attack on the east side of the river, the 16th & 25th was advancing "under the bank" of the river. This is due to the angle of the advance and the geography of Stones River. Zacharie and his regiment ended up splashing across the river with elements of the 2nd and 6th Kentucky regiments to its front. As the advance deepened, Gibson had only two regiments with him. Now as he advanced with one, the other was splashing across the river out of his control. To Zacharie's immediate front was the 6th Kentucky. The commander of that unit, Colonel Joseph Lewis, described the situation he and Zacharie faced: "When our line reached the fence, the alternative for me was either to be left entirely in rear of our lines and out of the fight, or to move by the right flank along on the edge of and under the bluff down the river. The second I adopted unhesitatingly."[47]

Guillet's regiment joined parts of Hanson's brigade to his front as they pushed up the river, joining parts of the 2nd Kentucky, 4th Kentucky and 41st Alabama regiments. The second line of enemy troops that they ran into was Colonel Benjamin Grider's brigade. Grider's regiments were deployed from right to left as follows: 19th Ohio, 9th Kentucky and 11th Kentucky regiments. It was Grider's brigade that was beginning to check and waver the Kentuckians. When Price's brigade broke and ran to the rear, Grider's regiments were ordered forward. Major Charles Manderson described the advance of his regiment along the river toward the Kentuckians: "We advanced up a gradual slope for about 200 yards, the lines in front of us pouring through our ranks in confusion; but the men preserved an excellent front, and rushed upon the enemy." Lieutenant Colonel George Cram echoed Manderson's description but went on to say that, by the "fourth or fifth round," the Kentuckians to his front began to break. It is into this firefight that Gibson went with the 13th & 20th Louisiana to bolster the Kentuckians. The matter was not decided by the intervention of Gibson, but rather by the units forced into the river bank by the angle of the advance. Grider's right regiment, the 19th Ohio, was flanked and was taking heavy fire from the river. This forced Grider and his men to fall back, and once the bank of the river was reached, confusion set in and the retreat became a jumbled mess as they streamed up the opposite bank.[48]

Pushing forward, Gibson reached a ravine, behind which was a hill that sat between the ravine and Stones River. From here the 13th & 20th Louisiana and "men broken from their commands" filled the ravine. The men Gibson was referring to were the scattered regiments of Hanson. After exchanging a few volleys, there suddenly came a "momentary lull" in the fighting. Across the river on a hill overlooking McFadden's Ford, the Federals were busy in rushing every available man and battery to the scene to stop the breakthrough. The lull Gibson described was the small opening of time in which Van Cleve's units were being allowed to clear the way for the parts of eleven different batteries, or 44 guns, to open fire on the Confederate line. Gibson said that when they approached the ravine, near the hill by the river, "the batteries of the enemy, posted on the opposite side, poured into our ranks without intermission. As soon as he was driven from the high ground on this side, his batteries played upon it. His batteries and infantry concentrated on every spot from which he was driven."[49]

The enemy counterattack was coming. Breckinridge's attack stalled out once it cleared Van Cleve out of the way and was then forced to absorb the shock of 44 guns blasting into its position. To the far right, the attack was unable to dislodge Grose's brigade. The attack had reached its peak. All of the top generals of Rosecrans' army were rushing about gathering units and beginning to push them towards McFadden's Lane. Posted behind the massive improvised battery atop McFadden's Lane were the brigades of Brigadier General Charles Cruft, Colonel Timothy Stanley, and Colonel John Miller. Behind these three brigades were the reforming regiments of Price and Grider's brigades of Van Cleve's battered division. Palmer was very active in organizing the counterattack and immediately pushed Stanley's and Miller's brigades splashing into Stones River to counterattack. Hazen's brigade, which was posted farther down the line to the right of Cruft, was ordered up toward Stones River also. Regiments were being grabbed from several spots and being thrown forward.

The first units to break were Pillow and Preston to Gibson's right. At the same time regiments from across the river began advancing. To remain in position meant destruction but retreating through the open field to the rear was just as destructive. The men made it through the intense fire, leaving most of their wounded in the wooded area along the ravine by the river. "I saw at once that we would be enveloped on the right and left," reported Gibson. "I ordered my command to fall back." With their position unbearable, soldiers began falling back in groups and finally in whole units. "The command fell back in some disorder, but without the slightest appearance of panic," said Breckinridge. "Scarcely any one could enter the open field to our right and rear without being shot down either by the infantry or by the batteries of the enemy," reported Gibson. Indeed, the retreat back to their lines was made under heavy Federal pressure, with the wounded being left on the field; one of them was Major Guillet, who led the 13th & 20th Regiment into action. The retreating Louisianians retraced their steps and regrouped themselves around the 32nd Alabama and Austin's battalion, which had remained east of the river, in their original positions, as a reserve. While retreating, Gibson went to grab the 16th & 25th Louisiana but discovered they had crossed the river. The men, isolated on the other side of the river, were not oblivious to the conditions; they were facing a counterattack of their own.[50]

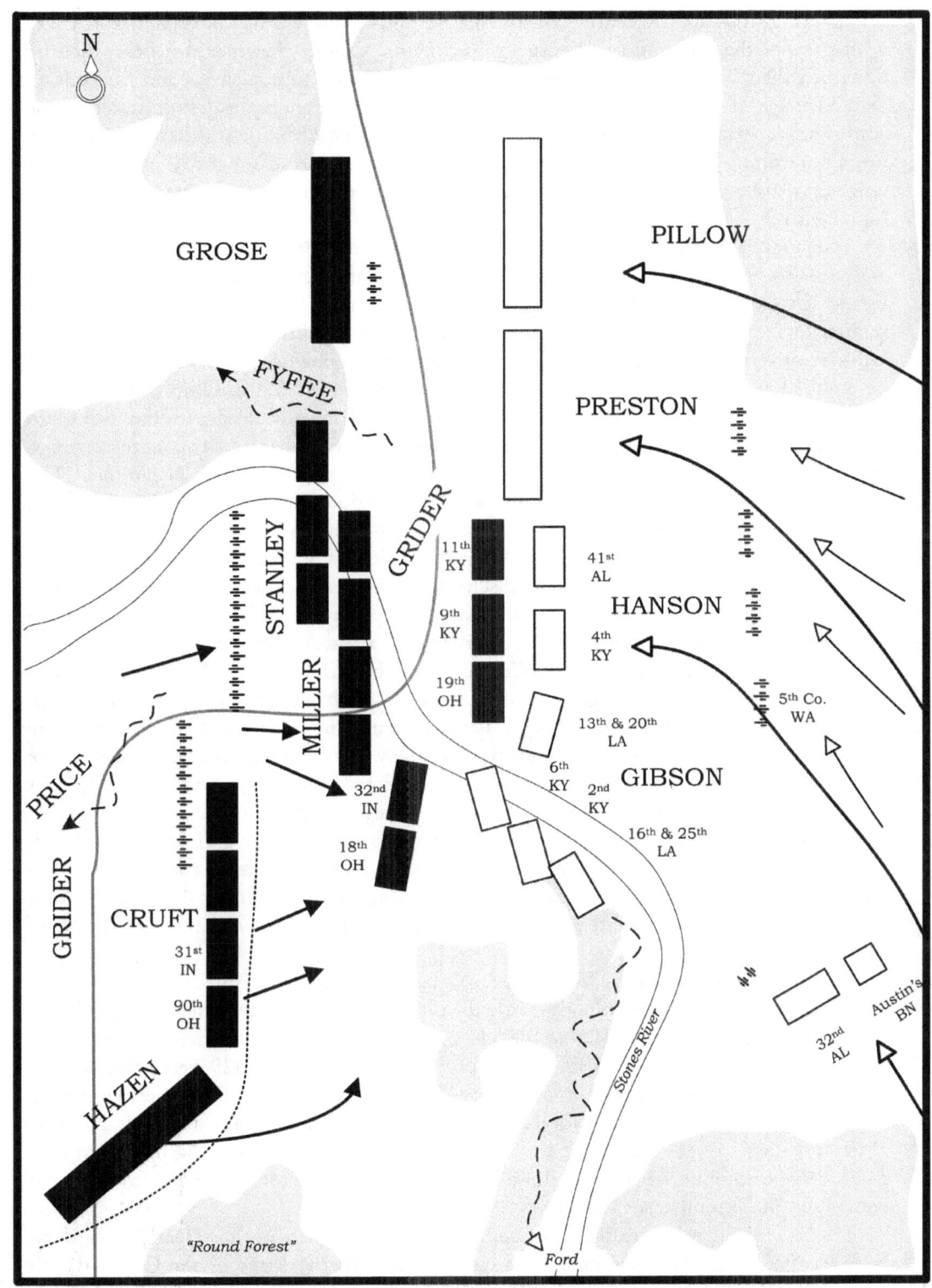

Gibson's Attack on McFadden's Ford, 4:00 P.M.–5:00 P.M.

During this time, Zacharie and his 16th & 25th Regiment had crossed Stones River with parts of the 2nd and 6th Kentucky Regiments. Colonel Lewis said it best when he described their situation: "On account of the want of space to maneuver, and the considerable change of direction that had to be made to face the enemy, as before stated, some confusion occurred after reaching the woods, and no line of battle was kept." The three units were pretty intermingled in the woods along the river and sought to use the picket fence they discovered as a means of cover to fire on the retreating, and soon to be advancing, enemy.[51]

General Palmer was instrumental in organizing a counterattack against the Confederates crossing the river. The Kentuckians and Louisianians were too close for comfort, and Palmer "determined at once to dislodge them." The first regiments he grabbed for the counterattack were the 18th Ohio from Stanley's brigade and the 32nd Indiana of Colonel W.H. Gibson's advancing brigade from the rear. These two regiments were sent forward before he grabbed two of Cruft's regiments, the 31st Indiana and the 90th Ohio. All regiments were ordered to fix bayonets and advance. The 32nd Indiana advanced with the 18th Ohio in support to its right. As the 32nd Indiana pushed the river bank, it encountered tough resistance with the Kentuckians and Louisianians "contesting every inch of ground." The 18th Ohio fired one volley and then fell back in confusion. Unaffected, the 32nd Indiana pushed forward with the help of the 31st Indiana and 90th Ohio approaching on its right. In the face of this pressure Zacharie and his men headed up Stones River to escape destruction. "The rebels had hardly time to discharge their pieces. They fled with the utmost speed." They found their way to the ford overlooking Wayne's Hill. Zacharie's unit made its way back to the brigade reserve, the 32nd Alabama and Austin's battalion.[52]

During the attack, Vaught had followed closely behind Gibson. When Van Cleve was ejected from his position, Vaught advanced his guns forward and placed them on the hill opposite McFadden's Ford. Immediately, Vaught opened fire on enemy batteries across the river, but he quickly ran out of ammunition. While waiting for ammunition to arrive, the infantry gave way and fell back. With pursuing Federals a mere fifty yards away, Vaught limbered up his guns and withdrew. When Vaught reached the belt of woods from which the attack began, he unlimbered his guns and went into battery. With ammunition on hand, Vaught helped stop the pursuing enemy. A combination of the intense fire from Confederate batteries and the confusion from night setting in saved the Army of Tennessee from a potentially devastating counterattack following one of the most poorly planned attacks of the war.[53]

Thus ended the Battle of Murfreesboro, a battle of lost opportunities for the Army of Tennessee, and an extremely bloody battle for the Louisiana Brigade. The attack on 2 January added another 159 casualties to the 544 men lost on 31 December, which brought the brigade's total casualties to 703. Of the 159 casualties on the second, 129 were from the 13th & 20th Regiment alone. Gibson reported that 14 of the regiment's 28 officers were wounded. Zacharie's regiment, although involved in the attack, was able to escape with only 25 casualties. The losses of the 32nd Alabama, Austin's battalion and Vaught's battery amounted to only five men. The brigade sustained a 43 percent loss in a total of about two hours of combat on 31 December and 2 January.[54]

Because the army retreated, that meant many wounded, and those tending to them, were left behind in Murfreesboro and were captured. In the Army of the Cumberland's provost marshal's report, he recorded that 459 men were captured from the units belonging to Adams' brigade. The 13th & 20th Louisiana was decimated at the Battle of Murfreesboro. Of an aggregate number of men placed at 452 men the regiment's total losses came to 351. The regiment listed 102 men missing in battle, but the provost marshal for Rosecrans lists 248 captured. That reflects a large number of men left behind that were probably wounded. Likewise, the 16th & 25th recorded 21 men captured or missing in battle, but a total of 121 were captured. The 32nd Alabama recorded 21 men on 31 December as captured or missing, but a total of 81 were captured. This disparity means that, of the 264 recorded by Adams as having been captured, those numbers actually rose by an additional 195, with the majority being wounded men left behind during the retreat.[55]

On the morning of 3 January, Bragg, with the concurrence of many of his generals, decided that the army must retreat. He directed that the army converge on the town of Tullahoma, forty miles south of Murfreesboro. At 10:00 P.M., Breckinridge's division pulled out of line and retreated south along the Manchester Pike. The brigade marched ten miles toward Manchester before halting for the day. The next day another ten miles were covered, eight miles the next and another eight miles before the small town of Allisonia was reached at the Nashville & Chattanooga Railroad. Continuing the last leg of the retreat, Gibson marched into Tullahoma on 8 January finishing a 57 mile hike in the winter. Despite the heavy casualties at Murfreesboro, the brigade began to rapidly recover its losses. When the brigade reached Tullahoma, its strength was up to 1,320 men, rank and file, present for duty. Just three days later, the number increased to 1,485. This rise in strength was probably due to stragglers or skulkers returning to their units, and the return of sick, furloughed or slightly-wounded men. Despite this increase in strength, the brigade had only 1,133 small arms available; the rest undoubtedly had been left on the battlefield around Murfreesboro.[56]

Symbolic of the Louisiana Brigade's fight at Murfreesboro, and also adding insult to injury, was the case of Roger Tammure of the 13th Louisiana. In the face of defeat, commanders often found the heroic deeds as a means to glorify something positive. In all battles, Gibson found the good to praise. In his report on Murfreesboro he made special mention of Roger Tammure, the color bearer for the regiment at Murfreesboro. Gibson noted him for his bravery and recommended his immediate promotion to lieutenant. Once the army was in Tullahoma, Tammure was given a three day leave of absence to a small town up the road, Winchester. As had been the case with the 13th Louisiana so often before, Tammure's three day leave was abruptly ended after one day because of his getting into trouble. Tammure went through Winchester "committing depredations in the neighborhood such as stealing horses." A squad of cavalry was sent out to investigate, upon which Tammure took flight. He was finally overtaken, in the words of Gibson, "within a few miles of Nashville," and put under arrest. He next attempted several escapes from the guard house and faced a court-martial, where he was sentenced to death for his crimes. The execution was never carried out because it looks as though Tammure finally made his escape and deserted. It is undocumented as to whether liquor was involved in Tammure's activities but judging from the history of the 13th Louisiana, it would be a reasonable guess that it was.[57]

CHAPTER 6

Retreat, Politics and to Mississippi: January–August 1863

> *"In obedience to your wishes, I have this day had a conference with the brigade commanders of my division, Generals Pillow and Preston and Colonels Trabue and Gibson ... it is their opinion that you do not possess the confidence of the army to an extent which will enable you to be useful as its commander."*
>
> — John C. Breckinridge to Braxton Bragg, Gibson's division commander, 12 January 1863

The defeat at Murfreesboro was the spark that lit a powder keg in the Army of Tennessee. In a series of events that took place over the next few months, cleavages already present among officers of the army were torn into gaping holes. Involved in this battle between officers was one of Braxton Bragg's enemies, Randall Gibson. Just days after the retreat to Tullahoma was completed, Bragg made an unprecedented move. Under severe criticism from Southern newspapers for the defeat at Murfreesboro, Bragg called his staff together on 10 January to read to them an article written in the *Chattanooga Rebel*. The article that he proceeded to read aloud claimed that he had retreated from Murfreesboro against the suggestions of his generals and that Bragg was to be replaced as commander of the army. With rumors floating around that Kirby Smith was to replace Bragg, the old, wiry general consulted with his staff on whether or not he had lost the confidence of the army and said that, if it were true, he would resign his position. When his staff agreed that he had lost the confidence of the army and suggested he resign, Bragg acted against their suggestion and raised the issue to a new level. He solicited the opinion of the top generals of his army.[1]

On 11 January, Bragg sent a letter to both Hardee and Polk and to the army's five division commanders: Breckinridge, Cleburne, Major General Benjamin Cheatham, Withers, and Major General John McCown. The purpose of Bragg's letter, he later claimed, was for each general "to commit to writing what had transpired between us in regard to the retreat from Murfreesborough." Bragg acknowledged the fact that his letter was brought about by criticism from within and without the army. Included in the letter was a statement that left the distraught general open to criticism: "I shall retire without a regret if I find I have lost the good opinion of my generals, upon whom I have ever relied upon as a foundation of rock." If set off balance by his staff's answer the day before, Bragg was knocked off of his feet when he received the replies to his circular letter.[2]

While Polk delayed giving his answer, probably hoping to avoid trouble, his two division commanders, Withers and Cheatham, sent a quick reply informing Bragg that not only did they support a retreat but, they were the two who originally suggested it. Polk, on 30 January, simply endorsed the letter written by Withers and Cheatham. It is most likely that due to the replies that Bragg received from Hardee's corps, Polk delayed his answer to keep himself clear of any controversy.[3]

Instead of reading the note as a request for them to "commit to writing" their recommendations regarding the retreat from Murfreesboro, several of the generals interpreted the letter as including an inquiry regarding the army's confidence in Bragg as commander. The reply from Hardee and his two division commanders was not what Bragg expected. Hardee wrote that he did not urge but did support a retreat; Cleburne avoided the retreat issue by stating that he simply followed orders, and Breckinridge supported Hardee's statement that he did not suggest but did support a retreat. But, all three generals surprised Bragg by saying that he had lost the confidence of the army and should step down as commander.[4]

Cleburne and Breckinridge took the issue a step further by consulting their brigade commanders on whether Bragg retained the confidence of the army. In his reply to Bragg, Breckinridge notified him, "In obedience to your wishes, I have this day had a conference with the brigade commanders of my division, Generals Pillow and Preston and Colonels Trabue and Gibson." Breckinridge said that although he and his commanders believed that a retreat was necessary, "it is their opinion that you do not possess the confidence of the army to an extent which will enable you to be useful as its commander. In this opinion I feel bound to state that I concur." Whether intentional or not, Gibson's involvement in Breckinridge's reply to the circular letter intensified Bragg's distaste toward Gibson.[5]

In less than two weeks, President Davis became aware of the ill feeling toward Bragg from the public and from within the army. To investigate the situation, Davis dispatched General Joseph E. Johnston, commander of the Department of the West, to the Army of Tennessee. "Why General Bragg should have selected that tribunal," wrote Davis to Johnston, "and have invited its judgment upon him, is to me unexplained." Johnston found himself in a delicate position, because if he found Bragg unfit for command of the army, for whatever reason, he was to personally take command of the Army of Tennessee. Instead of giving an objective, unbiased evaluation, Johnston allowed his personal feelings to influence his reports to Davis. Johnston believed that it would be dishonorable to take command of the army on the basis of an unfavorable report by him. Johnston reported that the condition of the army was better than ever before and that all seemed fine.[6]

"That circular contained but one point of inquiry, and it certainly was intended to contain but one," wrote Bragg angrily. He believed that this entire episode was "fomented by a few disappointed generals, who supposed they could cover their own tracks and rise on my downfall." He continued to write, "Finding themselves responsible for serious failings, they and their friends are moving all power to saddle me with the responsibility before official reports can put the matter right." Apparently Bragg felt as though Johnston's quick visit, lenient reports, and the fact that Davis retained him in command had vindicated him. This gave Bragg confidence to strike out against those who had spoken out against him. In late February, Bragg made his move against what he thought was a small group of a "few disappointed generals."[7]

Bragg moved against Gibson on 1 March. On that day, Bragg ordered Gibson to turn command of his regiment over to an officer of lower rank who had returned from conscription and recruitment duty in Louisiana. Gibson was to proceed to Louisiana and replace that officer on recruitment and conscription duty. The young colonel became livid and immediately wrote a letter of protest to the secretary of war, James Seddon. "I have this day received an order from Head Quarters of this Army which, without giving any grounds for my removal, relieved me of my command," Gibson angrily wrote to Seddon. Gibson argued further that he was replaced by an officer of lower rank who had been recalled from his duty. Trying to keep his language in a respectful tone, he wrote that "I proceed to obey the orders of the Commanding General but earnestly protest against it as arbitrary and unjust — as depriving me of my [illegible] as a soldier and degrading me in the eyes of my comrades in arms." Gibson was supported in his protest by Hardee, who wrote the Louisianian, "I know nothing of the cause of your being relieved. I suppose we may both make a reasonable conjecture. You owe it to yourself to make a protest in respectful language to the president."[8]

Gibson also pursued the matter through his good friend, William Preston Johnston, the son of Albert Sidney Johnston, and an aide to President Davis. "I suppose he thinks it his duty to drive me from the Army," Gibson wrote to Johnston. Gibson took a risk in protesting Bragg's order because since January, Adams had been leading a petition to have Gibson promoted to brigadier general. Even as early as October, in his official report of the Battle of Perryville, Adams had suggested Gibson's promotion. On 22 January 1863, while recovering from his wound received at the Battle of Murfreesboro, Adams sought the support of several other officers for Gibson's promotion. In a letter to Secretary of War Seddon, he included supporting testimony for Gibson by Patton Anderson, Gibson's former division commander; William Preston, a fellow brigade commander in Breckinridge's division; his corps commander, Hardee; and Gibson's former corps commander and prewar friend, Leonidas Polk. Adams' letter was followed the next month by a letter signed by several Louisiana legislators. Obviously Adams' attempt to promote Gibson failed when that officer was removed from his regiment in March and placed on conscript and recruitment duty. There is no doubt that it was a move by Bragg to keep Gibson from further promotion in his army and exile an insubordinate nuisance.[9]

It is possible that Adams was pushing for Gibson's promotion not only because he recognized Gibson as a capable officer but also because he sought duty closer to his wife and family in Mississippi. While Johnston was at Tullahoma, Adams apparently made a special request to him for a transfer to Mississippi. On 12 February 1863, Johnston notified Lieutenant General John C. Pemberton, commander of the Department of Mississippi and East Louisiana, that "Brig. Gen. Dan. W. Adams applies to be transferred to you. Have you an adequate place for him? also wounded." In the same letter, Johnston informed Pemberton that Brigadier General James Chalmers had been assigned to his department. On the next day, although Johnston issued orders reassigning Chalmers back to the Army of Tennessee, he made no mention of Adams. There was also no reply from Pemberton to Johnston about Adams.[10]

The story of Adams' return to duty after his recuperation and of who commanded the 13th & 20th Regiment after Gibson's departure remains sketchy. As of late January, Adams was still in Georgia recuperating from his wound. Gibson was listed as still commanding the brigade on 5 February. It is not known if Adams returned to duty in February prior to Gibson's removal on 1 March. The earliest date that confirms Adams' return to active duty is 22 April, when he was mentioned as temporarily commanding Breckinridge's division, while that officer was away. While Gibson was temporarily in command of Adams' brigade, Major Francis L. Campbell of the 13th Louisiana was listed as in command of the consolidated regiment during January. In March, though, Lieutenant Colonel Leon von Zinken, of the 20th Louisiana, was listed as commanding the 13th & 20th. When Gibson assumed command of the brigade at Murfreesboro von Zinken, being second-in-command, would have assumed command of the regiment. Instead, Major Guillet took command which documents that in late 1862 and early 1863 von Zinken was on detached duty. It appears that Von Zinken was the officer recalled from recruitment duty in Louisiana to replace Gibson in command of the regiment.[11]

The command structure of consolidated regiments within the Army of Tennessee seemed to create such a problem that Bragg was forced to address the issue in March. On 16 March, Bragg released General Orders, No. 56, which very likely came about due to the uproar caused by Gibson's removal. "Misapprehensions seem to exist in many corps of this army in regard to the recent orders of union on duty, or consolidation as it is erroneously called," the order began. Bragg tried to explain that the "union" of regiments for "temporary convenience and service in the field" created an excess of field officers. To bring these regiments back to a respectable strength that would require the use of all the regiment's field officers, the excess officers were "detached on recruiting, conscript, or other special duty." It was, according to Bragg, his intention, that when "the rank and file shall justify it," the consolidations would be broken apart and detached officers returned to field command. On 18 April, Bragg issued such an order, calling for officers of consolidated regiments with a strength of 400 men present for duty to return to their regiments and for the combined regiments to return to their original organizations.[12]

Neither the 13th & 20th nor the 16th & 25th Regiments were affected by Bragg's order of 18 April. Both units remained consolidated and Gibson was not recalled to his regiment. This is further evidence that Bragg worked to hinder Gibson. As of 21 May, Adams' brigade had 2,130 men

Lieutenant Colonel Leon von Zinken, 20th Louisiana (courtesy of Confederate Memorial Hall Museum, New Orleans).

present for duty. This was a jump from 1,410 present for duty on 5 February. Considering the fact that the two consolidated regiments constituted the majority of the brigade, it is reasonable to state that the 13th & 20th did reach a number of 400 men present for duty at some point. Even as late as 3 August, when the brigade's total present for duty dropped to 1,369 men, the 13th & 20th still listed 353 men present for duty. Despite the recall of officers on 18 April, Gibson did not return to command. Leon von Zinken was listed as commanding the regiment as late as 21 May. On 6 June Colonel Reichard, of the 20th Louisiana, was listed as commanding the regiment. Reichard remained in that position until 7 July, when he resigned his commission. Leon von Zinken then resumed command of the regiment again. Following von Zinken, Captain E.M. Dubroca, of the 13th Louisiana, was in command of the regiment by late July.[13]

Despite the civil war between the generals of the army, the Louisiana Brigade spent a peaceful time in Middle Tennessee after Murfreesboro. From middle January to late May, the brigade lay idle in Middle Tennessee, enjoying its longest period of inactivity during the entire war. Once reaching Tullahoma, the brigade remained in the vicinity of the town from middle January to late April. Slowly, the brigade regained its strength and spent most of its time fighting the routines of camp life: drilling and boredom. To pass the time, and to encourage more interest in drill, there were competitions between individual units. Gibson's regiment, the 13th & 20th Louisiana, earned a stellar reputation: "It is said to be the best drilled regt in the service." During this time, William Preston Johnston was sent out west by Davis, again, to inspect Bragg's army. In his inspection Johnston was invited to a drill review that involved Gibson's 13th & 20th Louisiana:

> On Monday, March 23, I reviewed Lieutenant General Hardee's corps at Tullahoma. I afterward, on the same day, saw Brig. Gen. B.R. Johnson drill his brigade, and witnessed a match or trial battalion drill between the Seventeenth Tennessee Regiment (Colonel Marks) and the Thirteenth Louisiana Regiment (Col. R.L. Gibson) and Twentieth Louisiana Regiment (Colonel Reichard), consolidated, and commanded by Lieutenant-Colonel Von Zinken. The Tennessee regiment was remarkable for fine stature, manly bearing, and steadiness of movement, but the rapidity and accuracy with which the Louisianians executed every maneuver at the double-quick was unequaled.[14]

Whether biased to his cousin and best friend or not, Johnston, showered the 13th & 20th Louisiana with praise over its maneuverability. This, of course, is a reflection of its commanding officer. No doubt this was a subtle hint to Davis that Gibson was an officer of caliber and meant to enforce the campaign to see Gibson promoted.

On 21 April the brigade received orders to change camp. Bragg ordered Hardee to move his corps from Tullahoma to Wartrace in anticipation of taking part in a demonstration against Murfreesboro. The brigade started leaving Tullahoma on the twenty-third, marched across the Duck River and encamped around Wartrace on the twenty-fifth. For the next month, the brigade remained in the Wartrace area, switching camps to Fairfield and then to Bellbuckle. "We have at last left Tullahoma. I am now camped here about 20 miles in the prettiest country," admired a Louisianian. "We found the greatest abundance of cold spring water all along the road the water here is excellent & plenty of shade trees."[15]

As the Louisianians were preparing to leave camp at Tullahoma to move to Wartrace, another regiment was attached to the brigade, the 19th Louisiana. When Bragg had moved the army from Tupelo to Chattanooga the previous summer, the 19th Louisiana had been detached from the brigade to join the garrison around Mobile. Since that time, the regiment had enjoyed months of peaceful duty around Pollard, Alabama. One soldier could only brag of how much good food he was eating and how much weight he was gaining: "This morning I weigh 190 pounds. Think I will get to 200 yet." On 14 April, the 19th Louisiana left Mobile for Tullahoma. After a week-long trip, the regiment reached Tullahoma on 21 April. The regiment finally reached the brigade's camps at Wartrace on the twenty-fifth, which Private Robert F. McAdams of the Nineteenth described as "a nice camping place." When the Nineteenth reached the brigade's camp, they were met with "glad shouting and cheers" from the remainder of their old brigade. A soldier of the 19th Louisiana concurred with his fellow Louisianians about Middle Tennessee: "We are in a cultivated and beautiful region, pleasing to the eye," but in relation to the local population, he said that he and his regiment much preferred the hospitality of Mobile.[16]

Regardless of the improvement in the scenery of their surroundings at Wartrace the brigade was "subjected d[illegible word] and constantly to drills," complained Rufus Cater of the 19th Louisiana. "Squad, company, skirmish, battalion & brigade, together with review inspections [illegible word] too tedious to enumerate." Colonel Augustus Reichard of the 20th Louisiana recounted a rare recorded event of a sham battle between Breckinridge's and Cleburne's divisions. Cavalry was brought up to scout out each opposing army and full battalions were deployed to act as skirmishers. Behind this wall of skirmishers came full brigades marching "in echelon of Battalions." The two armies pushed each other back and forth with countermaneuvering but the day proved to be Breckinridge's. "An opening is made in the centre by causing centre battalions to form in columns closed in mass on the right and left divisions. Breckinridge opens fire with his artillery and charges Cleburne's centre, which gives way in great disorder." These types of events increased the focus and interest in drilling. As the proficiency in drilling increased this naturally led to more competitions between other units.[17]

At one showdown between the 20th Louisiana and 17th Tennessee Generals Hardee and Breckinridge engaged in a friendly wager: "Hardee stakes his money on the 20th La. Maj Gen Breckinridge his on 17th Tenn. Hardee won." The Twentieth's success soon led to a challenge from the 4th Kentucky, and this showdown led to the biggest drill match of the season. In late May, Adams put his regiments against Brigadier General Benjamin Helm's Kentuckians. Officers and guests crowded around the parade ground as regiments were matched against each other to be judged by two colonels with General Hardee presiding over the event. The match-up was as follows: the 16th & 25th Louisiana versus the 6th Kentucky on the nineteenth; the 13th & 20th Louisiana versus the 2nd Kentucky on the twentieth; the 19th Louisiana versus the 4th Kentucky and on the twenty-first the 32nd Alabama versus the 9th Kentucky. The first three match-ups all ended in favor of the Kentuckians, a surprise to most. For Rufus Cater, it was not a surprise that his regiment lost to the 6th Kentucky: "We got 'out of practice' while at Pollard." Maury's Alabamians and the 9th Kentucky were not able to finish out the match because orders came down for Breckinridge's division to be ready to march. The men had to begin breaking camp and preparing themselves to be shipped out.[18]

On 23 May, Bragg issued orders to Breckinridge to prepare his division to move immediately for Mississippi. Desperate to save Vicksburg at the last minute, President Davis urged Bragg to send reinforcements to General Joe Johnston at Jackson, Mississippi. Adams was notified on the twenty-third to prepare his brigade to move and be at Wartrace by 7:00 A.M. the next day. Breckinridge had the entire division stack arms on the twenty-fourth and had them lined up near him while he stood on a stump to explain to the men the situation. Suspicions that they were going to Mississippi were confirmed and the men prepared

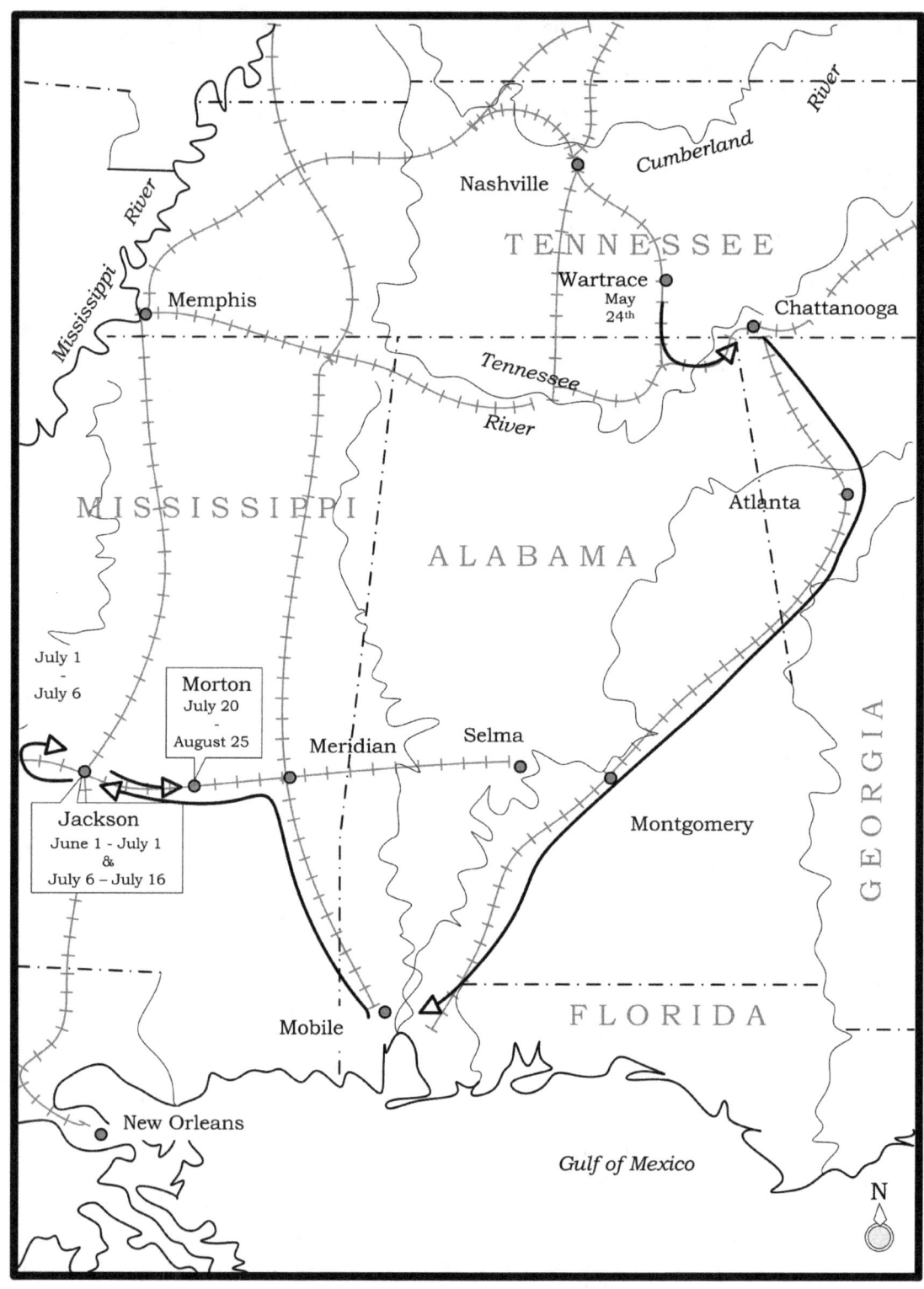

Movements of the Louisiana Brigade, January 1863 through July 1863.

to board their trains. During the months of idleness in Middle Tennessee, the men had acquired a large amount of personal belongings. Hardee issued orders to "reduce the personal baggage to the lowest point." Undoubtedly, the men lost a lot of their personal belongings in the quick removal from camp. The brigade broke camp early on the twenty-fourth and marched to the railroad at Wartrace, where the division was converging to leave for Mississippi.[19]

The ride back to Mississippi was a reversal of the journey taken by the brigade in August of the previous year. From Wartrace, the brigade traveled south to Chattanooga, across hilly North Georgia to Atlanta and then west to Montgomery, and then to Mobile. The regiments had to again ferry across Mobile Bay. From Mobile, the trains proceeded up to Meridian, Mississippi, and west to Jackson. On 29 May, the brigade detrained five miles from Jackson and continued the rest of the journey on foot. "We traveled in very good order with an exception of the cars they run off the track at Loachapoka, Ala., which resulted in two men of the Regt. being seriously wounded," wrote a member of the 32nd Alabama. On 1 June, Adams reached the outskirts of Jackson. The next day, the brigade marched into Jackson and set up camp. Once in Jackson, Breckinridge ordered Adams to picket southwest of town across the road to Raymond. The Louisianians were not impressed with Jackson. A little over two weeks before, Jackson had been sacked and burned by Grant's army as it was making its flank attack on Vicksburg. A member of the 16th Louisiana wrote to his wife describing Jackson: "I have never spent a sadder time than here; the town is almost entirely burned, the railroads are destroyed for two to three miles from town, and we hear constantly the monotonous sound, like distant thunder, of the broadsides of the Yankee gunboats." Remembering his stay in Mississippi the year earlier, where disease decimated his regiment, a member of the 19th Louisiana told his sister, "We have got back to Mis where we have to drink bad water."[20]

The Louisianians spent all of June at Jackson while Johnston organized his relief army for Vicksburg. On 30 June, Johnston prepared to push against Grant's army surrounding Vicksburg. During June, Johnston was able to scrape together a force of 28,000 effective men. On the morning of 1 July, Johnston began his advance toward the Big Black River, about midway between Vicksburg and Jackson, and north of the Vicksburg and Jackson Railroad. Anchoring the left of Johnston's advance was Breckinridge's division, which advanced along the railroad. Following behind Helm's brigade, Adams' brigade left Jackson before sunrise on the first. Intense heat and dry weather conditions claimed the lives of three men during the day's march. A soldier described the conditions as "weather hot, dust almost suffocating." Continuing the march the next day, Breckinridge pushed his division to Baldwin Station. While there, the division rested for two days before continuing the advance.[21]

On the evening of the fourth, Breckinridge ordered Adams to advance his brigade and picket the approaches to Baldwin Station. Due to a lack of suitable water for his men, Adams pushed his command a little farther than ordered and placed his brigade behind Baker's Creek, about 3 miles east of Edward's Depot. The severe heat wore down the Louisianians during the marching toward the Big Black. "The 4th and 5th [of July] was occupied in marching around the country, with seemingly no object in view but to keep moving," expressed a disgruntled member of the Washington Artillery. The rest of Johnston's army reached the ferries on the Big Black but found them to be heavily guarded. During June, Grant's army also grew in size. By the time Johnston began his advance from Jackson, Grant's army had swollen to 77,000 men. This allowed Grant to dispatch Major General William Sherman with seven divisions, 30,000 men, to guard his rear along the Big Black.

So, when Johnston reached the Big Black, he was met by Federals in equal strength. With the fords north of the railroad heavily guarded, Johnston ordered the army to prepare for a movement to the south of the railroad to attempt a crossing of the river in that direction. Events at Vicksburg, though, would drastically alter Johnston's advance.[22]

In the early hours of 6 July, Adams received urgent orders from Breckinridge to prepare his brigade to march at daylight. "Vicksburg has fallen," Breckinridge frankly wrote. Adams was to send his supply wagons ahead of him and retrace his steps back to Clinton. Johnston realized the danger his army faced and quickly fell back to Jackson. The situation was indeed dangerous for Johnston. As early as 3 July, Grant was making preparations to strike Johnston. Immediately upon the fall of Vicksburg, Grant had reinforced Sherman with six divisions, raising his force to 45,000 men. Grant's orders to Sherman were straightforward: "I want you to drive Johnston out in your own way, and inflict on the enemy all the punishment you can." On the sixth and seventh, Sherman began his advance across the Big Black at three points: two columns north of the railroad and one along the railroad. The march back to Jackson was not as leisurely for the Louisianians as the previous days. Beginning at daybreak of the sixth, the brigade marched almost continuously the entire day and into the night until the it reached Jackson. "A great many fell, some stretched on the side of the rode." An artillerist of Slocomb's battery added, "So great was the suffering of the Army that hundreds sank on the road side completely exhausted & every few hundred yards we would come across some poor fellow — lying dead on the road from sun-stroke."[23]

The Louisianians' misery increased as the brigade marched into Jackson. Pulling themselves into the city at about 10:00 P.M. on the sixth, the worn out men were met by a "heavy rain & storm." In the pouring rain, the men were allowed to bed down for the night in the mud. On the evening of the seventh, they were ordered to improve the old earthworks laid around Jackson two months earlier. Johnston deployed his four divisions in an arc around Jackson, with both of his flanks resting on the Pearl River, utilizing the extensive earthworks. Johnston deployed Breckinridge's division on the left of the army, facing south, with his left resting on the Pearl. Adams was placed on Breckinridge's right, connecting with the left of Major General Samuel French's division and across the New Orleans railroad. The Washington Artillery was deployed on top of the railroad, with two pieces on each side of the tracks. Immediately on the right of Slocomb's guns was the 19th Louisiana with the 13th & 20th Regiment to its right. On the left of Slocomb was the 32nd Alabama, and the 16th & 25th was on the extreme left of the brigade.[24]

On 10 July, Sherman commenced the investment of Jackson. Sherman ordered Major General Edward Ord's wing to invest Jackson from the west and southwest. From the Robinson Road, just south of the Vicksburg & Jackson Railroad, to the Pearl River, Ord deployed five divisions. Directly opposite Breckinridge was part of Brigadier General Alvin Hovey's Twelfth Division of the XIII Corps and Brigadier General Jacob Lauman's Fourth Division of the XVI Corps. Ord placed Hovey's division between the road to Raymond and the New Orleans & Jackson Railroad. Lauman was deployed to the right of the railroad with his right next to the Pearl River. Not until the late afternoon of 11 July did Hovey reach his position. Lauman, with only Colonel Isaac Pugh's brigade, camped behind Hovey for the night before proceeding to his position to the right of the railroad. On the morning of the twelfth, Pugh was ordered into line on Hovey's right and placed atop Bailey's Hill, behind Lynch Creek. On 12 July, Ord ordered Hovey and Lauman to press their men toward the Confederate line — not to bring on a major engagement but to push the Federal line closer to the Jackson defenses. Ord instructed Lauman to advance his line to within 1500 yards of the Confeder-

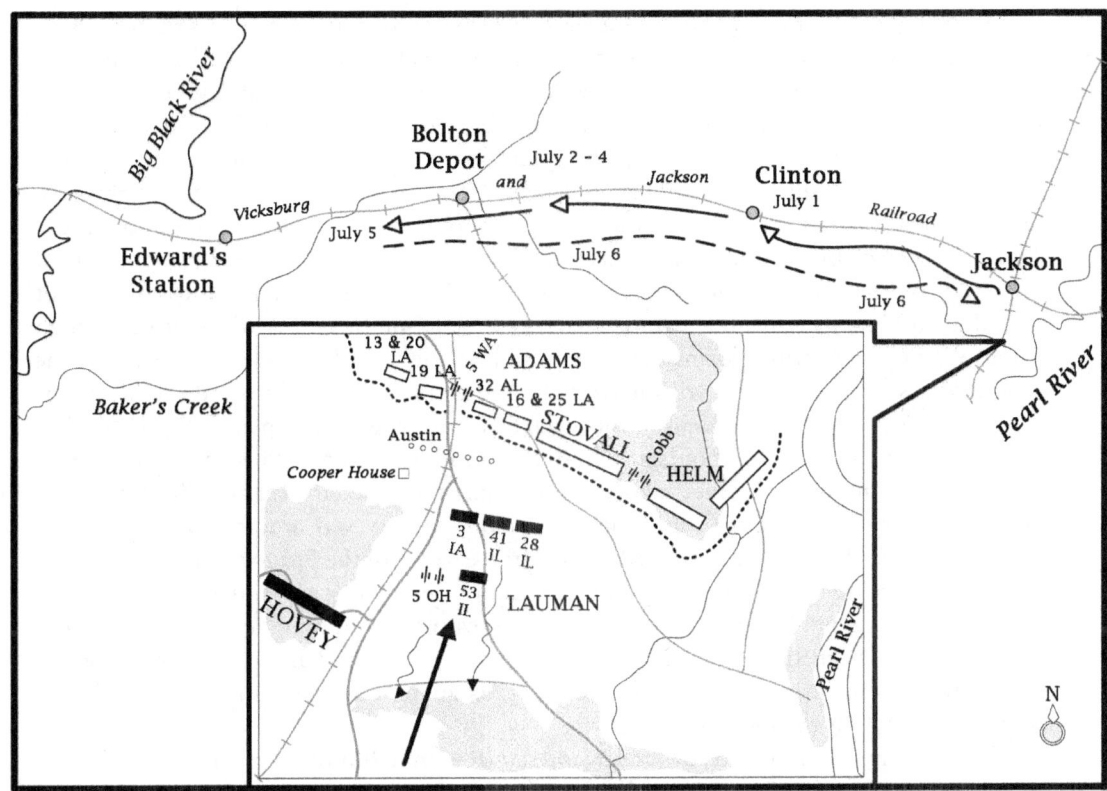

Jackson Campaign, July 1863. Inset shows the attack on Adams' position on 12 July by Lauman's brigade.

ate line, form on Hovey's right, and push his skirmishers "as near as they could get." Once at Bailey's Hill, Lauman ordered Pugh to push his brigade toward the Confederate line.[25]

During the encirclement of Jackson, Adams was busy strengthening his trenches. With Austin's battalion deployed far in advance of the works, men from the 16th & 25th Louisiana were given the task of clearing the fields before the trenches. As the men worked to clear the fields on the eleventh, Slocomb pushed forward a piece of the battery to harass Hovey's deployment. After disabling a piece of Federal artillery, Slocomb withdrew the gun back into the works. On July 12, as Pugh was preparing for his assault, men from the 16th & 25th were preparing to burn down a house in front of the trenches belonging to the Cooper family. Trying to help the family save as much of their personal belongings as possible, a group of men grabbed the Coopers' piano and carried it into the trenches and placed it in the small cotton bale redoubt that Slocomb's guns occupied. The piano was safely put behind the trenches right on the side of the guns and its close proximity was too tempting for the Washington Artillery.

Immediately members of the battery flocked to the piano and started playing and singing songs. The battery's bugler, Private Andy Swain, soon became the center of entertainment as he played numerous songs the men were familiar with. Soon, men from other units of the brigade drifted toward the music to take part in the excitement. The playing even attracted General Adams and the division's artillery commander Major Rice Graves. Suddenly, whizzing bullets and a loud cheer from the attacking enemy, interrupted the singing. Douglas Cater described the "novel scene" to his cousin: "While its soft notes were heard accompanied by the voice in song, shells were exploding and minie balls whistling around us. How vivid were home memories and reminiscences of peaceful days revived while the stern voice of war was breathing in the [illegible word] of the guns."[26]

Pugh had been advancing his brigade the entire time Adams' men were centering their attention on the Washington Artillery's festival. After crossing Lynch Creek, Pugh came upon the field razed by Adams. About 800 yards away, Pugh could see felled trees and obstructions made by the Louisianians, a clear indication that the Confederate line was near. Pugh hesitated and asked Lauman for further orders. Pugh had reached the appropriate spot to deploy on Hovey's right, but Lauman, in direct violation of Ord's orders, ordered Pugh to move forward. Austin's skirmishers put up a brief fight and quickly fell back into the works. Pugh's line of advance, with his left along the railroad, aimed toward the Washington Artillery's position. Immediately, Slocomb ordered his guns to open fire. Joining Slocomb was part of the 19th Louisiana and the 32nd Alabama. "The enemy opened a murderous fire on my whole line," wrote Pugh. Pugh's men tried to veer away from the blistering fire of the battery but Captain Robert Cobb's battery was ordered to support Slocomb in his pounding of the enemy. Major George Crosley of the 3rd Iowa, advancing with its left on the railroad and marching into the teeth of Slocomb's guns, described the conditions: "We were met by a perfect storm of grape, canister, and musketry. The timber and brush had been cleaned away in front of the enemy's works, and an abatis formed, which broke our line and threw the men into groups, thus giving the enemy's artillery an opportunity to work with the most deadly effect."[27]

"The enemy continued to advance steadily until within 200 yards, when, no longer able to endure the withering fire, principally from the artillery, they broke and retreated in disorder," reported Slocomb after the fight. Pugh was able to push his men forward, getting as close as 120 yards to the Confederate line before his brigade dropped to the ground for cover. "Our guns opened on them as soon as they came in sight with shell and changing to grape, then to shrapnel and double charges of canister as they came nearer. When in close range the infantry opened fire when they soon gave it up." Hovey, busy skirmishing with the Confederates in his front, was unaware of Pugh's desperate situation. Lauman attempted to reinforce Pugh by sending the 5th Ohio Battery to his support. It was the 5th Ohio Battery that had faced the Louisianians over a year ago at Shiloh at the Hornets Nest. Hickenlooper's guns made life miserable that day for the Louisiana Brigade and today was the day the Louisianians returned the favor. It was the Buckeyes' turn to taste the lonely feeling of attacking a well entrenched foe with no support. Before the

Pianist of the Jackson Trenches, Andy Swain, 5th Company Washington Artillery (courtesy of Confederate Memorial Hall Museum, New Orleans).

5th Ohio could properly deploy and support Pugh's men, Slocomb disabled two of the battery's guns and sent its crew scrambling for cover. After a fight of thirty or forty minutes, Pugh's brigade was "driven back in great confusion and with considerable loss." General Adams joined in on the fight by grabbing a nearby musket, mounting the brigade's works and firing off a couple of shots. Pugh's brigade began to break apart, some streaming to the rear and others clinging to the ground. Adams called a cease fire when groups of Federals began to wave their handkerchiefs. Quickly, men from Stovall's brigade to Adams's left and Austin's battalion jumped out of the works and began to mop up the repulse. Pugh's repulse was devastating. Stovall and Adams captured the flags of three of the four regiments in Pugh's brigade. Pugh brought into action about 880 men and lost 465 men killed, wounded and captured. Stovall brought in about 200 prisoners and Adams about 40. Adams suffered the loss of only two men, both wounded. One of the undocumented casualties of the day was Lieutenant Colonel Robert Lindsay of the 16th & 25th Regiment. As his regiment watched the Federals to their front get annihilated, Lindsay fell out from sunstroke under the Mississippi summer sun. Lindsay fought with overheating the rest of the campaign and, at one point, was unconscious for two hours. He soon took leave of the regiment to recover and he was not the only case. The heat cost the brigade many stragglers and captures in the coming days.[28]

Lieutenant Colonel Maury of the 32nd Alabama was one of the two men wounded. Captain John Kimball of the 32nd Regiment reported that Maury was leading his regiment "with his accustomed gallantry" when he was shot in the leg by a sniper at the close of the engagement. Command of the regiment fell on Kimball, and it remained so throughout his regiment's remaining months with Adams' brigade. Maury's tour was finished with the 32nd Alabama. By September, Maury had recuperated to take command of the newly formed 15th Confederate Cavalry out of Mobile. Maury's unit operated across Eastern Louisiana to Western Florida throughout the remainder of the war. He participated in the defense of Mobile in April of 1865, and his regiment eventually surrendered at Citronelle, Alabama, on 14 May 1865. Maury was not with his regiment, however. During the retreat, he fell and was kicked by his horse and remained in Mobile, nursing his wounds. Following the war, Maury engaged in "mercantile business" in Mobile and lived in that city until his death in 1869, due to acute gastritis.[29]

Immediately after Pugh's repulse, the 5th Company quickly jumped back to the Cooper piano. Musket fire and the thunder of artillery were quickly replaced by singing and cheering. Sergeant Hunter of the 19th Louisiana said, "Not being more than thirty yards to the left of our battery [5th Company] I often heard the boys of the battery during this time playing the piano which they had taken from a residence in front of us."[30]

Besides burying the enemy dead two days

Lieutenant Colonel Henry Maury, 32nd Alabama. Maury was wounded at the closing shots of the attack on 12 July at Jackson (courtesy of Alabama Department of Archives and History, Montgomery).

after the battle, the Louisianians sat idle for the remainder of the siege. On 16 July, Johnston issued orders for the army to retire across the Pearl River. The artillery was to begin falling back at 9:00 P.M. At 11:30, Adams began pulling his men out of line. The evacuation of Jackson was a wake up call for Louisianians who were frustrated with the war. Since the regiments had been sent to Shiloh back in early 1862, this was the closest the brigade had been back to Louisiana. The retreat out of Jackson was taking the brigade deeper into Mississippi and toward Alabama. As they retreated during the night, many men found their way out of the ranks and into the lines of the enemy. Whether on purpose or not, most of the men who deserted during the evacuation ended up as prisoners. The losses of the brigade in the siege were small, but the retreat took a serious toll. Brigade returns for the morning of 8 July during the siege, registered a total of 1,767 effective total men in the brigade. Returns for the morning of 19 July two days after the evacuation, the effective total was down to 1,488 men; a loss of 279 men. The vast majority of those lost were the city boys of New Orleans, the 13th & 20th Louisiana. Its numbers dropped from 8 July to 19 July from 407 men to 292; 115 men. The 20th Louisiana lost 77 men to desertion or straggling the night of the retreat. Of that number, nine were from its popular brass regimental band alone, and 18 were from its Company A. The 19th Louisiana maintained a strong reputation through the war but the Jackson Campaign saw the highest number of desertions at any point of the war. The first two days retreating from Jackson saw the regiment's effective drop from 445 to 373 with at least 25 men confirmed cases of desertions.[31]

Breckinridge marched his division along the old Brandon Road. The brigade marched until it reached Brandon, about twelve miles east of Jackson, around noon on the seventeenth. For part of the march the 19th Louisiana and a section of Slocomb's battery acted as the rear guard of the army. The retreat from Jackson was not any easier than the marching two weeks earlier when advancing toward Vicksburg. Suffocating heat, mixed with "clouds of dust" drummed up from the tramping of thousands of feet led to more straggling and desertions. Then there came the occasional thunderstorm in the afternoons that provided temporary relief from the heat. Wet feet and sloshing through muddy roads became an occasional inconvenience. The march was continued until the brigade reached Morton on the twentieth. At Morton, the brigade went into camp, dubbed Camp Hurricane, for the next month. Slocomb's battery, though, continued another twelve miles to Forest, where the battery went into camp. On 18 August, while at Camp Hurricane, Adams assembled the brigade early that morning into a three-sided square to witness the execution of Private J.S. Rogers of the 25th Louisiana. Rogers was a deserter from the 25th Louisiana that was caught and made an example of. It was a risk the men knew they faced if they left the ranks. Regardless of their contempt for deserters, it was a practice that brought sorrow and compassion for the condemned. The Jackson Campaign was over for the Louisiana Brigade. Even though the actual fighting around Jackson took but a handful of men the marching across central Mississippi took its toll. When the brigade was advancing toward the Big Black it had 1,827 effective total men for battle. When the brigade took roll on 29 July while at Camp Hurricane, it mustered 1,475 total effectiveness. That is a net loss of 352 men with the vast majority of this number deserting or straggling into captivity the night of the evacuation of Jackson. The 13th & 20th Regiment lost a total of 127 men captured or deserted in the campaign. The other regiments suffered a total drop during this period of the following: 32nd Alabama, 45 men; 19th Louisiana, 56 men; 16th & 25th Louisiana, 115 men; Austin's battalion, 9 men and the 5th Company 7 men. The longer the brigade rested at Camp Hurricane, the larger its numbers grew from men returning to duty.[32]

Taking advantage of the close proximity of his wife and family, Adams requested a ten-day leave on 29 July to handle personal business. With Adams away, Gibson assumed command of the brigade. As of 30 July, the day after Adams left to see his family, Gibson was listed in command of the brigade. He was not with his regiment during the Jackson Campaign, but he must have been stationed rather close for him to have been commanding Adams' brigade on the 30th. During the siege, Colonel Reichard of the 20th Regiment, commanding the 13th & 20th Consolidated in Gibson's absence, tendered his resignation due to a disease he contracted in Kentucky. He submitted his letter on 11 June and it was accepted on 7 July. When Reichard submitted his letter to the Inspector General Samuel Cooper, he clearly stated that Gibson had returned from recruitment duty and "may at any moment assigned to command of the regiment, by right of seniority." It is most likely that Gibson was operating in the area of Camp Moore in east Louisiana. Earlier in the year, Bragg designated a post in each of the states of Mississippi, Louisiana, Alabama, Georgia and Tennessee for the organizing of conscripts for his army. Officers placed on recruitment and conscription duty, such as Gibson, would have operated out of these posts.[33]

While encamped around Morton, Gibson took advantage of being free from Bragg's grasp by reinvigorating his request for a court of inquiry to investigate Bragg's official report of the Battle of Shiloh. Gibson sought written support for his case against Bragg's slanderous report from officers who were present during the assault on the Hornets Nest on 6 April 1862. Supporting Gibson's letter were statements from his aide-de-camp at Shiloh, Robert Pugh; Captain E.M. Dubroca, commander of the 13th Louisiana; the adjutant of the 13th Louisiana, Hugh Bein; and the former

Governor Henry Watkins Allen. When Randall Gibson requested a court of inquiry into Braxton Bragg's allegations against Gibson's competency, his appeal included testimony from the 4th Louisiana's former colonel, Henry Watkins Allen. Allen eventually was elected governor of Louisiana and served in that position until the end of hostilities in 1865 (courtesy of Confederate Memorial Hall Museum, New Orleans).

colonel of the 4th Regiment, Henry W. Allen. All supported Gibson's claim, saying the failure of Gibson's brigade to dislodge the Federals at the Hornets Nest at Shiloh was not due to Gibson's inabilities as an officer. Instead, as Bein wrote, it was due to Gibson's "want of artillery, the superior force of the enemy, his position, and the nature of the country through which we marched, the result was inevitable." Allen wrote that Bragg, his staff, and his escort all "retired to a ravine" when Federal artillery began to bombard the area. "I saw nothing more of them during that day," Allen continued. "No member of his staff ever rallied any of my men." Dubroca agreed that Bragg and his staff had no active role in keeping the brigade together. Cooper's reply to Gibson's request was that there was "no time to assemble a court of inquiry to examine into cases of personal or official difficulties between officers."[34]

David Tidwell, 19th Louisiana. Despite having the complexion of youth and innocence, Tidwell fought in, and survived, the arduous campaigns of 1863, including the Jackson Campaign (courtesy of the U.S. Army Military History Institute).

As the brigade quietly sat in Mississippi for part of June and most of August, events in Middle Tennessee were taking a bad swing for the Army of Tennessee. In early June, Rosecrans' Army of the Cumberland advanced from Murfreesboro. Through a series of skillfully conducted maneuvers, Rosecrans forced Bragg to evacuate Middle Tennessee, capturing Tullahoma on 4 July. For most of July and all of August, the Army of Tennessee remained around Chattanooga. With Rosecrans' army encamped across the Tennessee River, Bragg urgently wired Johnston on 21 August requesting reinforcements. On the twenty-second, the secretary of war ordered Johnston to send Bragg reinforcements immediately. Johnston replied to Bragg that he had ordered two divisions to the Army of Tennessee: Major General W.H.T. Walker's division and Breckinridge's division. On 25 August, Breckinridge began leaving for Chattanooga.[35]

CHAPTER 7

Chickamauga Campaign: September 1863

"In the charge that was made ... the balls would come as thick as hail, it was just like a storm coming the roaring of the cannons and muskets would drown the commands that were given to us. Oh, language is far short of me expressing to you how it was when the fight commensed."
— Private Ramy Lafitte, 19th Louisiana,
Co. I, 21 October 1863

Boarding railroad cars on the twenty-fifth, the brigade prepared for another week-long journey back to Tennessee. Traveling back through Mobile, Montgomery and Atlanta, the brigade reached the Chattanooga area on 1 September, disembarking at Tyner's Station, located east of Chattanooga. This was the second trip across the south for the brigade since May and was actually the third time since April for the 19th Louisiana to be flung across Georgia and Alabama. Crossing Alabama came at a price for the 32nd Alabama. Just like the New Orleans boys of the 13th and 20th Louisiana back in July, being close to home was too tempting for many. The number of men absent without leave in the regiment went from 80, when the regiment left camp in Mississippi, to 138 by the time the regiment reached Tyner's Station. Fifty-eight men deserted or went AWOL, which was 26 percent of the regiment. John Breckinridge's division was reunited with its old corps, Hardee's, when it returned to the army. William Hardee had been ordered to Mississippi following the fall of Vicksburg and Lieutenant General Daniel H. Hill had been placed in charge of the corps on 19 July. As the Louisianians settled into their new camp, Braxton Bragg remained in Chattanooga totally ignorant of William Rosecrans' next move. During the last week of August, Rosecrans was preparing to cross his army over the Tennessee River to the west of Chattanooga. Rosecrans' plan was to outflank Bragg by crossing at three points: Shellmound, Bridgeport and Carpenter's Ferry. It was Rosecrans' intention to move on Rome, Georgia, and force Bragg out of the Chattanooga area without a fight.[1]

Bragg had concentrated his entire army to the east of Chattanooga, facing the advance of Major General Ambrose Burnside's Army of the Ohio. Burnside had advanced from Kentucky, with his objective being Knoxville, Tennessee. Bragg believed that Rosecrans and Burnside would link up and cross the Tennessee between Chattanooga and Knoxville. "Almost accidentally," said D.H. Hill, Bragg learned of the crossing of heavy bodies of Federals to the west. It was not pickets from the Army of Tennessee that alerted Bragg of the enemy's movements but a citizen from Stevenson, Alabama. After several days of

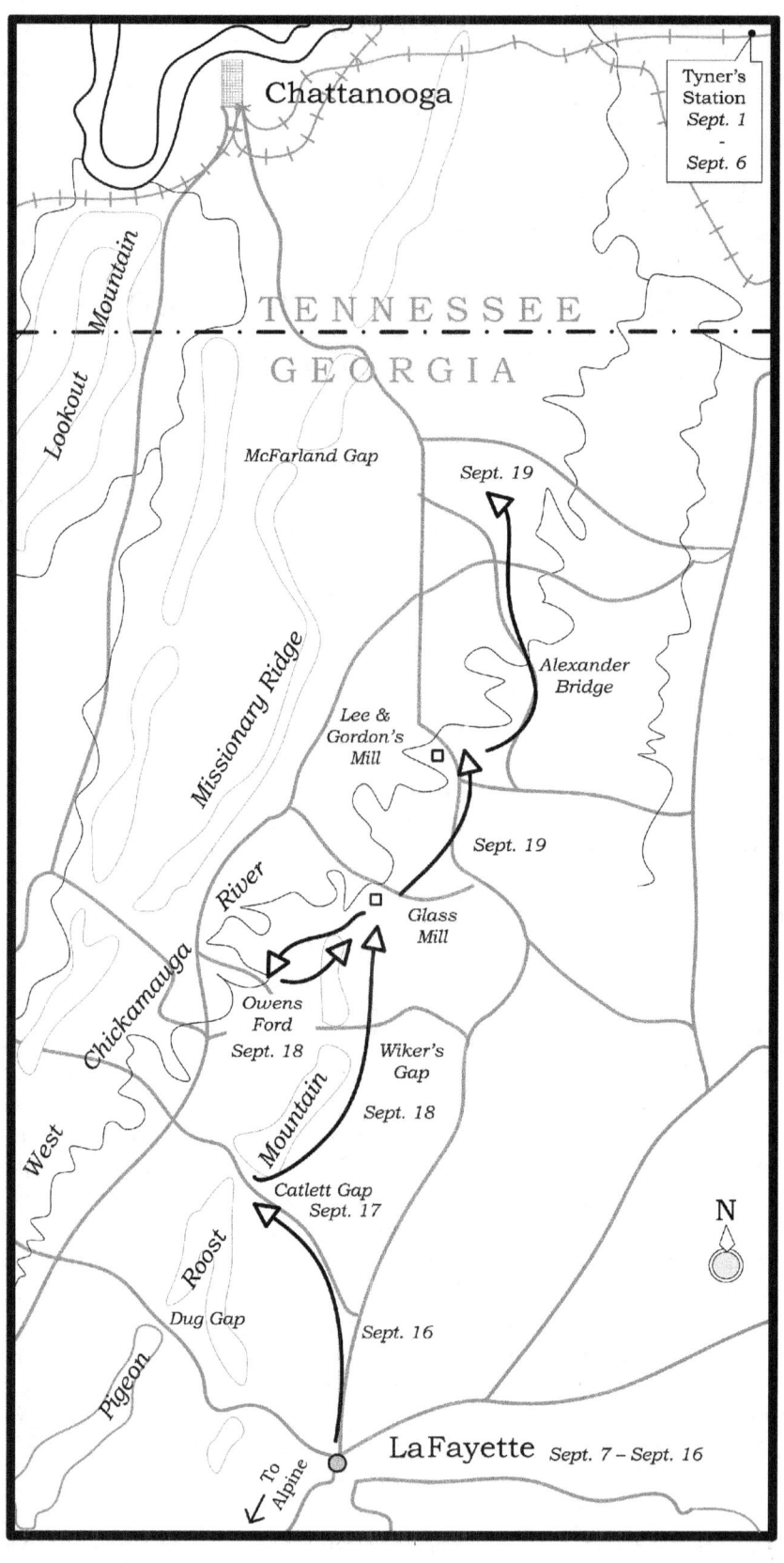

attempting to discern the true intentions of Rosecrans, Bragg decided to pull the army out of the area around Chattanooga and into Georgia. It had been the timely capture of a copy of the *Chicago Times* that had saved the Army of Tennessee from destruction. In an article in the paper, the full details of Rosecrans' movements had been published. Judging by the fact that several of the article's statements had already taken place (such as the crossing of a large number of troops to the west of Chattanooga), Bragg stuck to his only solid piece of intelligence and on 6 September ordered a retreat.[2]

On the night of the sixth, Adams and his men left Tyner's Station. Breckinridge's division was ordered to LaFayette, Georgia, where the division would guard the army's supply trains. After a footsore march across hilly north Georgia, the Louisianians were able to enjoy a rest at LaFayette. Bragg began to concentrate his army along Pigeon Mountain from LaFayette to Lee & Gordon's Mill located on Chickamauga Creek. Bragg then began a series of movements to try to destroy Rosecrans' scattered army. At the same time, Rosecrans believed that Bragg's army was in full retreat toward Dalton, Georgia. A collision between Rosecrans and Bragg was only a matter of time.[3]

As the two armies maneuvered, the Louisianians' dull stay at LaFayette was abruptly interrupted on the morning of the thirteenth. The right of Rosecrans' army had advanced deep into Alabama and had reached the town of Alpine, Georgia, located about twenty-five miles southwest of LaFayette. On the ninth, Brigadier General George McCook, commanding the cavalry that was leading the right wing of Rosecrans' army, occupied Alpine. That evening, Federal cavalry pushed to within several miles of LaFayette. To meet the threat, Hill ordered Breckinridge to post a sizeable infantry force across the Alpine Road. Breckinridge ordered Adams to move his brigade to the southwest of town and deploy skirmishers. On the morning of the thirteenth, McCook led four brigades of cavalry toward LaFayette. McCook's lead brigade, under Colonel Archibald P. Campbell, encountered Adams' skirmishers at about 8:00 A.M., 3½ miles outside of LaFayette. Campbell called up his lead regiment, the 9th Pennsylvania Cavalry, and ordered a charge. Although Campbell's quick show of force snatched eighteen Louisianians as prisoners, Adams' fire was too intense for Campbell to continue. Realizing that he faced greater numbers than he had expected, McCook fell back to Alpine, notifying his superiors of his discovery.[4]

It was McCook's accidental discovery of Bragg's army at LaFayette that alerted Rosecrans to the fact that Bragg was preparing for a fight and not retreating. Rosecrans earnestly began to concentrate his army, realizing that he was an easy target with his men spread across a 40-mile front. The skirmish at LaFayette also caused Bragg to concentrate his army at LaFayette. For the next couple of days, the Army of Tennessee sat idle around LaFayette while the Army of the Cumberland frantically worked to pull itself together. Finally, on the evening of 16 September Bragg issued orders for his army to advance. Bragg was going to outflank Rosecrans' left and cut him off from Chattanooga.[5]

With the bulk of Bragg's army moving farther north, Breckinridge's division was called out of Lafayette on the sixteenth and placed across Catlett Gap on Pigeon Mountain. Early on the seventeenth, Hill set his divisions in motion. Orders were given to move in support of Polk's corps, which was opposite Lee & Gordon's Mill on Chickamauga Creek. Breckinridge moved to Glass Mill on Chickamauga Creek the next day. That evening, a small Federal force began to cross the Chickamauga to the left rear of Breckinridge at Owen's Ford. Hill personally led Adams' brigade on a forced march to the ford, but the Federals

Opposite: **Movements of the Louisiana Brigade, 3–19 September 1863.**

quickly withdrew once a heavy force was present. Adams remained at Owen's Ford that night, returning to his division the next morning at Glass Mill.[6]

On 19 September fighting broke out between the Army of the Cumberland and the Army of Tennessee along Chickamauga Creek. As major fighting was erupting above Lee & Gordons' Mill, Hill made a diversionary move from Glass Mill across the Chickamauga. Helm's Kentucky Brigade was ordered to cross the creek. To help support Helm, Cobb's and Slocomb's batteries would cross the creek also. At 11:00 A.M., Slocomb deployed two guns above Glass Mill while he crossed the Chickamauga with his remaining four pieces. A sharp artillery duel ensued in which Slocomb and Cobb, deployed in the field in front of Glass Mill, caught the worst of the fight. Still trying to outflank Rosecrans' left flank, Bragg shuffled his units, as the battle raged, toward the right. In this shift, Breckinridge was ordered toward Lee & Gordon's Mill. The fight was quickly called off by Breckinridge; Helm, Cobb and Slocomb were ordered back across the creek. Slocomb was able to pull his guns back in a "crippled condition."[7]

From Glass Mill, Adams and his brigade marched to within three miles south of Lee & Gordon's Mill. Barely into place, the men were ordered to finish the three miles to Lee & Gordon's Mill to relieve Major General Thomas Hindman's division, which was deployed across the creek from the mill. "The division was hardly in position" when Bragg ordered Breckinridge to move his division from the extreme left of the army to the extreme right in order to take part in an early morning attack on the twentieth. By then, late in the afternoon, the Louisianians had once again trod through the small country roads to their destination. Breckinridge moved his division northeast along Chickamauga Creek until he reached Alexander's Bridge Road, at which point he marched north and crossed the creek at Alexander's Bridge. After continuing north for another two miles, Breckinridge, between 10:00 and 11:00 P.M., reached his destination, about a mile and a half to the right rear of the Confederate line. The Louisiana Brigade spent the first day of the Battle of Chickamauga marching from the extreme left flank of the army to the extreme right flank.[8]

Bragg initially planned to outflank Rosecrans' left so that he might cut him off from Chattanooga. Throughout the nineteenth, Bragg continually tried to make such a maneuver but failed to reach Rosecrans' flank. It was the deployment of Breckinridge's division on the right of Cleburne's division that finally outstretched Bragg's right flank over Rosecrans' left. The attack on the twentieth was to start with Breckinridge. Up before sunrise, Breckinridge deployed his three brigades on Cleburne's right: Helm on the left, Stovall in the middle and Adams on the right. Adams' brigade was deployed from left to right as follows: 19th Louisiana, 16th & 25th Regiment, 13th & 20th Regiment and finally the 32nd Alabama. Austin's battalion was deployed about 400 yards to the front of the brigade and was reinforced with a company from each regiment of the brigade: Company K of the 13th & 20th Louisiana, Company G of the 32nd Alabama, Company F of the 19th Louisiana and Company K of the 16th & 25th Louisiana. For the upcoming fight, Adams had 1,314 men in line.[9]

Adams had his brigade formed and ready by 8:00 A.M. but orders for the advance were not given until about 9:30. Austin moved his line forward about 700 yards and engaged enemy skirmishers. When Adams' main force came upon the skirmish line, Austin removed his battalion to form a reserve. Unknown to Adams and Breckinridge, Adams' brigade was actually advancing about two miles north of Rosecrans' main line. Marching forward, Adams came upon part of Brigadier General John Beatty's brigade. Extremely worried about his left flank, Rosecrans had begun shifting units from his right flank to his left flank early on

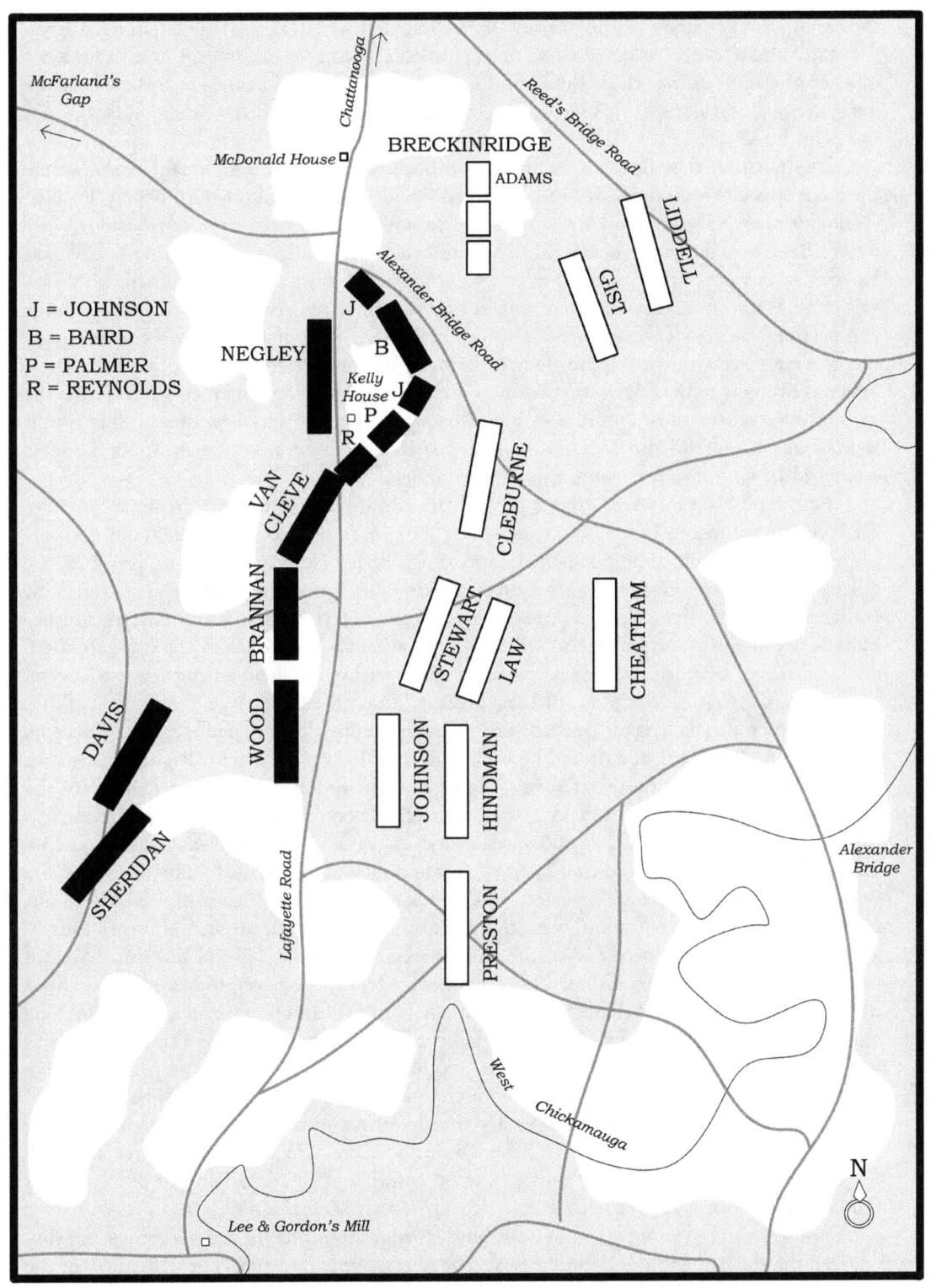

Battle of Chickamauga, 20 September 1863.

the twentieth. The first brigade to reach the Federal left was Beatty's, which had been given the unfortunate order to move from the main Federal line to occupy a ridge about one-quarter of a mile to the left of the Union line. Beatty protested having to leave his strong defensive position along Kelly's Field; he recognized the danger of being extended far beyond the main line.[10]

The position that Beatty was ordered to occupy was at the McDonald Farm, where the Lafayette-Chattanooga Road met the Reed's Bridge Road. Unknown to Beatty, his four regiments were advancing on a collision course with Breckinridge's entire division. Only two of Beatty's regiments, the 88th Indiana and the 42nd Indiana, reached the McDonald Farm. Beatty's other regiments, the 15th Kentucky and 104th Illinois, collided with Stovall's and Helm's brigades and were forced back to the main Federal line, creating a huge gap between Beatty's two regiments and the main line. Supporting the two Indiana regiments were three guns of Captain Lyman Bridge's Illinois Battery. One section of his battery was brought to the McDonald Farm, while the other section remained behind near the woods' edge where the Alexander Bridge Road met the Chattanooga Road. This meant Beatty was to defend the McDonald Farm, such an "imperative" position as Thomas described it, with two regiments and three cannons.

Before pushing forward, Adams pushed the 32nd Alabama forward to act as a reserve for Austin's reinforced battalion. After about 700 yards of wading through the undisciplined ground Austin came upon the Chattanooga Road. He instantly began firing at "the enemy's couriers, wagons, and ambulances," and ended up cutting off the 42nd and 88th Indiana Regiments line of retreat back to Kelly Field. Next erupted an intense skirmisher fight between Austin and elements of the 42nd Indiana. The Louisianians were stunned, and at first part of Austin's line was pushed back. Austin's line held strong against "several vain attempts" to push them out of their position along the road.[11]

As the Louisiana Brigade pushed west through the "thickly wooded" terrain, it became difficult to maintain brigade discipline with regiments losing alignment. Right after Austin was able to repulse enemy skirmishers, Adams gave the order for a general advance of the whole brigade on McDonald's Farm. Posted across the Lafayette Road, Bridge spotted Adams as he emerged from the thicket 400 yards away. "As soon as the battle-flags of the enemy emerged from the woods and there was no doubt about its being the enemy, I opened fire with my full battery," Bridge reported. The attack on the McDonald Farm was carried out by Austin's reinforced battalion, with the 32nd Alabama in support and Gibson's 13th & 20th Louisiana. Most likely due to the heavily wooded terrain, Gibson did not maintain line integrity with Gober's 16th & 25th Regiment. His march placed him somewhat ahead of the rest of the brigade. When contact was made with the Illinois regiments at the McDonald Farm, Gibson was met by "cheers and volleys from the enemy." The 42nd Indiana was no stranger to the Louisiana Brigade. The two had exchanged shots at Perryville almost a year before. Gibson immediately ordered a charge and slammed into the 88th and 42nd. "We fell upon him with such impetuosity that he broke in confusion, the men throwing away their arms and equipments," Gibson proudly wrote. His angle of advance seems to have taken him through the left flank of the 88th Indiana. The 42nd and 88th Regiments fell back to the west, from the Lafayette Road, towards McFarland's Gap.

Bridge's three guns were in a serious bind. Bridge attempted to order a retreat but discovered that he had enough living horses to haul away only one gun. The proximity of the Louisianians forced Bridge to abandon the one gun he could save: "The enemy was each moment closing his infantry in upon my front and right, firing as they advanced, and there

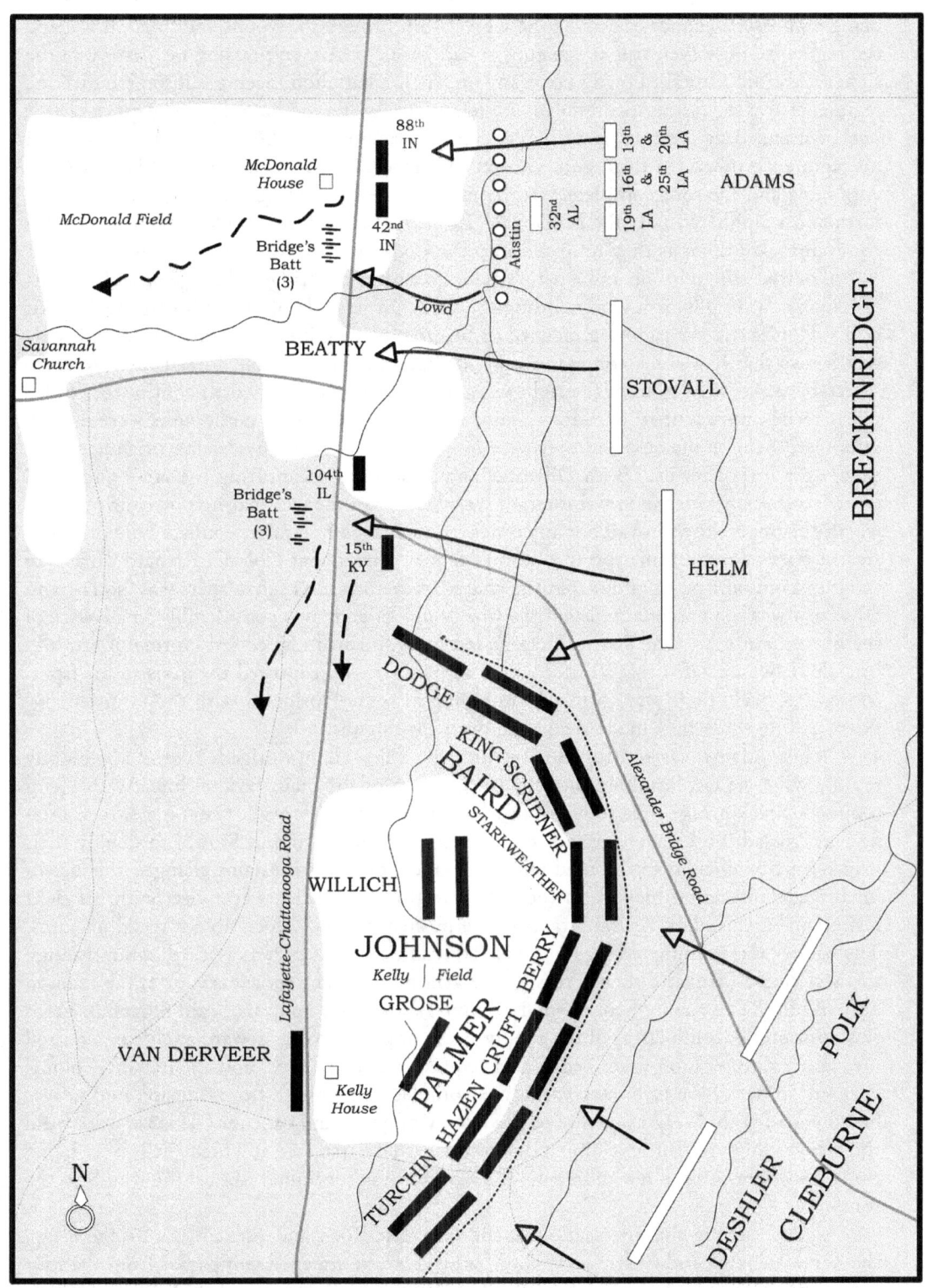

Breckinridge's Attack, 20 September 1863, 9:30 A.M.–10:30 A.M.

being no possible chance of getting these pieces off through the woods and brush, I ordered the remnant of my men still at the guns to fall back." The men pressing his battery to the right were from Captain Lowd's company of Austin's battalion. Seeing Gibson trounce the regiments near the farm, Austin moved his left company "forward rapidly." The quick charge by Lowd ended in the capture of two of Bridge's cannons and 86 men while Gibson and his regiment nabbed the third gun. Gibson described the McDonald fight: "The onset was admirable and the rout complete." To "complete" the rout, Slocomb's guns were brought forth and unlimbered near the McDonald Farm. As Beatty's men took to their heels, Slocomb pounded them as they retreated into the woods toward McFarland's Gap.[12]

Contradicting Gibson and Austin's claim to capturing Bridge's three guns is the report of Colonel W.S. Dilworth commanding the 1st & 3rd Florida of Stovall's Brigade. The 1st & 3rd Florida was the right regiment of its brigade, placing it near Adams' command. Dilworth says that it was his command that "charged the enemy" and forced them to leave "three brass pieces in front of the right wing of my regiment." Dilworth continued, "Judging it to be imprudent to withdraw many men from the ranks, as the guns were already safe, I left them on the field and they were removed subsequently by Adams' brigade, which came up a little after us." Both Dilworth and Austin claim capturing the same guns, and there is a lack of evidence to point either way other than the fact that no one confirms Dilworth's claim. Neither Stovall nor any other regimental commanders confirm Dilworth, but Austin does have confirmation in Gibson's report. Lieutenant Colonel Richard Turner of the 19th Louisiana pointed out that the charge of the brigade's skirmishers was "so fast and far that it was soon ascertained that the line of our brigade was considerably in advance of the line on our left." The line to Turner's left was Dilworth's 1st & 3rd Florida of Stovall's brigade. It would seem that Turner would remember who captured the guns to his front. More than likely there was an in intermingling of some Floridians with the Louisianians' skirmish line when they made their rush on Bridge's guns.[13]

While Adams was routing Beatty from the field, Helm's brigade had met a bloody repulse when he ran headlong into the breastworks of the main Federal line. With Helm repulsed, Breckinridge rode to his right to meet Adams and Stovall. Catching Adams after he had crossed the Lafayette Road, Breckinridge ordered him and Stovall to deploy their brigades perpendicular to the road and to advance southward. Adams changed the face of his brigade and rested his left on the Lafayette Road; Stovall did likewise, with his right resting on Adams's left. As the infantry were pushed forward, Slocomb advanced his guns. The battery was unlimbered on a piece of "favorable ground" past a ravine that ran through the McDonald Farm and then across the Lafayette Road. The spot was west of the road on a small hill. "The enemy here opened a heavy artillery fire upon us," said Slocomb. From this position, Slocomb engaged the enemy as the brigade moved forward and dropped itself into the ravine. Gibson described it as a "constant artillery fire," and Lieutenant Colonel Richard Turner of the 19th, who would be wounded in the thigh from this fire, said he was being pelted with, "very heavy fire of the enemy of grape and canister." It is very doubtful the fire was the type Turner claimed due to the extreme distance at which shells were being thrown in from. After a few moments, the advance was continued toward the woods to the south.[14]

Upon reaching the intersection of the Lafayette Road and Alexander's Bridge Road, the 32nd Alabama and Austin's battalion, with the four attached companies from the four regiments, were detached and placed across Alexander's Bridge Road facing west. Adams placed the three remaining regiments with the 19th on the left, next to the road, and the

13th & 20th on the right with the 16th & 25th in the middle. Farther south down the Lafayette Road the enemy was busy scrambling to shore up its left flank. As Beatty's 42nd and 88th Indiana Regiments were streaming to the rear, the 104th Illinois and 15th Kentucky had reformed across the Lafayette Road, facing north. Also, Colonel Timothy R. Stanley's brigade had been ordered to the Federal left to support Beatty. Meeting with Beatty as his brigade fell back, Stanley agreed with that officer to immediately form his brigade at right angles to the Lafayette Road. Stanley placed the 11th Michigan on his right, near the road, and the 18th Ohio on the left with the 19th Illinois in support to the right. Beatty retired his two regiments and reformed them to the rear of Stanley's line, with the 84th Illinois in support to the right. Stanley and Beatty were just completing their alignment when, Stanley remembered, "The line was hardly formed before the enemy advanced upon us in heavy force."[15]

Stovall faced an even bigger obstacle forming across the road. Not only was organized resistance met earlier, but there were substantially larger numbers marching to save the endangered Union left on this side of the road. Stovall's front was blocked by the extreme left anchor of the Union line, Colonel Joseph Dodge's brigade. Farther south the brigades of Colonels William Grose and Ferdinand Van Derveer were being thrown towards Stovall's advance, and backing them up were parts of Brigadier General August Willich's brigade and Colonel William Berry's brigade.

Onward pushed Stovall's small, but vicious, brigade of North Carolinians, Floridians and Georgians. Partially uncovered with no breastworks, Dodge's brigade put up token resistance and ran to the rear. Colonel William Grose's brigade was the first reinforcement to reach the north Kelly Field and take on Stovall. After exchanging several intense volleys, Stovall got the best of Grose and sent his men reeling to the rear also. Then things began to go wrong. Helm's brigade was unable to keep pace because it had run into King's and Scribner's entrenched brigades and part of Stovall's own brigade was detained by King's brigade. As Stovall's brigade pushed farther into Kelly's Field, about 75–100 yards so far, it was taking more flank fire on its left from King. Then across the field, barely 100 yards away, the brigade of Colonel Ferdinand Van Derveer emerged from its prone position in the dirt and hammered the disorganized advance with solid volleys. "The front line ... delivered a murderous fire almost in their faces," said Van Derveer. Stovall was in the firefight of his life. It did not take long for Stovall to break under the pressure. After firing into Stovall's men, Van Derveer's second line, joined by other units from Berry and Doge, charged headlong into the Confederates. Initial success turned into disaster for Stovall; his men broke and ran into the woods leaving Kelly Field in the hands of the enemy.[16]

All the while, Adams was pushing his brigade south. Adams managed to push about 100 yards farther south than Stovall by the time Stovall's brigade broke through the woods. Despite frustrating conditions of having to march about 800 yards through the heavy underbrush, described as "a dense thicket of underbrush and small saplings," and having taken steady artillery fire, the Louisianians' morale was up as they smelled victory in the air, something they tasted but never digested at Shiloh and Perryville. "The men scattered very much in the thick wood" but were "cheering as they came." Contact was first made with the skirmishers of the 15th Kentucky and 104th Illinois. When those two regiments fell back, their skirmishers were left to their own in the woods. The Louisianians unleashed a volley into these skirmishers and then were thrown forward in a wild charge. When within about 100 yards of Stanley's regiments, they were met with a surprise. Stanley had his men lie on the ground and had all the colors dropped. Colonel William Stoughton of the 11th Michigan

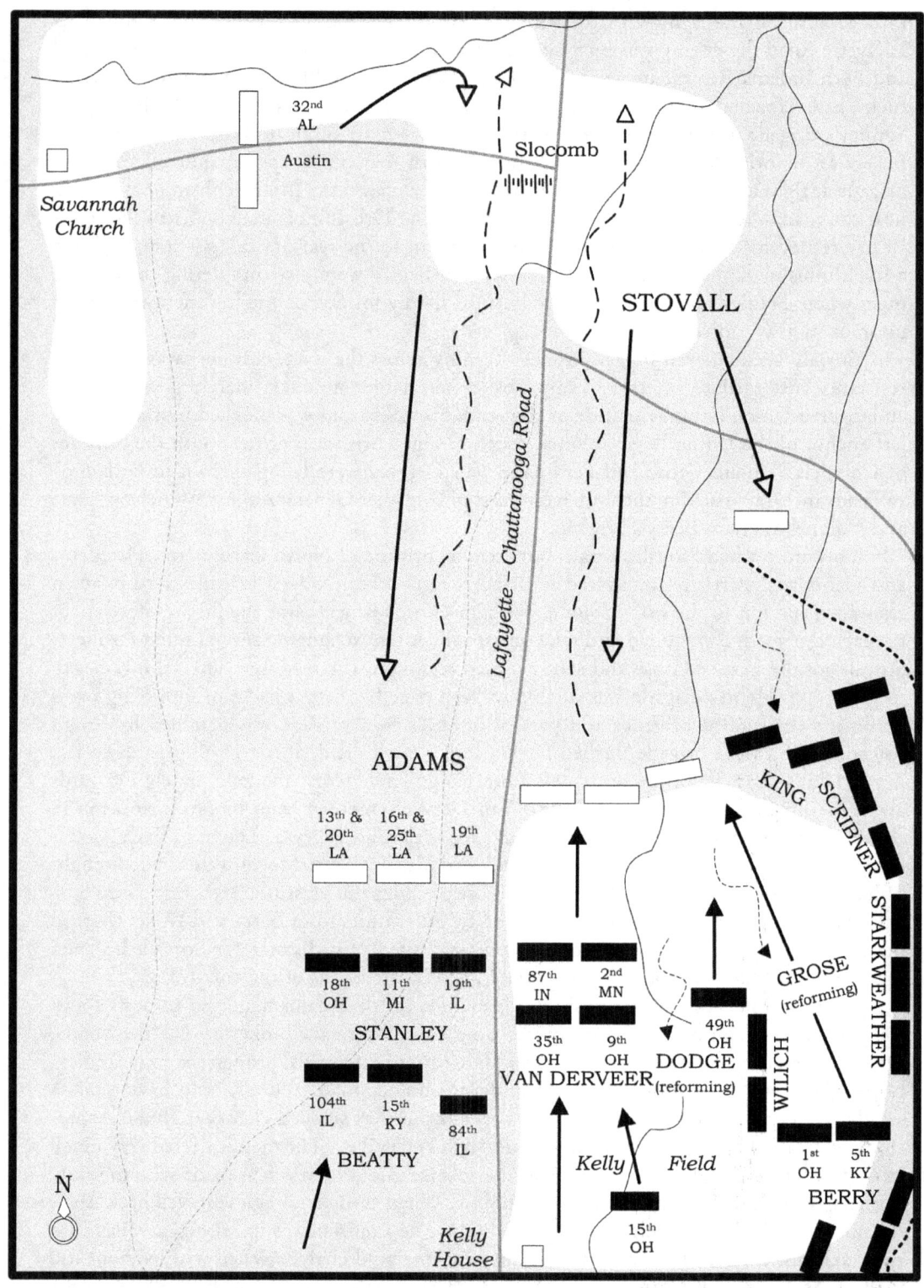

Attack on Kelly Field, 20 September 1863, 10:30 A.M.–12:30 P.M.

told his men, "Take aim at their legs.... Don't waste a bullet; pay strict attention to orders and we will make those fellows sing a different song." Suddenly, the 11th Michigan and 18th Ohio poured a "terrific and well directed volley" into the rushing Louisianians and stopped the men in their tracks. One source puts the firing taking place as close as two to three rods, or 20 yards. The 19th Illinois was quickly brought forward and put in line to bear weight on the Louisianians.[17]

Adams' brigade began to "waver" and soon "fled to the rear in the wildest confusion." Colonel Gibson described the scene of his regiment on the right: "While thus disordered, [we] received a terrific and unbroken volley from a second line that suddenly came up, flanking us on the right and sustained by a battery run out for its support. The whole line was checked. Some began to seek cover, and in a few minutes the command gave way in spite of every exertion." Colonel Gober, to the left of Gibson's 13th & 20th Regiment, was less descriptive but said it bluntly: "We came up on the enemy and were driven back." The fire was intense and deadly with a member of the 11th Michigan claiming the front ranks of the Rebels across him, 16th & 25th Louisiana, were all dropped. First Lieutenant George Walton of Company F of the 25th Louisiana, as did other officers, tried everything to push their men forward. For Walton, though, it would be his last time leading his men forward into combat. Gober wrote after the battle of Walton, "The last I saw of the gallant Walton he was some distance in front of his company shouting to them to advance." With the men falling back and Walton pushing forward he managed to make himself a prisoner and would not leave a Yankee prison until early 1865. Gibson and Gober suffered heavily from the surprise blast, and General Adams, who was following Gober's command, was hit in the arm by a minie ball. At first glance it appeared to all Adams simply suffered a minor wound.[18]

On Adams' left, the 19th Louisiana was still pushing forward as its sister regiments were wavering and falling back. Major Loudon Butler, who took command of the 19th Louisiana after Turner was wounded, led his men in the "most desperate and bloody charge that troops were ever called on to make." Butler was a full 100 yards ahead of where Stovall's men were and began to absorb the combined fire of all units nearby. Leading his regiment forward, Butler came under horrific fire from not only the 11th Michigan and 19th Illinois but also from across the Lafayette Road from the 87th Indiana. Captain Peter Troutman of that regiment described the fire it poured into Butler: "Our boys poured it into them at the left oblique and were the victors." The 19th Louisiana was devastated, with Butler being killed at the head of his men. A member of the regiment put his memories about Butler's death to paper fifty years after the battle, remembering, "Butler was the only officer in the brigade who dared to enter the charge horseback. His neck was broken by a grape-shot, and in pitching forward at the instant of death his sword fell several feet nearer the enemy." Suddenly Captain Hyder Kennedy was given command of his regiment in a most desperate situation. "Seeing myself almost deserted," said Kennedy, "and in the face of a most destruc-

Lieutenant Rufus Cater, 19th Louisiana. Cater was killed at Chickamauga on 20 September leading his men into Kelly Field. Rufus' brother, Douglas, came across his body that night and slept next to it before he buried him the next day (courtesy of the Cater Family).

tive fire, I had no alternative left me but to order a retreat." The dead and wounded were left behind as the Louisianians bolted for safety.[19]

The 19th Louisiana was gutted from the charge into Kelly Field. The left side of the regiment had none or next to no cover from the woods and was not afforded the patchwork protection of the thicket. Captain Winfrey Scott of Company B described the disaster that unfolded as his regiment attempted to push forward, "...when within a hundred and fifty paces, we opened a terrific fire upon them and loaded as we advanced ... a most dreadful fire was opened on us by their artillery, and their infantry their artillery shot canister, grape and leaden balls ... the shell, canister, and grape flow fast and thick, our boys fell on the right and left, but on we went, with nothing to shelter us but the unseen arm of God until we got I suppose within 90 or 100 yards of them, when our line ceased to advance...." Scott continued with a detailed account of the result of his and Captain John A. Bruton's Company B: "Capt. Brutons & Capt. Scotts Co's suffered more largely, than any others in the Regt. the former losing 25 killed & wounded out of 38 carried into action; the latter 21 out of 33. Both of the Commanders wounded. Capt. Bruton severely in the shoulder; since died. Capt. Scott was shot in the calf of the leg; missing the bone, now rapidly improving. Likewise all the other commissioned Officers in both companies wounded slightly, except one in each."[20]

Stanley did not hesitate to take advantage of either the tactical situation or the chance to gloat: "Our volleys were destructive to them, and I attribute their utter rout to the skillful fire and impetuosity of my brigade." The tide had turned, and it was now time to take advantage of it. With Adams' advance checked, Stanley and Beatty "simultaneously gave the order to advance, then to charge." "The troops rushing forward with a shout drove the enemy on the run." The seven small regiments that Gibson and Stovall brought to Kelly Field were too few for the weight of Stanley's, Beatty's and Van Derveer's brigades, plus parts of Berry's, Willich's, King's and Dodge's reformed brigades.[21]

As the brigade recoiled a short distance into the woods, Gibson and Gober were able to rally their regiments for another advance. Gibson grabbed the colors of his regiment and earnestly commanded his men back into line. Gober was able to do the same with his 16th & 25th Regiment but missing from the realignment was General Adams, who had been following behind the unit. Seeing that Gober's regiment was rallied, as his own, Gibson prepared to renew the advance when Colonel Gober rode up and notified Gibson that Adams was missing, and his whereabouts were unknown. Adams was directing his brigade from behind the 16th & 25th Regiment when he was hit in the arm. Gibson had noticed Adams looking at his arm as the brigade advanced but thought that, since the general remained on the field, it was but a minor wound. Gibson, being the senior officer in the brigade, took command in Adams' absence. Gibson turned command of the 13th & 20th over to Captain Dubroca, and he quickly sought to ascertain the situation that the entire brigade faced. Gibson's position was dangerous. Only the 13th & 20th and the 16th & 25th had been able to reform themselves. To the left, Gibson was totally unsupported, and he found himself isolated with the 19th Louisiana "unreformed" and Stovall's brigade "driven back." Driving hard to his front and flank came the Union counterattack. To stay meant destruction.

Gibson ordered a retreat to Slocomb's guns to rally his disorganized units. Colonel Stanley pushed the dazed Louisianians hard: "The enemy fled in dismay.... We thus drove them for a half mile or more, strewing the ground with killed and wounded, and taking a large number of prisoners." A significant number were captured in the retreat, and all the wounded were left behind in enemy hands. Those that could walk were all collected under a detail from the 11th Michigan and herded to the rear, and before the day was out, found themselves marched into Chattanooga.[22]

One of the many wounded left behind in the quick retreat was Adams. When the 16th & 25th fell back under pressure from Stanley, the wounded Adams was unable to keep up with his men and was forced to stop and rest at the foot of a tree due to the loss of blood. He was taken prisoner as Stanley's regiments pursued the Louisianians. Adams' capture was credited to the 19th Illinois. Stanley came upon Adams, and they exchanged introductions. Adams asked for a stretcher to be carried to the rear, but Stanley, caught in the excitement of pursuing the disorganized Louisianians, offered his apologies for not being able to order one up and continued on his pursuit. The capture of Adams officially went to Captain James Guthrie of the 19th Illinois. This created a controversy after the war with many units claiming to be the captors of Adams.

The author of a history on the 11th Michigan's role at Chickamauga challenged all other claims as to who captured Adams: "We ask them to produce their proofs, and if they can't do that, to come up like gallant comrades and give us the credit that rightfully belongs to us." This demand was not met with his own proof. The 11th Michigan was able to produce Adams' sword, pistol and field glasses: "Simeon D. Long, of Company D, secured one of General Adams' revolvers; John Spitler, his field glasses, and the lamented Sergeant-Major Snyder, his sword." In 1907, Captain Borden Hicks of the same regiment contradicted the story that Sergeant-Major Snyder took Adams' sword. Hicks claims he carried not only his own sword but also Adams,' "looking savage as a meat ax," in the pursuit of the Louisiana Brigade back toward McDonald's Farm.[23]

To muddy the waters more, there is the 5th Kentucky and 105th Ohio, the latter bearing more credit. Colonel William Berry reported that when he sent one of his regiments, the 5th Kentucky under Captain John M. Huston, to help in repelling the breakthrough behind Kelly Field, it actually captured Adams, "struck the enemy in their flank, and drove them pell-mell for a mile and a half, capturing many prisoners, among them General Adams." Most likely, part of the 5th Kentucky covered the very ground already cleared by Stanley's regiments, and because Adams was left behind, it was their assumption they had captured him.[24]

The 105th Ohio gives a very descriptive account of its interaction with Adams. The 105th Ohio did not reach this part of the battlefield until very late in the afternoon. They were part of a counterattack designed to throw back Liddell's division that had crossed the Chattanooga Road. It was not until late in the afternoon that an officer of the 105th Ohio came upon Adams. The young officer was Lieutenant Albion Tourgee. Tourgee was in charge of collecting the wounded of his regiment and came across Adams leaning against a tree. What caught Tourgee's attention was Adams crying out for help against three Union soldiers who he said were robbing him. Tourgee said that Adams "was loading them with imprecations of unique and vigorous character." "Their conduct and his condition seemed to justify the charge," said Tourgee, and having been a prisoner of war who had suffered the same conditions, Tourgee intervened. As the three skulkers melted away, the lieutenant and an assistant loaded Adams onto a horse. Adams at first tried to resist, saying that moving him was too dangerous, but Tourgee felt like it was a ploy to stay behind and hopefully be rescued by a friendly unit. Tourgee noticed that Adams' wound had been dressed and thus his reason not to be moved must have an alternative reason. Although angry at first for being moved, Adams became thankful, considering the circumstances he faced all day of being robbed of his belongings. He wanted to give Tourgee something as a token of his appreciation, but the "damned rascals had not left him even a sleeve-button"; all of his personal belongs had been taken. Adams offered a button off of his coat and told Tourgee that if he were ever in Adams' position in the war, then he was to present this button and Adams promised to see to his care personally. Tourgee, in return, offered General Adams his knife in which to use in cutting tobacco while a prisoner.[25]

Meanwhile, Gibson was aiming for the "favorable ground" the Washington Artillery was deployed on to rally his mangled regiments. Upon taking command of the brigade and seeing it hopeless to stand near Kelly Field, Gibson placed the retreat north of the three Louisiana units in the hand of Gober. Gibson and staff members then went about trying to rally and form a new line behind the small hill Slocomb stood on. The brigade's assistant inspector general, Captain John Labouisse, and Gibson rode forward and, with the help of Slocomb, were able to help rally parts of Stovall's regiments to the east of the road. Labouisse was then sent to recall Austin and Kimball's units. Austin had spent the time during the attack "watching the movements of the enemy's cavalry." Austin had partially beat Labouisse to the punch. Seeing elements of the brigade filtering from the woods south at a high rate, he foresaw the desperate need to send organized support to protect Slocomb's guns. He quickly sent Major John Kimball and his 32nd Alabama and Captain Andrew Handley's company of the 19th Louisiana to support the Washington Artillery. Pulling back, Austin threw himself into position on the far right of the brigade. The remainder of the brigade used him and the 32nd Alabama as a guide point to rally, reform and lay low as the enemy drew closer.

Following hard on the heels of the Louisianians was Stanley's brigade. First Lieutenant Adolphe Chalaron of the Washington Artillery saw Adams' horse "dash riderless and madly out past our guns." It was foreshadowing of what else was to come out of the woods. A couple of hundred yards to the south, men

Second Lieutenant Thomas M. Blair, 5th Company Washington Artillery. Slocomb's Battery saved the Louisiana Brigade from destruction after its repulse from Kelly Field. Lieutenant Blair was one of the gunners killed protecting his brigade on 20 September (courtesy Louisiana Historical Association collection, Manuscripts Collection 55, Series 55-FF, Photographs, Louisiana Research Collection, Tulane University Libraries).

were pouring out of the woods heading north toward the battery. Slocomb patiently allowed the retreating regiments to take refuge before he unleashed the power of New Orleans. Slocomb pounded Stanley as he emerged from the wood line of the McDonald Farm, only a few hundred yards distance. Stanley stopped immediately and quickly withdrew under the heavy fire. The Washington Artillery then became the target of several Federal batteries around Kelly's Field. In the ensuing firefight, alone and facing at least three enemy batteries, the 5th Company lost 8 men killed, 16 men wounded and 13 horses. With his ammunition almost used up, Slocomb received permission to retire to the rear. The Washington Artillery's stand allowed the Louisiana Brigade to avoid a complete disaster by a counterattack of parts of at least four enemy brigades. Austin was recalled and redeployed on the brigade's right. With the brigade's guns safe and the regiments rallied, Gibson pulled back to McDonald Farm.²⁶

As the brigade fell back, Austin's battalion was detached to assist General Forrest in retarding the arrival of enemy reinforcements from Rossville Gap. Austin remained with Forrest for most of the day and, when ordered to rejoin the brigade by Breckinridge, Forrest refused to release the battalion until it was relieved by another unit. Austin was not relieved until 10:00 P.M. and didn't rejoin the brigade until the morning of the twenty-first.²⁷

John W. Labouisse, 13th Louisiana. Labouisse was promoted to the staff of the brigade by the time of Chickamauga and received praise from Gibson for his performance at that battle (courtesy of Confederate Memorial Hall Museum, New Orleans).

The brigade rested before it was ordered farther to its left to about where the brigade started its day. Breckinridge's division was reformed behind Walker's corps. Walker had moved up during the fight and was facing southwest toward the Federal line surrounding Kelly Field. Breckinridge placed his division about 600 yards behind Walker. Reaching its new position, safe from enemy fire, Gibson had the brigade stack arms and rest. There the brigade sat while Slocomb replenished his caissons from the captured guns near the McDonald Farm, and Austin's battalion maneuvered in the woods on the far Confederate right.

Stovall's and Adams' flank attack was the catalyst that led to mass confusion in Rosecrans' army and opened the door for a smashing, successful attack on the Union center. To meet the threat on his left, Rosecrans detached several brigades. At 11:00 A.M., Rosecrans mistakenly ordered a division out of line in the middle of his front to reinforce his left. Coincidentally, at 11:10 A.M., the long awaited Confederate attack began. By 1:00 the entire Federal center and right wing had been routed off the field or pushed north. To capitalize on the situation, Bragg attempted to put pressure on the Federal left again.

Bragg ordered Polk to push the right wing into action about 2:00 P.M. What next transpired was the epitome of the problems that plagued the Army of Tennessee. Bragg ordered the right wing to attack and, for hours, absolutely nothing transpired. As wing, corps and division commanders squabbled and argued about gaps in their lines and proper line of attacks the hours of the day slipped by. This gave the Federals time to stabilize their line.

By 3:30 the attack was still slow in coming as squabbling prevailed. When the attack finally did start, instead of it being a full coordinated attack, it was disjointed. An attempt was then made to simply wear the enemy's ammunition out. All the while the Louisiana Brigade sat in reserve with stacked arms from about 1:30 to about 5:00.

Finally, a general advance was ordered and parts of four divisions were ordered forward. Sometime after 4:00 P.M., Gibson was ordered to form his brigade and push it toward the enemy line surrounding Kelly Field. As Gibson's men prepared themselves for the advance, Colonel Leon von Zinken reported to Gibson and took command of the 13th & 20th Regiment. Zinken was serving as inspector general for Breckinridge's division and had been active on the battlefield all day. He was aware that Adams' capture forced Gibson to relinquish command of their unit and received permission to relieve himself of his position and take command of the 13th & 20th Louisiana.[28]

The units in Gibson's front (brigades belonging to the divisions of Brigadier Generals St. John Liddell and States R. Gist) advanced in a west to southwest direction so that their attack brought them west across the Lafayette Road, the area that Adams and Stovall reached earlier in the morning. This put Gibson on the front line as it advanced to attack Brigadier General Absalom Baird's division posted around Kelly's Field. Marching in support of Gibson to his left were the brigades of Brigadier Generals George Maney and Marcus Wright of Cheatham's division with Helm's Kentuckians following in reserve. The brigade was arranged as follows for the afternoon attack, from left to right: 13th & 20th Louisiana, 19th Louisiana, 32nd Alabama and 16th & 25th Louisiana. After passing over two ranks of fellow troops from Brigadier General John Jackson's brigade and units of Gist's division, the Louisianians headed back into the fight at about 4:45 P.M. Several batteries were also organized to provide support to the new attack. Whether or not the 5th Company of Washington Artillery took part is not known. The battery rejoined the brigade about 3:30, but whether the battery was deployed to assist in the afternoon attack is not known.[29]

At 4:45, what remained of the Federal army was trying to retreat from around Kelly's Field. The right flank of the Army of the Cumberland was completely shattered, and Major General George Thomas, commanding the remainder of the Federal army in the field, finally ordered a retreat. Starting from the right, each brigade tried to extract itself from the fight. Absalom Baird's division anchored the Federal left. As late as 5:00 P.M., Baird had no idea that the right of the Federal line had collapsed. "At 5 o'clock it [firing to the Federal right] had almost ceased, but I was still ignorant of the course of events upon the right, and had no idea that any portion of the troops had given way. An officer then arrived, with orders ... to withdraw our troops and fall back," reported a surprised Barnes after the battle. Baird's situation became more hazardous when the officer commanding the brigade in the center of his line, Colonel Benjamin Scribner, refused to fall back because he did not believe that the army was in retreat. In the face of an actual coordinated Confederate attack, Baird, along with Colonel Sidney Barnes' supporting brigade to his left, was having difficulty extracting his men. Baird described the situation at about 5:00 P.M.: "Just as this order reached me [to retire] ... another attack, the most violent of all, upon my portion of the line. This time the enemy used artillery, and concentrated the fire of three batteries upon us, while his infantry pressed on with the utmost vigor."[30]

Gibson and his men were completely ignorant of events across the line and farther away on the battlefield. Following Liddell's men, the Louisianians were forced to oblique to the left to prevent themselves from being raked by flank fire from Baird's artillery. The Louisianians moved "slowly, carefully, and with all precision" toward the enemy's breastworks, with

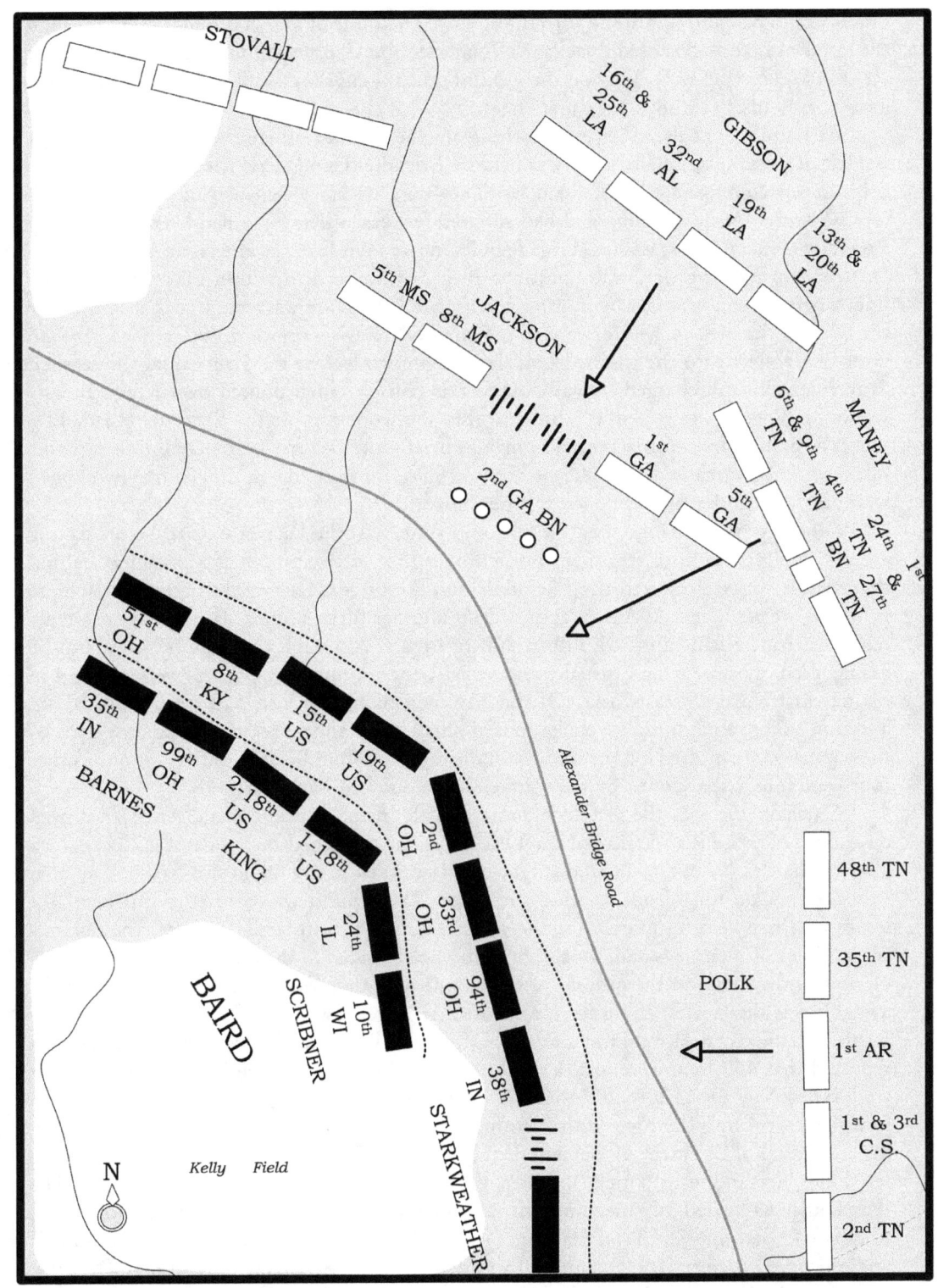

Afternoon Attack, 20 September, 5:00 P.M.

orders not to halt and return fire with the enemy. Their line of march brought them through the ranks of Ector's Texans and Jackson's Tennessee and Georgia regiments. Passing through Jackson's men, who were lying on the ground exchanging shots with Baird's line 150 yards away, the Louisiana troops were met "heartily" with cheers.[31]

As Baird's right flank began to retire from the field, as ordered, Gibson's brigade hit the left of Baird's line. Baird's left was held by Brigadier General H. King's brigade. King's brigade was composed of U.S. Regulars. The Regulars had been instrumental in Helm's repulse earlier in the morning and had suffered few casualties. King had been able to stop Brigadier General John Jackson's brigade in its tracks soon after the afternoon assault began. "Moving in perfect order," the Louisiana Brigade advanced to within 60 yards of King's line, when Gibson was met by a "most terrific fire." The line wavered, but "cheered on by the officers, the men rushed forward to the charge." King's worn down brigade was able to pour two volleys into the thinned Louisiana regiments before the Louisianians unleashed "a terrific yell" and charged forward. As fast as Gibson's men poured over King's breastworks the Regulars retreated at a full run into the woods across the Lafayette Road. Elements of Baird's division attempted to make a brief stand behind their second line of works but were quickly brushed aside. In the ensuing fight, the excited von Zinken had two horses shot out from under him as he led his men forward.[32]

Gibson pursued King's men for 50 to 60 yards past the Lafayette Road before calling a halt. The 13th & 20th Regiment poured over the works and left 150 prisoners behind them as they chased the retreating Regulars into the woods. During the night, thirty more prisoners were taken, and Austin rounded up another fifty the next day. Gibson excitedly reported that he had captured 300 to 400 prisoners. Although that number seems to be exaggerated, most of King's casualties, especially the numbered captured, were suffered in his retreat from the breastworks. Of the 839 men that King lost, 523 were captured. In addition, Gibson captured several hundred small arms and at least six cannons. Two of these guns were captured by Austin early in the morning from Bridge's battery, and the other four were found abandoned by von Zinken as he pursued King's brigade.[33]

Chickamauga was the second bloodiest battle in the entire war and left both armies devastated. Private R.L. Lafitte of the 19th Louisiana described the scene of Chickamauga after the battle: "I saw the awfullest sight that I ever saw in my life in this battle. The men was piled up on top of one another for miles. The ground was covered with them like leaves." Lafitte went on to describe the wounded in the rear of the lines near the doctor's tents: "Piles of men, legs and arms high as my head almost ... the doctors would cut them off and throw them on the ground just the same as if they were throwing pieces of sticks away. It was the hardest thing for me to see that I ever saw before." Brigade losses at the Battle of Chickamauga were tremendous. Of the 1,314 men carried into the battle, Gibson reported that 429 men were lost, a total of 32 percent of the brigade. Most of the losses were suffered by the 13th & 20th, 16th & 25th and the 19th Regiments. The 13th & 20th Louisiana went into the right with 275 men and lost 16 killed, 64 wounded and 44 missing for a total of 124 men; 45 percent of the regiment. The 16th and 25th Louisiana mustered 293 men and lost 110 men (16 killed, 63 wounded and 31 missing) or 36 percent. The 19th Louisiana fielded 349 men and lost 28 killed, 106 wounded and 19 missing for a total of 153 or 43 percent. The 32nd Alabama (4 wounded), Austin's battalion (6 men wounded) and Slocomb's battery (11 killed and 20 wounded) casualties totaled only 41 men.[34]

Possibly the greatest loss to the brigade was the wounding and capture of Dan Adams. The wounded general was carried back to Chattanooga where he underwent surgery on 23

September. A combination of Bragg's friendship with Adams and Bragg's intense dislike for Gibson prompted Bragg to attempt to secure Adams' exchange following the battle. On 28 September, Bragg wrote to Rosecrans requesting the parole and return of Adams. Adams' wound, though, precluded his removal from the U.S. Hospital in Chattanooga. Rosecrans replied to Bragg's letter the next day apologizing for not being able to exchange Adams due to the severity of his condition. Writing to his wife, on 27 September, Adams was nonetheless positive about a quick recovery from his wound: "The surgeon thinks I am doing very well & I hope, in fact feel that I am." It would take four weeks after Adams' surgery for him to be sent through the lines with his parole. To Bragg's chagrin, Gibson remained in command of Adams' brigade. Adams went to La Grange, Georgia, and had to wait for almost another year before he was exchanged and made available for duty. "Old Pelican" never returned to his Louisiana Brigade. Instead, once exchanged, Adams served, for the remainder of the war, in the Department of Alabama, Mississippi and East Louisiana, where he commanded a brigade of cavalry. He ended the war at Meridian, Mississippi, where he was paroled on 9 May 1865.[35]

Chickamauga was the greatest victory of the war for the Army of Tennessee, yet it became the catalyst that would engulf the high command of the army into its own civil war, one that would affect Randall Gibson. The Army of Tennessee, rocked by two days of the bloodiest fighting it had yet experienced, was in no shape to organize an effective pursuit of Rosecrans. Not until mid-afternoon of 21 September was the army set in motion in pursuit of Rosecrans, who by this time was digging his army in at Chattanooga. The march on Chattanooga was very slow, taking two days to complete. By 23 September, when the Army of Tennessee reached the Chattanooga Valley, the Army of the Cumberland was already dug in around Chattanooga.[36]

CHAPTER 8

Chattanooga Campaign: September–December 1863

"I do regret exceedingly, my dear, to have to inform you of our severe reverse, which the Army of Tenn. met with at Missionary Ridge. In fact to tell the plain and simple truth we were completely whipped and route from a strong position on the Ridge, which ever one thought almost impregnable against any Yankee force that Gen. Thomas could send against us."
— Sergeant James Christian, 16th & 25th
Louisiana, Co. G, 7 December 1863

Bragg mulled over what to do next: Prepare for a siege? Encircle the city? Cross the Tennessee River and cut off the city? Order an all-out assault on Rosecrans's trenches? Despite several meetings with his top subordinates to discuss the army's next move, Bragg never developed a sound plan for the retaking of Chattanooga. Bragg's indecisiveness became a rallying point for the anti–Bragg faction of the army. On 4 October, Lieutenant Generals James Longstreet, Simon Buckner and D.H. Hill organized a petition to President Jefferson Davis calling for the removal of Bragg from command of the army. In all, twelve officers signed the petition, Gibson being the only officer below the rank of general to do so.[1]

President Davis was so concerned about the petition that he immediately made a special trip to the siege lines around Chattanooga. On 9 October, Davis arrived at Bragg's Headquarters and began to investigate the situation. Gibson took advantage of Davis's visit to try to get his case for promotion directly to the president through Breckinridge. "As a sensitive man General, I begin to feel as if the failure to promote was equivalent to censure, and that I ought not to continue much longer in the position I have so long held," wrote Gibson. "I appreciate the indelicacy of this communication but experience has taught me that we must lookout [illegible word] for ourselves and the severe blows I have received while seeking to serve my country, I think justify me in the endeavor to gain a position which will enable me to ward them off." Officers of the Louisiana Brigade drew up their own petition on behalf of the young colonel. Initiated by von Zinken, and signed by fifteen other officers of the brigade and later endorsed by Adams and Breckinridge, the following petition was forwarded to the president:

> We the undersigned officers having long been associated with Col. R.L. Gibson, 13th La. Regt, now in command of the Louisiana Brigade, Army of Tenn., respectfully recommend him to be appointed Brigadier General.
> He is the oldest officer of his rank by far in commission from Louisiana & we deem it but right while expressing our confidence in him as commander & our cause sense [sic] of his long

service constant devotion to duty & in our view of the conspicuous gallantry & skill which has characterized him on the battlefield to commend him to the President as are officers justly entitled to promotion.[2]

If Breckinridge ever brought Gibson's case before the president, or if the president received the petition from the brigade is not known. Perhaps Davis did not take Gibson's case into consideration because, before leaving Chattanooga, he had decided to keep Bragg in command of the army. Perhaps Davis thought it especially inappropriate for one of the petitioners against Bragg to be promoted. Following the departure of the president, Bragg took revenge against the officers who spoke out against him. He either transferred officers to other departments or punished them during a reorganization of the army. To break up the blocs of generals who were against him, Bragg implemented a massive reorganization of the army on 12 November. The Louisiana Brigade was separated from its old division, a solid force of the anti–Bragg faction. The brigade was attached to Major General Alexander P. Stewart's division. Leaving Breckinridge's division meant that the 5th Company and the brigade would be separated from each other. The separation caused "quite a commotion," and Colonel Wesley Winans of the 19th Louisiana drew up a petition asking that the brigade and the battery remain together. Nothing came of Winans' petition. "I was sorry to leave our old division," E.J. Ellis of the 16th Louisiana wrote, "but I believe Gen Bragg knows best and acts for the best." Bragg's intentions were not "for the best" as Ellis naively believed.[3]

There were more immediate effects on the brigade's structure in the reorganization. The 32nd Alabama was transferred out of the brigade and placed in the Alabama brigade of Henry Clayton. In Clayton's brigade, the 32nd was consolidated with the 58th Alabama. To fill the vacancy left by the 32nd, the 4th Louisiana Battalion was assigned to Gibson.[4]

Private James Deas, 32nd Alabama. Chickamauga was the last battle in which the 32nd Alabama served with the Louisiana Brigade. The regiment served with the brigade from Murfreesboro through Chickamauga. Private Deas' youth disguises the fact he served in all the regiment's battles with the Louisiana Brigade. During the Siege of Chattanooga the 32nd Alabama was transferred out of Gibson's brigade (courtesy of Alabama Department of Archives and History, Montgomery).

The 4th Battalion was under the command of Lieutenant Colonel John McEnery. The thirty-year-old Virginia native became an adopted son of Louisiana at the age of two when his family moved to Monroe, Louisiana. At age 14, McEnery was sent north for schooling at Hanover College in Indiana and then returned to Louisiana where he graduated from the University of Louisiana in New Orleans with a law degree. Politics became his interest. McEnery served on the Ouachita Parish Police Jury and was even appointed to serve in the State Land Office in 1857 by President James Buchanan at the age of 24. He served in this position until the start of hostilities in 1861. This tie or connection to the land office was because of his father, Mathew McEnery. Mathew McEnery had been serving in the register of land office in Monroe of which he was appointed to by President John Tyler in the early 1840s.[5]

When the war started McEnery helped to organize the Ouachita Blues and was elected captain. With the mad rush on Louisianans to get to the front before the war was over many companies did not organize into regiment, but rather, were shipped to the front as independent companies. The Ouachita Blues was one of these companies. When it reached Richmond, Virginia, it was a homeless unit until the 4th Louisiana Battalion was organized. The unit was organized in Richmond on 10 July 1861 with a total of five companies mustering in 561 men. Four of the five companies were from North East Louisiana, and the fifth company, Company E, was from Natchez, Mississippi. The 4th Battalion was the only unit of the brigade that was not formed in Louisiana.[6]

Its record up to November 1863 proved to be unique in relation to its sister units, as well. Upon being formed in Virginia, it remained in that state through early 1862. Up to that point the battalion did miscellaneous duties around Richmond like guarding Libby Prison and serving as President Jefferson Davis' bodyguard. The 4th Battalion saw the elephant during brief service in western Virginia during the fall of 1861. From Virginia the battalion was transferred to the Department of South Carolina, then to Georgia and on to Florida. During their bouncing around between Savannah, Georgia, and Wilmington, North Carolina, a fifth company was attached to McEnery's battalion, the Ouachita Blues. The Blues were organized in the spring of 1862 and were sent east to join McEnery. The vacation on the coast ended with U.S. Grant's bold move on Vicksburg in the summer of 1863. The Fourth was part of the relief force that was pulled together at Jackson, Mississippi. It was sent as part of Colonel C.C. Wilson's Georgia Brigade and once at Jackson it was attached to Major General W.H.T. Walker's division.[7]

In the Jackson and Chickamauga Campaigns the 4th Battalion served with Wilson's Georgia Brigade. The Battle of Secessionville was the only serious engagement the battalion had been in prior to this time. Although only lightly engaged prior to Chickamauga, the battalion proved its fighting spirit. Take the situation of Private Thomas Henderson of Company A. He was captured during Chickamauga, but after his brigade was able to rout the enemy that had just captured him, Henderson was able to make his escape, pick up one of their rifles and then, in turn capture six of his former captors.[8]

When the battalion was attached to Gibson, it was a shadow of its former self because of the Battle of Chickamauga. Private John McNeil of Company A was on detached duty during the Chickamauga Campaign and did not rejoin his battalion until 18 October, during the Siege of Chattanooga. McNeil described his unit: "I am now with the Batt., what is left of it, about one-hundred in camp. We lost twenty-seven of our Company.... The highest Officer in our Company is Third Sergeant." H.J. Lea of Company F of the battalion said, "Having lost in battle every commissioned officer, killed or wounded, except one lieutenant," Gibson had to appoint Major Samuel Bishop of the 20th Louisiana to temporary command and Captain John McGrath of the 13th Louisiana as his second in command. Chickamauga was only a foreshadowing of what was in store for the 4th Battalion outside of Chattanooga.[9]

Frustrated by the whole series of events while under Bragg's command, Gibson considered resigning from service. He wrote his cousin, an aide to President Davis, William P. Johnston: "It was only the hope that Genl Bragg would be removed that delayed me taking this step but since it is now clear that he will remain with the Army of Tenn and that so long as he commands I shall be Kept in exile, I feel that this or resignation is the only course for me to take. Under no circumstances could I ever serve under him again." In fact, the day before the reorganization of the army, Gibson wrote Cooper asking to be transferred to the Trans-Mississippi Department. Before Cooper could reply to Gibson's request, the siege of Chattanooga had begun to fall apart, and military events in the last week of November forever changed Gibson's difficult situation with Bragg.[10]

While Gibson battled Bragg, the men of his brigade spent their time battling the conditions around Chattanooga. Following Chickamauga, the Louisianians settled into camp outside Chattanooga in Chattanooga Valley between Missionary Ridge and Chattanooga Creek. Chattanooga Creek ran down the middle of Chattanooga Valley and emptied into the Tennessee River at the base of Lookout Mountain. A Louisianian noted that rations were cooked at the wagons, five miles away, and "of course the food is always cold" and "I hear but little complaints except when the rations are short which is (I regret to say) frequently the case." "The army was diminished daily by sickness brought on by insufficient and poor food," remembered a Louisiana veteran after the war. Worse, the men were still without tents. To protect themselves from the rain, the men "split boards and made shanties." Without tents, the men made small, very crude log cabins to protect themselves from the rain. Another Louisianian described to his wife, "It is extraordinary to see two armies such as ours confront the other in plain sight, and no one fire a shot; the guards talk and exchange newspapers, and nothing disturbs our tranquility except an occasional bomb which falls in our vicinity." Captain John McGrath said that his men, only 100 yards apart on the skirmish lines, openly traded with the Yanks, "the boys exchange tobacco for coffee ... they meet the yankees at night."[11]

The conditions around Chattanooga demoralized the Louisianians. Desertion while on picket duty proved a routine problem. Alfred Lacey Hough of George Thomas' staff wrote to his wife, "We had yesterday 11 men from one Company of Louisianians come to us, they all say that thousands would come in if they dared make the attempt." It's probable that the group of deserters was from the 13th & 20th Louisiana. The regimental rolls show that at least 12 men deserted to the enemy while on picket duty during this time. During this same two month period the 16th & 25th Louisiana showed only one deserter, Austin's battalion had two and the 19th Louisiana had four. Fraternization with the enemy pickets did not dissuade this practice. While on picket duty one Irishman from the 13th Louisiana discovered that the enemy picket across from him was an Irish friend serving in an Ohio regiment. From their conversation, he learned that his cousin was also serving in the Ohio regiment. Permission was granted, and the Louisiana Irishman was allowed to visit his friend for half an hour. A deserter from the 32nd Alabama, Thomas Kearney, attested to the condition of his regiment, and possibly the brigade, to his captors: "As far as my acquaintance goes, the men are very much disheartened. Would take peace on most any terms. A great many of the men of my regiment's terms of service will be out in a few months, and the men will not stay any longer in the service. A number that I know would leave now, but as their time is so near out, they prefer serving their time out. We get about the same rations we have had.... Our division has not been paid off for five months." Gibson was forced to address the high desertion rate with an order in early November that drastically changed procedures for the skirmish line. Men were forbidden to cross skirmish lines anymore and anyone who did was to be arrested. Also, whole companies no longer went out on picket duty but rather one officer picked men from different companies, and an additional officer was given the assignment of constantly patrolling the different outposts.[12]

On 1 October Gibson wrote the assistant adjutant general of the army urging the return of all men detached from his brigade. "I beg to bring to your earnest attention the condition of the Louisiana regiments of this command," Gibson wrote. "There are now more men serving in this part of the Confederacy outside these regiments than with them.... If this be not done, these regiments must disappear." Gibson was very affirmative in his letter, possibly trying to state the fact that his brigade was in bad shape. The 13th & 20th Regiment did not muster even 200 effective men for service by November. By the end of November, Gibson would be able to muster fewer than 800 men for battle.[13]

During late September, October and early November, while Bragg contemplated what he should do against Chattanooga and battled his own officers, the Federals busily worked to rescue the Army of the Cumberland and Chattanooga. U.S. Grant had personally arrived in Chattanooga determined to expel Bragg from the area. Instead of spending needed time tightening the noose around Chattanooga and developing strategically placed trenches, the siege was neglected. Worse, Bragg spread his army too thin. The main Confederate line, which ran from Lookout Mountain two miles below Chattanooga across Chattanooga Valley to Missionary Ridge, covered a distance of about four miles. The right of Bragg's line rested at the north end of Missionary Ridge, at Chickamauga Creek. Along this entire line, Bragg had only seven divisions of infantry, less than 40,000 men, to defend his line and to conduct the siege of Chattanooga.[14]

On the night of 23 November, it became evident that Grant was threatening both ends of Bragg's line—at Lookout Mountain and at the north end of Missionary Ridge. To meet the pressure on the right, Bragg pulled Walker's division from its line in the Chattanooga Valley. Stewart's division was the only division deployed between Chattanooga Creek and Missionary Ridge. Deployed in a single rank, Stewart covered about two miles of ground, dangerously overstretched. Gibson did not hesitate to notify Stewart of the problem: "The troops of this brigade will not more than cover the line of the entrenchments from the artillery to the creek upon our left; even then, they are not all formed in two ranks." Gibson further warned that, because the brigade was reduced in numbers, half of the brigade would be on picket duty which would leave the left flank near Chattanooga Creek vulnerable. In addition to not having enough men, the Louisianians were placed behind "very inferior works" and did not have any proper entrenching tools.[15]

Despite the danger that loomed, Gibson's brigade was posted as skirmishers 1,200 yards in advance of the division. With the fight for Lookout Mountain taking place, the brigade remained on picket duty until just before dawn of the twenty-fifth, when Gibson received orders to retire to Missionary Ridge. With Lookout Mountain taken by the Federals on the twenty-fourth, Bragg recalled all his forces in Chattanooga Valley and Lookout Mountain to Missionary Ridge. Major General Carter Stevenson's and Brigadier General John Jackson's divisions were relocated to the northern end of the Confederate line. With the 16th & 25th Louisiana in the lead, Gibson retired to Missionary Ridge. Stewart placed his divi-

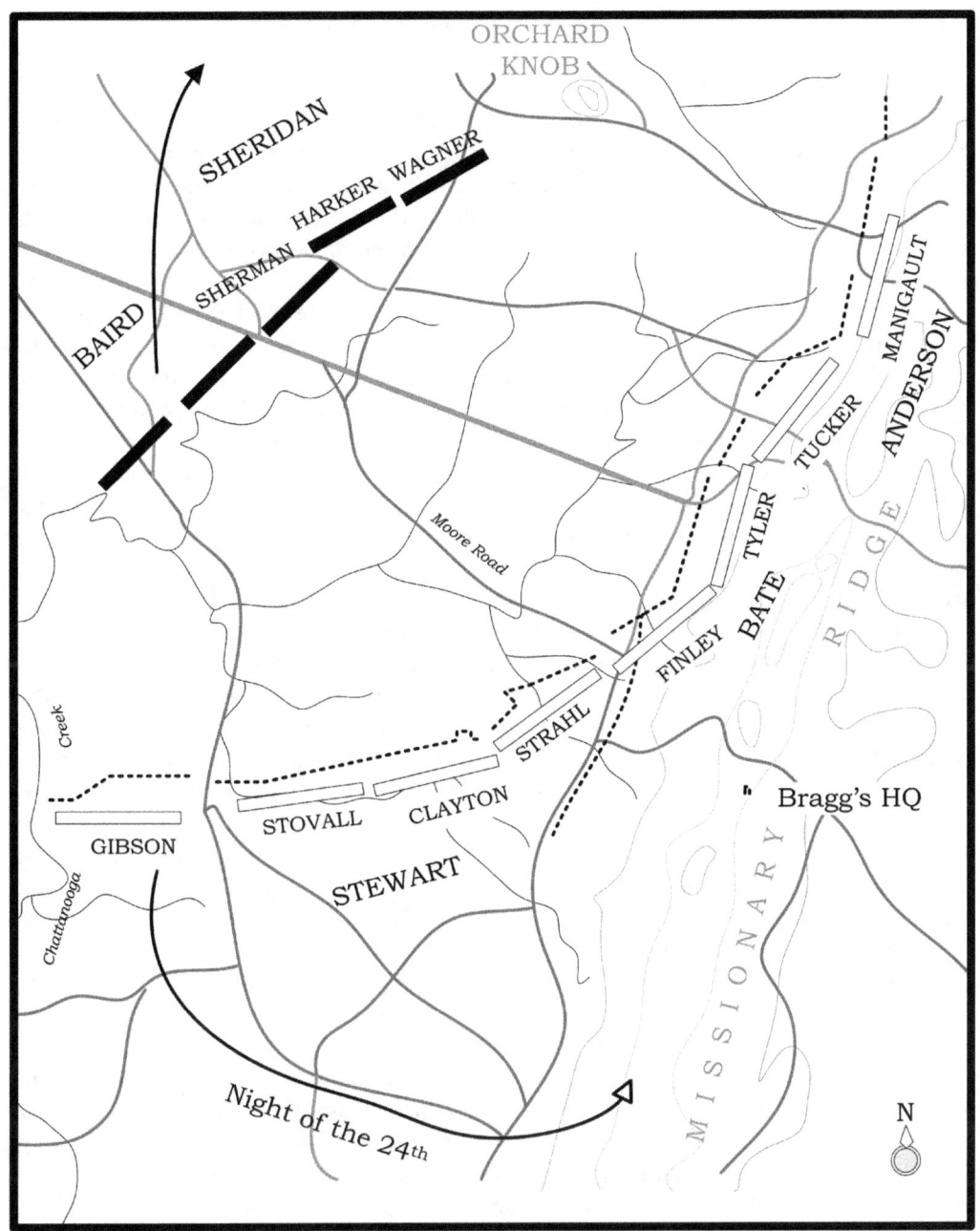

Chattanooga Area, 24 November 1863.

sion along the south end of Missionary Ridge with orders to hold the ridge from Moore Road to Rossville Gap, a total of two miles. Stewart's 4,979 men had to hold two miles of ground while Bragg had massed the rest of his army, over 30,000 men, north of Moore Road to defend just four miles of the ridge. Once atop Missionary Ridge, Gibson was placed on the left of Stewart's line. The Louisianians stacked their arms near Breckinridge's headquarters on the south end of Missionary Ridge and proceeded to cook the five days' rations supplied to them the day before.[16]

Around 1:00 P.M., Gibson was ordered to proceed farther up the ridge and report to

Brigadier General James P. Anderson, who was commanding Thomas Hindman's division. Anderson was posted in the middle of the Confederate line, north of where Moore Road crossed Missionary Ridge. After a march of about a mile, Gibson reached Anderson and was placed on the left of Anderson's line. Problems began to arise concerning the deployment of units along Missionary Ridge next to Moore Road. William Bate's division, posted to the south of Moore Road, with its right resting on the road, was ordered to move right so that it could fill a gap between his and Anderson's divisions. While shifting right, Bate came upon Gibson and halted to see if he was to form on Gibson's left. Gibson had to be pulled out of line, let Bate's men file past, and march back to his left and reform on Bate's left. All of these movements were taking place as Grant's forces were advancing across Chattanooga Valley. Peter Cozzens described Bragg's quick reaction on 25 November: "Nearly two months of benign neglect gave way to a few hours of frenzied improvisation."[17]

The shuffling of units put Gibson on the south side of Moore Road, with his right resting near the road in front of army headquarters. Given the area that he had to defend, Gibson formed his entire brigade into a single rank and moved into line along the crest of the ridge. Sitting to Gibson's right was Captain Robert Cobb's Kentucky Battery, which had been deployed in front of Bragg's Headquarters at the Moore House. From right to left, Gibson's brigade was aligned as follows: Austin's battalion, 13th & 25th Regiment, 4th Battalion, 19th Regiment, and the 16th & 25th Regiment on the extreme left. To help strengthen the line, a section of artillery was placed between the 4th Battalion and the 13th & 20th Regiment. Altogether, Gibson had only 764 men present in the line. The only cover available to protect the men was "incomplete and hastily-formed breastworks composed of logs and a little dirt." Worse, the right side of the brigade didn't have the luxury of even that modest cover. The last minute deployment of the brigade did not allow Gibson time to properly deploy his men. Army headquarters actually sat on a large swell in the ridge and, thus, practically blocked Gibson's view of his left flank when on his right and vice versa. It was a very difficult situation to coordinate the actions of five regiments deployed in a single rank snaked along the ridge.[18]

Matters along the Confederate left-center were further confused by the defensive scheme developed by Breckinridge and Bragg. Not only was the Confederate line spread too thin but orders were given that regiments, or parts of regiments, were to be deployed at the base of the ridge while the remainder of the units were deployed at the top of the ridge. To complicate the defense of the ridge more, units posted at the base of the ridge were not to give stiff resistance to the enemy. Instead, they were to fire one volley and retire up the ridge and rejoin their units. The splitting of brigades only disrupted unit cohesion and the command structure and thinned out the Confederate line even more. When Bate was redeployed north of Moore Road, the units of his division posted at the base of the ridge, the 1st & 3rd Dismounted Florida Cavalry, 4th Florida and 7th Florida of Brigadier General Jesse Finley's brigade, were given orders by Breckinridge to remain in position. So when Gibson was deploying his regiments in front of army headquarters, the three Florida regiments were deployed at the base of the ridge to his front. North of the road were deployed the remaining units of Finley's brigade.[19]

To the left of Gibson was Brigadier General Otho F. Strahl's brigade. Strahl, too, had to post his brigade in a single line. Worse, due to the confusing defensive scheme developed by Bragg and Breckinridge, Strahl only had two regiments on the crest of the ridge with him, the 24th and 19th Tennessee Regiments. Strahl's other regiments were posted at the base of the ridge in front of his position. With so few units to man the crest of the ridge, another gap emerged between Strahl and Gibson. To fill the gap, Lieutenant William McKenzie's Eufaula Battery was placed to the left of the 16th & 25th Louisiana, and a section of McCall's battery was placed to the right of Strahl's right regiment, the 19th Tennessee.[20]

Stewart was present to witness Gibson deploying his brigade in front of Bragg's Headquarters then galloped off to check the left flank further down the ridge. As Gibson was making his dispositions, he noticed that the Federals began their advance in the valley toward the ridge. Also, the 13th and 20th Louisiana and Austin's battalion were suddenly marching to the right oblique, away from the brigade front. Gibson rode to investigate. The gap from Moore Road to Gibson's right was supposed to have been filled with units of Bate's division but were kept north of the road to plug other gaps. As the Louisiana Brigade was moving into line, officers of Bragg's staff ordered Gibson's right two regiments to fill the gap. This forced Gibson to reposition the rest of his units farther to the right to complete the line. This last minute change by Bragg left a large gap of about 100 yards from Gober's 16th and 25th Louisiana with McKenzie's Battery and Strahl's right. Stewart, who had ridden south to check other brigades, was never notified of the change.

Advancing toward the Confederate center along Moore Road was the division of Major General Phillip Sheridan. Directly across from Gibson was Colonel Charles G. Harker's and Colonel Francis T. Sherman's brigades. Harker's brigade, nine regiments strong, was deployed into three lines. Sherman, with just as large of a brigade as Harker, was also deployed in five lines. The eighteen regiments of Harker and Sherman numbered around 6,000 men. To the right of Sheridan was the division of Brigadier General Richard W. Johnson. Johnson's left brigade, in line to the right of Sherman, was Colonel William Stoughton's 1,500 muskets. Facing these odds were Strahl's 974 men and Gibson's 764 men, a total of 1,738 men. Deployed at the last minute, overstretched in single ranks, protected by "temporary breastworks" and outnumbered 4 to 1, the odds were not stacked in the Confederates' favor.[21]

At about 3:00 P.M. Sheridan's division began its advance across the 800-yard open field to the base of Missionary Ridge. Once clear of the woods, the march across the field was met with shot and shell from the batteries around Bragg's Headquarters. Although not very effective, the fire of the Confederate guns was described as "the most fearful tornado of bursting shells" by Captain Edward Bates of the 125th Ohio. Colonel Sherman referred to the barrage as "a most terrific fire of artillery." Most of the exploding shells, though, exploded above the advancing lines; as one officer put it, "The enemy annoyed us all they could with their batteries." If anything, the exploding shells only increased the anxiety of Sheridan's men of what lay ahead of them. Soon, the march across the field turned into the quick step and eventually a dead sprint for the line of Confederate works at the bottom of the ridge.[22]

Finley's Florida troops put up token resistance, as ordered, and scampered up the ridge as the skirmishers of Harker and Sherman slammed into the first line of works. The Federal skirmish line pushing up the ridge was composed of Harker's 42nd Illinois and three companies from each of Sherman's three lead regiments: 36th, 73rd and 44th Illinois regiments. As the line at the base of the ridge fell apart, the batteries around the Louisiana brigade turned from shot and shell to canister, raking the ridge with a shower of death.

Colonel Daniel Gober and his 16th & 25th Louisiana watched in frustration and horror as the Florida boys in front were gunned down as they ran for their lives up Missionary Ridge. The Louisianians sat helplessly as they watched the Florida regiments in their front get swallowed up by the enemy. One of the Florida regiments in front of the

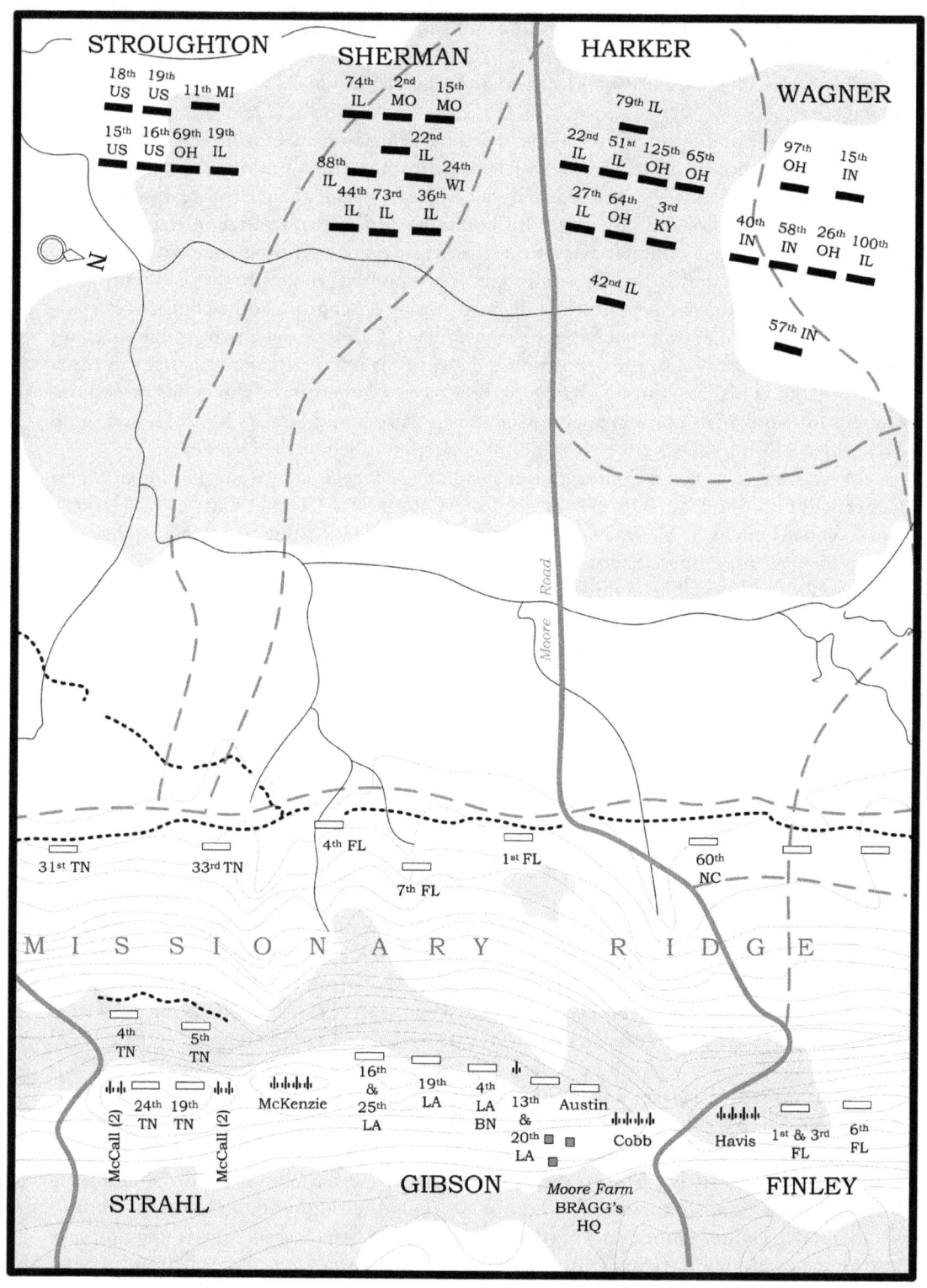

Attack on Missionary Ridge, 25 November 1863, 3:30 P.M.

Louisianians, the 4th Florida, was almost wiped out of existence, escaping up the ridge with only 18 of its 177 men. A large portion of the surviving Floridians made their way up the ridge across the front of Gober and into the gap between Strahl and Gibson. So last minute were the changes on the right of the brigade, the 13th & 20th Louisiana and Austin's battalion were just forming into line on the crest as the enemy skirmishers were already past the first line of works and were pushing up the ridge. "We had scarcely formed," said Major Francis Campbell, "before we became actively engaged with the enemy, whose first line had already cleared the low entrenchments and was well up the slope of the ridge before we had gotten into position."[23]

With Finley's regiments out of the line of fire, the 16th & 25th Regiment prepared "to share no quarter." "As soon as they [Sherman's skirmishers] came in range," wrote Gober, "we opened fire upon them, and the roar of cannon and volleys of musketry for several minutes was truly deafening." The fire was so intense that Gober was forced to repeat his orders to his company commanders in person because his voice could not be heard over the roar of his men's fire. Major John Austin withheld the fire of his little 78 man battalion until the enemy were within 200 yards. Although small in number, Austin's battalion was a unit of handpicked sharpshooters. Their fire was with "great precision and effect." The "enemy wavered and fell back in the most disorderly manner," reported Austin. The roar of the cannons and the intense fire of the Louisianians made calling out orders almost impossible. Because of the intense noise, Colonel Winans of the 19th Louisiana divided his regiment under Captains Winfrey Scott and Michael Person so that they could help repeat the orders that the colonel yelled out. The adrenaline-filled enemy skirmishers pushed to within 200 to 250 yards of the entire line before they were forced to fall back to the second line of works to collect themselves, wait for help and above all else catch their breath after fighting at a run for over a mile. Just as the Yanks were pushed back, Colonel Winans was shot in his neck. Several of his men attempted to see to their colonel, but after a few steps to the rear the young colonel was dead. Command of the 19th Louisiana passed to Captain Scott.[24]

Gibson rode the length of his line urging his men not to waste their shots: "Fire at his feet and to do so carefully and deliberately." Realizing that resupplying the men with ammunition would be almost impossible, Gibson issued orders to "hold the position at all hazards" and to use the bayonet and stones if necessary. Confusion with ordnance officers would prove fatal to all of Gibson's regiments. Almost immediately, once the engagement commenced, there were calls for more ammunition. On 22 November, while Stewart's division was posted in Chattanooga Valley, the corps quartermaster was ordered to bring up wagons to allow the men to cook their rations. Receiving a subsequent order to move the wagons across Chickamauga Creek, five miles away, the quartermaster got confused and immediately withdrew all of the division's wagons, including the ammunition wagons, across the creek. Also, while his brigade was on picket duty on the twenty-fourth, Gibson specifically called for a supply of ammunition but never received it. He did send a detachment to the rear for ammunition, but the only rounds it could acquire were the wrong caliber or were of poor quality powder that only clogged up the guns.[25]

With their skirmishers at a standstill, the successive waves of Harker and Sherman began to cross the first line of works at the base of the ridge. Practically every regiment dropped to the ground at the base of the ridge and took cover in the ditches or in the shanties on the side of the hill as they caught their breath after their quick march to the ridge. The rest was but a few minutes, and then the advance up the ridge began. Once the different lines slammed into the works at the bottom of the ridge and began their attack, any semblance of regimental identities quickly dissipated. John Shellenberger of the 64th Ohio described the situation: "The two lines were intermingled without regard to regimental or company organization." Captain Samuel Rexinger of the 15th Missouri said, "Here our lines became broken on account of the obstacles, and we struggled up the hill as best we could, each man for himself." Major Campbell of the 13th Louisiana described it best when he called the fused advance of some 18 to 20 regiments in his front a "moving mass of beings."[26]

Sheridan's units became more intermingled as they attempted to use whatever cover they could find to shield themselves from the Louisianians' fire. "The whole mountain seemed to vomit forth grape, canister, and musket balls," remembered the famed Colonel Emerson Opdycke of the 125th Ohio; whose regiment advanced against the left of Finley and right of Gibson. About 250 yards from the base of the ridge was a second line of works that seemed to stretch across the front of Gibson and Strahl. This turned out to be a rallying point for retreating skirmishers and for the advancing regiments to stop and rest. From that point to Gibson's line, the ridge was at a 40 degree angle. An officer in Sherman's brigade described the situation: "The men took advantage of all obstacles in the way for shelter, and thus advanced steadily toward the top of the ridge. The fighting fierce and severe, but owing to the formation of the ground my men were able to screen themselves partially from the deadly volleys that were being hurled at us at every step of our advance." "At several points along the line my troops were ascending the hill and gaining positions less exposed to the enemy's artillery fire," was how Major General Gordon Granger described his men's advance against Gibson's line. In Austin's front the jumbled units of Harker and Sherman "scattered among trees and rocks," and were "forced to take refuge ... behind all obstacles." The sharpshooters of Austin's small unit put forth a small but consistent and deadly fire.[27]

The intermingled regiments snaked up the ridge in the forms of inverted v's. "Each regiment in following its colors slowly up, got into the form of two sides of a triangle, the apex of which was the flag." There was no organized advance, but rather a race between the color bearers of the various regiments to see which regiment would be the first to reach the crest of Missionary Ridge. Sheridan described the advance: "The right and right center [Harker and Sherman] were approaching the second line ... led by twelve sets of regimental colors; one would be advanced a few feet, then another would move up to it each vying with the other to be foremost." Sherman remembered that the color bearers of his regiments took the lead in the uphill fight, "each bearer wishing to be the first to place the banner of his regiment upon the last of the rebel works." "Each regiment tried to surpass the other in fighting its way up a hill" was the observation of Granger from Orchard Knob in the rear. A Louisianian described the scene before his unit: "They marched right up to our fortifications in seven lines, squalling and yelling like the very devil was after them."[28]

The color bearers, being at the apex of these inverted v's, naturally became targets of the Louisianians. Colonel Gober watched as Sherman's "color-bearers would run from tree to tree until they were in advance and then stick the staff in the ground and lie close to the first object that would protect them ... I heard several men during the progress of the fight cry out, 'There, I killed a flag-bearer! Didn't you see him fall?'" The struggle of the 74th Illinois's flag to make it to the top of the ridge was a prime example of the day's work for Sherman's flag bearers[29]:

> In that charge [Up Missionary Ridge] the new flag of the Seventy-fourth was borne by Chas. E. Allen, of Company E. He soon fell truck by a minie, but the colors had hardly dropped from

his nerveless grasp before they were seized by Alba Miller, of Company C, who carried them but a short distance, when he, too, was hit and severely wounded, and the falling flag was grasped by Corporal Compton, of Company D, who soon after fell, mortally struck, about a rod below the crest of the ridge. The dangerous emblem, which seemed to be a favorite mark for the for the enemy, was snatched from the dying Compton by Corporal Fred Hensey, of Company I, who soon planted it pierced by fifteen bullet holes, upon the rebel works.[30]

With the enemy's first line repulsed and his successive waves beginning to push forward Gibson rode over to the left flank to ascertain the situation. Once there, Gibson met with Gober who was looking to his left flank. Gober pointed out how the enemy to his front were using the ravines and contours of the ridge to make their way toward the Eufaula Battery, which was limbering up and pulling back because it had exhausted all of its 206 rounds of ammunition. Worse, the troops supporting the battery, scattered fragments of the Florida regiments, were close to breaking. There were no men to spare, and Gibson echoed the orders of Stewart and told Gober to "hold on to his position with the bayonet." When the company commanders started calling for ammunition, Gober ordered his company commanders to "let their men use stones until the enemy came near enough and then the bayonet." As Gibson rode back to check on his endangered right, he remembered, "For some time everything went well along the entire line." Not all was well — both flanks were about to be turned, and the men in line were resorting to throwing rocks.[31]

Pushing up the ridge in the face of McKenzie's Eufaula Battery was part of Colonel William Stroughton's brigade. Stroughton, as did Sherman and Harker, divided his brigade into demi-brigades to help make command easier. The left wing of his brigade, the 19th Illinois and 69th Ohio and the 11th Michigan, was under the command of Colonel Marshall Moore. The fire of McKenzie's guns, Strahl's Tennessee boys and Gober's regiment were able to stop the 19th Illinois and 69th Ohio in their tracks, but not for long. McKenzie limbered up and moved his guns off the ridge with Stroughton's men twelve paces away. Once clear, though, the Florida troops were quick to scatter. Despite the attempts of Stewart's staff officers, they quickly crumbled and were swooped up. Stewart was behind Strahl's right regiment, the 19th Tennessee, when the Florida rabble "gave way, and the enemy rushed in taking Gibson and Strahl in reverse." So quick was the breakthrough by the 19th Illinois and 69th Ohio that one of McKenzie's guns was abandoned on the side of the ridge as the men made their escape.[32]

Gober watched in horror as his left was now completely left unsupported. A company from the 16th & 25th Regiment was pulled out of line and thrown perpendicular to the line. Less than a hundred yards to the south were the six hundred rejoicing men of Moore's demi-brigade. Stroughton's regiments reformed themselves and began to flank Gober. The attack on Gober's position was intense, and Sherman's men were pressing hard. So close were Sherman's men to his front that officers were using their pistols, and men "who were without ammunition, with bayonets fixed, held their guns in the left hands and threw stones with their right." Sherman described the fighting: "Every foot being contested by the enemy. Rocks were thrown upon our men when the musket ceased to be of use, but to no purpose." Sergeant James Christian of the 16th & 25th said, "Men actually, after shooting away their last cartridge, gathered up stones and knocked the scoundrels down as they climbed over the breast works." Rocks were no match for a determined foe four times your number.[33]

The 16th & 25th Louisiana was now on the verge of facing destruction. Gober gave the command to retreat, and due to the proximity and severity of the fight, the left wing of the regiment "was almost annihilated" in the attempt to retreat. Sherman reported that,

Captain E.J. Ellis, 16th Louisiana. The very opinionated and patriotic Ellis was captured on Missionary Ridge on 25 November 1863. In one last of defiance before going into captivity, Ellis threw this sword down Missionary Ridge so it could not be won as a trophy (courtesy of Louisiana State University Archives, LSU Libraries, Baton Rouge, LA).

when within ten yards of the Louisianians' line, his men were "thrown forward as if by some powerful engine" and swept the works. In a mad scramble for safety, the color sergeant was shot and captured; three captains and seven lieutenants were also wounded or captured. Captain John Ellis' company was hard to hold in line with all the confusion. Unsure of the course of events to his left, Ellis did not want an unjustified, hasty retreat. The 16th & 25th was about 30 or 40 yards below the crest of the ridge and therefore could not see Moore's units pushing north up the ridge along the crest. Attempting to keep his unit from bolting, Ellis and company were hit from shot from behind, atop the ridge. At that moment Ellis ordered a skedaddle, but it was too late. Ellis and "all but two or three" men of his company were captured. A frustrated and angry Ellis, in "very bad grace" refused to give his sword to a Union officer and threw it down the ridge before surrendering.[34]

As the left flank of the brigade was on the verge of getting turned and destroyed, Gibson was riding over the swell at headquarters to assist the right of the brigade. When Gibson reached the 13th & 20th Louisiana, word came from Major Austin that he was worried about his right flank because the troops north of the road "had thinned out" and "had frequently recoiled." The left flank of Brigadier General J. Finley's Florida Brigade, the 1st & 3rd Florida, was thrown into disarray when the skirmishers at the base of the ridge in his front, the 60th North Carolina, retreated in the face of Wagner's and Harker's brigades. The 60th North Carolina was rallied with some difficulty and pushed into action on the left of Finley between Cobb's battery and Finley's left at the Moore Road. Finally, it was sent north along the ridge, making Austin even more anxious. Austin was not impressed. It was "clear to his mind that they would give way altogether before long," and he requested help in securing his right before the units to his right gave way. Gibson took Company B of the 13th & 20th Louisiana on the extreme left of the regiment and redeployed it on the right side. Captain Eugene Blasco's company was also the largest company of the 13th & 20th, so Gibson was able to extend his right and help close the gap between Austin and Finley.[35]

Corporal Elias Murphy, 16th Louisiana (courtesy of L.F. Jacob).

The detachment of Blasco's company, the largest in the regiment, simply put more strain on Major Campbell's command to cover its overextended front. Ammunition for the 13th & 20th Regiment was in such short supply that the men were hurling stones like Gober's command, "those of my command who had exhausted their ammunition assisting their comrades by hurling stones down the ridges." Suddenly, Finley's 1st & 3rd Florida broke to the rear "without waiting to come to a hand-to-hand encounter." Harker's right, led by his 64th Ohio and 125th Ohio and Sherman's left 36th Illinois and 22nd Illinois, pushed into the gap aiming for Cobb's guns. While steadying Campbell's and Austin's men, Gibson witnessed the gunners to the left of Campbell's regiment breaking to the rear. Due to the concave shape of his line and the outbuildings from Bragg's headquarters Gibson was totally ignorant of events on his left. Gibson rode down the line and went to push the gunners back into place but he witnessed the men of the 74th Illinois of Sherman's brigade pushing through gap left by the 4th Battalion and artillerists. Colonel Jason Marsh of the 74th Illinois reported that he was shocked to find that when his men finally reached the crest, the Confederate line crumbled: "For some unaccountable reason they either fled or surrendered instantly upon the first few of our men reaching them, not even trying to defend their battery."[36]

Once Gober was flanked from his position, each successive unit was forced from their positions or be captured. Captain Scott of the 19th Louisiana was directing the fire of his unit in an oblique right angle and appeared to ripping into the flanks of the 44th and 88th Illinois Regiments with some success. Scott was proud of his momentary victory: "Our men were ready for them and gave them a right oblique fire, which they were not able to stand." Colonel George Chandler and his 88th Illinois were forced to drop to the ground, take cover and wait for help to push against the 19th Louisiana before they could proceed. The help was not long in coming. Captain Scott said, "No one seemed to dream of being driven from our position" until he heard the calls for retreat to his left and then saw the left wing of his regiment in full retreat. The exasperated captain attempted to rally his men at the top of the ridge behind their line "but found we were under an enfilade fire," and Scott ordered his men "to get from there as quick as possible."[37]

Major Samuel Bishop's 4th Louisiana Battalion was next. It appears that the 4th Battalion was not heavily engaged during most of the battle. This is most probably due to the geography of the ridge, which funneled the climbing columns in other directions. Bishop said his battalion was in a "position of watchfulness" until he saw the 19th Louisiana breaking to the rear and the regiments of Moore and Sherman pushing up the ridge. "I discovered the entire left giving way and three of the enemy's colors in the rear of the regiment ... which broke, as did I, in considerable disorder." Private Zachariah Smith of the 4th Louisiana Battalion remembered, "Our left gave way the Yanks were coming in pretty fast and in a few minutes the whole left give way and regular run commenced ... it appeared a marecal how any of us got out of such a shower of bullets." The rout was on. The breakthrough of Stoughton's and Sherman's men now threatened Campbell with capture. The routing of Finley's brigade left Austin totally exposed to a conglomeration of units from both Harker and Sherman.[38]

In Bate's report of the battle, he alludes that his left was turned. This suggests that the Louisianians failed to hold their part of the line, which resulted in Bate's flank being turned. "In seeking to rally the right I did not see the exact time when the flag went up at the left of General Bragg's headquarters," wrote Bate. The position he wrote of, "at the left of General Bragg's headquarters," was the position held by the Louisiana Brigade. To help clarify this point Bate refers to the reports of his subordinate commanders. Reports from Austin and Gibson clearly state otherwise but it's the report of Phil Sheridan that helps clarify the problem: "When I crossed the rifle-pits on the top the Confederates were still holding fast at Bragg's headquarters, and a battery located there opened fire along the crest, making things most uncomfortably hot." Sheridan goes on to describe the fight around Bragg's headquarters as the Confederates' "last position."[39]

The 13th & 20th Louisiana and Austin's battalion were the last two units that remained in line. It was the stand of these two regiments in front of Bragg's headquarters that Sheridan spoke of. The battery unleashing hell on Sherman's and Harker's men was Cobb's battery to Austin's right. Realizing capture was imminent, the two units were ordered back. Gibson and his staff assisted Austin and Campbell in rallying their units in the rear of Bragg's headquarters and prepared for a counterattack. Captain Stuart of Gibson's staff grabbed the Hardee flag of the 13th & 20th Louisiana, and with Gibson at his side, they began to lead the reformed regiments forward. Major Campbell rode up to inform Gibson that his right was turned and now taking enfilading fire. After just a few steps, Captain Stuart tapped Gibson on the shoulder and pointed to their left. Just fifty yards to the south was a Federal battle line marching at right angles to his left, across the crest of the ridge. Both of Gibson's flanks were by then turned, and the enemy was swarming in his rear. "If the command had remained a minute longer, it [would] have been captured." "I saw then that instant retreat was necessary, that nothing could be done," Gibson wrote after the battle. The command began to fall back in confusion, leaving behind hundreds of men to be captured. Men were streaming down the hill in every direction. Also, in the confusion, the 15th Indiana of Wagner's brigade captured the colors of the 13th Regiment. The 13th's was the first flag of the Louisiana Brigade to be captured in the war.[40]

The retreat of Gibson left the gunners of Cobb's Kentucky Battery on their own. Cobb's guns were recorded by several attackers for the intense and deadly fire they subjected the attackers to. When the crest was reached, Cobb's guns became a target for all the regiments to aim for. Elements of the 64th Ohio, 125th Ohio and 36th Illinois were the first to hit the battery. The Kentuckians proved to have as much fight in them as their guns unleashed

13th Louisiana's Hardee Flag captured by the 15th Illinois at Missionary Ridge (courtesy of the Chicago Historical Society).

earlier. Outnumbered and outflanked, the battery was captured after a quick and deadly hand-to-hand fight.

While the brigade was retreating down the Crutchfield Road, Gibson was not to be found. Gober believed Gibson had been captured and took command of what remained of the brigade. At a small ridge about a 1,000 yards to the rear of Missionary Ridge, Gober reached a rear guard being formed under the direction of Bate. Gober rallied as many men possible from the brigade and put them in line supporting Captain Slocomb's gunners of the Washington Artillery. The 5th Company lost all six of its guns on Missionary Ridge and commandeered two abandoned cannons. In almost a prophetic manner, when the Washington Artillery and the brigade had been separated in Bragg's reorganization in November, the artillerists had been told by their fellow Louisianians, "Boys, you will lose your guns to-day; we will not be there to stand by you." Major Austin said after the war that when he met up with Slocomb he said, "Well, Ned, I have lost my guns for the first time.... If your battalion had been there, it would not have happened." With a handful of ammunition, a determined Slocomb told Austin, "I will right here on this hill, wipe out what happened on the other."[41]

The details of the rear guard are sketchy and surrounded by controversy, but it appears as though Bate was able to rally remnants of Finley's brigade to the left of the Crutchfield Road and Tyler's brigade to the right. The actual placement of the two guns under Slocomb and where the pieces of the Louisiana Brigade reformed are not clearly described. According to the report of Major Campbell of the 13th & 20th Regiment the Louisianians were placed in support of Slocomb's left piece. Bate also reported that part of Adams' command was to the left of his position. Gober lent some men to Slocomb to assist in manning the guns and dispatched Austin to the front as skirmishers.[42]

The Louisianians were not long in waiting. After taking Missionary Ridge Sheridan set about organizing his mingled command to pursue the chaos in front of him. "His disorganized troops, a large wagon train, and several pieces of artillery could be distinctly seen fleeing through the valley below within a distance of half a mile." "It was with difficulty that we could sufficiently control the men so as to reform our lines, and follow up the retreating foe," remembered a rump seared Harker. Joining in the "unbounded enthusiasm" after taking the ridge Sheridan and Harker both jumped on and straddled two guns from Cobb's battery. Unfortunately for Harker his gun was searing hot from having just been fired resulting in his uniform being singed and preventing him from riding a horse for two weeks. Each passing moment that his division celebrated only gave time for the Confederates to reform, and Sheridan knew it. Elements of Wagner's and Harker's brigades were sent down the Crutchfield Road in pursuit. Harker, now disabled from his "famous artillery ride," sent Colonel Opdycke with his demi-brigade in pursuit.[43]

It looks as though when the various regiments from Harker and Wagner hit Bate's ridge, only token help was given by Opdycke. Colonel Henry Dunlap of the 3rd Kentucky, part of Opdycke's command, boasted that they "speedily drove them after considerable firing." The hour long fight was more intense than Dunlap let on. Two regiments of Wagner's brigade bore the brunt of this fight, the 97th Ohio and 40th Indiana. Their memory of the rearguard stand was a little more descriptive. Colonel John Lane of the 97th Ohio remembered, "It was apparent from the murderous fire to which we became exposed that the enemy had chosen a strong position and intended to maintain it … we could not advance without almost certain destruction. The fight continued over an hour, resulting in the loss of a large proportion of those counted in the aggregate of killed and wounded." Lieutenant Colonel

Elias Neff echoed Lane: "The battery had been placed in position here by the enemy, and was vigorously worked during our advance. To storm the hill with the force we then had was clearly impossible.... The rifle-balls passed in almost every direction, front and flanks ... it seemed certain that annihilation or capture awaited." Neff reported that 45 percent of his losses in the Battle of Chattanooga were from the firefight at sundown. Gober testified to the intensity of their stand: "We kept up the fire until we checked the advance of the enemy and exhausted the ammunition we had picked up on the roadside."[44]

Wagner's two regiments, slightly supported by various regiments or parts of others, were in a desperate situation. To dislodge the Confederates, Wagner sent the 26th Ohio and 15th Indiana on a flank attack. The right of the line was turned by these two regiments and quickly retreated from the ridge. Colonel Gibson returned to the brigade sometime before the flank attack hit. When the order to retreat from Missionary Ridge was given by Gibson, he rode to the left of his line, being ignorant of events because of the terrain, to attempt to rally the men there: "I determined to go off to the left where I presumed the left regiments would be found." In the process of trying to rally his men, Gibson got separated from most of the command. After little success, Gibson rode to the right toward the Crutchfield Road where he "heard the cannon." He reached the brigade at sundown and Wagner's flank attack after the sun had rested to the west.[45]

The brigade fell back to Chickamauga Creek where General Stewart deployed the brigade to the left of the road to help form a rearguard for the rest of the army to retire. After remaining in line in the shivering cold, the brigade was allowed to retire across the creek and continue its retreat for another hour to Chickamauga Station, where it was allowed to rest. Finally, the Battle of Chattanooga was over for the Louisiana brigade.[46]

Colonel Wesley Winans, 19th Louisiana. Winans was killed on Missionary Ridge steadying his men against Sheridan's attack. Winans was the highest ranking officer killed during the battle (courtesy of the Horner Family).

The Battle of Chattanooga was the worst defeat the Army of Tennessee had suffered to date. The losses in Gibson's brigade were heavy. Of 760 men that fought in the battle, 33 were killed, 88 wounded and 232 captured for a total of 363 causalities. The 13th & 20th Louisiana fielded 212 men and lost 3 killed, 23 wounded and an estimated 83 were captured for a total of 109, over 50 percent losses. The losses of this regiment exemplify how casualties were low until they were torn off the ridge. Major Campbell attested to this fact when he reported that, in the retreat, his "loss was far heavier than it had been during the whole previous engagement." Out of the 244 men in the 19th Louisiana, 7 were killed, 23 wounded and 13 missing for only 43 casualties. Austin's battalion of 78 men lost 9 killed, 20 wounded and 31 captured for an amazing 79 percent loss. Symbolic of Austin's terrible losses was the death of the battalion's color bearer, Thomas Willbanks, who was "obliterated" by an exploding shell. The 4th Battalion lost 5 men wounded and 28 missing for a total of 33 men.[47]

Included among the dead was Colonel W.P. Winans of the 19th Louisiana, killed at the front of his regiment. Winans' body was left on the field due to the sudden collapse of the Confederate line. General Hardee sent inquiries across the line to Thomas' army looking for Winans' body. Being the highest ranking officer to die in the battle on the Confederate side, he would be hard to miss or get confused with other fallen officers. Most likely, Winans' personals were stolen off his body, much the same way that Adams was robbed three months prior at Chickamauga.[48]

In camp in Dalton, Georgia, after the battle, Gibson sat down and wrote his report of the battle: "The officers and men all did well whilst on their fields.... I sincerely believe it was reserved for Missionary Ridge to witness the best fight this command ever made." The Battle of Chattanooga, though, proved to Gibson's benefit. Following the battle, Bragg did not hesitate to tender his resignation as commander of the army. Trying to ease his friend's misfortunes before the catastrophe on Missionary Ridge, William Johnston wrote to Gibson, "B. cannot last forever. he is too complete of a failure. Hold on grimly. Do your duty & all will be well." Johnston's prophetic words came to fruition after Chattanooga with the appointment of Joe Johnston as the new commander of the Army of Tennessee.[49]

CHAPTER 9

With Joe Johnston: December 1863–July 1864

"We are still quietly resting in our winter quarters, waiting for the spring campaign to open with its qualifying marches and honorable battles. We anticipate a very active campaign in the department next summer, which the Generals are making great preparations to me."
—Sergeant-Major Robert W. Wells, 4th Louisiana
Battalion, 14 February 1864

From Chattanooga, the Army of Tennessee limped thirty miles to the southeast into Dalton, Georgia, where it spent the winter of 1863 and 1864. Following Braxton Bragg's resignation, Randall Gibson's friends pushed in earnest for his promotion. Louisiana Confederate congressmen bombarded the secretary of war with letters. Daniel Adams, who had been pushing for Gibson's promotion for a year, sent another letter of recommendation dated 8 December. Attaching their names to the new recommendation were Alexander Stewart, William Hardee and John Breckinridge. D.H. Hill sent his own letter of recommendation on 9 January 1864. Marcellus Stovall sent another recommendation in January of 1864, endorsed by Thomas Hindman and Joseph E. Johnston. Johnston's support for Gibson's promotion came with a single statement: "I believe that Col. Gibson deserves promotion," and it was quick in forthcoming. On 25 January 1864, James Seddon relented and recommended Gibson's promotion to brigadier general. On 1 February, the Confederate Congress approved Gibson's promotion with his rank to date from 1 January.[1]

Gibson's promotion secured his position as commander of the Louisiana Brigade. Following Bragg's resignation on 2 December command of the army was temporarily turned over to Hardee. Davis offered Hardee permanent command of the army, but he declined. On 16 December Davis ordered Johnston to Dalton to take command of the Army of Tennessee. Johnston immediately tried to improve the condition of the army: furloughs were granted and winter quarters were ordered built. On 14 December the brigade was up to 682 effective men. There was a serious shortage of small arms, only 416, most having been thrown away while retreating from Missionary Ridge. Worse, there were 553 pairs of shoes reported as "actually needed." The *Mobile Advertiser* printed a request to Louisiana refugees living in Mobile, "in behalf of the soldiers of Adams' Louisiana Brigade," urging them to form a relief association to provide the destitute men with clothing and shoes. The *Daily Constitutional* of Augusta, Georgia, repeated the plea for shoes in March saying 500 men were "suffering for shoes." Supplies were rolling in, though, to re-equip and clothe the men after the rough months of September through November. The equipment of the regiments was also seriously depleted and in disarray. Quickly, though, the brigade was reequipped and rearmed. For example, on 1 December the 13th & 20th Louisiana received 200 sets of accoutrements, 324 knapsacks, 300 haversacks, 315 canteens, 315 straps and 20 rifle muskets. In April the 16th Louisiana received 25 Austrian rifles with bayonets, 8 cartridge boxes, 30 belts, 41 cap pouches, 30 bayonet scabbards, 26 waist belts and 2,000 rounds of cartridges.[2]

The months spent relaxing helped the sick and wounded return to duty; perhaps Johnston's furlough policy induced more men to remain with their regiments once they had been allowed to visit their families. The brigade's strength began to steadily rise as each month passed. From mid–December to the beginning of May, Gibson's effective strength rose from 682 men to 917 men. A soldier in the 19th Louisiana wrote home hoping the Confederate Congress would "order out 100 000 negroes" to replace the losses the army had suffered. Despite the losses and defeats incurred, the morale of the brigade increased during the winter. "We are all in good spirits and good condition," boasted a Louisianian. Another soldier told his friends at home, perhaps to ease their war weariness, that "the condition of our army was never better than it is now. The health of the troops is very good. And all are inspired with patriotism anew." John McGrath of the 13th Louisiana relates the mood well to his wife: "It is now three years since I have buckled on my armor and joined the army ... although I have endured the hardships ... and yet I am ready and willing to struggle on, fight on until our independence is achieved." Another Louisianian said defiantly, "We are not, we will not be whipped. Liberty and independence must be will be ours." Meetings held by the individual companies of the 19th Louisiana, where they held votes of unanimous consent to reenlist "for the war," showed signs of "reanimation" and determination. Morale was on the rise.[3]

Conditions were improving and the spirit of the men was exhibited in a massive snowball fight on 22 March 1864. It was somewhat a rematch of a similar battle the Louisianians fought during the winter of 1862–63 at Murfreesboro between their division, Breckinridge's, and Cleburne's divisions. On this particular snowy morning the Louisianians found themselves gripped in an epic battle against their former division, now under the command of Bate. The morning started with a skirmish of fighting between the Mississippi and Alabama gunners of Major J.W. Eldridge's Artillery Battalion. Fighting to an impasse, the two batteries joined forces against Captain Charles Fenner's Louisiana Battery. Fenner's Battery was a veteran group formed from the ashes of Dreaux's old 1st Louisiana Battalion. It had only recently joined the Army of Tennessee and this was no doubt a welcoming from their comrades. Just as all groups had fought to a standstill the deadlock was broken "...when, looking down the road in our rear, we saw two regiments of infantry [the 16th and 25th Louisiana], approaching us rapidly and fully armed for the fray. They came over for the purpose of whipping out Fenner's battery." The batteries rallied to Fenner's side and made a stand. A Mississippian of Stanford's Battery recalled, "The conflict was a desperate one," and resulted in another stalemate. A truce was called and an alliance was made to unite forces to strike the nearest camp. The rest of the Louisiana Brigade was called to arms and with snowballs filling every arm and haversack, the Louisianians and Eldridge's Battalion, "formed in line of battle and deployed skirmishers in front." It seems the feisty Louisianians had provoked a major engagement with their attempt to joyfully "welcome" Fenner's Louisianians to the army. Deserters seem to have spread the word, for when the invaders approached the camp of Brigadier General Thomas Smith, of Bate's Division, the

Tennessee and Georgia boys were formed in a line of battle and armed with snowballs. Smith was soon joined by Kentuckians from another camp which resulted in the mustering of Stewart's entire division. By the end of the day the Louisianians were masters of Smith's camp. It was a great escape from the reality of war and reflected a psychological recovery from Missionary Ridge. The Mississippian who recounted this event summed up his impression of the day's battle: "Our army here is in splendid fighting trim. Full confidence is felt in our gallant commander. The troops are in good spirits, and their physical condition unsurpassed. If the Yankee host of Thomas see fit to try our mettle, they will find us ready, and will assuredly meet with something warmer than a snowball reception."[4]

Another major morale booster was a revival that swept the South in the winter of 1863 and 1864. It is believed that the defeat at Chattanooga was such a psychological blow to the Army of Tennessee that it never got over it, and thus the ground

Brigadier General Randall L. Gibson. Once Bragg resigned as commander of the Army of Tennessee, Gibson received his long sought promotion to general (courtesy of Confederate Memorial Hall Museum, New Orleans).

was ripe for revival. John B. McFerrin was one of the rods that stoked the growing religious revival in the army since mid–1863 and was especially active at Dalton. In reference to Chattanooga, Mcferrin said, "The army of Gen. Bragg never overcame the demoralization of that day.... Nowhere else in life have I ever witnessed to wonderful a revival as that at Dalton from December, 1863, to May, 1864." Again, the very descriptive John McGrath shared information on this within the Louisiana Brigade: "A revival took place in this army this spring and a majority of the troops joined the church and now where ever you turn you see soldiers holding prayer meeting. The other day I was passing along the fortifications and saw a regiment formed in Columns of Companies with their flag and music, kneeling in prayer appealing to the Throne of Mercy.... Was it not a beautiful sight to see those stalwarth warriors with uncovered head and bended knee."[5]

Bringing the brigade's strength up was in part due to the attachment of another regiment to the brigade, the 1st Louisiana Regulars. This regiment had been organized on 5 February 1861 with Henry Gladden as its colonel and Daniel Adams as lieutenant colonel. The regiment was transferred to Confederate service on 13 March and sent to Pensacola, Florida. The regiment remained at Pensacola until February of 1862, when it was ordered to proceed to Corinth, Mississippi, to be part of Bragg's relief column. The regiment left Mobile in late February and arrived in Corinth in early March. In the organization of the Army of the Mississippi, the Regulars were attached to General Gladden's brigade, Jones Withers' division of Polk's I Corps. When at Corinth, men of the regiment proved very creative in getting their hands on whiskey, something long denied while at Pensacola. J.E. Carraway of the 19th Louisiana relates how "our Irish" were responsible for creating havoc in Corinth. He blames most of the problems on the Irish of the 1st Regulars, "composed exclusively of Irish." "Pandemonium reigned and the sleeping officers and men were ordered from their slumbers into line, and the cause of the warwhoops investigated." Martial law was declared because of problems from the whiskey, men were bucked and gagged, thrown into the guardhouse, and force was used to find out how so many men were able to get their hands on whiskey. It was found out that the men crawled under saloons and bored holes in the floors until they penetrated the floors where the barrels of liquor sat. Kettles were used to carry the drinks but were too small for what the barrels held. "The barrel having in it rather more than the kettles would hold, they undertook to drink the overflow and save the kettles for future use. The overflow being enough to make all hands drunk, drunk, drunk."[6]

The regiment remained part the first brigade of Withers' division up through early 1863. In that time period the regiment fought at Shiloh, in the Perryville Campaign and at Murfreesboro. On 10 January 1863 the regiment was put on provost duty, which it performed until 25 August when the Regulars were temporarily consolidated with the 8th Arkansas of Cleburne's division. Following the Battle of Chickamauga, the regiment was separated from the 8th Arkansas and returned to provost duty, mainly guarding army headquarters. The effective fighting strength of the regiment had been depleted by January of 1864, when it had dropped to only 57 effectives. The regiment's commander at that time, Colonel James Strawbridge, wrote to Samuel Cooper asking the regiment be allowed to go back to Louisiana to rebuild, a request that was denied. By early April its effective total had risen to 100 men. On 16 April at the request of Gibson, the 1st Regulars were attached to his brigade.[7]

When assigned to the brigade, the Regulars were under the command of S.S. Batchelor. Batchelor was a dentist turned warrior. He served as captain of Company H from the start of the war until February of 1863; he was then appointed major. Taking command of the regiment was risky business. The unit's previous commanders all ended in unfavorable conditions. The regiments' first colonel, Henry Gladden, was promoted to brigadier general and was killed at Shiloh. His replacement, Daniel W. Adams, was wounded in the eye at Shiloh and later promoted. Lieutenant Colonel F.H. Harrar Jr. led the Regulars at the Battle of Murfreesboro and was mortally wounded and died. The regiment's colonel, John Jacques, faced a court-martial and was cashiered in early 1863. Upon the dismissal of Jacques, Major James Strawbridge was promoted to colonel and was later captured.[8]

The attachment of Batchelor's small unit could provide only small relief to the inability to rebuild the strength of the Louisiana Brigade. A major obstacle to regaining losses from the campaigns in late 1863 was the breakdown of the prison exchange cartel between the two sides. In previous battles the Louisiana regiments always saw the return some of

Samuel L. Bishop, 20th Louisiana (right), is pictured with two fellow Confederate officers (courtesy of Confederate Memorial Hall Museum, New Orleans).

their missing losses by the paroling and exchanging of prisoners. Men captured at Shiloh, Corinth and Perryville were mostly exchanged from October through December of 1862 with some of these men rejoining the ranks in time to fight at Murfreesboro. The large number of men captured at Murfreesboro were exchanged between March and May of 1863 and rejoined the ranks for the Jackson Campaign. These patterns of exchange did not fit the mold for every soldier captured but it was the predominant trend by a large margin for each campaign.[9]

Events changed in mid–1863 and the cartel was ended. From that point forward men captured were not exchanged. Instead, they were sent north to remain in northern prisons. This was a devastating blow to the Louisiana Brigade in its ability to maintain its numbers. The reason being is that the campaigns of 1863 saw a large number of men captured: Jackson (close to 300), Chickamauga (95) and Chattanooga (232). Faced with long prison terms more and more men turned to taking the oath to the U.S. government and thus ended their fighting careers. They also turned to galvanizing—enlisting in the United States armed forces. The city companies showed a tendency to galvanize whereas the country companies were less likely. The result is that throughout the war small numbers from the 16th, 19th and 25th Regiments switched sides and joined the enemy. The immigrant filled city companies of the 13th and 20th Regiments and Austin's battalion (the remnants of the New Orleans based 11th Louisiana) yielded larger numbers of galvanizers. Of the three latter units an estimated 387 took the oath and of that number 180 galvanized. That is in contrast to the northern and rural regiments which saw around 72 men take the oath and about 61 galvanize. Most of the Louisianians who chose to wear the blue enlisted in the U.S. Navy or in U.S. Frontier Regiments. There were a few isolated units they joined such as the 34th Kentucky, 7th Indiana Cavalry, 12th Michigan Battalion and even a group of Germans from the 20th Louisiana joining the ranks of the heavy German roster of the 32nd Indiana Infantry. Longer spans in prison also resulted in many deaths from disease while prisoners of war and was also a catalyst that encouraged galvanizing. All of these factors led to a serious drain on the Louisiana regiments to replenish themselves in the last two years of the war.[10]

Another drain on the manpower of the brigade was the rising number of men who remained in Louisiana while on furlough. It was a temptation that many men succumbed to and joined other units closer to home. For example, Lieutenant James C. Murphy of Company G of the 13th Louisiana tendered his resignation from his regiment as an officer so he could enlist as a private in a cavalry company based in Louisiana. Others, such as Colonel Gober, sought transfer and received it through official means. Beginning in February of 1864, Gober, with the aid of General Gibson, began pushing for his promotion to general. This push was quickly endorsed by generals who were commanded by Gober in the past such as Daniel Adams, John C. Breckinridge and Patton Anderson. Gober penned his frustration and true intentions to Louisiana's representative from Gober's St. Landry Parish and a former member of the 18th Louisiana, Lucius J. Dupré: "I want it distinctively understood that I am not fighting for promotion if I had had no higher aspirations than that I should have remained at home with my family; but at the same time it is humiliating to know that two of my juniors have been promoted over me. There are some two thousand Louisianians in Leiut. Genl. Polk's department, in brigades from different states. Is it not due the state of Louisiana, that these troops should be put in a Brigade made up exclusively of Louisianians?" From February through April the push went from Gober's trying to obtain a promotion to his transferring closer to home. Gober partially succeeded by being ordered to report to Polk's Department of Alabama, Mississippi, and East Louisiana, with his assignment being the collection of absentees from the ranks of the regiments in Gibson's brigade. Finally, on 3 May while on duty in East Louisiana, Gober received a telegraph from Polk assenting to his request to serve in the department and raise troops for operations in that area. Gober immediately began the recruiting of a regiment of

James Lingan, Austin's battalion. Lingan joined Austin's battalion from the 11th Louisiana in August 1862 until his wounding and capture at Ezra Church (courtesy of Jack McCormack).

mounted infantry, which became known as Gober's Regiment. Gober served the remainder of the war in the East Louisiana region serving in several different units with his men until their surrender in May of 1865. After the war, Gober made his way to Kentucky where he practiced medicine until his death in 1889 in Frankfort, Kentucky. Gober's departure left a void to be filled in his regiment, something common with several of the regiments at this time. Command of the 16th & 25th Louisiana fell upon Colonel Joseph C. Lewis of the Twenty-Fifth. Commissioned lieutenant colonel of the 25th Louisiana when it was formed, he became the commanding officer of that wing of the 16th & 25th Regiment when Stuart Fisk was killed at Murfreesboro.[11]

The command structure was more complicated for the 13th and 20th Regiments. From rolls and reports of the brigade it appeared as though the 13th and 20th Regiments began the spring campaign independently again. Beginning on 17 April and throughout the entire campaign, they appeared separately on morning reports. Increased numbers on their rolls was not the reason for separating the units again. Their combined total as of May was only 148, and this was well below the 16th & 25th and 19th Regiments, which fielded 233 and 278, respectively. Exact reasons are unknown for the justification of reestablishing the units, but what is known is that both regiments entered the field with new commanding officers. The Gibson–von Zinken era at the command of the consolidated 13th & 20th Regiment came to an end at the beginning of 1864.[12]

The 13th Louisiana's new commanding officer was Major Francis Lee Campbell, recently promoted to lieutenant colonel. Campbell was twenty-five when the war started and was a native of South Carolina from a family with a rich history. Young Campbell attended the United States Military Academy in Maryland and, by the outbreak of the war, was in New Orleans enlisting in Aristide's and Avegno's battalion of Zouaves. Campbell started the war as a captain in the 13th Louisiana and was wounded in the shoulder at Shiloh. In December 1862, Major Stephen O'Leary retired and Campbell was promoted to fill his vacancy. Even though Campbell is shown commanding the regiment on at least two occasions, and facing a court-martial for unknown reasons, he managed to retain a relatively low profile. He was not present with the regiment, or not mentioned in any reports, at Murfreesboro, Jackson, or Chickamauga. In November of 1863 he is shown as commanding the regiment and leading it through the Battle of Chattanooga. In early 1864, Campbell began a writing campaign, like Gober, for promotion. The position of colonel was forthcoming to Campbell before the year's end.[13]

Francis L. Campbell, 13th Louisiana. Campbell emerged in 1864 as the new leader of the 13th Louisiana. He began his tenure as leader of the regiment before the Atlanta Campaign and served in that position throughout the remainder of the war (courtesy of Confederate Memorial Hall Museum, New Orleans).

Filling in as Campbell's second-in-command was Captain Edgar Martin Dubroca. Dubroca brought experience to the table for the 13th Louisiana. He had commanded the regiment on several occasions before. He led the regiment at Shiloh after its officers were all wounded; he led the regiment for a significant time during the Mississippi adventure prior to Gibson's return to the unit, and he led the regiment at Chickamauga before Leon von Zinken excused himself from Breckinridge's staff and led the regiment. The 13th Louisiana's original lieutenant colonel, Aristide Gerard, was still detached from the regiment and thus command duties always, not of their rank, fell on the shoulders of Campbell and Dubroca. When Gibson assumed command of the brigade on two different occasions, full command fell on their shoulders: a major and captain doing the duties of a colonel and lieutenant colonel. Dubroca wrote his frustration to Samuel Cooper in August of 1863 and put forth a request for promotion. Gibson did likewise in January of 1864 and had Gerard removed from the rolls and Campbell and Dubroca promoted to lieutenant colonel and major, respectively. Dubroca's promotion was well deserved and long overdue. When Campbell was promoted later in the year, Dubroca advanced in rank also. The 13th Regiment was in solid hands for the remainder of the war with the Campbell-Dubroca combination. Adding to the solid command of the regiment was the promotion of the one legged Michael O. Tracy to major, another outstanding and well deserved promotion.[14]

Leon von Zinken assumed his duties with Breckinridge's staff again after Chickamauga, which left Campbell as ranking officer of the consolidated 13th & 20th Regiment. Once the regiments began operating independently again, command of the 20th Regiment fell on the shoulders of Major Samuel L. Bishop. Bishop, a boilermaker before the war, joined the Twentieth as an officer in the Jameson Light Guards, of which company he became the captain. He was made major of the regiment while at Jackson in 1863. He was absent from Chickamauga, and during the siege, he was appointed temporarily to take command of the 4th Louisiana Battalion, that unit being without any officers due to Chickamauga. By seniority Major Campbell outranked Major Bishop, and thus the command of the 13th & 20th Louisiana Regiment went to Campbell in late 1863 — two majors commanding a consolidated unit. Perhaps Gibson's remedy to a possible officer conflict was to separate the two units, each commanded by a major. There did not erupt an urgency on the part of the officers of the 20th Louisiana as did those of the 13th Louisiana in demanding rectification of positions and promotions. Bishop entered the Atlanta Campaign as a major with Captain Samuel Sutton operating as his second-in-command. Even after Bishop was wounded during the campaign, he was replaced by a captain, and the 20th Louisiana remained to be commanded as such.

The 19th Louisiana's field officers were all killed or wounded at Chickamauga and Chattanooga: Lieutenant Colonel Richard Turner wounded at Chickamauga; Major Loudon Butler killed at Chickamauga, and Colonel Wesley Winans killed on Missionary Ridge. Commanding the regiment in this vacuum was its newly promoted major, Hyder A. Kennedy, who had led the regiment at Chickamauga after Turner and Butler were disabled. Kennedy's family moved from Alabama, where Kennedy was born, to Claiborne Parish prior to the war. When the war broke out, the twenty-

Edgar Martin Dubroca, 13th Louisiana (courtesy of the West Baton Rouge Historical Association).

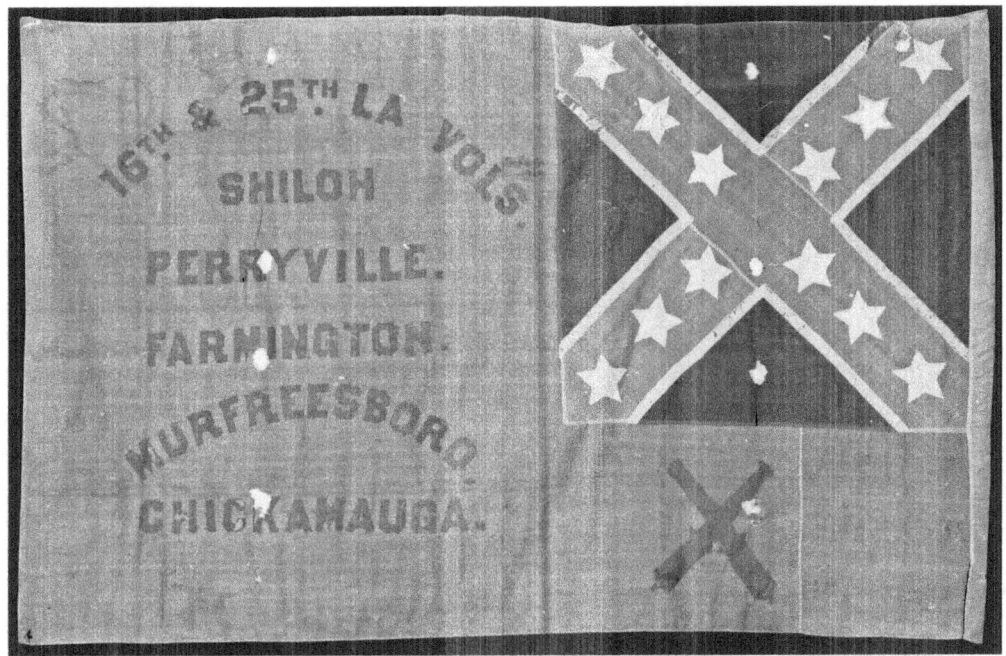

16th & 25th Louisiana's Second National Flag (courtesy of Kentucky Library and Museum, Western Kentucky University, Bowling Green).

one-year-old Kennedy was at school at the University of North Carolina. He made his way back to Louisiana, became captain of the Claiborne Volunteers and mustered in with the 19th Louisiana. Turner healed from his wound, was promoted colonel and retook command in January of 1864. When the campaign began in May, Turner was absent from the regiment "on detached service with the military court" for Hood's corps. Kennedy led the regiment until 13 May upon which Turner returned.[15]

The Louisiana Brigade was witnessing many changes: a new army commander, new corps commander, new units assigned to the brigade (4th Battalion and 1st Regulars), new unit commanders and many promotions for several officers, including Gibson. The Louisiana Brigade was taking on a new look, but the changes did not stop there. Once Johnston took command of the army, he tried to implement a major change, the adoption of a single flag for the entire army. Prior to early 1864, regiments and batteries had carried flags that were designed by their respective corps or department commanders. Polk's and Hardee's former corps each had their own respective flag. When regiments from Van Dorn's and Kirby Smith's departments were eventually added to the Army of Tennessee, they also brought their own flags with them. The reinforcement of Bragg's army in the Chickamauga Campaign brought new flag variants from the Department of Alabama, Mississippi and East Louisiana and the Department of Georgia, South Carolina and Florida. By the time Johnston took command, the Van Dorn and Smith flags appear to no longer have been in use since their respective departments and armies no longer existed. The chaos in Confederate flags in the West was very symbolic of the confusion and chaos that plagued this department through most of the war.[16]

When the regiments had been formed they carried with them the first national flag of the Confederacy. Common across Louisiana, and the whole South, ladies in communities made flags for the departing companies. When the regiments were formed at Camp Moore, or in the New Orleans area, they did not have on hand regimental flags to hand out. Instead, a

Second National Flag of Austin's battalion (courtesy of Confederate Memorial Hall Museum, New Orleans).

company flag was picked and became the flag company. This was almost standard operating procedure early in the war for most units. For example, the 16th Louisiana's regimental flag up through early 1862, and possibly carried at Shiloh, was Company D's First National Flag.

Beauregard attempted in early 1862 to implement a standard flag like Johnston. Coming from Virginia in early 1862, Beauregard attempted to implement what is known as the Cassidy Flag. It was a variant of the St. Andrews's cross flag, the most profound difference being the large yellow bunting border on the three exterior sides of the flag. Between February and through late March, 132 of these flags were ordered for the Army of the Mississippi forming at Corinth. Bragg ordered flags for his men, which included Gibson's brigade, on 8 March. The first to receive these flags were to be Bragg's troops from Pensacola; they were the only force not with a battle flag already. Polk's and Hardee's troops were already bearing their own specific flags. Fifty of these flags were delivered to Bragg, thirty of which were designed for infantry units. Bragg had in his command only 20 infantry units at the time, but by the time of Shiloh it had reached a total of 30.[17]

On 27 March 1862 General Bragg issued an order that said that units were to "furnish each other accurate detailed descriptions of the battle flags in use in their divisions respectively, which descriptions will be read on parade to each regiment, separate battalion and squadron of cavalry, independent troop or company, of their several commands for three successive days, and will otherwise accustom their men to these battle flags, which for the present, must be used." This explains the flurry of accounts in early April in which officers were constantly showing the men the different flags. The three main flags that were paraded around by officers were Hardee's, Polk's and the Cassidy Flag. The Cassidy Flag was also referred to as Bragg's, or Johnston's or the battle flag. There are two documented cases where Ruggles' division was drawn up on 4 April near Monterey and shown all of the different battle flags including "Gen. Johnston's battle flag," which was a reference to the Cassidy Flag. It is documented that the Cassidy Flags were present before Shiloh but an exact date of issuing to the Louisiana Brigade is not documented. In an account on 2 April while marching through town toward Grant's army, a veteran wrote, "They passed headquarters in review of General Johnston and staff the battle flags were given to those who were without them." The Cassidy Flag was carried by the brigade until late 1862.[18]

When the Louisiana Brigade was created in August of 1862, it was assigned to Hardee's corps and remained with that corps until its transfer to Stewart's division in November of 1863. Hardee had been carrying his distinct blue flag with a white oval and border since 1861 and, thus, it would only make sense that the corps quartermaster issue all regiments in the command Hardee pattern battle flags. The only question is when was the Louisiana Brigade issued Hardee Flags? Were they issued at Chattanooga in August or after the Perryville Campaign? That is unknown, but they were issued Hardee Flags. There are two Hardee Flags in existence that bear this testimony: The 5th Company of Washington Artillery and the flag of the 13th Louisiana captured at Missionary Ridge by the 15th Indiana.[19]

The exact date that the brigade was issued Hardee Flags is not known. It is believed they were issued flags before Perryville, but that is not confirmed. Private Jacob Gall of Company D, 19th Louisiana, had a role in making the flags for the corps. In May 1863, he was detached to serve as Hardee's personal tailor. Hardee sent him to Enterprise, Mississippi, to make 34 "Battle Flags" for Hardee's command. This, of course, would have accounted for all the regiments of the Louisiana Brigade.[20]

There are three Union sources that lend evidence to the Louisiana Brigade carrying Hardee Flags from the Battles of Perryville, Murfreesboro and Chattanooga. At Perryville, a member of the 42nd Indiana wrote an article for the *Daily Evansville Journal* in which he described the flags that were advancing on his position as "the blue flag with a single star waved all along their lines." The only regiments across from the 42nd at that time were Cleburne's and Adams' Louisiana Brigade. There were no unit flags with a "single star" but possibly the Hoosier got it mixed up with the white oval in the middle of the flag. All of the enemy flags to his front were Hardee Flags. At Murfreesboro Captain Jerome Cox of the 10th Indiana Battery made this statement as Adams' brigade moved on his position on 31 December 1862: "We held our fire until they were within 400 yards, when we could completely see the devices on their colors." This obviously suggested the oval on the blue flag of the Hardee pattern.[21]

Sheridan's report on the Battle of Chattanooga, prior to the assault on the Confederate line, is another example. He saw enemy regiments across from him, moving from the right to near the Moore Road, "waving their blue battle-flags." The units Sheridan saw moving from his right to the Moore Road were part of Stewart's division. Posted directly south of the Moore Road were three brigades of Stewart's division: Adams's, Stovall's and Strahl's. Prior to the November reorganization, Adams and Stovall were part of Hardee's corps (then under the command of Hill). Strahl had been part of Polk's corps and thus carried the flags of that officer. Sheridan's division made contact with Strahl and Gibson but not with Stovall. Thus, when Sheridan spoke of "blue flags" in his front (moving from the right toward the Moore Road), he must have seen the flags of Gibson's brigade.[22]

The flag that Johnston adopted was a variant of the St. Andrew's battle flag carried by the Army of Northern Virginia. Johnston's new flag was identical to the Army of Northern Virginia flag except in its shape. Instead of being square with fringe, Johnston's flag was rectangular with no fringe and had thirteen stars. Every regiment in the brigade was issued a "Joe Johnston Battle Flag." Confusing Johnston's plan was that units in the Army of Tennessee also began ordering Second National Flags for their units. Gibson's brigade was one that did so in November of 1863 before the Battle of Chattanooga and the reorganization of the army took place. He ordered flags for all the infantry units and the 5th Company. After the reorganization the 32nd Alabama and Washington Artillery were no longer part of the brigade but still received their flags. On the Second National Flags, names of battles and inverted cannons were ordered. It is believed these flags were kept for reviews, or other events, and not carried into battle.

Another twist came in July of 1864 when the 4th Louisiana and 30th Louisiana were attached to the brigade. These two regiments were part of the Department of Mississippi, Alabama and East Louisiana and carried another variant of the St. Andrews flag. It was a square flag with only 12 stars and no bunting. The 4th Louisiana Battalion, which joined the army from the Department of Georgia, South Carolina and Florida, was issued a flag before the Battle of Chickamauga. The flag they were issued replaced the stars and bars, but there is no description included of the new flag. If issued before going to Georgia for Chickamauga, then it would have been a flag similar to the 30th Louisiana's. The 4th Battalion, though, was issued a Joe Johnston flag after its arrival with the Army of Tennessee. The 30th Louisiana, though, carried its Department of Alabama, Mississippi & East Louisiana flag through August of 1864. In that month the 30th Louisiana lost its flag at the Battle of Ezra Church and replaced it with another 12 star pattern flag. Both the 4th Regiment and 30th Battalion are documented carrying 12 star flags as late as December of 1864. The two flags the 30th Louisiana carried in 1864 and the 4th Louisiana's flag were all the same department style, but all three were different. The first of the 30th's flag had "30th La" in inscribed in the middle of the flag, while the flag it carried from early August through mid–December did not have the "30th La." Also, both flags were different with the 4th Regiment's stars gold and the second flag of the 30th Battalion silver. One last difference is that neither flag of the 30th Battalion had battle honors inscribed on them, whereas the 4th Regiment's flag was inscribed with honors for Jackson, Port Hudson, Baton Rouge and Shiloh. Despite the variants that existed, all regiments in the brigade after mid–1864 carried some sort of flag that contained the St. Andrew Cross pattern.[23]

The only break in the monotony around Dalton was a demonstration against the Confederate position in February. Major General George Thomas, having replaced Rosecrans in command of the Army of the Cumberland, created a diversion toward Dalton while Sherman made a major thrust on Meridian, Mississippi. On 23 February Hindman ordered Stewart to deploy his division along Rocky Face Ridge, with his right resting on the gap through which the Western and Atlantic Railroad crossed. A small advance was made on Stewart's position on the twenty-fourth but Gibson's brigade was never involved in any fighting. Only one man was wounded in the brigade during Thomas's brief excursion from Chattanooga. When Austin was sent forward on the twenty-seventh with skirmishers from Stovall's brigade, Thomas had already fallen back to Chattanooga.[24]

In May of 1864 Gibson's Brigade was organized as follows:

> 1st Regulars — Major S.S. Batchelor
> 13th Louisiana — Lieutenant Colonel Francis Campbell
> 16th & 25th Louisiana — Colonel Joseph C. Lewis
> 19th Louisiana — Colonel Hyder A. Kennedy
> 20th Louisiana — Major Samuel Bishop
> 4th Battalion — Lieutenant Colonel John McEnery
> Austin's battalion — Major John E. Austin.[25]

9. *With Joe Johnston: December 1863–July 1864*

Left: 13th Louisiana's Joe Johnston Flag (courtesy of the Museum of the Confederacy). *Right:* 4th Louisiana Joe Johnston Flag (courtesy of Louisiana State Archives, Office of the Secretary of State).

In May, conditions for Gibson's brigade changed drastically. When a Louisiana soldier wrote that "the Spring campaign will soon begin and I tell you we are prepared for it," he had no idea what was in store for him and his comrades. In May, William T. Sherman, leading a combination of three Federal armies at Chattanooga, began an advance on the Army of Tennessee. On 7 May the brigade was called out of camp and ordered to Rocky Face Ridge and posted on the left side of Mill Creek Gap where the Western & Atlantic Railroad crossed the ridge. Sherman continually tested Johnston's defenses on the ridge. Because the brigade was posted near one of the two major gaps on Rocky Face, there was constant skirmishing with Federals for five days. In what became standard procedure for Sherman during the entire Atlanta Campaign, he tested Johnston's defenses, found they were too strong and moved to outflank the Confederate position. On the night of 12 May Johnston began his first retreat, ordering his army to fall back to the town of Resaca. Stewart's division was deployed to the north of Resaca, across the railroad to Atlanta, with his left next to Major General Carter Stevenson's division and with his right resting on the Consauga River. Johnston's army was deployed around Resaca in the shape of an upside down fishhook, facing west and north. On 15 May Stewart was ordered to make a counterattack against elements of Major General Joseph Hooker's XX Corps, which had just been repulsed by Stevenson. Stewart organized his division into two lines, with Gibson being deployed in the second line behind Henry Clayton's brigade. The Confederate attack moved in a large left wheel hoping to catch the flank of Hooker. The attacked ended up being more of a grand maneuver than an attack. Orders soon arrived to call off the

19th Louisiana Joe Johnston Flag. In a postwar photograph the 19th Louisiana's identity is shown in a different manner from both the 4th Battalion and 13th Regiment (courtesy of LSU–Shreveport Archives, Noel Memorial Library).

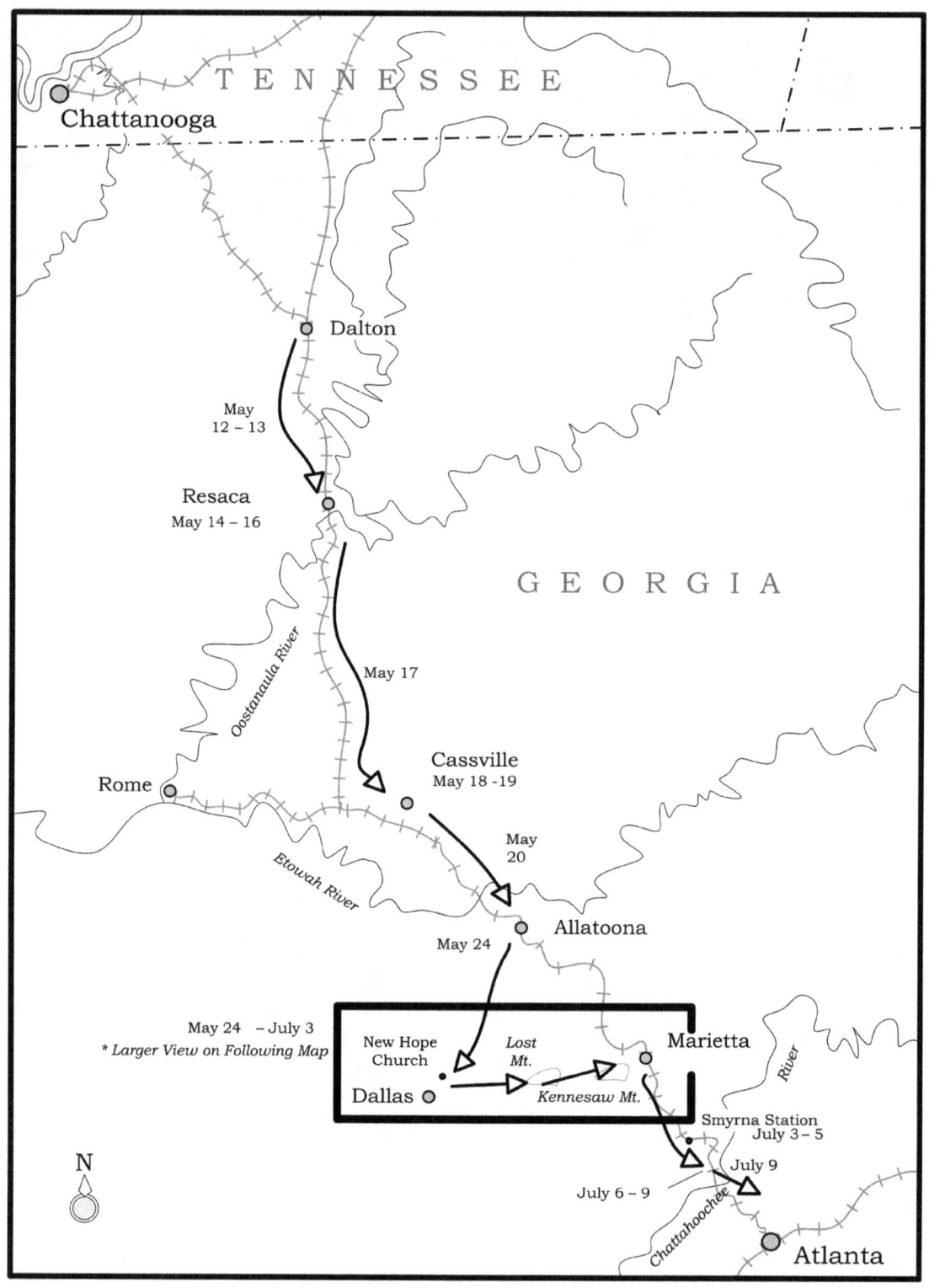

Movements of Louisiana Brigade, 7 May to 9 July 1864.

attack. Gibson fell back to his original position after firing only one volley at the enemy. The attack saw very few losses but one important loss was Lieutenant Colonel McEnery of the 4th Battalion. McEnery was severely wounded and never returned to duty with the battalion. Once recovered from his wound, he, like so many from the brigade, was ordered to report to the Trans-Mississippi Department where he served under Brigadier General Harry Hays. When the war was over, McEnery went into law and became very active in Louisiana's postwar politics. He was elected to the state legislature but was later removed for being a former Confederate. In 1872 he won the gubernatorial election over William Kellogg but was eventually thrown out of office by a presidential order from then President Ulysses S. Grant. McEnery kept up his resistance against Reconstruction rule while living in New Orleans where he died in 1891. After the wounding of McEnery, command of the battalion fell to Major Duncan F. Buie.[26]

Again, Sherman found the defenses around Resaca too strong and eventually outflanked that position on 15 May. On the night of the sixteenth, the Army of Tennessee quietly withdrew across the Oostanaula River, with Gibson commanding the rear guard of the army, composed of his and Stovall's brigades. The retreat was continued to the town of Cassville. On 19 May the army was drawn up to undertake a massive counterattack against Sherman. After much hesitation, the attack was called off; a retreat was ordered that night, and the men fell back across the Etowah River, to the town of Allatoona. Fighting for the brigade up to this point had been light. The brigade only took part in skirmishing for the entire time. Austin's battalion had taken part in almost constant fighting on the skirmish line from 7 May to 19 May. Losses of the command up to 20 May were only 17 killed and 75 wounded. Sherman recognized the natural defenses of Allatoona. The town was located behind the Etowah River and atop mountainous terrain. Sherman decided to outflank Johnston to the west, directing his army toward the small town of Dallas.[27]

Ordered to meet Sherman's flank movement, the brigade broke camp on the twenty-second and marched toward the southwest. Gibson, leading the division's march toward Dallas, was approached by Colonel E.H. Cunningham of Hood's staff as the brigade was nearing a crossroads near a small church named New Hope. Cunningham ordered Gibson to send skirmishers forward up the Pumpkin Vine Road to form a picket line and attempt to halt and feel out an approaching enemy force. Gibson deployed the brigade to the right of the road leading to Dallas along a "considerable eminence" and threw forward Austin's battalion, reinforcing it with Lieutenant J.E. Carraway's Company B of the 19th Louisiana. Austin was to act as support to Colonel Jones' 32nd & 58th Alabama Regiment of Henry Clayton's brigade. Jones' regiment was already deployed in the woods ahead and was supporting Confederate cavalry resisting an enemy advance across Pumpkin Vine Creek about three miles ahead. The Alabamians were waiting in the woods for support when Austin arrived. Stewart's division was halted near New Hope Church and began entrenching as Jones and Austin pushed their way through the woods.[28]

Jones pushed his regiment up the Pumpkin Vine Road, with Austin deployed across the road to his left. Altogether the two units numbered a little over 300 men: Jones with 250, Austin with 45 and Carraway's numbers are unknown. Hoods' orders to Jones were to "press vigorously forward, make the enemy develop their strength." Picketing Pumpkin Vine Creek ahead was the 9th Texas Cavalry, under Colonel Dudley W. Jones, of Brigadier General Lawrence Ross' brigade. Jones' cavalry was pushed aside by advancing elements of Major General Joseph Hooker's XX Corps of the Army of the Cumberland. Crossing the creek down the New Hope Church Road was Brigadier General John Geary's division.

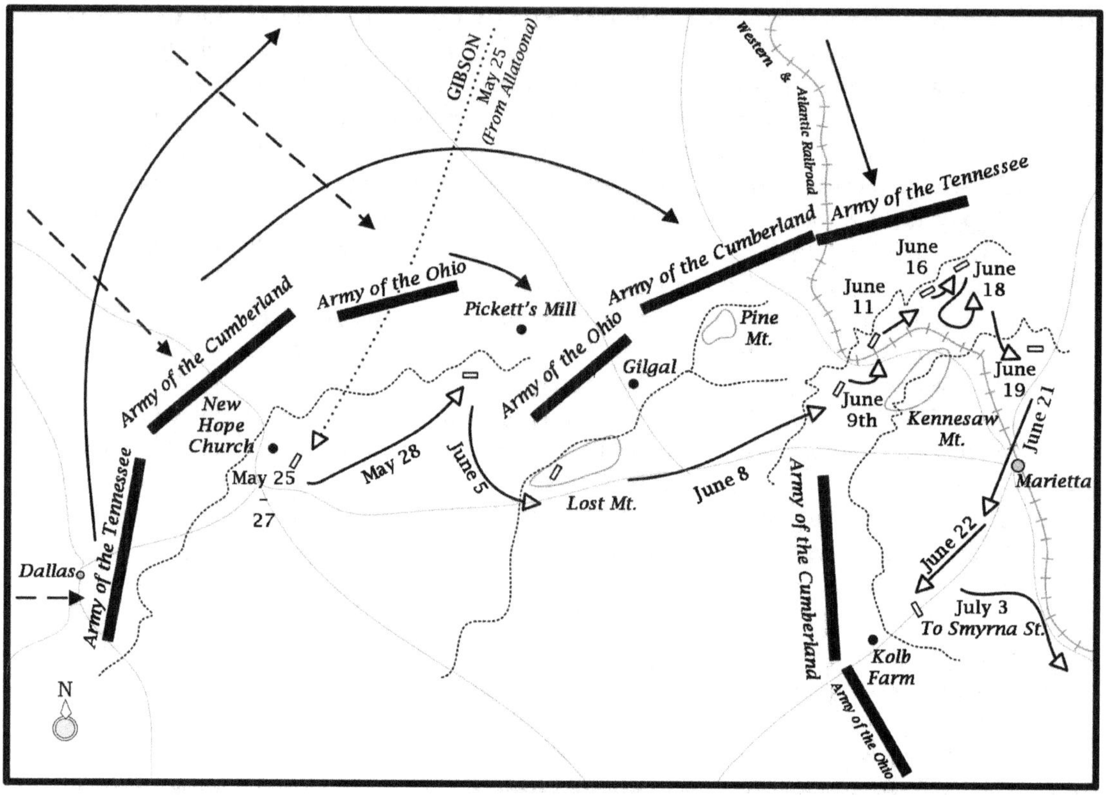

Movements of Louisiana Brigade, 25 May to 3 July 1864. This inset of the campaign map shows the constant moving and marching the Louisiana Brigade underwent from when it arrived in the Marietta area on May 25 to when it evacuated the area on July 3 toward the Smyrna Station.

Colonel Samuel E. Hunter, 4th Louisiana (courtesy of Camp Moore Historical Association).

Colonel Charles Candy and his brigade were given the task of crossing the ford and pushing the Texans back. Candy deployed his 7th Ohio as skirmishers with the 28th Pennsylvania and 5th Ohio in close support. Marching up behind the brigade were the 66th Ohio and 148th Pennsylvania regiments.[29]

Contact was made with Candy's advancing brigade between 10:00 and 11:00 A.M. about two miles from Pumpkin Vine Creek and about one and one-half miles from Stewart's Division. The ground over which Austin and Jones met Candy was advantageous to their severe shortage in numbers. Austin described the terrain: "The woods were thick and ground uneven"; Carraway said, "The country was heavily wooded. Besides this there were ravines and undulations." The first enemy that the Louisianians came upon were actually members of Hooker's and Geary's staffs and their bodyguards. It did not take long to scatter this group; one volley sent the group scurrying for cover of their line. Geary quickly called on Candy's skirmish line, the 7th Ohio, to push forward to check Jones and Austin. The Confederates crossed over a small ridge and made contact with the Buckeyes. Austin's fire was so intense that it required Candy to start deploying his brigade to assist the troubled 7th Ohio.[30]

Candy responded by deploying the 28th Pennsylvania to reinforce the 7th Ohio, and he brought up the 5th Ohio down the Pumpkin Vine Road in column so it could easily be deployed, as needed, on either side of the road. The remaining regiments of Candy's brigade were deployed to the right of the road, opposite of Austin, and immediately pushed forward. "A brisk fire was opened and kept up for some time," said Colonel Ario Pardee of the 148th Pennsylvania, opposite Austin. Austin was forced to gradually fall back and sent word to Jones of him doing so but Jones had already taken things into his own hands. Jones threw his Alabamians into a charge against the 7th Ohio. "Almost immediately a furious charge was made upon us," said Geary, who was nearby with the skirmishers. The 5th Ohio, which was marching in close support of the 7th Ohio and deploying 28th Pennsylvania, was thrown into confusion, and the right wing of the regiment almost broke from the field. "The enemy advanced and poured a heavy and galling fire in the entire line. It fell most heavily on the Fifth Ohio Volunteers," reported Candy. Jones' line was severely outflanked, though, and fire from his right ripped through his ranks. Jones was able to exchange shots for about 10 to 15 minutes before he pulled his regiment back.[31]

Jones' bold move did buy Austin time to rally his unit and push it back again, but Candy's numbers were too great. Moving up and down the ridges, ravines and heavily wooded terrain was now a benefit to Austin's small detachment against the cumbersome lined regiments now pushing against him. Carraway described the scene as his company and Austin's battalion fought their way back through the woods toward Gibson's line: "Our little battalion fell hurriedly back until we had crossed the first ravine, when we halted, about-faced, waited until they were in plain view, when we again fired into them. The result was a charge from the Yankee line. Again we fell back until another place suitable to make a stand was found, when as before we halted and fought again in this way." Candy halted his units once they took the ridge over which Austin's and Jones' men had emerged and began entrenching. Candy's skirmishers, though, were not up against just any skirmish line. Austin's men were a hand-picked lot known for their sharpshooting skills. Austin described the nightmare he inflicted on the enemy skirmishers as they attempted to pursue him: "He now attempted to throw forward skirmishers, but they were driven in by our fire, and their officers in vain tried to urge them on. The line of battle again charged us, and we retired slowly, fighting them back stubbornly.... The enemy's line was again halted for adjustment ... and skirmishers urged forward by command and oaths, but without effect. They were driven in as before." Austin was able to escape to the safety of Gibson's line and Candy began consolidating his position.[32]

Gibson's line was about 1,000 yards from where contact was made with Candy. Jones had been in a serious fight from about 11:00 A.M. to noon, and it was at this time that Austin and Carraway were rushed to the scene. The Louisiana Brigade was deployed across the Pumpkin Vine Road, north of the road to Dallas, between noon and 1:00 P.M. It is here the brigade sat, providing a buffer between the division preparing its position and the skirmish line trying to check an enemy advance. Once Austin had extracted himself from Candy's

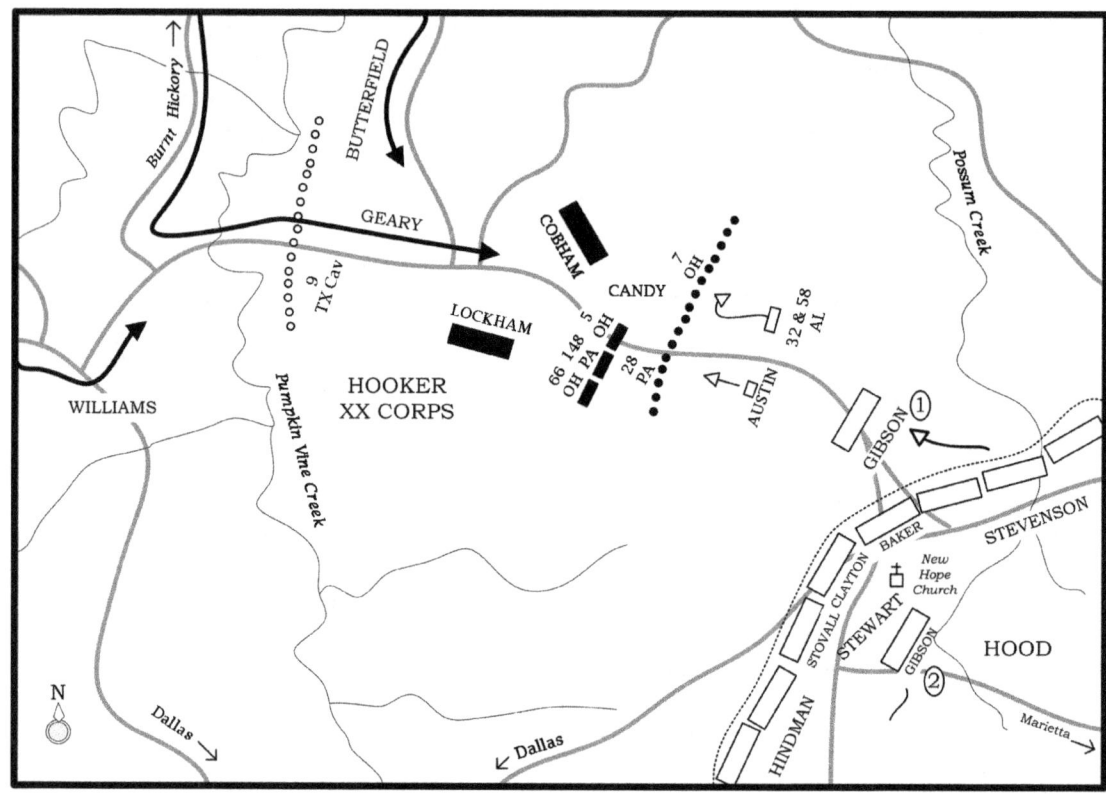

Battle of New Hope Church, 25 May 1864.

push, Gibson sent the 16th & 25th Louisiana to him and ordered him forward again at around 2:00 to 2:30 P.M. Behind this strengthened line, Gibson pushed his brigade forward, along with Jones, to "develop" the enemy's line and strength. As Austin went to work on Candy's line, Gibson said, "My skirmishers were ordered to charge ... chasing the enemy to his barricades." Pushing to within about 200 yards of the ridge line Candy was holding, Gibson was able to report Candy was "developing a strong position." For about an hour the Louisianians kept up a "scattering fire," and by doing so kept the lead elements of the Army of the Cumberland bottlenecked in the rough terrain. Pressure soon came that forced Gibson to pull his brigade back to New Hope Church. Once Geary made serious contact, Hooker began concentrating his other two divisions, under Brigadier General Alpheus Williams and Major General Daniel Butterfield. Also, Geary's other two brigades had arrived on the scene and were beginning to field into line on Candy's flanks. At about 3:30, Williams' jaded division arrived on the scene and proceeded to push the Louisianians back toward New Hope Church. "Driving the enemy before us," said Williams, "and forcing back his strong skirmish line and heavy reserves at double-quick." By about 4:00 P.M., Gibson abandoned the field and moved into the main line.[33]

The small but lengthy skirmish on the part of the Louisiana Brigade was the most action the brigade had seen up to this point in the campaign. Austin lost 15 of his 45 men in the 4 or 5 hour exchange, Company B of the 19th Louisiana lost 7 wounded; the 25th Louisiana lost 6 men wounded and 2 missing for a total of 30 out of about 85 Louisianians engaged. Judging from the reports of Candy's regiments concerning the skirmish, it looks as though Candy lost 9 men killed and 75 wounded for a total of at least 81. Jones' losses are unknown.[34]

Once back to Confederate lines, Stewart ordered Gibson to fall in behind the division to act as a reserve. The brigade was placed in line behind Stovall's brigade, with the right of the brigade just passing New Hope Church. The day was not over, though, for the Louisianians. "We had hardly taken post," said Gibson, "when the enemy advanced in great force." Once Hooker had all three of his divisions in place, he continued his push on Stewart's position. He massed all three of his divisions in columns of brigades and tried to push his way through Stewart's line. The brunt of the attack fell on Clayton's and Stovall's brigades to Gibson's front. Lying in reserve for the two hour ordeal cost the brigade several casualties. The ground over which Hooker's corps was attacking required his men to cross over "an elevated position" and down into a "hallow" from which the ground rose into another elevated position that Stewart's division occupied. Stewart described the result: "Our position was such that the enemy's fire, which was very heavy, passed over the line to a great extent." The problem with this situation, for the Louisiana Brigade, is that the brigade was subjected to a serious amount of fire. Also, to Gibson's right was the division's battalion of artillery, which was the main target of Hooker's cannons. One of the casualties was Major Samuel Bishop of the 20th Louisiana, who lost his right arm during the battle. After Hooker was repulsed, some of the Louisiana regiments were ordered to replace some of Stovall's and Clayton's in the front line. The 16th & 25th Louisiana replaced one of Clayton's Alabama units the next morning and simply filled into the trenches the Alabamians had built the previous day and night. Campbell's 13th Louisiana and Kennedy's 19th Louisiana did not enjoy such amenities. For whatever reason, Stovall's brigade did not erect breastworks prior the Battle of New Hope Church for the four hours they sat in line. So, during the night, Campbell's and Turner's regiments had the privilege of relieving the Georgians and building breastworks for them.[35]

Gibson reported his losses from the seventh to the twenty-fifth at 220 men killed, wounded or missing. Subtracting the 92 casualties suffered up to the twentieth, Gibson lost 128 men at the Battle of New Hope Church. Austin's small battalion, which began the campaign with just 60 men, lost 15 killed and wounded at New Hope Church, bringing his total losses since the seventh to 23. New Hope Church was actually the only significant fighting that the brigade was involved in up to that point and for two months after that.[36]

The brigade remained in the works along the Dallas–New Hope Church–Pickett's Mill front until 4 June. After the Battle of New Hope Church, the brigade remained near the church for two days, spending their time building breastworks. After building up Stovall's front, the regiments spent time building a line of works for themselves about 150 paces to the rear of Stovall. The whole time the work was done under a very harassing fire from the enemy. Captain Robert Keen described the two days around New Hope Church on the 26th and 27th of May: "We remained in this position [Stovall's former line] day and night until the morning of the 28th being constantly annoyed by an enfilading fire from the enemy's sharpshooters in front of the right of our brigade, rendering it extremely hazardous to send the necessary details for water." The 16th & 25th Louisiana, having relieved the 36th Alabama of Clayton's brigade, was in a serious bind itself. Its "whole front swarmed with the enemy's sharpshooters, and confronted by a heavy line of skirmishers, whose fire was a great annoyance." The enemy fire prevented about 80 of the Alabamians from leaving their works, and while Lewis moved his regiment to fill the works four men were wounded.[37]

On 28 May Stewart's division was shifted to the right of the line to meet the ever expanding growth of Sherman's army. This time the Louisiana Brigade was put on the front line, and Stovall's Georgians got to enjoy sitting in a reserve position for a few of days. The next three days the brigade busied itself, again, with building breastworks and continually skirmishing with the enemy. On the morning of the thirty-first Stovall relieved Gibson, and the brigade was pulled back about 200 yards for the men to rest but rest was not easy. The men were put back in the trenches on the night of 1 June and went back to fighting the enemy skirmishers and intense rains for the next two days. During this time the trenches were flooded and without practically any protection the Louisianians passed a very miserable two days. As one Louisianian wrote, "It has been a very disagreeable day. Much rain."[38]

Finally, the brigade was ordered out of the trenches and marched east during the night of 4 June. The downside of being able to evacuate the "ditches" was that it was done in a downpour of rain. Sherman realized that frontal assaults on the lines around Dallas–New Hope Church–Pickett's Mill front were not realistic and began maneuvering his armies to get around Johnston's flank. The march on the night of the fourth and early part of the fifth was to a new position at Lost Mountain. Once settled, the wet and dogged men were issued rations of whiskey. In prior days, whiskey meant trouble, but for men exposed to the elements for weeks it brought warmth and refreshment that the elements weren't supplying.[39]

The movement toward Lost Mountain was to reestablish a new line to prevent getting flanked on the right by grand sweeping movement of the Armies of the Tennessee and the Cumberland. Sherman's goal was to reestablish control of the railroad to Chattanooga for his supply line. Gradually his line crept more and more to the east toward the railroad with his goal being Marietta. This meant the Louisiana Brigade's stay at Lost Mountain was short lived. On 8 June the brigade was ordered east and positioned close to the railroad, only to be moved the next day across the railroad to meet the expansion of the Army of the Tennessee. The next nine days (9 June to 18 June) saw Gibson's men continually change positions to the east as part of Johnston's attempt to keep his right flank secure. Even though it was a time of little fighting, it was one filled with constant movement and constant rain, as exemplified in the diary of Lieutenant Emmett Ross of the 20th Louisiana[40]:

    Thursday, June 9, 1864

We marched and countermarched until dark.

    Friday 10

We moved again this morning.... We have considerable rain again today.... We have orders to move again in the morning.

    Saturday, June 11, 1864

We moved again this morning to the right and built new breast works — We have had much rain.

    Sunday 12

Much rain today. We are still occupying our trenches.

    Monday, June 13, 1864

We are still occupying the trenches, have had much rain all the forenoon.

    Tuesday 14

Read orders to hold ourselves in readiness to move.

    Wednesday, June 15, 1864

We made a reconnoicance in our front this morning ... moved out again this afternoon and formed in line of battle.

    Thursday 16

We moved again this morning.

Friday, June 17, 1864
"It is cloudy today — We have orders to hold ourselves in readiness to move.
Saturday
We marched this morning at 4 o'clock to an extreme left through much mud and water. It has rained very hard. We were formed in line of battle about 2 o'clock P.M.... At 6 o'clock P.M. we moved again towards our right, and bivauked at 10 o'clock at night.
Sunday, June 19, 1864
Rain last night-this morning the sun came out yet the clouds are threatening.... We marched at 5 o'clock.

Lieutenant Carraway of the 19th Louisiana also elaborated on the conditions the men faced while on the march: "Not a tent in the regiment, or brigade for that matter, but we must if possible keep the three days' rations dry. That which we had in our haversacks must be cared for. No man had more than one blanket, and ordinarily two men slept together." Lieutenant John Kendall of the 4th Louisiana found brushing his teeth to be the biggest obstacle, but not due to the lack of toothbrushes: "One of our greatest inconveniences was as to our teeth. Here water became the problem again. As for toothbrushes, there was no difficulty, for they were plentiful in every clump of woods. The twigs of the hickory or the gum, splintered at one end into a sort of tassel, made good toothbrushes. But it amounted almost to a question of convenience, this matter of wasting precious water indulging in such a refinement as brushing the teeth." As if things couldn't be more frustrating for Kendall, his prized horse was wounded, which led to its death, during this time. What made Kendall's horse such a prized possession was that it once belonged to the famed poet-turned soldier Colonel William Lytle of the 10th Ohio. Lytle, who had faced the Louisianians at Perryville and was captured by them, had been exchanged and was later killed at Chickamauga, where his horse was taken. Finding the good in a bad situation Kendall wrote, "However, we made soup and beefsteak of his remains."[41]

During this constant maneuvering Gibson received news of the death of a dear friend, General Leonidas Polk. On 14 June Gibson's prewar friendship with Leonidas Polk came to an end. On that day he and other top ranking generals were on top of Pine Mountain and were spotted by none other than Sherman himself. Sherman ordered rounds thrown at the large body of officers and staffs to disperse them. Polk was nearly cut in half by one of the rounds thrown in their direction. Gibson had visited the general the night before, spending some time in his tent discussing various issue and topics; he was even attempting to be transferred to Polk's corps.[42]

On the nineteenth, the brigade fell back and formed part of the right wing with the army's line anchored by Kennesaw Mountain. The brigade stayed north of Marietta until 21 June when it was moved to the southwest of town to support a movement on Kolb's Farm set for the next day. The brigade sat idle during the Battle of Kolb's Farm and remained on the lines to the southwest of Marietta until Johnston evacuated the area on 3 July. The army's retreat brought the men to a new line at Smyrna Station and then to the Chattahoochee River where slaves had been busily working to build works for the army. From 5 July to 9 July Gibson occupied part of the left wing of the army near where the left flank anchored itself on the Chattahoochee.

On 9 July the brigade crossed the Chattahoochee and entered a line of works posted behind Peach Tree Creek to the north of Atlanta. For about the next two weeks the brigade remained active along this line, marching and countermarching to meet the sprawling threat of Sherman's advance and continually going on picket duty. Other than those circumstances, some men were able to make trips into Atlanta for various reasons. The close proximity to civilization led to the Irish of the 1st Regulars getting their hands on liquor again. Not since the regiment hit the streets of Corinth in 1862 had there been problems with the Regulars and whiskey. On the thirteenth, there was "great excitement" in the Regulars' camp: "All hands drunk." The past two months' stress of marching and fighting, in the words of Colonel Hunter, "this exhausting campaign. It is enough to wear down a constitution of iron constraint."[43]

There were, however, other important matters that took place outside the brigade that affected the Louisianians during their stay in the Peach Tree works. One was the attachment of two more Louisiana units to the brigade: The 4th Louisiana Regiment, under Colonel Samuel Hunter, and the 30th Louisiana Battalion, under Lieutenant Colonel Thomas Shields. On 3 June the secretary of war ordered the transfer of these two units, which was effected on 19 July. For the 4th Louisiana it was a reunion, even though Robert Patrick of that regiment said, "It has created a great dissatisfaction in the 4th." That regiment had been part of Gibson's original brigade in April of 1862, having fought with the 13th and 19th Louisiana Regiments at Shiloh. Following Shiloh, the 4th had been transferred to Edwards's Depot, Mississippi, where it reorganized itself. Briefly stationed around Vicksburg, the 4th Regiment was attached to an attack force to retake Baton Rouge from Federal forces. At the Battle of Baton Rouge, 5 August 1862, the regiment's colonel, Henry W. Allen, was wounded and would never return to his regiment. Lieutenant Colonel Samuel Hunter was promoted and took command of the regiment, a post he would hold until late 1864. Following the Battle of Baton Rouge, the regiment performed duties at Port Hudson on the Mississippi and then became part of Johnston's relief army in June and July of 1863. The regiment remained part of the Department of Mississippi, Alabama and East Louisiana for the rest of 1863 and early 1864. During service in this department, Hunter's regiment was assigned to Brigadier General William Quarles' brigade. In May of 1864, Quarles' brigade was sent to the Army of Tennessee.[44]

The 30th Louisiana Battalion was originally in state service, but in the form of a full regiment. The Sumter Regiment, as it was nicknamed, was organized in December of 1861 in New

Lieutenant Colonel Thomas Shields, 30th Louisiana. Shields and his regiment joined the Louisiana Brigade in the middle of the Atlanta Campaign. Shields' regiment suffered horribly at the Battle of Ezra Church on 28 July 1864, with Shields being killed in the charge on the enemy works (courtesy of the U.S. Army Military History Institute).

Orleans and then was transferred to Confederate service for ninety days in March 1862, during the Confederate concentration to stop Grant's capture of Fort Donelson. Gustavus Breaux was its original colonel, Thomas Shields its lieutenant colonel and Charles Bell its major. Breaux was a thirty-three-year native of Louisiana who was working as a lawyer in New Orleans before the war. He led the regiment until February 1863, when the 30th Regiment became the 30th Battalion, and thus the position of colonel was removed, leaving Breaux with no position. He served the remainder of the war in southwest Louisiana. While under Breaux's command, the regiment was part of the New Orleans garrison until that city was evacuated in April of 1862. Being a New Orleans recruited unit, it ended up losing three companies and part of a fourth in the evacuation. Once at Camp Moore, the regiment underwent a reorganization and was officially recreated by the addition of more companies to bring it up to strength. The new Company B was a conglomerate of several decimated companies. Two independent companies were added, the Richard Musketeers and Pickett Cadets. Another ninety days organization was merged into the new Thirtieth. The Orleans Guards Battalion was raised in New Orleans and sent north to Corinth. It had fought at Shiloh and, at its end of service, was sent back to Louisiana but could not get back to New Orleans. The unit was disbanded at Camp Moore, and from its ashes, Private Louis Fortin organized a company of 92 men. Fortin was made its captain, and the unit was attached to Breaux's regiment where it became Company F. Once organized, the regiment fielded 804 men. Soon afterwards, Company K was furloughed home, which was in the New Orleans area, and that company ceased to exist upon the

Anatole Gauthier, 30th Louisiana. The 30th Regiment went through several company level changes that eventually resulted in it being demoted from a regiment to the 30th Battalion. One of the company changes came with the addition of a new Company F, the Orleans Guards. The Orleans Guards were men recruited from the disbanded Orleans Guards Battalion. Gauthier was one of the 92 men who joined the new Company F (courtesy of Edward G. Gauthier).

men entering enemy occupied territory. Therefore, the regiment operated with only nine companies.[45]

The regiment remained in Louisiana over the next year participating in the Battle of Baton Rouge and helping in building the defenses at Port Hudson. In May 1863, the regiment was ordered to reduce itself to a battalion, and two of its companies were disbanded and distributed throughout the remaining seven companies. At this point, Lieutenant Colonel Shields, a native Ohioan, took command and was in this position when the regiment joined the Louisiana Brigade in July of 1864. In the same month, the 30th Louisiana joined the 4th Louisiana as part of Samuel Maxey's brigade, as it was sent to Jackson to assist in Joe Johnston's buildup to help Vicksburg. From this point on the regiment's movements mirrored that of the 4th Louisiana. The attachment of the 4th and 30th brought the total number of units under Gibson's command to ten: 1st Regulars, 4th, 13th, 16th, 19th, 20th, and 25th regiments and Austin's, 4th, and 30th battalions. Gibson's brigade, in mid–July, mustered 1,115 effective men. Due to the decline in numbers, it is believed, that for either most or part of the campaign, several of the smaller units were consolidated with others. For example, the 1st Regulars was combined with the 13th and 20th Regiments for a time and by August it is suggested that the 1st Regulars and 4th Battalion were operating under Major Austin's command with his battalion.[46]

The other major event that took place during this one week window was one of more drastic consequences: the appointment of John Bell Hood to command of the Army of Tennessee.

Chapter 10

Battles for Atlanta: July–September 1864

"With the change of our commander came a change in tactics on our part. From being constantly on the retreat we have to some extent assumed the offensive and having turned up on the enemy there is no telling where or how hard we will have to fight."
—Colonel Samuel E. Hunter, 4th Louisiana,
letter to wife, 24 July 1864

On 17 July President Davis relieved Johnston with Lieutenant General John B. Hood. Braxton Bragg had been sent west by Davis to relieve Johnston of his command. Rumors flew wildly with Bragg's arrival in Atlanta. "I have no doubt old Bragg has had something to do with this," swore a critical Louisianian about the change in command. Chief Musician of the 19th Louisiana Douglas Cater also thought Bragg was the cause of Johnston's fall: "He [Bragg] appeared upon the scene and used his influence against our General Johnston." Hood had come west with James Longstreet's I Corps of the Army of Northern Virginia in August of 1863 to reinforce Bragg prior to Chickamauga. After being wounded at Chickamauga, Hood remained in Georgia when Longstreet's corps eventually made its way back to Virginia. Once recuperated, Hood was ordered by the secretary of war to report to Johnston for command of a corps in the Army of Tennessee. The corps that Hood took command of consisted of the divisions of Stewart, Stevenson and Hindman. Replacing Hood in command of his corps was Major General Benjamin Cheatham, previously a division commander in Hardee's corps. Division leadership had changed in June when Leonidas Polk was killed at Kennesaw Mountain. Stewart was promoted on 23 June to lieutenant general and given command of Polk's corps. Taking Stewart's position as division commander was Brigadier General Henry Clayton. Stewart had earned the respect of the Louisianians. "His quiet way enlisted the love of the division," admired a member of the 19th Louisiana. Clayton's appointment, as can be suspected, was not met with widespread enthusiasm: "His appointment does not give gen'l satisfaction," was how a member of the 20th Louisiana bluntly described his feelings.[1]

Hood immediately went on the offensive against Sherman. The Louisiana Brigade was lucky enough to have missed the first of Hood's three attacks along Peach Tree Creek on 20 July. Even though readied to support the attack, and even ordered forward to support the right flank of that attack in the evening, the brigade was withdrawn back to the works north of Atlanta. Colonel Hunter described the role of the brigade during the Battle of Peach

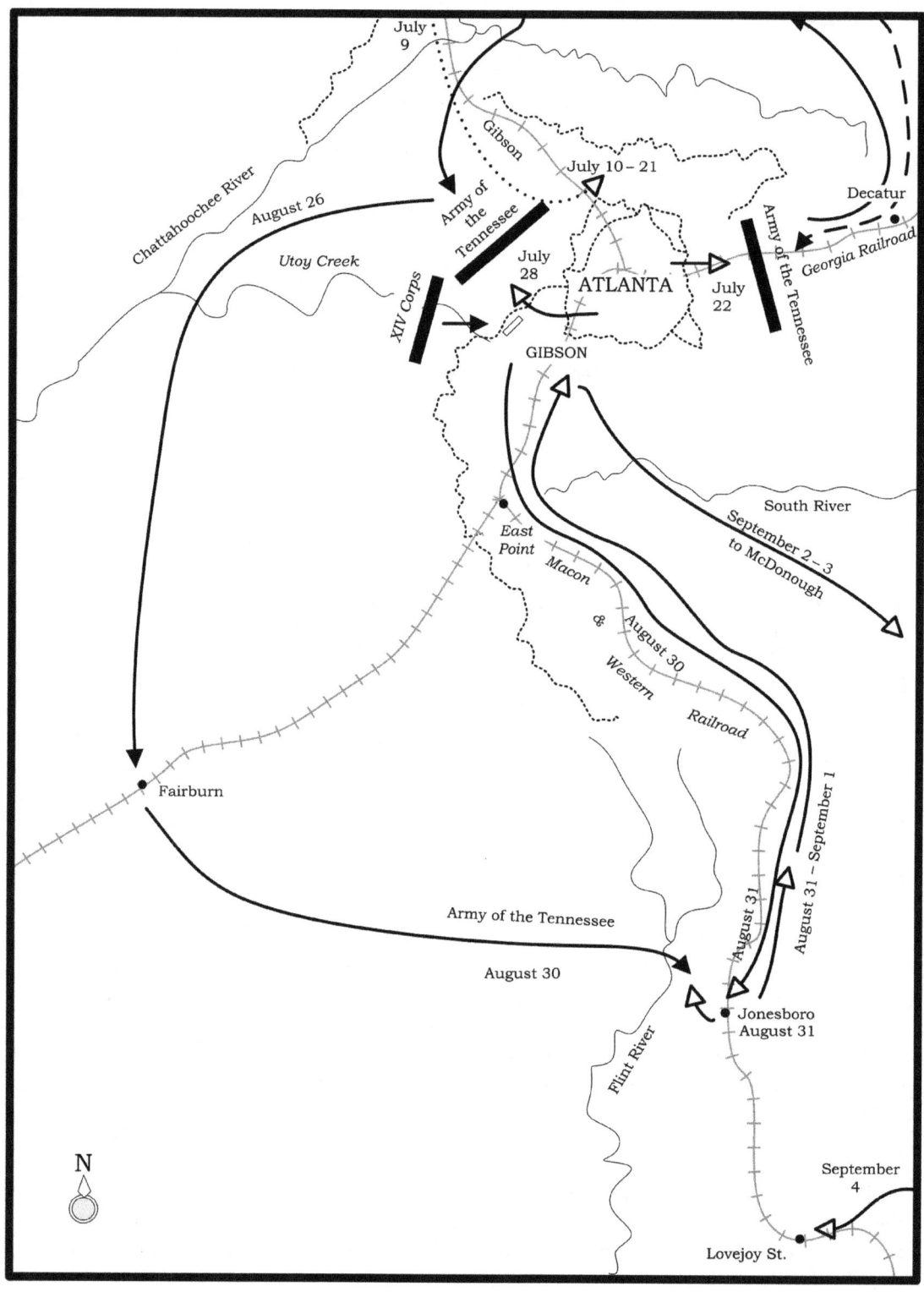

Movements of Louisiana Brigade, 9 July to 1 September 1864.

Tree Creek: "Orders to be ready to advance on the enemy's works.... The day wore away however and to our great relief no order came." The brigade was not so lucky in the week that followed. One of Sherman's armies, the Army of the Tennessee under Major General James McPherson, had marched to the east of Atlanta and turned back west so as to invest the city from the east. After an intense fight with part of Hardee's corps on the twentieth, McPherson occupied a line of crude works, built by the Confederates, about one mile from Atlanta. Hood drew together a flank attack on McPherson's position, which lay about one mile east of the city. Hardee's corps was to make a long march on the night of 21 July and hit McPherson in the left flank. Cheatham's corps, deployed on the east line of the city's trenches, was to make a frontal assault once Hardee opened the attack.[2]

Although the initial attack by Hardee on 22 July was successful, it did not begin at dawn, as expected, but rather around noon. Hood ordered Cheatham out of the Atlanta trenches at about 2:00. From right to left, Cheatham's corps was deployed as follows: Stevenson's division, Hindman's division (under the command of Brigadier General John C. Brown) and Clayton's division. At 4:00 P.M., Cheatham ordered Clayton out of the trenches around Atlanta to support Brown's advance. Clayton moved his division out of the trenches and deployed it into two lines perpendicular to the railroad that ran east through Decatur. Baker and Stovall were deployed in the first line with Gibson and Baker in the second, Gibson behind Stovall and Jones behind Baker. Between the two lines was a heavily wooded area that afforded protection for the Louisianians as they formed up for the attack. This belt of woods opened up 300 yards short of the enemy line.[3]

Holding the right end of McPherson's line were the divisions of Brigadier General Morgan L. Smith and Brigadier General Charles Woods. Smith's division, under the command of Brigadier General Joseph Lightburn, was deployed across the Georgia Railroad with Lightburn's brigade to the north of the railroad and Colonel Martin's brigade to the south of it. Placed across the railroad was Battery A of the 1st Illinois Battery. Deployed on the right of Lightburn was Battery H of the 1st Illinois Light Artillery. Woods' division was deployed to the right of Lightburn. Colonel James Williamson was to Lightburn's right. Deployed in the middle of Williamson's line was the 4th Ohio Battery. To Williamson's right was Colonel Milo Smith's brigade. The entire Federal line occupied breastworks built by the Confederates the day before. When the Confederate attack began, Lightburn's and Woods' men were in the process of reversing the Confederate works.[4]

Brown's division advanced against the front of Lightburn's line. The right of Brown's line, Brigadier General Arthur Manigault's and Brigadier General Jacob Sharp's brigades, succeeded in penetrating Lightburn's line. As Brown engaged Lightburn, Clayton advanced his division in support. Stovall's and Holtzclaw's brigades charged into the Federal works in support of Manigault. Clayton moved Gibson to support Brown to the south of the railroad. As Gibson was advancing to assist Brown, the Federals were trying to reverse the Confederate breakthrough. Woods pulled his division out of line and deployed it parallel to the Georgia Railroad, facing south. Lightburn's brigade was able to reorganize itself, and with help from the Federal left, he was able to organize a counterattack. Lightburn and Woods converged on Brown's and Clayton's men and forced them back. Before Gibson was able to engage the enemy, he was met by the retreating elements of Brown's division. Just as the Louisianians were "nearly to their works," Clayton pulled Gibson back and reformed his division to the rear. The brigade was able to, again, avoid major combat. The only fight that day was Ross Emmett's fight with the truth by boastfully writing home about the Battle of Atlanta, "Made good use of my sword and Navy 6." Hardee's corps was eventually

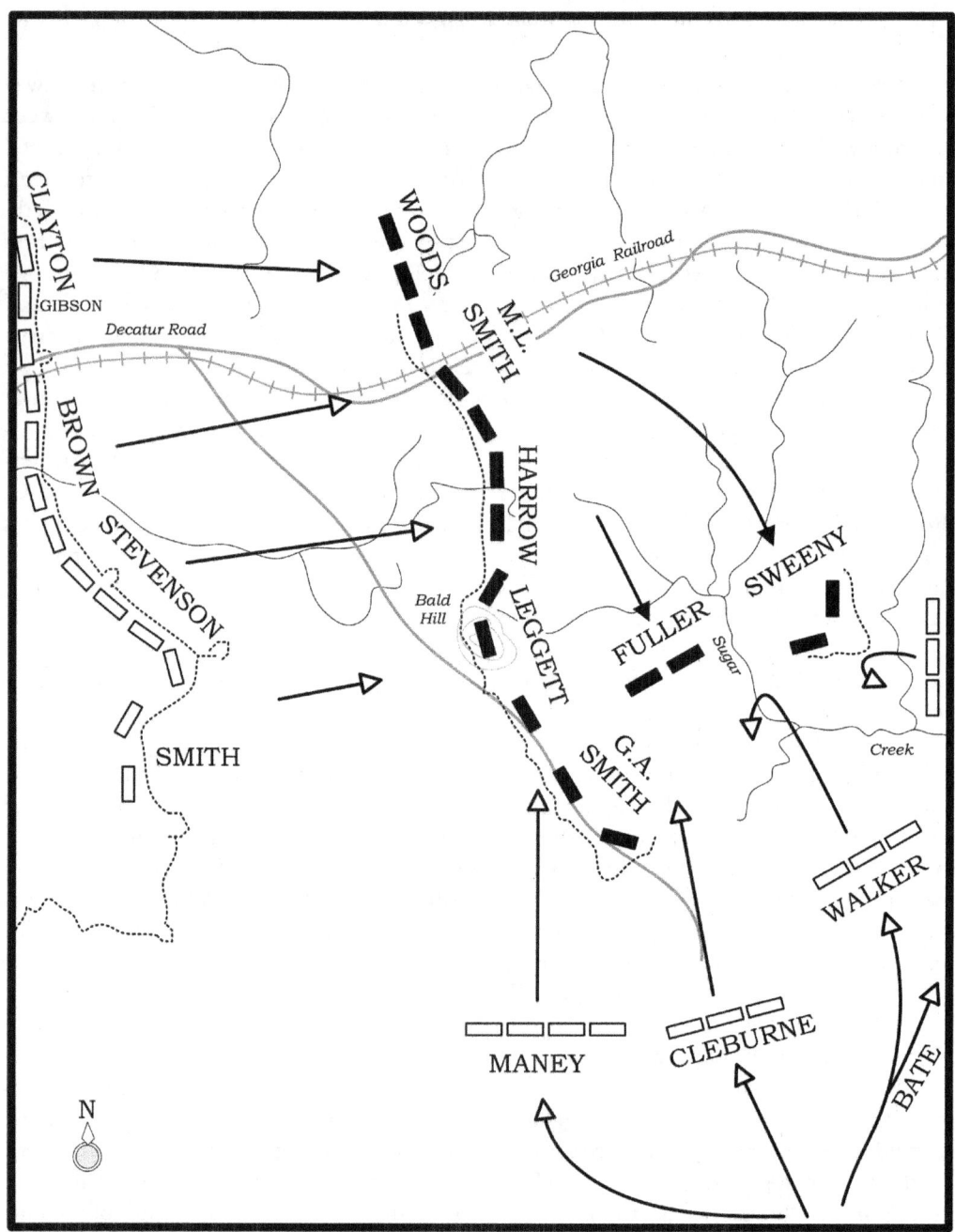

Battle of Atlanta, 22 July 1864.

repulsed due to Hood's tardiness in supporting his attack with Cheatham. The time lapse between Hardee beginning the attack and the commitment of Cheatham allowed the Federals to switch units from their front line to their left flank and back. Gibson pulled his men back to the "ditches" around Atlanta to await their next movement.[5]

For the next five days, the brigade occupied the trenches to the east of Atlanta. On 27 July Gibson was pulled from the trenches east of the city and marched through Atlanta to the Marietta and Peach Tree Creek roads. His movement was part of a larger move by Hood

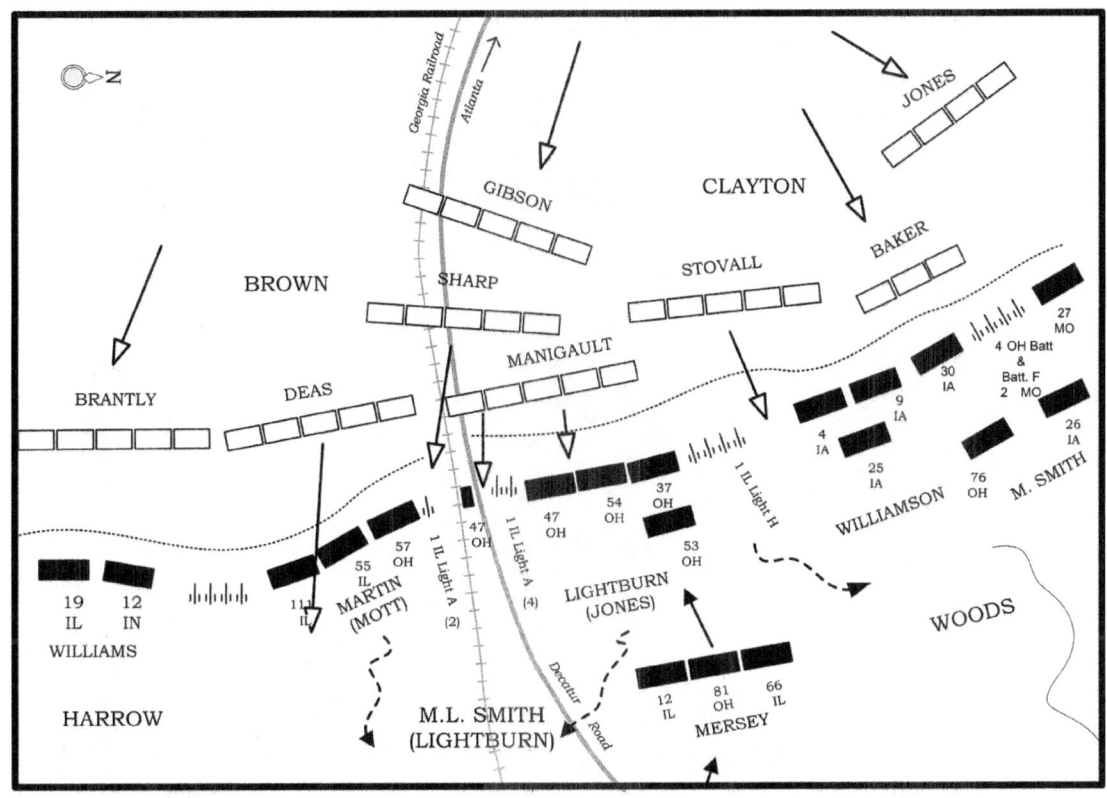

Battle of Atlanta, Clayton's Attack, 3:30 P.M.–5:00 P.M.

that included all of Clayton's and Brown's divisions. They were moved west of the city to meet another flanking movement by Sherman. Sherman moved the Army of the Tennessee from the east side of Atlanta to the west side. Trying to prevent Sherman from cutting the last railroad into the city, the Macon & Western Railroad, Hood sent parts of two of his corps to halt the Federal thrust. On the twenty-seventh, Clayton's and Brown's divisions were pulled out of line and marched to the Lickskillet Road, southwest of Atlanta. A new commander was also appointed to command the corps on the twenty-seventh, Lieutenant General Stephen D. Lee. Lee prepared to lead his corps into battle on the day after taking command.[6]

At 11:00 A.M. on 28 July, Lee left the Atlanta works to attack the Army of the Tennessee. Moving out along the Lickskillet Road for about a mile, Lee deployed his two divisions: Brown to the left of the road and Clayton to the right. The division was deployed facing north, almost parallel to the Lickskillet Road, with Gibson posted on the left, Holtzclaw on the right and Baker in reserve. Gibson deployed his brigade in a belt of woods near the road, which he described as having a "remarkably dense overgrowth." Austin and his battalion were sent forward to "develop the enemy thoroughly." On Gibson's left, next to the road, was the 13th (and possibly the 20th Regiment), then the 30th Battalion, the 19th Regiment, the 4th Battalion and the 16th & 25th on the right of the line. The alignment of the 1st Regulars and 4th Regiment are not known, but it is believed that the Fourth was somewhere on the right. The Louisianians knew they were in for a fight: "We heard skirmishing to our front. We began to smell the biggest kind of rot," said a member of the 19th

Eloy Campbell (brother of Leon; see page 48), 16th Louisiana. Campbell was one of the few casualties suffered on 22 July 1864 in the Battle of Atlanta. While recuperating from his wound Campbell deserted his regiment (courtesy of Camp Moore Historical Association).

Louisiana. As Austin's men pushed the enemy to their front back toward their lines, Brown's division to the left was making its attack on the enemy line.[7]

After deploying his brigade, Gibson rode over to Holtzclaw's brigade to confer with Clayton, who was supervising its deployment. After receiving last-minute details for the attack, Gibson rode back to his brigade only to find it gone. In Gibson's absence, Lieutenant Colonel E.H. Cunningham, the assistant inspector general of the corps, had issued orders to Colonel Leon von Zinken to advance the brigade. There is no explanation why

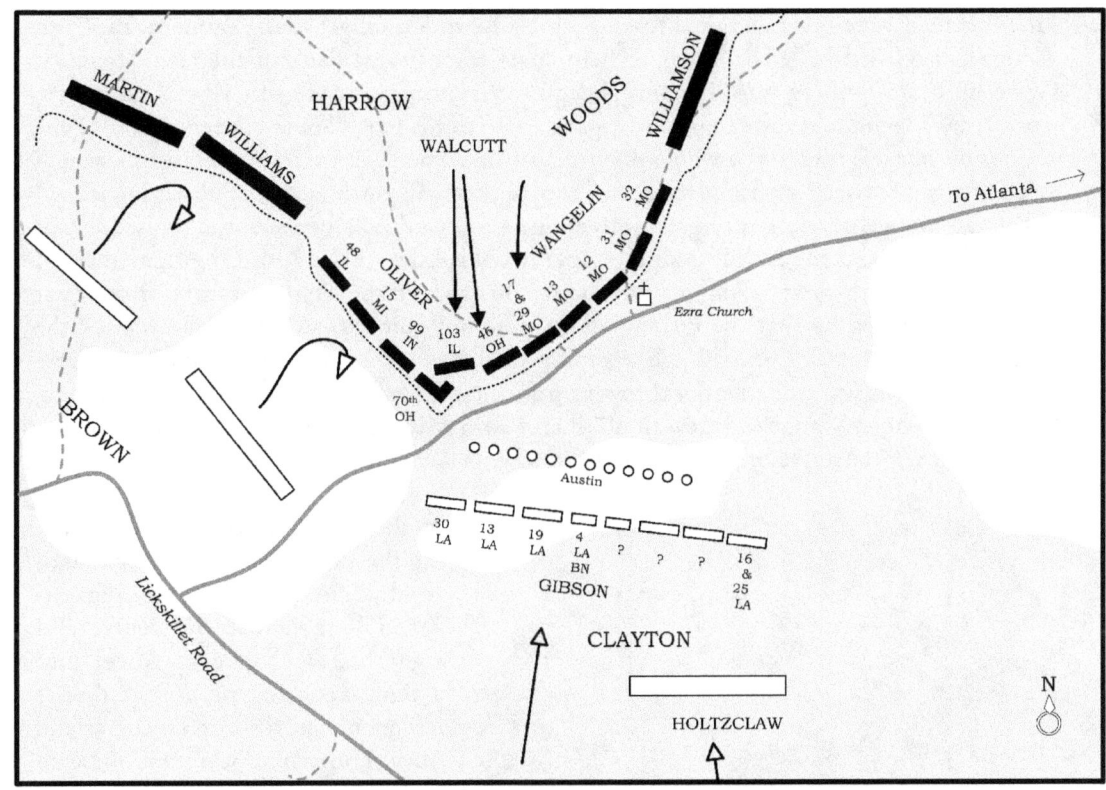

Battle of Ezra Church, 28 July 1864, 11:00 A.M.–1:00 P.M.

Cunningham issued orders for the brigade to move forward except for the possibility that as Clayton was preparing his division for the attack, Brown's division was being repulsed. Perhaps Cunningham was trying to send help to Brown before his attack was beaten back. Whatever the reasons, Gibson blasted von Zinken in his report of the battle. The orders were "improperly repeated and obeyed by Colonel Leon von Zinken ... who was not, in my absence, the senior officer present with the brigade, and who should have awaited orders from some superior in command."[8]

Gibson hurriedly tried to stop his brigade: "I galloped through the woods to overtake the command, but heavy firing soon told me that it had struck the enemy in strong force." The "strong force" that the Louisiana Brigade hit was a combination of Colonel Hugo Wangelin's and Colonel John Oliver's brigades. These two brigades marked the point where the First and Fourth Divisions of the XV Corps of the Army of the Tennessee met. Their lines were perpendicular to each other and thus formed an angle in the Union line: one side facing east and the other facing south. Wangelin's brigade, forming the right of the First Division, faced east and was thrown into line at about noon. From left to right his regiments in the front line were the 33rd Missouri, the 31st Missouri and the 12th Missouri. In reserve were the 3rd Missouri and the 17th and 29th Missouri regiments. Just outside his line to the left sat Ezra Church, which had its pews raided by Wangelin's men for their breastworks. The pews were stacked, knapsacks were piled behind them, and the Yanks began digging to reinforce them.[9]

Rolling into line to the right came Oliver's brigade of the Fourth Division. Across the line, his men were put to work throwing up breastworks. Oliver's left regiment, the 70th Ohio, had refused its left in order to help cover the exposed flank of the 12th Missouri. With units still pulling into line and generals attempting to make sure dispositions were correct, Wangelin had to realign his brigade more to his left: "Some concentration of the troops on our left caused the whole line to close up some distance to our left again, which created a gap between my right regiment, the Twelfth Missouri, and the Fourth Division." That gap Wangelin referred to grew into about a 100 yard hole between the refused left of the 70th Ohio and the 12th Missouri. Captain Louis Love of the 70th Ohio remembered that the gap was bigger, saying it was "about 200 yards to the right and front of the First Division, but finding that the First Division were not going to advance I threw back the left of my regiment." Even though a gaping hole was left in the Union line there were already temporarily, crude works thrown up for new units to be thrown behind. To partially fill the hole, Wangelin threw the 17th and 29th Missouri regiments. As the Louisiana Brigade struck the angle of this line, reinforcements were on the way to fill the gap.[10]

William Dixon, 4th Louisiana. Dixon ran away from home in early 1862 to join the 4th Louisiana Regiment. He served faithfully with his regiment until his wounding at Ezra Church. After the war, young Dixon returned to his studies in St. Francisville, Louisiana (courtesy of Camp Moore Historical Association).

The angle of Gibson's advance resulted in his left regiments approaching the angle of the enemy line. This resulted in the left becoming engaged long before the center and right had a chance to wheel into action and bring support. Gibson's left regiments, the 13th Louisiana and 30th Louisiana, were the first to make contact. These two regiments marched opposite of Love's 70th Ohio of Oliver's brigade and the gap to his left. The ground over which they advanced was clear open fields until they reached a small ridge opposite the Buckeyes about 100 to 200 yards away. At this point, until the Union line was reached, the Louisianians had to advance in a "dense wood" that was described as "covered by a thick growth of small trees." Gibson described the woods as being so dense that he could only see a few paces ahead. The terrain helped to make up for the deficiency of the crude works Love's regiment recently threw together. The gaping hole to Love's right was soon filled up by the addition of two regiments from Brigadier General Charles Walcutt's brigade. His brigade was in reserve, and once Lee's jumbled attack began, his brigade was dispersed to points needed. The two regiments sent to fill the gap were the 46th Ohio and the 103rd Illinois. The 103rd Illinois was posted to the right of Wangelin's Missourians, and shortly afterwards, the 46th Ohio filled into line on the right of the 103rd Illinois, but the gap was too small. So, part of the 46th Ohio was put into line behind Love's 70th Regiment. Adding to the woes of the Louisianians as they advanced over very disagreeable terrain Walcutt's regiments were armed with breech loading rifles. A bright note for the day was that there was little enemy artillery on the field facing the angle of the enemy line. The Army of the Tennessee was so concerned about its right flank being turned that the majority of its artillery was posted in that sector. The Louisiana Brigade was able to avoid an artillery pounding similar to the Hornets Nest and Round Forest.[11]

Due to the heavy undergrowth in the advance, the regiments to the 13th and 30th Regiments' fronts held their fire until the Louisianians were close. "They wisely reserved their fire until we were close to their line," said Lieutenant F.O. Trepagnier of Company G of the 30th Louisiana, "when they poured such a terrific and destructive fire at short range into our line that our men were actually mowed down." The fire from the angle was destructive, but the Louisianians pushed forward to within 20 to 25 paces. There the flag of the 30th Louisiana was planted in the ground and members of its color guard and color company attempted to keep it up. Oliver watched as the 30th Louisiana made its stand with its colors posted so close: "New and largely augmented columns of the enemy came pouring in upon us, with the same results, however, as before, although their colors were planted within twenty paces. Their front lines were broken up by deadly musketry, their columns staggered, halted." It was here, with the Thirtieth's flag in his hand and cheering his men on, Colonel Thomas Shields was killed. Not far from this, Major Charles Bell also went down. Trepagnier went on to describe the total destruction of his unit

Lawson Rheams, 4th Louisiana, wounded at the Battle of Ezra Church (courtesy of Camp Moore Historical Association).

at the hands of the 103rd Illinois and 46th Ohio's breech loaders: "Fourteen line officers out of 20 present had also fallen, either killed or wounded. The color bearer and all the color guards were shot down; only 6 members of the color company and only 3 members of the company on the left of the colors were uninjured. All of the officers of these two companies were either killed or wounded." As the regiment was forced to retire, its flag was left behind on the battlefield because no one was around to bear it. It was an intense fight that Love described as an attack with "greater fury."[12]

The rest of the brigade advanced at the quick step across the field, over the ridge and into the dense overgrowth beyond. "We that were in the ranks could see nothing," remembered R.F. Eddins. Struggling to make their way through the obstacles, the Louisianians were met by a volley just 80 yards away from Walcutt's and Wangelin's regiments. "A terrific fire was opened upon them that no mortal could stand, " said Wangelin. That was as close as the center and right of the brigade came to the Federal line. It was at this juncture in the battle Gibson found his regiments. He described finding his men trying to exchange fire with Oliver and Wangelin with "much energy and obstinacy," but it was doing no good. It was a lopsided fight that Gibson knew his outnumbered brigade could not win; he called on help from his division commander. Clayton was near by and had watched the Louisianians' advance. Even as Gibson advanced, the men to his left were retiring, and when a plea for help came from the Louisianian, Clayton was fully aware of the situation on hand. His response was to immediately send Baker's brigade into action to assist the Louisiana Brigade. The dense underbrush, though, impeded a quick advance from the Alabamians, and Gibson had no choice but to pull his men back. The alignment, improper angle of advance needed and strict orders on zones of attack were all reasons for Clayton's third brigade not having been committed to the fight. Gibson pulled the men back into a ravine on the other side of the small crest opposite of the Union line to reform. Once the men were collected, the brigade fell back to a position about 400 yards from the enemy trenches.[13]

Following behind Gibson's battered regiments as they retreated, skirmishers of the 46th Ohio came upon the flag of the 30th Louisiana lying among the dead and wounded. Wangelin reported that he buried 72 Confederates in his immediate front after the battle. The brief fight with Gibson cost Wangelin only 1 man killed and 34 wounded. The Louisiana Brigade did not fare as well as its enemy. Due to the angle of advance of the brigade, the left of the brigade was badly chewed up, whereas the 16th & 25th , 4th Regiment and the 4th Battalion escaped with few casualties. John Bass of the 4th Battalion reported the losses of the battalion at 12 killed and wounded and estimated the losses for the brigade at almost 400. Gibson never reported his casualties at the Battle of Ezra Church. Private Eddins of the 19th Louisiana placed the losses of his brigade that afternoon at 480 men killed, wounded and missing and Captain S.A. Hightower, Company C of the 19th Louisiana reported his own regiment lost 125 men. Included in the Nineteenth's losses were Colonel Turner and Lieutenant Colonel Kennedy who were both wounded. To confuse the report of losses more Douglas Cater of the same regiment said the Nineteenth lost 48 men and the whole brigade lost 200 men. A member of the 4th Louisiana reported his regiment's losses at 82 out of 240 men and claimed that the brigade lost 540 of 900 effective men. The muster rolls of the 20th Louisiana stated that it went into battle with 46 men and 12 officers and survived the battle with only 18 men and 6 officers. On 18 July, the brigade's effective strength had been 1,115 men. On 29 July, the day after the Battle of Ezra Church, the brigade's effective strength was 763, a loss of 352 from 18 July. Captain Hightower best explained the condition of the brigade following Ezra Church when writing to Colonel Hyder Kennedy: "I am left with only seventeen men this morning. The Company is a sad picture to look at." Kennedy had himself been wounded in the wrist in the battle and his brother John, serving in Company C, was last seen loading and firing his rifle beside his brother. John was wounded and captured.[14]

William Oake of the 26th Iowa and part of his unit were sent out to bury the dead the day after the Battle of Ezra Church. The area that he and his unit were working was about 200 plus yards to the right of his position in line, which would have placed them burying the dead in front of Wangelin's brigade, where the Louisianians fought the previous day. While on burial detail, Oake left a very good description of the destruction wrought on the Louisiana Brigade. Oake noticed impressions in the ground from cattle and horses from a time when it was wet and how they were filled with human blood. Along the fence separating the field and the woods in front of Wangelin's line, he said the enemy dead were lying in rows. "During my three years of service I don't think I ever saw a field where the timber and underbrush were cut down by bullets as it was at the battle of Ezra's Church," said Oake. Major Abraham Seay of the 32nd Missouri, Wangelin's brigade, backed up Oake's description of the situation to the brigade's front: "Here the dead lay in unbroken lines; I may say in heaps."[15]

The 30th Louisiana suffered severely at Ezra Church. Not only was its flag captured, and its color guard decimated, but it also lost Lieutenant Colonel Thomas Shields and Major Charles Bell. Captain Arthur Picolet of Company D was immediately promoted to major to fill the command void of the 30th Battalion. After the battle, stories of the 30th Regiment losing its flag made headlines in the North in *Harper's Weekly* and the *Cincinnati Commercial*. In *Harper's Weekly* a Union soldier is depicted taking the regiment's flag from a wounded Confederate and the flag is a 2nd National Flag. In Vicksburg's pro–Union *Daily Herald*, a story appeared based off of a correspondent from the *Cincinnati Commercial*. In that story the 30th Louisiana's flag is described as follows: "The border is of buff moiré antique, the ground work is of beautifully fine red worsted, and the diagonal bars of blue silk, edged with white, and dotted their entire length with stars." This description was in fact the 30th Louisiana's flag issued from the Department of Alabama, Mississippi, and East Louisiana. Either the 30th Louisiana was not issued a Joe Johnston flag upon joining the army or declined to use it.[16]

Wounded at Ezra Church was a long stay member of the brigade, Colonel Leon von Zinken of the 20th Louisiana. A shell fragment shattered his hand and forearm. The wound prevented him from retaking command of his regiment and he was retired from field command. After recovering Zinken was placed under the command of Major General Howell Cobb's district in Georgia and was assigned to command the post of Columbus, Georgia. Zinken served at this post until the close of the war. Zinken's last taste of fighting came at the very closing of the war when Major General James Wilson's massive column of cavalry ripped through Alabama in 1865 and reached Columbus. Zinken's forces were meager and did not stand up to Wilson's well equipped veterans. In preparation for the Battle of Columbus, fought on April 16, 1865, Zinken had wired a request to the secretary of war, and his old commanding officer, John C. Breckinridge that, if allowed, he could raise a brigade of "negroes" within a "short time," because they "offered daily to volunteer." Unfortunately for Zinken, and more importantly for the Confederacy, this was an issue that they waited too long to address and agree to. After the defeat at Columbus, Zinken was captured and paroled. Zinken lived out his days in New Orleans until 1871, working as an auctioneer, appraiser and city inspector.[17]

The flag of the 30th Louisiana captured at the Battle of Ezra Church (courtesy of Confederate Memorial Hall Museum, New Orleans).

Hood's attack at Ezra Church did halt Sherman's advance for a few days on Hood's last railroad entering Atlanta. To protect that supply line, Hood deployed Lee's corps to the southwest to Atlanta. Following the Battle of Ezra Church, the brigade fell back to the Sandtown Road, near Utoy Creek, to the southwest of Atlanta. Clayton's left rested on the Sandtown Road, and Gibson formed the extreme left of Clayton's line near the Baugh House. Due to the amount of ground the brigade was forced to cover the regiments were deployed in a single line. One company of the 4th Louisiana, which still numbered around 30 men, defended 100 yards of the line. To compensate for this disparity, the brigade was ordered to remove all of the trees to their front and create an "impassable abattis" of felled trees. Behind this natural barrier, small redoubts were built across the front of the line that were manned by three to four men for the picket line.[18]

The brigade was in position for a few days before Sherman began stretching his army to the southwest of Atlanta in an attempt to cut off its last rail line, the Atlanta & West Point Railroad. The force assigned to take the railroad was Major General John Schofield's Army of the Ohio and two divisions of Major General John Palmer's XIV Corps of the Army of the Cumberland, a total of 25,000 men. The goal of the movement was to aim

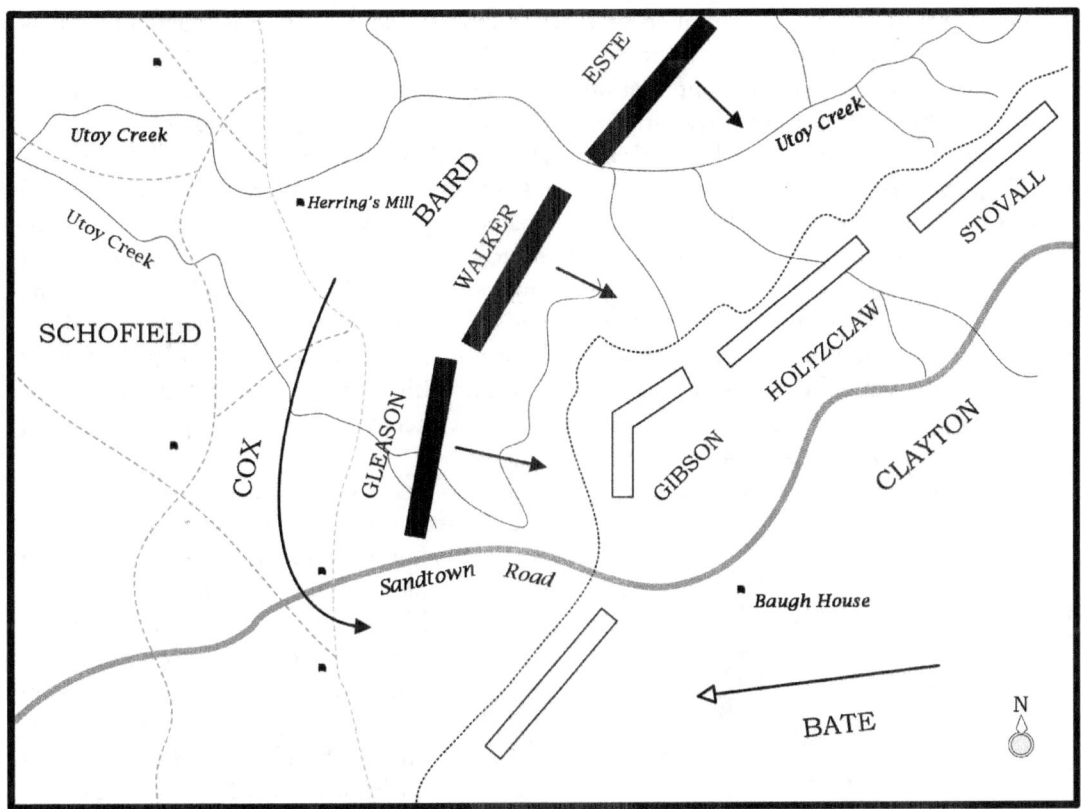

Siege of Atlanta, Operations on the Utoy, 3 through 7 August 1864. Union forces were very active in the month of August with the 3rd through the 7th being some of the most active. Union positions were not static due to their continual attempt to flank the left of the Confederate line. Union dispositions shown above are for 5 August. Movements of Bate's division and Cox's division in the latter parts of the day are shown.

for East Point about six miles below Atlanta. This grand flanking movement brought Schofield's force to Utoy Creek to the southwest of Atlanta by the night of 2 August. Schofield's line of march was not turning out to be a quick flank movement as Sherman envisioned. Instead, Schofield's current line of march was toward East Point, across the Utoy and down the Sandtown Road area toward Clayton's thin line. To prevent Clayton's left, the Louisiana Brigade, from being flanked, Hood rushed divisions from Hardee's corps and deployed them south of the road.[19]

The Battle of Utoy Creek, 3 through 7 August was not really a set battle. Instead, it was a series of small scale engagements along the Utoy Creek–Sandtown Road area in search of the flank of the Confederate line. With each day's advance, the Union lines inched closer and entrenched as they went: "The enemy cautiously pushed forward his lines toward ours, erecting new lines of works as he advanced." Schofield's advance put the skirmish lines a mere 75 yards in front of the Louisianians. Construction of redoubts along the Louisianians' skirmish line was still underway when the Battle of Utoy Creek began. A small detachment of three men from the 19th Louisiana were forced to lay prostate with one pick as they built their redoubt while taking fire from an enemy picket. "That Fed was having a picnic all by himself." Once their redoubt was complete, the men each took a shot at the picket and sat as proud champions of their accomplishment, only to be moved to a new location to undergo the same work.[20]

Skirmishing along the front intensified with the first major push on Gibson's front coming on 5 August. Pushing down on Sandtown Road from Herring Mill, along Utoy Creek, was Brigadier Absalom Baird's division of Palmer's XIV Corps. Opposite of Gibson during this push was Baird's right brigade, Colonel Newell Gleason's. Baird's men had pushed across Utoy Creek on the third and were prepared to push Clayton's line, but deployment confusion and command seniority tethered Baird's advance. It was not until the evening of the 4th that Baird pushed his men to the Sandtown Road. Gleason's brigade was given the job of feeling out Clayton's line and performed an excellent job in capturing several of the skirmishers' redoubts to Gibson's front. With no support marching to his flanks from other divisions, Baird pulled Gleason back for the night. With his front cleared, Gibson reoccupied his skirmish line, and orders were given for the men to "fight to the last" rather than give up their positions so easily.[21]

Somehow in the early hours of the fifth, skirmishers of Gleason's brigade were able to sneak up to within yards of the picket line of Gibson's brigade and make a "sudden assault." Gleason accredited the stealthy move to having moved over and having fought on the same ground the evening before. The Louisiana units on skirmish duty were caught off guard but put up a stiff fight. Two heavy lines of skirmishers, followed by solid reserves, fell on the 16th & 25th Regiment, the 4th Regiment, and Austin's battalion, which were on picket duty. Members in both units blamed supporting elements from other brigades for allowing the enemy to swing around and capture a lot of the men in the redoubts. About 100 men were captured along the skirmish line by Gleason's quick rush: at least 24 from the 4th Louisiana and at least a dozen from the 13th Louisianian, 18 from Austin's dwindling unit and the remainder from the rest of the brigade. Both W.H. Duff of the 25th Louisiana, who was captured, and Gleason agreed that orders to hold the line to the last extremity allowed for men to be captured more than anything. The small, obstinate fight on the fifth cost Baird about 83 men, with 26 being in Gleason's command. Fighting along the Utoy continued for the next two days, with the bulk of Schofield's advance now falling upon

Captain Louis Fortin, 30th Louisiana. Fortin was killed by a sharpshooter in the trenches south of Atlanta during August (courtesy of Confederate Memorial Hall Museum, New Orleans).

Bate's division to Gibson's left. With the Confederate left extended and the railroad protected, the two sides dug in.[22]

For the next month the brigade remained in this position, mainly digging trenches. "I have become expert in the use of the spade & axe," a Louisianian truthfully joked in a letter home. For the month of August, Sherman busied himself with besieging Atlanta. One Louisiana soldier wrote, "We built works here [Sandtown Road area], but were much exposed to the fire of the enemy's artillery. This practically confined the men to the ditches; it was not comfortable there, but at least one was safe." "They shell us constantly," wrote another soldier. Douglas Cater of the 19th Louisiana described the conditions of trench life: "Our clothes were soon the color of the clay in which we were protected from shells and minie balls. We could not leave the ditches in the daytime without danger of being killed at any moment." Despite the conditions the men were subjected to in their recent battlefield defeats, Gibson's Louisianians were still regarded as top-notch troops. A Captain Jordon from one of Clayton's Alabama regiments deserted to the enemy on 13 August and gave detailed information on the location, strength and morale of as many units as he could. When the deserter got to Gibson's brigade, he said that "his [Gibson's Brigade] is counted the best fighting brigade in the corps [Lee's Corps]."[23]

Colonel Hunter related the conditions he regiment faced to his wife in the trenches on the Sandtown Road:

[We are] compelled by the enemy's shot & shell to remain most of the time in the ditches and after [illegible word] being very muddy and disagreeable on account of daily rains a [illegible word] soldier has need of all his patience & philosophy to keep his courage & spirits up. My poor regiment has suffered so much during the last week that I have been somewhat despondent. Two shells struck in the ditches where my men were on the 7th. Two men were killed outright—five more died of their wounds & two more had their legs amputated and others were wounded more or less severly—16 in all.[24]

Despite being under orders by Hood himself to refrain from firing, "except in cases of necessity," the Louisianians tried to make life difficult on their counterparts. Gleason, whose brigade was in front of Gibson for most of August, does not elaborate on the conditions of his regiments, but Baird does:

The necessary location of our camps was such that they were constantly exposed to the enemy's fire, and there were few points at which a man could show himself without the risk of being shot. On certain portions of the line a temporary truce would be arranged with the troops that chanced to be in front, whilst at others a vicious skirmish would be kept up, and for days the men would be imprisoned in their trenches, not daring to show their heads above the parapet, and this varied by the fire of artillery or more active demonstrations begun by one or the other party.[25]

During one of the armistices that Baird referred to, Captain Louis Fortin, commanding officer of the 30th Louisiana by default due to all other officers being killed our wounded, was shot by a Union sharpshooter and later died.[26]

On the night of 25 August Sherman left the siege lines around Atlanta and made a wide sweeping movement to the west of the city. Hoping to end the stalemate around Atlanta and boost support for Lincoln's reelection in just a few months, Sherman decided to cut loose from his supply line and march the bulk of his army against the Macon & Western Railroad. Hood did not catch onto Sherman's move until the evening of 30 August because Hood, as many others, believed that Sherman had abandoned the siege. Quickly,

Hood reacted by sending Lee's and Hardee's corps south to the town of Jonesboro to intercept Sherman.[27]

The fourteen mile march to Jonesboro was an "exceedingly fatiguing" march on the night of 30 August. Clayton's division marched into Jonesboro about midday and was given two hours rest before being called into formation. The rest the Louisianians got to enjoy was the building of breastworks parallel to the railroad, about 200 yards to the west of it. Clayton formed two of his brigades, his other two having been temporarily detached to Stevenson, in the second line of the Confederate attack on the right. Gibson was posted to the left of Jones' brigade. The brigade was placed to the west of the railroad toward Atlanta and north of the Fairburn Road that headed west to the Flint River. In front of Gibson was Brigadier General Zachariah Deas' brigade of Major General James P. Anderson's division. The Louisianians were posted a mere thirty to forty yards behind Deas' Alabamians. The actual alignment of the Louisiana regiments is only partially known. The 30th Louisiana was in the center of the brigade, and the 4th Louisiana and the 16th & 25th Louisiana were on the right of the brigade in an unknown order. It appears the 13th and 20th Louisiana Regiments may have been on the left of the brigade. The alignment of the 1st Regulars, Austin's battalion and the 19th Louisiana are not documented.[28]

Opposite the Louisiana Brigade's position was the Army of the Tennessee, which had remained in its position around Ezra Church until 26 August. That night, it first moved west, almost to the Chattahoochee River, and then headed south to the town of Fairburn on the Atlanta & West Point Railroad. The army then headed east, its destination being the town of Jonesboro on the Macon & Western Railroad. The Army of the Tennessee crossed the Flint River, about two miles from Jonesboro, on the afternoon of the thirtieth and were issued orders: "Strong works to be made during the night." The unit posted opposite of the Louisiana Brigade was the Second Division of the XV Corps, commanded by Brigadier General William Hazen. Hazen was no stranger to the Louisianians. Hazen was deployed to the north of the Fairburn-Jonesboro Road. His Second Brigade, under Colonel Wells Jones, had its right resting on the Fairburn Road and facing east. Jones' line turned to the northwest at an angle and provided flank fire across the front of Hazen's First Brigade, under Colonel Theodore Jones.[29]

The First Brigade's front was mostly at a southeast to east front, and then its left flank was refused in the opposite direction, forming an angle. The reason Hazen's line was in a motley shape was that he had ordered Theodore Jones' brigade forward to take a "commanding eminence" about 800 yards to the front of his line. After throwing several regiments to the front for the divisions' skirmishers Theodore Jones wheeled his brigade "to the front and right," and by doing so his left sat at the crest of the hill that Hazen wanted occupied. Jones was now in a very exposed position with his left hanging open to Lee's corps and a large gap emerging between his right and Jones' Second Brigade. The regiment on Jones' left, on top of the hill, was the 127th Illinois. Its line was refused in an attempt to cover its flank. The majority of Jones' line now formed a right angle with Jones' Second Brigade. Forming next to the 127th Illinois, forming the other part of the angle, was the 55th Illinois. To the right of that regiment was the 57th Ohio and then the 116th Illinois. These regiments were facing more of a southeast direction. The latter of the two was pulled back from the skirmish line to help fill the gap to the right of the brigade.[30]

Hazen described his line as "light" and having "considerable intervals." Unfortunately for the attacking Louisianians, Hazen requested and received reinforcements to bolster his

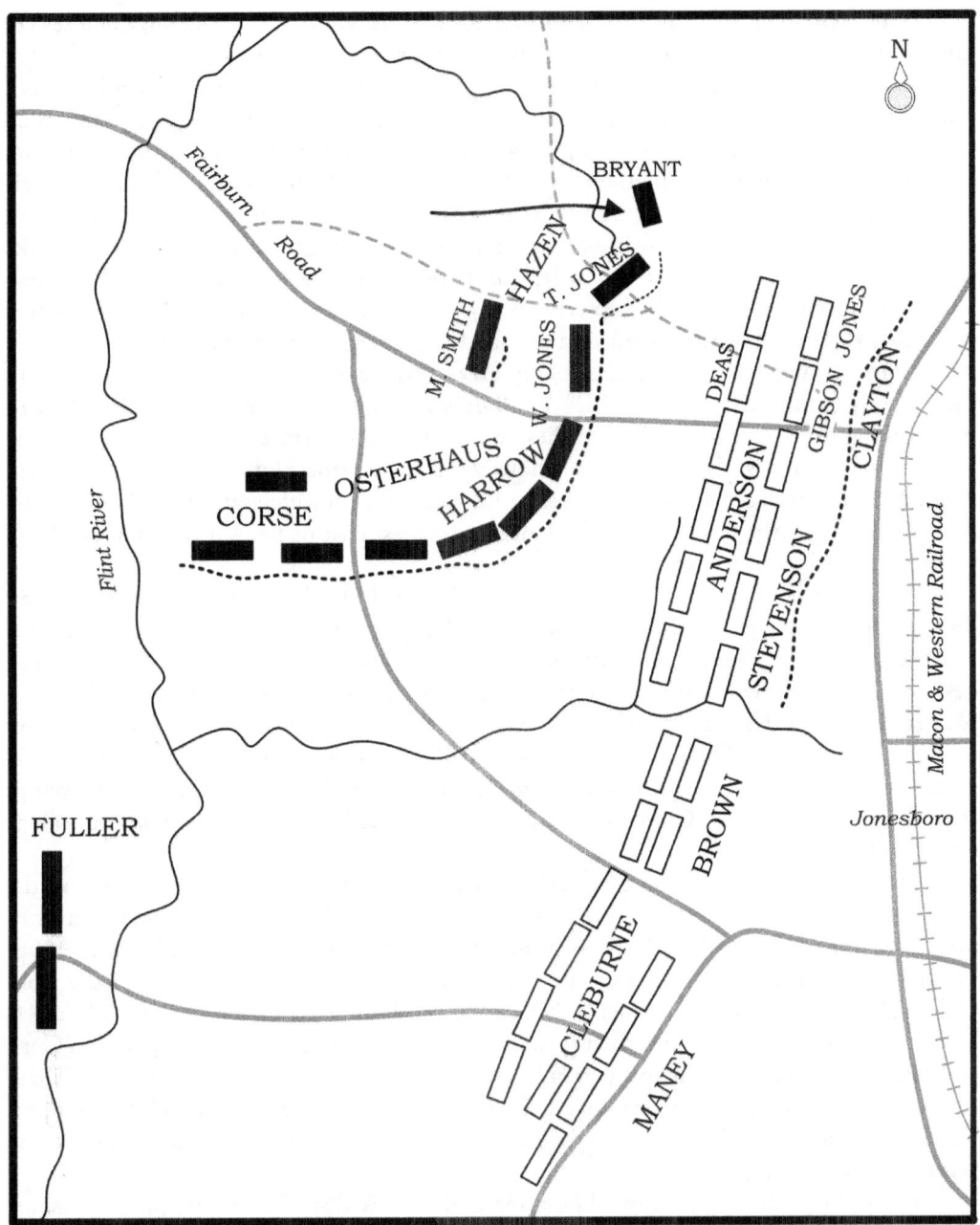

Battle of Jonesboro, 31 August 1864.

exposed line. Five regiments were sent to his aid that were placed on his left flank and thrown into his line where needed. To make matters worse for the upcoming fight for Gibson's brigade, Hazen's two batteries, Batteries A and H of the 1st Illinois Light Artillery, had been brought across Flint River and thrown into battery. Battery H was posted near the left flank to strengthen that end of the line, and it appears that Battery A was placed somewhere between the two brigades. Jones' brigade and supporting regiments hurriedly dug in as the Louisianians formed into line outside their breastworks for the attack. The longer the day drifted the harder the work that lay ahead for the Louisianians.[31]

Hardee, in temporary command of Lee's and his own corps, did not launch his attack until about 2:00 P.M. Given an entire day to build breastworks, with their right anchored on the Flint River, the Federals occupied a rather strong position.. Every passing minute allowed for the enemy to strengthen their defenses. General Anderson described the position opposite his, and Gibson's, front: "The enemy was strongly posted on the crest of an irregular ridge, and that his position was rendered still stronger by a line of breast-works which he had thrown up before our arrival, and upon which he was still at work." The terrain upon which the brigade had to cross was just as non-flattering to an attacker: "There was but little cover for our assaulting lines, and the ascent in some places was moderately steep, but not rugged, affording the enemy great advantages in the ground in addition to those derived from his breast-works." The Louisiana Brigade's trenches were in a belt of woods along the railroad, and it is in these woods the men formed up for the attack. The woods continued west for quite a bit before the terrain turned into a field that stretched about 300 yards into a thicket, "low brush and small trees," in which sat Jones' First Brigade. At the tree line to the thicket, a picket fence ran across most of Jones' front at about forty yards from his line of works.[32]

Gibson's brigade pushed forward at about 3:00 behind the advance of Deas. Gibson pushed into the charge just thirty to forty yards behind the first line. What occurred next was the product of Hood's bold attacks around Atlanta the month before. General Lee described what he saw: "The attack was not made by the troops with that spirit and inflexible determination that would insure success." Colonel Jones in the brigade next to Gibson reiterated Lee's words: "The men seemed possessed of some great horror of charging breastworks, which no power, persuasion, or example could dispel." Deas' brigade was not exempt from this type of behavior. Gibson said that Deas' men faced a "withering fire" and "recoiled" once it hit them.[33]

The Louisianians were close enough to witness the effectiveness of Jones' fire on the men to their front. As the front line began to fall back, Gibson could see that groups of men were beginning to waver in the advance. Gibson rode to the color bearer of the 30th Louisiana, grabbed its flag, ordered his staff forward with him, and "dashed to the front and up to the very works of the enemy." "Great enthusiasm" swept the ranks of the Louisianians, and "the whole brigade rushed forward." Riding to the right of the brigade was General Clayton; he had his hat in his hand cheering the men forward. Once clear of Deas' retreating units, the Louisianians were pelted with their first "terrific volley" of the fight. The Louisianians absorbed the blow of this first volley and pushed forward under strong exertions from yelling officers.[34]

The right of the brigade, 4th Louisiana and 16th & 25th Louisiana, pushed against the angle of the 127th Illinois and 55th Illinois and the 57th Ohio. The brunt of the attack fell upon the 55th Illinois and 57th Ohio. Luckily for Hunter's and Lewis' units there were few obstacles in their way to reaching Jones' line. "The way was clear, a little abattis & a small picket fence being the only obstacles." With sword in hand, Colonel J.C. Lewis pushed his 16th & 25th Regiment forward into the fire of Jones' angle. Hunter's 4th Louisiana bore down on the very angle itself. "When we opened upon them," said Colonel Samuel Mott of the 57th Ohio, "many fell, but with a stubbornness and determination that showed no value was attached to human life, the gaps were soon closed, as if by magic. Onward they came, with firm step and compressed lip." Casualties were mounting and the officers used

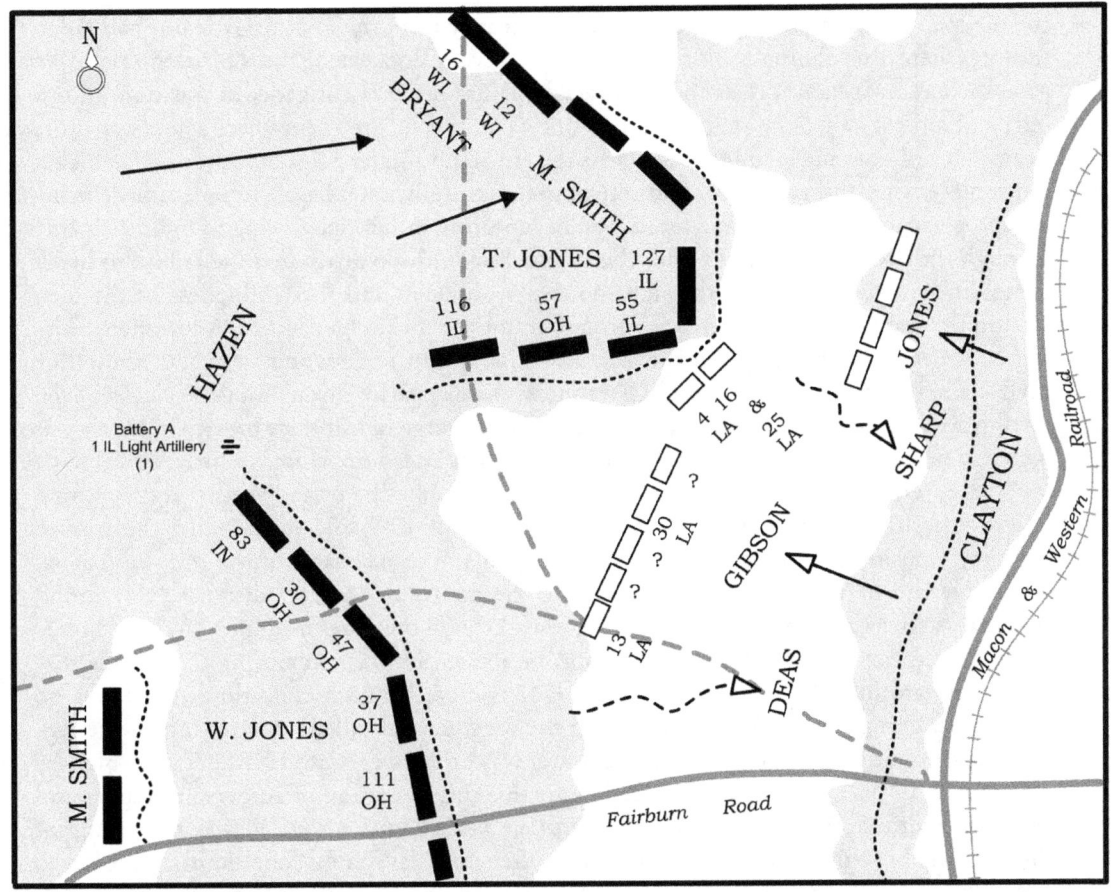

Lee's Attack, Battle of Jonesboro, 31 August 1864, 4:00 P.M.

every exertion to keep the men going. A Hoosier of the 55th Illinois described the enemy to his front: "Every man yelling like a demon incarnate." Colonel J.C. Lewis was shot and mortally wounded "within a few paces of the enemy," while leading the 16th & 25th Regiment against the 55th Illinois and 57th Ohio. Along with Lewis, Major Robert Oliver of the 16th Louisiana was mortally wounded. Oliver would live out the day before dying a prisoner of the enemy. Jones ordered the 55th Illinois and 57th Ohio to fix their bayonets and prepare to meet the Louisianians' rush. Accounts vary as to how far the charge actually went. They go from actually entering the angle of Jones' line, to a few paces, to ten yards. There is collaborating evidence that the Louisianians did pierce Jones' trenches if for only a few moments. Parts of Hunter's and Lewis' regiments did reach the works but were too few to make a difference. Gibson said, "A few of the men got up to the works of the enemy and some inside of them," and most of those who did venture too close became prisoners.[35]

The left part of the brigade's advance was not as easy as that of the right. Their pathway was not as wide open and clear. As the brigade got close to the thicket line, it "encountered abattis and a dense growth of underbrush which prevented them from attacking up to the works." As the regiments struggled through these obstacles, they took serious flanking fire from the part of Wells Jones' regiments that faced in a northeast direction. One of the regiments in this line, the 30th Ohio, was actually from the First Brigade but had fallen into line here after falling back from skirmish duty. A Buckeye of the Thirtieth said, "We gave the enemy a flank fire as they advanced against the First Brigade, in position on our left, and almost at a right angle with our line. The loss of the enemy here again was quite heavy." It did not take long for men across the entire Louisiana Brigade to stop at the picket fence picket line and take cover and return fire. Naturally, men began to return fire during this process, and soon more and more men began firing rather than trying to fight their way through the obstacles and push onto the enemy line. Gibson attributed the failure to break Jones' line to having to fight through too many obstacles and the willingness of the men to stop their advance to exchange fire from behind the picket fence line. "A few men, halting at the fence and lodging in the skirmish pits, began to fire, and soon the whole line fired, halted, and finally gave way." Clayton, who was nearby throughout the charge, even having a horse shot from under him, described the charge of Gibson's brigade: "Never was a charge begun with such enthusiasm terminated with accomplishing so little."[36]

An interesting event during the battle occurred while the brigade was tied down for a few minutes in front of the enemy works exchanging fire. While encouraging the men to hold their position, General Anderson came upon the color bearer of the 13th Louisiana. Anderson said he found the bearer in rear of the main line "a short distance." He found the man "with a number of men scattered about through the pines near him." When Anderson inquired as to what the man was doing, he replied he was attempting to rally his regiment forward but was, so far, unsuccessful. Obviously, in such conditions, there was no time for skulking and shirking of duty, and the wiry general called upon officers of the regiment, but none were found. Worse, the bearer was ordered forward by Anderson, "but few responded" to his call. Gibson forever fought this interpretation of Anderson's report and spent years attempting to seek, "*The vindication of the 13th La Regt.*" It was the urging of Gibson that brought to surface a report from General Clayton on Jonesboro, and it led to nothing but an affectionate memory of the Louisianians. Regardless if correct or not, the left part of Gibson's brigade did stall out and quickly turn to taking cover to exchange fire rather than push forward from their protection.[37]

The brigade fell back to their works where Gibson prepared his men for a second charge. The optimistic brigadier said his men met his rally calls to renew the advance and "every officer and man was in his place and ready to advance." The Battle of Jonesboro, though, was over for the Louisianians. It was the bloodiest fifteen minutes of the war for the brigade. In that time span, Gibson's brigade had suffered heavily, again. Gibson did not provide an official statement on his brigade's losses for the Battle of Jonesboro, but he and Clayton did state that his losses were half the number of the brigade. Assistant Surgeon John H. Bass wrote in his journal that the brigade lost 172 men, and the 16th & 25th Regiment lost 43. Colonel Hunter gave a very detailed casualty list for the 4th Louisiana, putting his losses at 64 out of its 104 men: 12 killed, 35 wounded and 17 missing. Numbers for the whole brigade, though, have to be drawn from the musters taken before and after the battle. On 28 August the brigade's effective strength was listed as 697 men. On 8 September a week after the battle, that number was 549, by which time stragglers and perhaps the slightly wounded had returned to the brigade. After the war in a letter to General Clayton, Gibson said he lost 224 men.[38]

On the evening of the thirty-first, Lee's corps was called back toward Atlanta, leaving Hardee to defend Jonesboro with only one corps. On 1 September, Hardee was forced to withdraw after a day-long battle with the Army of the Tennessee and elements of the Army of the Cumberland. The loss of Jonesboro and the last rail supply line for Atlanta caused Hood to order the evacuation of Atlanta. Orders were given to all forces to meet up with Hardee's corps at Lovejoy Station on the Macon & Western Railroad, below Jonesboro. Lee, on his way to Atlanta, was stopped by Hood. Hood ordered Lee to retreat south to Lovejoy Station, where the army was designated to regroup. Lee's corps, with Clayton in the lead, marched toward the town of McDonough, located just east of Lovejoy Station. The brigade reached McDonough on the third. On 4 September, Gibson and his men reached Lovejoy Station. The Atlanta Campaign was finally over. Nearly four months of constant marching and skirmishing had finally ended but not without serious losses.[39]

CHAPTER 11

Tennessee Campaign: September–December 1864

"[T]rying to seize a stand of colors and lead the brigade against the enemy. The color-bearer refused to give up his colors and was sustained by his regiment. I found it was the color-bearer of the Thirteenth Louisiana. It was Gibson's Louisiana Brigade. Gibson soon approached at my side and in admiration of such conduct I exclaimed: 'Gibson, these are the best men I ever saw; you take them and check the enemy.'"

—Lieutenant General Stephen D. Lee, Corps Commander, on the Battle of Nashville

Constant marching and fighting from May through September took its toll on the Louisiana Brigade. Gibson began the campaign with 917 and peaked out over 1,000 with the addition of the 4th Regiment and 30th Battalion. Four days after regrouping with the army around Lovejoy Station, Gibson listed his effective strength at 549 men. "My regiment only numbers 80 muskets for duty, not ⅓ of what I brought up here," said Colonel Samuel Hunter of the 4th Louisiana. Hunter was sent by Gibson to Mobile, a large Louisiana refugee haven, in an attempt to find shoes for the men. In the process of trying to procure shoes, Hunter was able to gain an audience with the department commander, General Richard Taylor, who pushed forth 500 pairs of shoes. With only 549 men present for effective duty, that meant practically every man in the brigade needed a new pair of shoes; not a surprising fact after four months of marching and fighting.[1]

With such drastic losses and hardships also came a new wave of faces in positions of command within the brigade. Only three officers that commanded their units in May made it through the Atlanta Campaign: Major John E. Austin, Colonel Samuel Hunter of the 4th Louisiana and Colonel Francis Campbell of the 13th Louisiana. A long stay officer in the brigade, Major John Austin, was issued a 125 day leave of absence by General John B. Hood in late September. Austin never returned to duty with his battalion but was apparently active in the Trans-Mississippi Department. He was paroled in Shreveport in June of 1865 and made his way back to New Orleans where he practiced law until his death in 1878. Command of the battalion went to 1st Lieutenant A.T. Martin of Company B, a transfer from the 11th Louisiana with Austin in August of 1862. The 1st Regulars, 19th Regiment, 20th Regiment, 4th and 30th battalions all emerged from the campaign with captains in command: William Quirk, Camp Flournoy, Alexander Dresel, T. Alexander Bisland and H.P. Jones, respectively. Douglas West of the 1st Regulars was promoted to major after Ezra Church and placed in command of the regiment but was given a furlough by Hood.

Command of the regiment then fell on Captain Quirk's shoulders. Camp Flournoy was promoted to major soon afterwards.²

Command of the 16th & 25th Louisiana had remained a stable force under Fisk, Gober and then Lewis for the majority of the war, with then Major Frank Zacharie filling in as commander during Murfreesboro with Stuart's death. The 16th & 25th Louisiana ran into the command disaster after Atlanta that its former consolidated sister regiment faced, the 13th & 20th Regiment. To fill the vacancy left by Lewis' death, Frank Zacharie was promoted to colonel and his vacancy was filled by the promotion of Calvin H. Moore to lieutenant colonel. Captain W.F. Mellon was mentioned for filling the vacancy for major. Both Zacharie and Moore, though, were in Louisiana on detached duty at this time, and Mellon had just tendered his resignation due to the inability to serve in the field. Command of the 16th & 25th Regiment fell on the shoulders of Lieutenant Colonel Robert Lindsay until Zacharie's return. Likewise, Major Frank Raxsdale had been absent from the regiment on various duties since December 1862 and returned to the regiment in time for the Atlanta Campaign only to get wounded in early July. Afterwards, he was

Major Frank Raxsdale, 16th Louisiana. Raxsdale continually remained detached from his regiment on recruitment duty from late 1862 to early 1864. Raxsdale returned to his regiment to participate in the Atlanta Campaign but was wounded. He left the regiment to recuperate and remained absent for the remainder of the war (courtesy of Camp Moore Historical Association).

detached again and, thus, left another void in the command echelon of the 16th & 25th Regiment. Lindsay operated in this manner until November when Zacharie returned to the army, and the two regiments were split into separate units. All during this time, there were repeated attempts by several of these officers to push themselves for promotions to the next position, regardless of being active with their unit or not.

Promotion was big to the officers of not only the Louisiana Brigade but throughout the Southern culture. It was prestige and honor at stake, and to these men, most of affluent and politically powerful families, not to receive promotion, when available, was a dishonor to them. This was exemplified in earlier chapters with the struggle of Randall Gibson and his quest for brigadier general. Officers serving in his brigade were no different, and Gibson was very proactive and supportive of correcting the roles of his regiments and pushing for promotions. In regards to the 16th & 25th Louisiana, Frank Zacharie explained the importance of promotion in a letter to his father: "I should be a poor soldier were I destitute of ambition. Napoleon says I think that every true soldier should have his eye on the *baton* of the Marshall's and of course I look forward to promotion as gratifying to my pride and with an honest wish to do the country service." Oddly, Zacharie boasted that generals such as Daniel Ruggles, Patton Anderson and Daniel Adams would all "recommend me

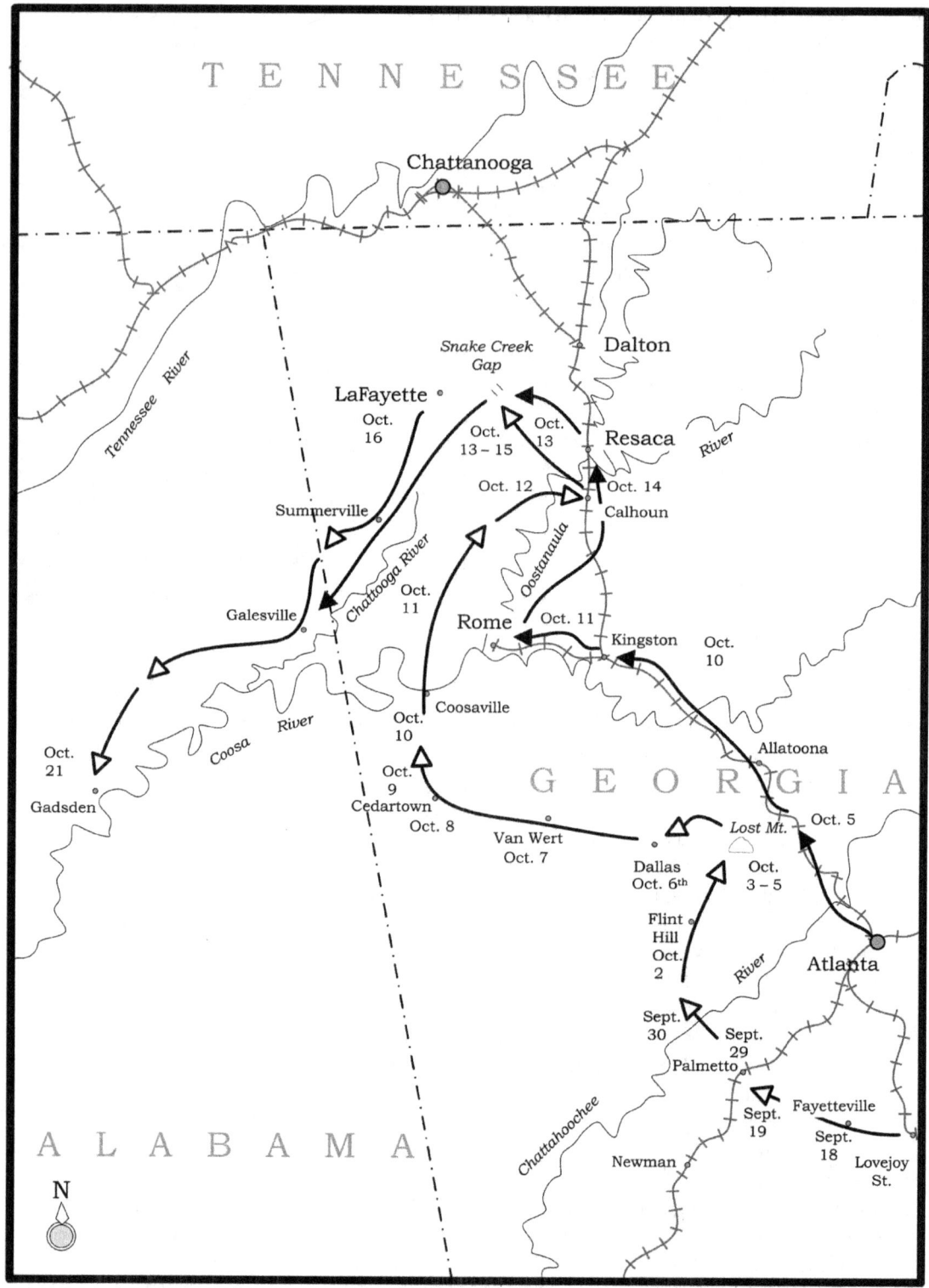

Movements of the Louisiana Brigade, 18 September to 21 October 1864.

for the position ... of Brig General of volunteers" but left out Randall Gibson, an officer he fought with and was commanded by for two years. The glaring omission of Gibson raises concerns of whether Zacharie was questioning Gibson's leadership qualities when he told his father, "I could fill the position of Brig. General of Volunteers as well as some now occupying that position." Zacharie's father was a well known and profitable merchant before the war and engaged in blockade running during the war. He made sure that Zacharie's letter was forwarded to the proper contacts in Richmond, and young Zacharie's promotion was not long in arriving.[3]

With his army barely pulling itself together around Lovejoy Station, John Hood suggested to President Jefferson Davis on 6 September an offense against Sherman's supply line to Chattanooga. The rest at Lovejoy Station was not long enough for the Louisianians. On 18 September the brigade left camp and marched to Palmetto, to the west of Lovejoy Station, where it arrived the next day. Hoping to restore the morale of the Army of Tennessee after the fall of Atlanta, President Davis made a special visit to the army. Unknown to the brigade, Hood was preparing to initiate an offensive campaign. Davis arrived at Palmetto on 25 September to discuss Hood's proposal and try to boost the morale of the army. After an impromptu tour of the front lines and of the army itself, the president was serenaded in the evening by the 20th Louisiana's renowned band. The Twentieth's band performance attracted soldiers from several commands and it culminated in a huge rally with large speeches by generals and politicians. Davis agreed to Hood's plan to strike Sherman's supply line and left Hood the option of doing what he thought best. On 29 September the army broke camp at Palmetto and marched north. "Hood's campaign has commenced. Hostilities are resumed," one Louisianian noted in his diary. Randall Gibson and his men crossed the Chattahoochee River that afternoon at Pumpkin Town.[4]

From the Chattahoochee, the march was made at a north to northeast path toward Lost Mountain. Passing through Flint, the brigade reached the Lost Mountain vicinity on 3 October. The brigade enjoyed building breastworks the next couple of days, while other troops demonstrated along the railroad. The demonstrations resulted in small gains and a major setback at Allatoona where a small garrison whipped a division of Stewart's corps. Hood cut out attacking the railroad in this area and looked elsewhere. The march was continued on the sixth with the army passing the Dallas–New Hope battlefields. The Louisianians continued on a northwesterly to northern march through Van Wert, Cedartown, and finally to Coosaville on the tenth, where the brigade crossed the Coosa River below Rome on 11 October. The marching and weather conditions were taxing on the men, observed a Louisianian: "The men suffer a great deal with their feet but keep up their spirits." The men were on the move, advancing and bringing the fight to a place of their choosing. On the horizon were stores of Yankee goods at depots on the railroads to replace their rations of cornbread and beef.[5]

On 12 October Hood made his move toward the Dalton and Resaca garrisons. The Louisianians took part in the move to scare the Resaca garrison into surrendering. The brigade crossed the Oostanaula River and were placed near Calhoun, on the Western & Atlantic Railroad, below Resaca, thus cutting it off from Sherman. When the garrison refused to surrender, possibly emboldened by the valiant stand at Allatoona Pass days earlier, Lee, per orders under Hood not to risk an attack if an opportunity was not available, ordered his corps back to rejoin Hood's army. On the thirteenth, the brigade recrossed the Oostanaula and headed back north. The 4th Louisiana took the liberty to liberate Calhoun of any supplies they could find before leaving. Hood withdrew his army into the mountains and passed west of the Dalton and Resaca area, with Gibson's brigade stopping to help man Snake Creek Gap.[6]

"So far everything goes on quietly on our ride," a surprised and relieved John Bass noted. The brigade's discipline was intact, and only about twenty men appeared to be AWOL during the two weeks of hard marching. Despite starting out in rainy and muddy conditions, with little to no protection, the march north brought renewed spirits, but not new provisions to the Louisiana Brigade. "Troops healthy & good spirit & short rations," said John Bass of the 16th & 25th Regiment. Colonel Hunter of the 4th Louisiana, whom Gibson had sent to Mobile to get shoes for the brigade, arrived at Newnan, Georgia, to find the army had marched north. After walking 55 miles, Hunter caught up with the army and made this observation: "We are having a very disagreeable time. Last night a heavy frost fell.... We have very little to eat. Bread and beef and not much of that." Lieutenant John Kendall boasted that the men became very accustomed to living without tents and became experts at setting up blanket shanties. Despite these conditions, which were becoming more of the normal way of life for the brigade, Hunter did say his men were "in fine spirits."[7]

This was a major goal of Hood's campaign. He, and other leading generals of the Army of Tennessee, were convinced, as evident in reports from Jonesboro, that the men in the army had lost their ability to be aggressive and, more importantly, to attack breastworks. Stephen Lee, who was Gibson's corps commander, said, "I regarded the *morale* of the army greatly impaired after the fall of Atlanta, and, in fact, before its fall the troops were not by any means in good spirits. It was my observation and belief that the majority of the officers and men were so impressed with the idea of their inability to carry even temporary breastworks that ... they regarded it as recklessness in the extreme. Being impressed with these convictions they did not generally move to the attack with that spirit which nearly always insures success." Lee's solution? "In view of these facts it was my opinion that the army should take up the offensive, with the hope that favorable opportunities would be offered for striking the enemy successfully, thus insuring the efficiency of the army for future operations." Douglas Cater of the 19th Louisiana provided a different opinion to Lee, from a rank-and-filer perspective. Lee had taken command of the Louisianians' corps right before the Battle of Ezra Church in July and made little preparation for that battle. He sent Gibson's brigade into action totally unsupported, which resulted in a very high casualty list for the Louisianians. Cater remembered a speech Lee gave to the brigade in which he said, "'Soldiers, you can take temporary breastworks, you must and you shall take temporary breastworks' ... it made me feel like he had lost respect for us." Hesitating to attack an entrenched foe is an obstacle in itself for an officer to overcome. Following orders from a leader you have no faith in might be a greater one. "He was not in the charge on foot with a musket when our men were forced back.... He certainly had no more at stake than the rest of us." Perhaps Lee's problem in battle was not Yankee breastworks. Unprepared and uncoordinated attacks at Ezra Church lead to dispirited results and attempts at Jonesboro. The result of both situations was bloody repulse and defeat. Instead of finding fault in himself, Lee attributed defeat at those two battles only to the lack of "spirit and inflexible determination that would insure success" reflected by his men.[8]

Despite the army's improved spirits, as evident with the Louisianians, Hood was to be disappointed. Regardless of all the things Hood was not, and was limited to, he had stolen a march on Sherman and gotten in his rear. Hood's army was between Sherman and Chattanooga, and if disposed in a strategic position, he could force the decisive battle that he sought so badly. He kept the army for two days near Lafayette ready to give battle, but his generals advised against it. "I had expected that a forward movement of one hundred miles would re-inspirit the officers and men in a degree to impart to them confidence, enthusiasm, and hope of victory, if not strong faith in its achievement."[9]

On the fifteenth, Hood put his army in motion to the southwest, toward Alabama, to avoid Sherman's pursuit. The brigade passed Ships Gap and moved in a parallel route with the Chattooga River, reaching Summerville on the seventeenth. In contrast to a dispirited Hood, the brigade was in "fine spirits" as they marched away from Sherman. A member of the 19th Louisiana said, "Our troops are again in good spirits—no straggling with the army." The army reached Gadsden, Alabama, on 21 October where it was met by the commander of the Military Division of the West, General Pierre Beauregard. Beauregard had seen first hand the condition and spirit of the army the night before through a simple conversation with an unsuspecting soldier of the 30th Louisiana. While the young Louisianian was warming himself by a fire, he was engaged in a conversation by Beauregard, who was sitting close by. "My young friend, you seem to be badly shot," said Beauregard referring to the man's worn out shoes. "Yes, we are, many of us, in this condition; but let another fight come on with the Yankees, and we will all have new shoes." As John Bass marched and pitched camp near Gadsden, he wrote, "The health of the army was never better & the spirits are good. Hood & Beauregard have full confidence." Beauregard, accompanied by Hood, made their way to the different units in the army and gave speeches to build morale. He was joined in giving a pep speech to the Louisianians by Gibson, Hood, Bate, Clayton and Cleburne. Douglas Cater went on to say that Hood was met with "a loud cheer," and "the army are getting better satisfied with him as commander." The issuing of new clothes and shoes did much to improve the condition and morale of the men. The shoeless men were able to shed their cowhide moccasins and put on socks and shoes again. Hood was a restless commander and immediately set his sights on pushing into Tennessee.[10]

It was at this point that Sherman decided to abandon the pursuit of Hood. He had aggressively pushed after Hood with six full corps. Sherman was frustrated with Hood's ability to move faster than him, due in part to Hood sending the majority of the army's supply wagons and reserve artillery to Jacksonville, Alabama. Hood had jumped the gun on Sherman, gotten ahead of him and was moving faster. When Sherman reached Resaca on 14 October he said, "I determined to strike Hood in flank, or force him to battle." He sent part of his army to Snake Creek Gap to tie Hood down and attempted to flank him. Again, the Army of Tennessee was moving faster and was able to make its way to Gadsden. Sherman gave chase to Gaylesville, Alabama, before he called a halt. It was apparent to Sherman that Hood had no intention of giving battle: "He evidently wanted to avoid a fight." Beginning on 26 October Sherman began preparations to meet Hood's apparent move into Tennessee and to begin his own move into Georgia for the Atlantic Coast. Preparing for Hood in Tennessee was Major General George Thomas, formally of the Army of the Cumberland. Sherman reinforced Thomas' forces with his own V and XVIII Corps.[11]

As Sherman moved back into Georgia, Hood was moving the Army of Tennessee north. On 22 October Gibson's brigade began its march toward the Tennessee River. The first two days were spent passing ridges and mountains. Originally, the point of crossing was not far from Gadsden, at a place named Guntersville. That crossing was delayed and moved west because Hood was waiting the arrival of Major General Nathan Bedford Forrest's cavalry to begin his invasion. Over the next week the brigade marched through Sumerland and

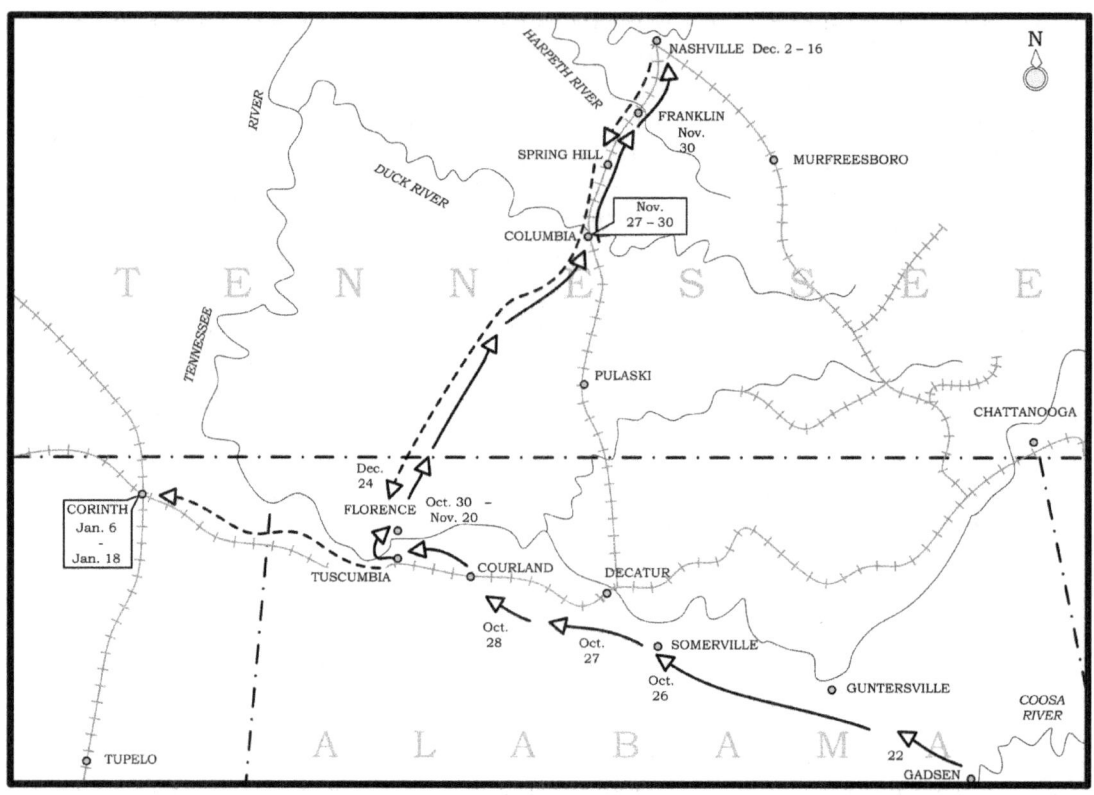

Movements of the Louisiana Brigade, 23 October to 18 January 1865.

Courland before arriving at Tuscumbia on 30 October. Across the river lay the town of Florence, the town in which Hood planned to cross the Tennessee River.

Lee's Corps led the army's march, and once its lead elements reached Tuscumbia, he ordered Gibson's Louisianans to the river to take Florence. Another division of Lee's corps, Major General Bushrod Johnson's, crossed a few miles up river. Pontoon boats were ordered forward for the Louisianans to cross the river. Gibson ordered gathered detachments from several units and put them in charge of Colonel R.H. Lindsay. The pontoons sat between 17 to 19 men each. Filing into the bows of the boats were sharpshooters from Austin's battalion to provide covering fire. As the Louisianans made improvised paddles from "fence pickets and boards from houses nearby," Clayton brought forward several pieces of artillery near the old railroad bridge to provide a covering.[12]

Across the river was part of Brigadier General John Croxton's Federal Brigade of cavalry. Croxton was defending about a twenty-four mile area along the river and believed that Hood's crossing was going to take place east of Florence at Bainbridge. The majority of his forces were dispatched to that region to meet the anticipated crossing. Croxton's two worst units, the 10th and 12th Tennessee U.S. Cavalry, were garrisoning Florence. These two regiments were "so badly mounted and so carelessly managed" that they fielded only 200 men to guard the town. From the Louisiana Brigade's side of the river, the pickets along the river seemed "perfectly indifferent, or ignorant" of the coming attack. They were, for it was believed that the crossing was going to take place miles to the east. As preparations were being made to cross the river some of the Louisiana boys went down the bank of the river and started talking with the enemy. The Tennesseans along the bank occupied a brick warehouse and were "leisurely lolling about the old house, some in shirt sleeves, others sitting quietly on the river bank, talking with the 'Johnny Rebs.'" Spying the enemy 1,000 yards away along the banks, Lindsay worried about having to wrest the brick warehouse away from the unsuspecting enemy. "I had but little hope of ever reaching the north bank," Lindsay admitted.[13]

The artillery was let loose on the enemy cavalry, and the Louisiana navy was unleashed into the river. The Tennesseans did not make much of a stand and "skedaddled." Once on the other side of the river, Lindsay formed his men up, dispatched Lieutenant Thomas Pegues of the 16th Louisiana with five men to deal with the warehouse on his flank, and then ordered the men forward in a charge up the hill into Florence. Lindsay, who had to leave his horse on the opposite shore, took the liberty of taking a horse from a fleeing Yank and rode forward with his men. The Union cavalry dispersed and left town as quick and suddenly as the Louisianians burst on the scene. Lee described the crossing as "handsomely executed and with much spirit." The entire affair cost the brigade only one casualty. Andrew Devilbiss of Austin's battalion was the victim of friendly fire. As the men pushed up the hill into Florence, he was hit in the back by a round that fell short from Confederate cannons from the opposite shore. The citizens of Florence welcomed the return of Confederate troops to the city, and the Louisianians were welcomed as heroes, especially by the women. The men did not complain about the attention. The men "were met with the wildest enthusiasm by the ladies. All seemed overjoyed

Andrew Devilbiss, Austin's Battalion. Devilbiss enlisted in the 11th Louisiana at the start of the war in John Austin's Company. When Austin created his sharpshooting battalion, Devilbiss was picked for the select unit. Devilbiss served his country faithfully, even earning the Confederate Medal of Honor for his actions at Murfreesboro on 31 December 1862. Devilbiss was the only casualty during the attack on Florence, Alabama — a victim of friendly fire from artillery across the river. Lieutenant A.T. Martin wrote home to Devilbiss' wife with these words, "I have known Andrew since the commencement of the war, and his only wish seems to have been to see his boys and have them with him once more."

to meet us." "The town, with all its pretty women, etc., was ours," said Lieutenant John Dicks of the 4th Louisiana. The men were given clothing, food and parties as forms of thanks from the women. According to Lindsay the men were "given leave of absence for twenty-four hours," and he mused, "Need I say that the officers and soldiers had a good time?" That night, Johnson's advance elements encountered Gibson's pickets around town. A fight almost began because Johnson did not know the town had been captured. The Confederates quickly identified each other and rectified the situation.[14]

The Louisianians remained in Florence for almost a month while Hood stockpiled supplies and awaited the arrival of Major General Nathan B. Forrest's division from West Tennessee. For about three weeks, the brigade was able to enjoy somewhat of a break from marching. Brigade returns show that the 16th and 25th Regiments were unconsolidated like its sister units, the 13th and 20th Regiments, prior to the Atlanta Campaign. Again, the decision is not understandable, for their combined total of effective men was only 138 men. The only other explanation was the return of Colonel Frank Zacharie of the 25th Louisiana. Gibson's brigade was organized, with 660 effective men, as follows:

> 1st Regulars—Capt. S. Sutter (26 men)
> 4th Louisiana—Col. Samuel E. Hunter (103 men)
> 13th Louisiana—Colonel Francis Campbell (34 men)
> 16th Louisiana—Colonel Robert H. Lindsay (75 men)
> 19th Louisiana—Major Camp Flournoy (140 men)
> 20th Louisiana—Captain Alexander Dresel (23 men)
> 25th Louisiana—Colonel Frank C. Zacharie (62 men)
> 4th Louisiana Battalion—Captain T.A. Bisland (45 men)
> 30th Louisiana Battalion—Major Arthur Picolet (92 men)
> Austin's battalion—Captain W. Q. Lowd (24 men).[15]

On 20 November, the march north was resumed, but only after precious weeks had passed. Hood's goal was Nashville, and he set his army in motion toward Columbia, about halfway to Nashville. After a week of marching through rainy and bitterly cold weather, Gibson's brigade reached the outskirts of Columbia. The town, located in a bend of the Duck River, was heavily defended by about 20,000 Federal troops. Rather than attack the prepared Federals, Hood decided to flank the town and move toward the Harpeth River. Hood took with him two corps and one division of Lee's corps. Clayton's division, along with most of the army's artillery, remained outside Columbia, giving the impression that an attack was on its way.[16]

Hood's plan to cut off the Federal force in Columbia from Nashville was interrupted at the town of Spring Hill. The Army of Tennessee ran into several Federal units defending the town. Hood was unable to dislodge the Federals and simply waited until the next morning to renew the attack, without having secured possession of the Franklin-Columbia Turnpike. During the evening of 29 November, the Federal garrison evacuated Columbia and retreated north toward Franklin. On the same evening, Clayton's and Stevenson's divisions were ordered across the Duck River. The morning of 30 November bore bad news to Hood: the Federal garrison at Columbia had slipped past him in the night and had reached Franklin. Furious, Hood ordered an immediate pursuit. Coming to within two miles of Franklin, Hood ordered an attack on the Federal position entrenched around the town, much to his subordinates' dismay. The attack would traverse two miles of open ground, against an entrenched enemy and without artillery support. The majority of the army's artillery was far to the rear with Clayton and Stevenson. Over 6,000 Confederates, including 12 generals, were lost that horrible afternoon in Hood's rash attack. Lee's two trailing divisions arrived on the battlefield late in the evening on the 30th, and Hood had them drawn up in line, ready to attack. "We found that bloody and disastrous engagement begun, and were put in position to attack," wrote Clayton, "but night mercifully interposed to save us from the terrible scourge which our brave companions had suffered." Seeing the effects of the repulse, a disgusted Randall Gibson told Lindsay, "The whole thing is inexplicable. Some one blundered."[17]

Allowing his battered army to rest on 1 December Hood completed his march to Nashville on the next day. Upon passing the carnage of Franklin, a member of the 19th Louisiana described what he saw: "The ditch in front of the enemy works with dead, dying and wounded Confederates ... they were lying with their scarred faces upturned amidst heaps of dead Federals. The scene was awful to look upon." Everything Hood was able to restore in the army's confidence died with so many men on the field of Franklin. Gibson's brigade was saved the slaughter of Franklin, and since its leaving Florence over a month before, its only role had been marching with little skirmishing. Colonel Hunter's prediction in a letter to his wife before the brigade left Florence seemed to be coming true: "I do not think we will have much of any fighting to do on this campaign." Almost prophetic, but the campaign was not yet over. The most fighting the brigade did was against the elements. The men were limited to blankets for their cover at night, their clothing was wearing out from the constant movement, and rations were short. A private of the 4th Louisiana, Gustave Wolf of Company D, braved the repercussions of the brigade's provost officer, Lieutenant Alfred Clark of the 20th Louisiana, described as a "harsh and very severe officer." He broke ranks while on the march in search of food. His breaking of protocol paid off when he found a hog at a nearby farm, but its owner was not willing to let it go and there emerged a showdown. A "compromise" was met, and the starving soldier and farmer cut the hog in half. Wolf returned a conqueror and hero to the men of his regiment. His punishment by Clark was well worth the meal. On the march between Florence and Nashville, the 4th Louisiana Battalion was detached to guard the army's pontoon bridge over the Duck River. The detachment of the 4th Battalion lowered Gibson's effective strength by about forty-five men. The 25th Louisiana was also detached when the brigade reached Columbia. The regiment was given prisoner detail, and while the brigade marched north to Nashville, the Twenty-Fifth marched prisoners as far south as Meridian, Mississippi, before they boarded cars for Mobile.[18]

For the next two weeks, while outside of Nashville, the Louisianians dug trenches and fought the cold weather. The brigade was lucky to miss a lot of fighting for the better part of the month. Numbers in the regiments, though, did decline. Leaving Florence with 660 men the brigade's effective total was down to 548 by 10 December while outside Nashville. The majority of the depleted numbers was Zacharie's 25th Regiment detached with the prisoners, around 62 men. As for the remaining 50, very few were absent due to being sick. The vast majority were able for duty with the brigade, except for 15 men who were under arrest from the 16th Louisiana for unknown reasons. Considering the severe weather conditions, coldness and rain, combined with improper shelter, the men only using blankets, along with a scarcity in consistent food and poor clothing, it is amazing the Louisiana Brigade did not lose more men the two weeks it sat outside of Nashville. During this two week window, Thomas had been concentrating troops from throughout Tennessee and Kentucky. By the second week of December, he was prepared to take the offensive against Hood.

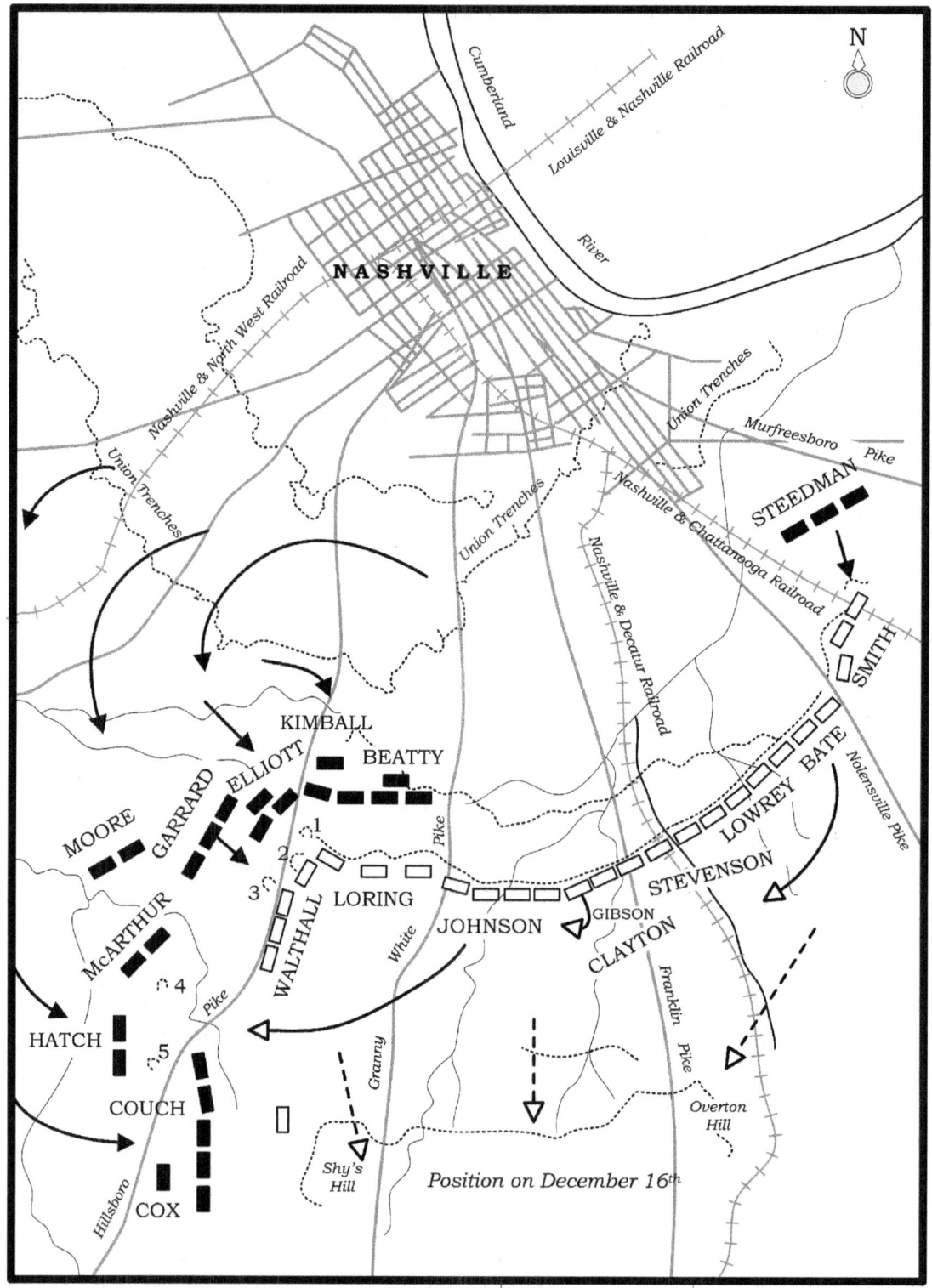

Battle of Nashville, 15 December 1864.

On the morning of 15 December, Thomas marched his army in a huge left wheel so that it struck the left flank of Hood's army. Outnumbered, Hood's left was able to hold on for a part of the day but soon gave out. Lee's corps, on the right of the army, was forced to send units to help anchor the crumbling left flank. At 2:00 P.M., Gibson was ordered out of line, sent to the extreme left of the corps, and ordered to deploy in a single rank and cover as much ground as possible. To hold back the Federal attack, Hood had taken units from the left of Lee's line, B.R. Johnson's division, and sent them into the fight farther to the left, leaving holes in the middle of the Confederate line. Soon, Federal soldiers appeared on Gibson's left flank, forcing him to reform his brigade at a right angle to Lee's position. Gibson threw forward Lieutenant Martin with Austin's battalion to engage the enemy. The arrival of night stopped Thomas's victorious troops, and Gibson escaped an impending disaster. At about midnight, Lee pulled his line back 2 miles.[19]

During the night Clayton was given responsibility for holding the right of the army. He anchored his line on Overton Hill. Overton Hill was described as a "well-intrenched position" by the Federals as they approached it. Stovall was the rightmost brigade of the division and army. He was entrenched on the east-northeast sides of Overton Hill. Next to Stovall was Holtzclaw's Alabamians covering the northern-northwest slopes with his left resting on the Franklin Pike. These two brigades were entrenched along the slopes with a massive abattis to their front. Clayton capped off the Overton Hill defenses with two batteries: Stanford's Battery under Lieutenant McCall faced north and Captain William McKenzie's Eufaula Battery. Posted to the left of this fortress, across the Franklin Pike, were Gibson's Louisiana units. Luckily, the Louisianians had a stone wall to their front that they quickly and easily improved. To the left of Gibson was Major General Carter Stevenson's division, with Brigadier General Edmund Pettus' brigade next to Gibson. The geography of Gibson's position was described as a "declivity of the ridge forming a gap through which the turnpike passes." That meant both Holtzclaw and Pettus enjoyed a high elevation and stronger defensive position. Flanking Gibson on his right was a stone wall that ran along the turnpike. Posted about 300 yards to the entire front was a strongly entrenched skirmish line. It was in this defensive position that the Louisianians waited on the morning of 16 December.[20]

Rolling down the Franklin Turnpike toward Gibson was Brigadier General Thomas Woods' IV Corps. The farther Woods marched south, the larger the gap that emerged between his right flank and the left flank of Major General Andrew Smith's divisions from the Army of the Tennessee. Woods fixed this issue by throwing his First Division, which was in reserve, into line on the right. As Woods approached the Confederate position, he was deployed as follows: Brigadier Samuel Beatty's Third Division was on Woods' left on the east side of the Franklin Turnpike, opposite of Overton Hill; to the west of the right, forming Woods' center and right, were Brigadier Generals Washington Elliott's Second Division and Nathan Kimball's First Division. Elliot's left flank followed along the turnpike as he headed south. Woods pushed his line until it was about 600 yards from the Confederate trenches. Batteries around the Louisianians immediately began dropping shells which prompted Woods to also employ his artillery. Appearing opposite Gibson's skirmishers at about 11:00 A.M. were the skirmishers of Elliott's First Brigade under Colonel Emerson Opdycke and Beatty's Second Brigade under Colonel Sidney Post. By 1:00 P.M. Gibson had to reign in his skirmishers "when it was discovered that preparations were being made to charge us in force." Once the skirmish line was taken Union regiments immediately began converting that line into a defensive position for themselves.[21]

When the picket line was taken along the Confederate front, Elliott's division, guiding on his middle brigade, Colonel John Lane's, kept pushing forward, "flushed with the success of the previous day, the desire to rush forward without orders," reported Elliott. In doing so Opdycke's brigade did not advance directly on Gibson, but rather his advance came across the front of Pettus and on the left of Gibson. By guiding on Lane, as ordered, Opdycke's left flank became dangerously enfiladed by Gibson, Holtzclaw and Stanford's guns. Lane and Opdycke were able to push to within about 100 to 150 yards of the Confederate line before the fire became too strong. The boldness and "great spirit" of this attack was soon brought into reality. It was "checked by heavy volleys of musketry with shot, shell, and canister." The two brigades pulled back and began entrenching themselves under fire at about 150 yards. Opdycke's left was dangerously exposed, being "not connected with other troops." To fix the problem Opdycke threw forward his second line to cover his flank; this line faced to the southeast opposite Gibson and Holtzclaw. From this close position the regiments of Opdycke and Lane "kept up an incessant firing" on Pettus and Gibson, thus keeping them occupied and tied down. Colonel Lindsay spoke first hand of the effect of the "incessant firing": "A ball went through the rim of my hat. Again while looking for sharpshooters a ball passed through my hat, coming out at the crown, and the third shot tore a V-shaped hole in the shoulder of my overcoat." For about the next hour and a half this "constant fire" was kept up along with an artillery bombardment from the four batteries supporting the attack in this sector. Stevenson described the bombardment on this sector as "an artillery fire which I have never seen surpassed for heaviness, continuance, and accuracy." Adding to the misery of Pettus and Gibson were the creative members of the 36th Illinois. Members of this regiment wheeled a gun from Battery G of the 1st Ohio Artillery up to the Confederates' skirmish line and began blasting away at a mere 300 yards.[22]

At 3:00 P.M. a major attack came to Gibson's front from Beatty's division. When Elliott advanced and pushed close to Pettus' and Gibson's front, Beatty had halted at the Confederate skirmish line to reconnoiter Overton Hill to his front. Thus, the left flank of Opdycke was exposed he pushed himself almost into a perpendicular line to Gibson's front. Although Clayton's line was formidable, Woods' ambition to make a name for himself was greater. He decided to push an attack directly at Overton Hill with the support of Major General James Steedman's motley Provisional Detachment to his left. Starting with Beatty's division, Wood ordered his corps forward. Gibson's front partly faced the advance of Beatty's division, which was stacked in columns of brigades; the lead brigade was under Colonel Sidney Post with Colonel Abel Streight's brigade directly behind him. Post's brigade ran into the abatis and could go no further, but still he pushed his second line forward. Streight was pushed forward into the mass of bluecoats pressing their way into and through the abatis. It became mass confusion with the two brigades becoming totally jumbled and losing all cohesion. Streight said the brigades "seemed to waste away, until all became intermingled in one mass." Gibson and Holtzclaw's men were "firing rapidly and low" at the easy targets, with Post being one of their victims and Stanford's guns "swept the hillside with canister." Adding to the punch in the Confederate fire was the reinforcement of two brigades from the extreme left of Hood's line. These regiments filed into place just as the enemy was hitting the obstructions to the front. It did not take long before Beatty's two attacking brigades melted away before his eyes. His men slowly trickled to the rear and then, suddenly, a mass retreat took place: "Large numbers of men from both brigades commenced running to the rear." Gibson was very discreet in his report on the Battle of Nashville, but

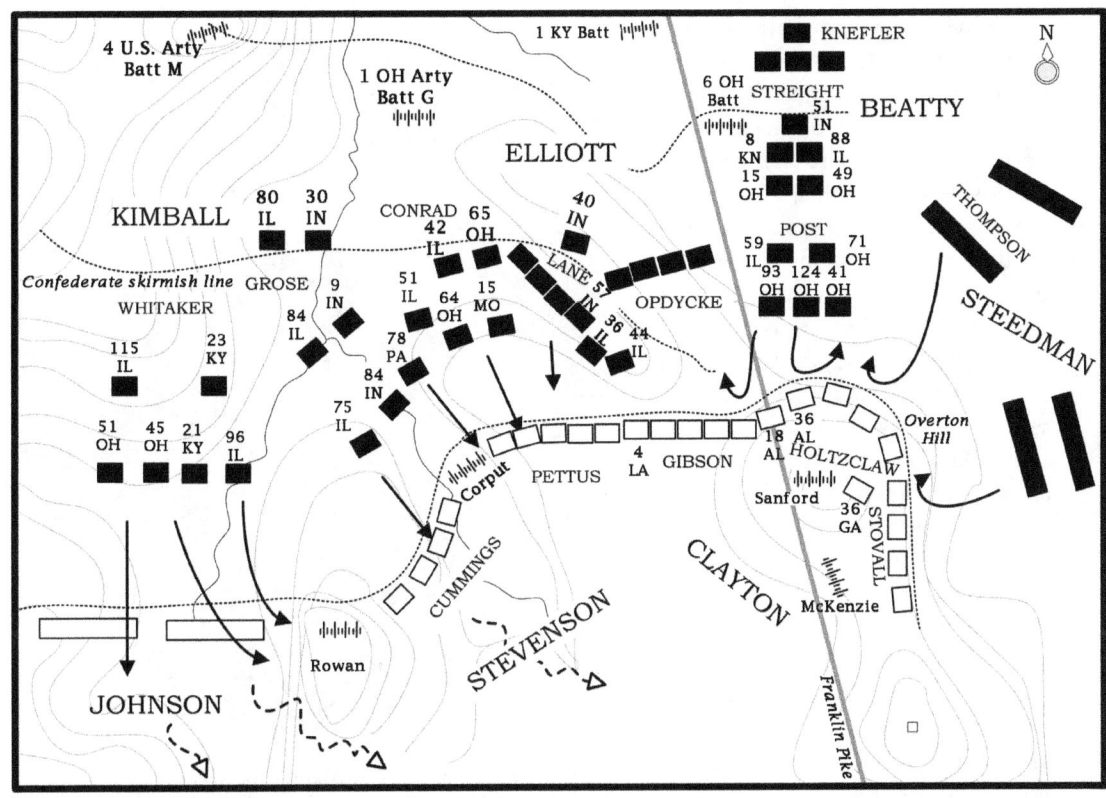

Stand on Overton Hill, Battle of Nashville, 16 December 1864, 3:00 P.M.–5:00 P.M.

one detail he gave us was on the attack at 3:00 P.M. He said that the attackers got to within 75 yards of his line but after a "few minutes broke and fled." Once the Yanks hit the abatis to the front, they stood for only 10–15 minutes under the fire before retreating. Post's and Streight's regiments bolted to the rear and reformed themselves behind Beatty's last brigade, Colonel Frederick Knefler's brigade.[23]

After stalling Beatty's advance, Gibson noticed troops "double-quicking toward the rear" on his left. Fearing the worst, Gibson sent one of his aides, Lieutenant Cartwright Eustis, to confer with Pettus, on his left, to cooperate in sealing the part of the line that had been broken. When Eustis returned to inform him of his conversation with Pettus, Gibson noticed "the enemy was observed already upon our rear." What Gibson did not realize was that the entire left wing of Hood's line had crumbled, and the troops "double-quicking" to the rear were part of the center of the line giving way. In just moments, Stevenson's division began to crumble before Gibson's eyes. Woods was witnessing the collapse of the Confederate line from behind Kimball's line and quickly ordered his corps forward. Progressively from right to left the IV Corps pushed forward. Woods broke through to the left of Stevenson and rolled his left flank up fast. Gibson attempted to save his brigade by deploying Lindsay's 16th Louisiana as a skirmish line along the trenches. This would have allowed the rest of the units to retire but the tidal wave of terror that had already crushed Pettus and now flew across the Louisianians. "Confusion prevailed over everything," said Gibson. Opdycke's and Knefler's brigades crossed the works where the Louisiana Brigade had held its position, and before them was a mass of fleeing Confederates.[24]

One of the Louisianians' adversaries, Captain Charles Clark of the 125th Ohio of Opdycke's brigade, described the attack on the afternoon of the sixteenth: "The enemy was literally swept out of his whole line so rapidly as to loose a great part of his artillery and thousands of prisoners. It was a second Missionary Ridge." Clark's observation eerily resembles the prediction Douglas Cater of the 19th Louisiana made in a letter written in the early hours of 15 December: "Our Generals are expecting an attack from the enemy. If it be the case, another Missionary Ridge affair would not surprise me. I would not say this if the battle of Franklin had not taken place but we have good works and may repulse the enemy — if so Nashville will be ours — But hark! There is a cannon — another — and still another. The battle commences on the right of our position. We will see the results." It was an uncanny similarity: the Army of Tennessee lacked confidence in its commander; it was "laying siege" to an enemy army; it faced harsh conditions with improper supplies, and it was coming off a bloody battle in which it held the field on both occasions but remained licking its wounds for weeks to come because of severe losses.[25]

William Jackson, 4th Louisiana Infantry, captured in the trenches of Nashville on 16 December 1864 (courtesy of the U.S. Army Military History Institute).

Almost the entire Army of Tennessee was running from the field. Besides a handful of other organizations, Clayton's division was able to pull off with most of its units semi-intact. Lee frantically ran among the troops hoping to stop the rout. During this chaotic period, Lee came upon Gibson's brigade. Wanting to stall the pressure from pursuing Federals, Lee turned to the color bearer of the 13th Louisiana and demanded his colors: "Give me the colors. I wish to lead this regiment and brigade to drive back the enemy." "No," answered the color bearer, who was supported by members of his regiment. "General, it is not necessary to expose yourself in that way; point in the direction you desire these colors to be borne, and we will carry them forward as long as there is a shred of them or a man left." Stunned in admiration, Lee turned to Gibson, who had just ridden up, and said, "Gibson, these are the best men I have ever saw." Gibson's reformed line was near Mr. Overton's home next to the Franklin Pike and provided token but semi-organized, resistance. Stovall's brigade, which was still intact, and McKenzie's battery provided enough resistance along the pike for Gibson to fall back. About a mile from the trenches is where Clayton brought his division into line supported by Pettus, the 39th Georgia and McKenzie's battery.[26]

Clayton was able to pull his division back to within five miles of Franklin at Hollow

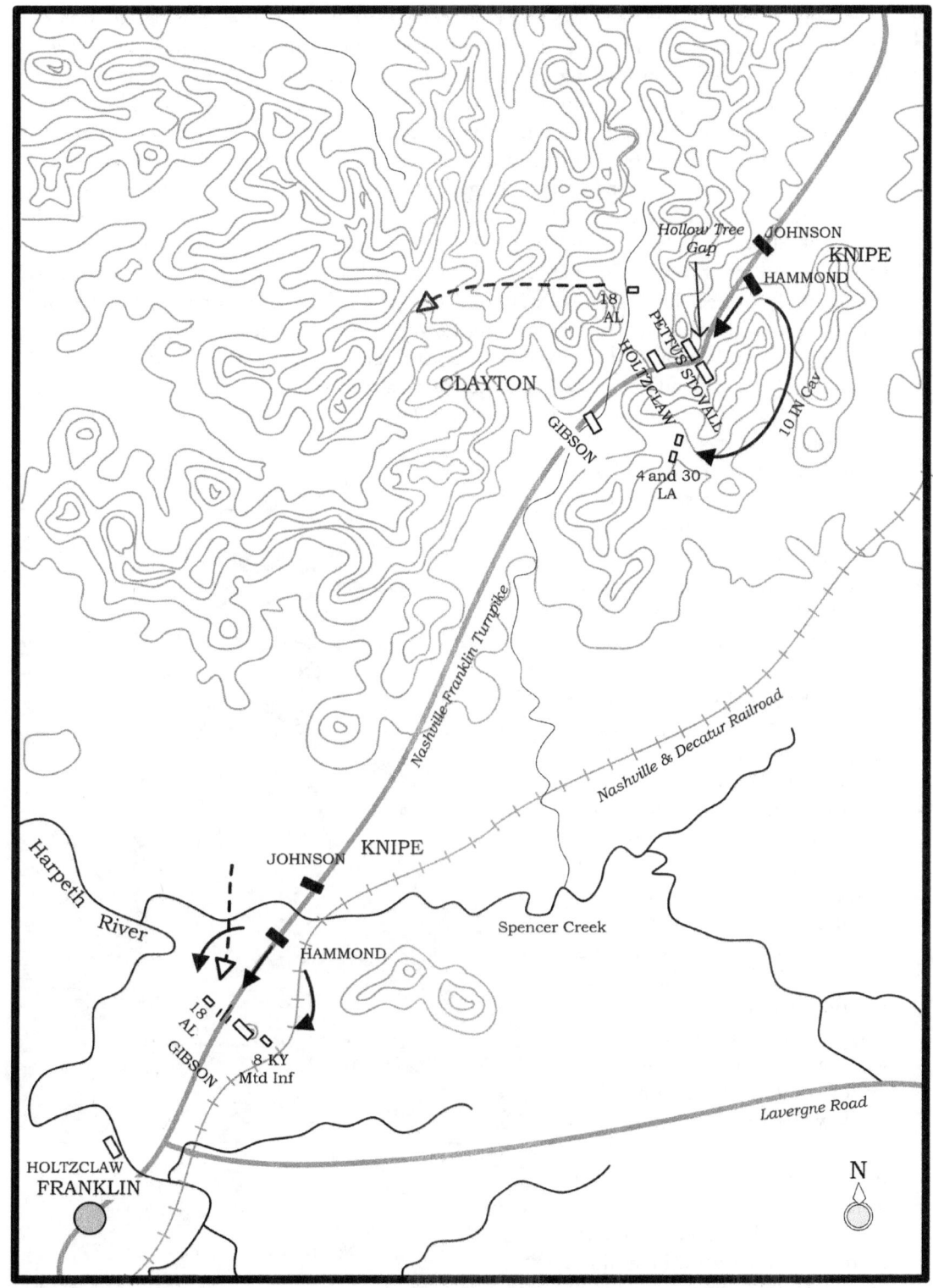

Hollow Tree Gap, 17 December 1864.

Tree Gap, where the Granny White and Franklin pikes met. The brigade was able to settle down at about 2:00 A.M. The brigade escaped on the sixteenth, but 17 December dwarfed the action and tribulations the brigade faced outside of Nashville. The men got three hours of sleep before being put back into line. Early on the seventeenth, Clayton deployed Stovall and Pettus across the pike at Hollow Tree Gap with Gibson and Holtzclaw in reserve. Gibson was posted about 600 yards south of the gap with only about 315 men left in the brigade's ranks. Just a week before, the brigade mustered 548 men on roll which suggests that around 200 men were captured or lost during the sixteenth. In order to protect his flank in Hollow Tree Gap, Clayton ordered Gibson to forward a force to protect his right flank. Gibson sent forward Colonel Hunter with his 4th Louisiana and the 30th Louisiana Battalion. To protect his left flank, Clayton threw one of Holtzclaw's regiments, the 18th Alabama, into another small pass. Pushing down the pike at the rear guard was Union brigadier general Joseph Knipe's division of cavalry. Leading his push was Brigadier General John H. Hammond's brigade. Confederate cavalry to Clayton's front was easily scattered and chased into Hollow Tree Gap at about 9:00 A.M. Hammond's lead regiments, the 10th Indiana Cavalry and 19th Pennsylvania Cavalry, were blasted at close range and sent running down the pass. Their pursuit momentarily stalled, Hammond found a pathway around Lee's right flank and sent word to Knipe of his discovery. The pathway the Federal cavalry came charging up was the very pathway Hunter was defending. Hammond pushed up the path with part of the 10th Indiana Cavalry and crashed into the unsuspecting Louisianians. The 4th and 30th Regiments were totally decimated by Hammond's quick push. About 75 men were captured as was Colonel Hunter. Lee and Clayton realized the pressure was being put on their isolated position and at about 10:00 A.M. began pulling their force out of the gap. Part of Knipe's division was already working its way around the Hollow Tree Gap area. A hasty retreat was made for the Harpeth before the entire force was swallowed up.[27]

During this time, Gibson had marched south toward Franklin to intercept enemy cavalry approaching the Franklin-Nashville Pike

Trasimond Landry, 4th Louisiana, captured at Hollow Tree Gap (courtesy of Camp Moore Historical Association).

from both sides. It's unknown which units these are due to the limited amount of reports from Knipe's division and the brevity of the ones that are available. Gibson reports that he easily dismissed the units approaching the pike. He drew the Louisianians into line across the pike on a small hill about 1,000 yards from the Harpeth and its crossing into Franklin. Joining him came the 18th Alabama which had been cut off in the retreat from Hollow Tree Gap. The regiment ran through the hills north of the river and skirted Knipe's regiments. "Exhausted with running around the enemy's cavalry," the 18th Alabama reentered the Franklin-Nashville Pike close to Gibson's position. Gibson stopped the regiment and threw it into a skirmish line with the 16th Louisiana to help protect a section of Bledsoe's Missouri Battery.[28]

Riding on the heels of the 18th Alabama and the retreating elements of Clayton's division were Knipe's troopers. After punching through Hunter's command near Hollow Tree Gap, he pushed the 9th Indiana Cavalry down the pike, with the 10th Indiana Cavalry and 4th Tennessee (US) in close support. Pushing in behind him came Johnson's three regiments. An avalanche of cavalry was about to swallow the Louisiana Brigade up. "The enemy, 5,000 strong," said Gibson, "charged in three columns ... one in front, one in rear upon the left flank, and one in rear upon the right flank." Brigadier General James Chalmers was in charge of the cavalry defending the rear of the army and had bolted when hit by Hammond's men in the morning. His regiments attempted to make another stand between Hollow Tree Gap and the river as Clayton's division pulled back but were scattered by Hammond's victory-flushed men. When Brigadier General "Abe" Buford's division of cavalry arrived from Murfreesboro on the Lavergne Road they were dealt the same blow was Chalmers. A disaster was unfolding in front of Gibson. To slow the enemy cavalry, he had Bledsoe's section begin pumping rounds down the pike at the center column. Instead of

Thomas Bickham, 4th Louisiana, captured at Hollow Tree Gap (courtesy of Camp Moore Historical Association).

arresting the aggressive moves, it simply encouraged the enemy to push their horses harder and close the gap with the Louisianians faster.[29]

To avert total destruction, Gibson ordered the artillery to make a run for the Harpeth, ordered the 18th Alabama and 16th Louisiana to cover the front, and he pulled his remaining regiments out of line with orders "to move to the rear and to fight as they went." Enemy cavalry was closing in on the brigade fast. "My command fought its way to the river, entirely surrounded" was not an exaggeration by Gibson. The 9th Indiana Cavalry, formed in column and charging directly down the pike, came to within 100 yards of Bledsoe's guns as they were attempting to cross the river. Colonel Campbell's 13th Louisiana unleashed a volley that delivered a strong punch and "broke up" the Hoosiers. Clayton blamed the disaster that unfolded on the morning of the seventeenth squarely on the cavalry: "I think no one to blame but our cavalry, who, all the day long, behaved in a most cowardly manner." There were two units, the 8th Mounted Kentucky Infantry and 100 or so cavalry rounded up by a mysterious Colonel Falconnet who charged into Gibson's pursuers. Holtzclaw was able to provide minimal support with his line drawn up across the river; the only fire provided coming from Bledsoe's other section of artillery next to the brigade. His presence dissuaded Knipe from crossing the river in force, though. The run to the river cost the brigade 10 men killed, 25 wounded and only 5 captured. Losses totaling 40 men is not a staggering number but it is a staggering loss when Gibson's brigade numbered only about 250 men when it made its stand north of the river.[30]

The day was not over, though. Stevenson's division took up the rear guard action south of Franklin, and the Louisiana Brigade was spared the torturous rear guard duty for most of the remainder of the day. About six miles south of Franklin, Clayton halted the division, just shy of Spring Hill, and redeployed it across the Franklin Turnpike facing north. Gibson was on the right of the road because of the increase of heavy firing to the rear where Stevenson was fighting off Wilson's divisions. Clayton marched to Stevenson's rescue on the West Harpeth River with Holtzclaw's brigade and left Gibson in charge of his and Stovall's brigades. Near sunset, as Stevenson was fighting for his survival and slowly falling back, a column of enemy cavalry appeared off to the left of Gibson's flank. He immediately wheeled his left regiment around and then threw Stovall's Georgians into line parallel with the pike, with their right on Gibson's refused regiment. Wilson had ordered Brigadier General Richard Johnson's division to try to strike the retreating enemy in flank at Spring Hill, while the majority of his force pushed down the Franklin Pike and kept the rearguard busy. The exact force or size is unknown, but judging from Gibson's report, it was at least two regiments to a full brigade. Gibson reported that a few volleys from his line "cut the charging column, and a part of two regiments continued down the road, while the rest fell back into the woods."[31]

The fighting on the seventeenth was the last rear guard duty that the brigade took part in. The retreat from Nashville was the worst march of the war for the Louisianians. In the rainy, cold and usually snowy days, the brigade marched 137 miles from 17 to 26 December, when it finally recrossed the Tennessee River: "I thought the march was hard as we advanced but the retreat surpassed anything I have ever experienced or even read. Rain, snow, wind, *mud*, all added together with the marching." The 4th Louisiana reported: "The suffering from the extreme coldness of the weather was very great on account of [the men] being badly clad and many of the men being completely barefooted, in consequence of which in many places their tracks were left bloody." On Christmas morning, the brigade was forced to cross a creek with water up to the men's waists. Once across the 150-yard-wide creek, the men were not allowed to build fires to warm their freezing clothes. Instead, the men were quickly marched to the Tennessee River, where they spent most of the day digging breastworks out of the frozen ground. It is no wonder that a cold, miserable Louisiana soldier wrote in his diary on the twenty-fifth, "Christmas, and a miserable one."[32]

The retreat from Tennessee was continued for several weeks after the battle. After crossing the Tennessee River, the brigade marched west along the Memphis & Charleston Railroad until it reached Burnsville. From there the brigade undertook leisurely marches until it reached Tupelo, Mississippi, on 6 January. Lieutenant Kendall of the 4th Louisiana was very bitter about the Nashville Campaign. After the war he wrote, "Everything in the campaign was stupidly managed. We lost it because the men were so badly provided for that they would not accomplish the heavy tasks demanded of them." The same Douglas Cater that praised hope and confidence in Hood back in October at Gadsden, Alabama, spoke differently once he made it safely to Corinth, Mississippi: "Gen Johnston demoralized me but [was] willing to give Hood a trial." Cater was not unfounded in his frustration: "This grand army which retreated to this place from Corinth two & a half years ago ... again reaches this place a demoralized wreck. Nearly all without shoes & with worn out garments and added to this a ear of corn in each man's haversack to check the awful epidemic — hunger."[33]

The Army of Tennessee was broken from the Nashville Campaign, never to be an effective fighting force for the remainder of the war. Gibson never reported an overall loss of his command for the campaign. Muster rolls show that on 10 December, just prior to the Battle of Nashville, Gibson had an effective total of 548 men. The next muster was not taken until the brigade reached Tupelo. By 8 January, the effective strength of the brigade had dropped to only 262 men. Comparing brigade muster rolls from November while at Florence to those from Corinth in January, the span of the Nashville Campaign, there were an additional 365 men recorded as prisoners of war. Colonel Hunter and Lieutenant Colonel Pennington of the 4th Louisiana, along with most of the regiment, were captured. Captain Alexander Dresel, commanding the 20th Louisiana, was captured, and Lieutenant Martin commanding Austin's battalion was lost in the trenches at Nashville as was Captain Picolet commanding the 30th Louisiana and most of that unit. Gibson's brigade remained a shadow of its former self when most of its regiments had encamped at this same town almost two years earlier. To worsen the morale of the brigade even further, it was rumored that they were to be shipped to Georgia to oppose Sherman. Instead of Georgia, Gibson informed his men that they were going to Mobile, news which brought "great rejoicing." Before leaving Tupelo, the brigade listened to Hood give a farewell speech. Douglas Cater of the 19th Louisiana admitted it "made one feel badly," but Cater was very perceptive in sizing up the general when he said, "I liked him for his bravery and untiring energy but he lacked caution and seemed to care nothing for the lives of his men."[34]

CHAPTER 12

End of the War: January–May 1865

"I am ashamed of many of the people of the south, in the male population ... fine brave men were left in the field to meet the enemy while at least two thirds of the men who could fight had become tired and quit. Such men do not deserve freedom."
— Private Douglas Cater, 19th Louisiana,
16 May 1865

The year 1865 brought on the last five months of the war for the Louisiana Brigade. The men of the brigade were unaware of the ending struggle but were not naive to think the disaster of 1864 under Hood was not a foreshadowing of events. When January rolled around, the Louisianians were happy to simply be in camp away from Thomas' pursuing cavalry. At Tupelo for the first part of January, the brigade slowly licked its wounds and prepared for the next spring that was sure to bring more campaigning.

On 18 January, the Louisiana Brigade left Tupelo and proceeded to Vernon, Mississippi, arriving seven days later. The railroad was of no use, and the trip was made on foot. From Vernon, Gibson was ordered to proceed to West Point, where the brigade could board cars for Mobile. Between 25 and 28 January the brigade reached West Point and left on 1 February, reaching Mobile on the night of the next day. On 3 February the brigade was put into "comfortable log huts" for winter quarters, with a soldier of the 20th Louisiana reporting, "The men are in good spirits." Furloughs were given, some back to Louisiana and others for shorter terms for the immediate areas. The month of February and early March was the first real down time for the brigade since May of the previous year. There were temporary lulls in September and November, but the year 1864 was the toughest on the brigade to date.[1]

A reorganization of the brigade took place in February due to the lack of numbers. The 1st Regulars and 16th and 20th Regiments were consolidated into one unit under Lieutenant Colonel Robert Lindsay of the 16th Louisiana. Lindsay's regiment had an effective total of 103 men. The 25th Regiment and the 4th Battalion merged to form another unit under Colonel Francis Zacharie. Zacharie's unit had an effective strength of 141 men. The 4th and 13th Regiments and the 30th and Austin's battalions were combined to form a third unit under Colonel Francis Campbell of the 13th Louisiana. Campbell's command had an effective total of 140 men. Only the 19th Louisiana, under Major Camp Flournoy, was able to escape consolidation. The 19th Louisiana had maintained the ability to keep high numbers throughout the war, and even as late as 1865, it was able to avoid consolidation with

12. End of the War: January–May 1865

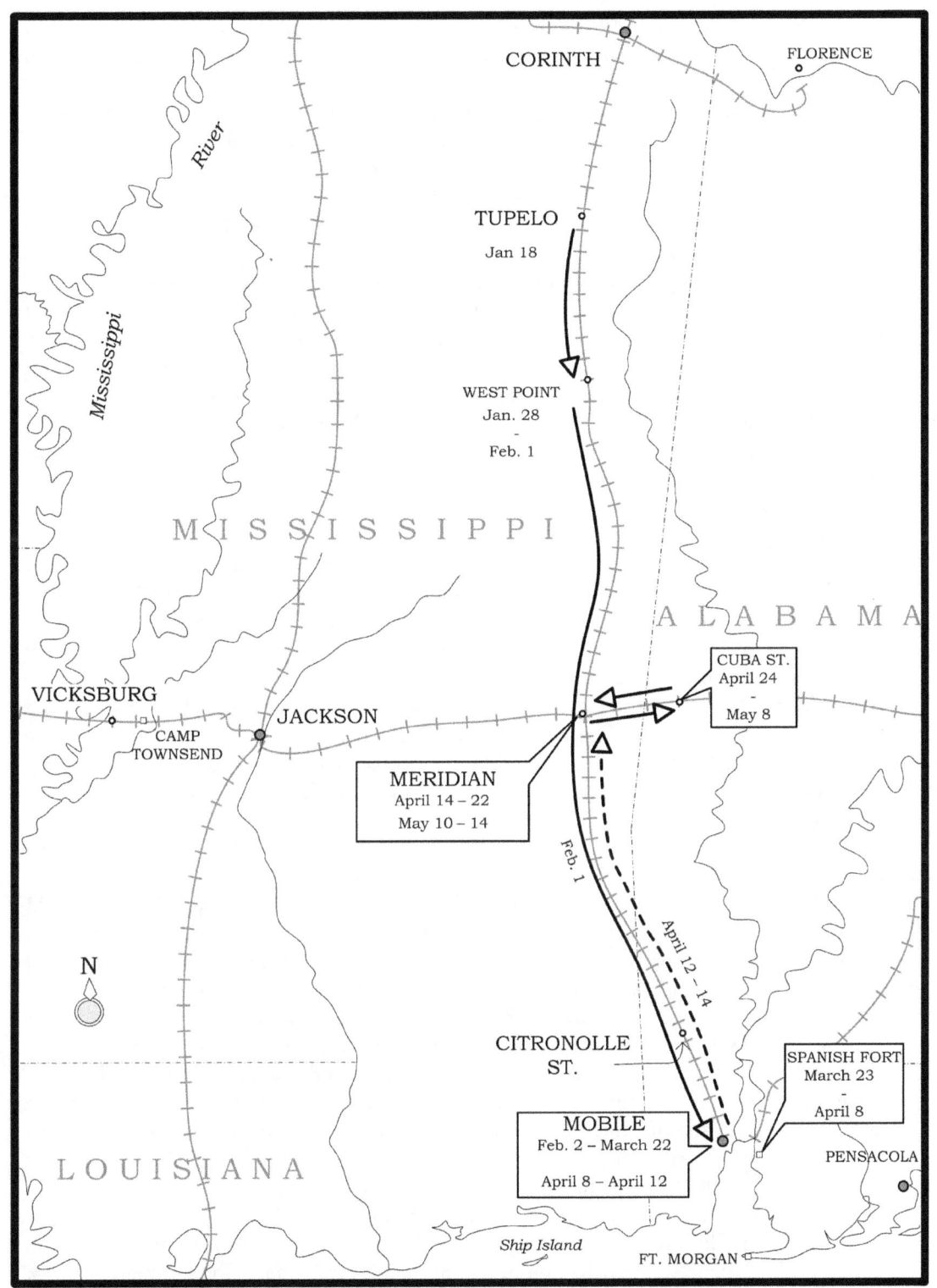

Movements of the Louisiana Brigade, December 19 January–10 May 1865.

any other unit. Flournoy fielded 141 men in his regiment. In all, Gibson's brigade, as of 15 February, had risen back up to a strength of 525 men, this number increasing to 550 by 10 March.[2]

In desperation to fill the ranks of the brigade, officers began petitioning the government to recruit from enemy prisoners. In December, Major Michael O. Tracy of the 13th Louisiana requested permission to recruit foreigners from enemy prisoners. Tracy said, "The Federal Government refuses to exchange. A great many of these men are willing to join our army." Colonel Francis Campbell, of the same regiment, had made the same suggestion to Samuel Cooper the month before. He wanted to recruit Irish from the enemy ranks because his regiment "is chiefly composed of that class, (Irish)." Their argument was the fact that their regiment had been cut off from the city it was raised in, New Orleans; their regiment was predominately filled with immigrants, especially of Irish, and the regiment had only about 100 men which "will shortly cease to exist." Even Colonel Leon von Zinken, from his post in Columbus, Georgia, petitioned Braxton Bragg in Richmond to allow him to recruit foreigners from enemy prisoners to refill the 20th Louisiana, another heavy laden immigrant regiment. With Germans and Irish making up the largest numbers of foreigners in the Union Army and combined with the fact that there was a sizeable number conscripted, their plan may have worked. No documentation allowing or disallowing the plan has been found.[3]

The relaxation from being away from the active front came to an end at the end of March. Major General R.S. Canby, commander of the Military Division of West Mississippi, was reinforced and ordered to make a move on Selma or Montgomery, Alabama. Instead of marching his army overland from the New Orleans area, Canby's plan called for his army to be transported across the Gulf of Mexico and landed on the east shore of the Bay of Mobile. From there he would reduce the works on the east side of the bay, Blakely and Spanish Fort, and thus force the evacuation of Mobile. Next, he planned to move against Montgomery. Canby received 22,000 reinforcements from various commands out west. When he made his move on southern Alabama, he hit its sandy shores with a little over 45,000 men.[4]

To oppose this juggernaut was the 10,000 man garrison of Mobile under Major General Dabney Maury. Of that force only 7,700 were infantry and artillerymen. Maury dispatched the majority of this force, 4,500 men, to the east shore to contest Canby. On 22 March the Louisiana Brigade was ordered to Spanish Fort, where Gibson was placed in charge of the post. Spanish Fort was one of three redoubts. The other two redoubts, Redoubt 2 known as Fort Blair and Redoubt 3 known as Fort McDermott, were built to protect Spanish Fort. Gibson was not impressed with what he was given charge of: "The three redoubts gave no mutual support, with the exception of two guns in Redoubts 2 and 3, and no crossfire could be obtained." In addition, the entire line to defend was about 3,500 yards. Upon examining the works, a glum Gibson described the scene: "There were 400 yards on the extreme right, in front of which the forest had been cut down, but no defensive works constructed; about 350 yards in the center, across a deep ravine, in front of which was only a slight curtain partially complete, and about 600 yards on the extreme left with no works of any kind, and the dense forest covering that flank untouched."[5]

The size of Gibson's garrison did not help alleviate the general's anxiety. His brigade, placed under Colonel Campbell's command, numbering 575 men. The Louisianians were placed in the works between McDermott and Blair on the right of the line. Already posted at Spanish Fort were four companies of the 22nd Louisiana Consolidated Infantry. These were exchanged and reorganized Louisiana prisoners from the Siege of Vicksburg. These 340 men were manning the guns in Spanish Fort proper and Fort McDermott. Also joining the garrison was Captain Cuthbert Slocomb's 5th Company of Washington Artillery. Since their departure from the brigade back in November 1863 the 5th Company had participated in all of the major battles of the Army of Tennessee that the Louisiana Brigade was associated with. At Nashville the battery lost its guns when its infantry supported deserted them. While in Mississippi licking their wounds, they were spared the order to go to North Carolina but, instead, were ordered to report to Mobile to temporarily operate as infantry. Slocomb's 90 strong force was placed in Fort Blair, in the center of the defensive perimeter, where it was given eight guns to man. Manning the center and left of the line was Brigadier General Bryan Thomas' Alabama Reservists. Rounding out the garrison, posted to the center and left of the line, was Captain J.W. Phillips' battery and Lumsden's battery under Lieutenant A.C. Hargrove. In all it was about 2,500 men.⁶

Late war photograph of General Gibson (courtesy of Camp Moore Historical Association).

For the Mobile Campaign, the Louisiana Brigade was organized as follows:

Colonel Francis Campbell
1st &16th & 20th Louisiana — Lieutenant Colonel Robert Lindsay (117 men)
4th Battalion & 25th Louisiana — Colonel Frank C. Zacharie (140 men)
19th Louisiana — Major Camp Flournoy (152 men)
Austin & 30th Battalions & 4th & 13th Louisiana — Colonel Francis Campbell (166 men).⁷

What Gibson and his men lacked in numbers, tools and established works, they made up for with determination and hard work. Gibson's first inspection led him to the conclusion that "it was apparent that an immense work with the spade, pick, and ax was before us." He immediately put the garrison to work building and improving works. What the men faced was a total lack of entrenching tools. Gibson continually kept requesting more tools from Maury in Mobile and Brigadier General St. John Liddell commanding the post at Blakely. On 27 March alone Gibson made at least four requests for more tools and included this statement to Liddell: "I have said so much about the absolute necessity of an ample supply of intrenching tools that I will not annoy you any more." The Louisianians worked day and night from the time they arrived at Spanish Fort to the day they left. In front of Campbell's works, trees were cut down up to 1,000 yards away to provide a clear line of fire for the artillery. When contact was made with enemy skirmishers on 27 March they were already worn down from three to four days of constant laboring. Work now had to commence not only night and day but also under enemy fire.⁸

Canby began his march north on 17 March. The XIII Corps left Fort Morgan, at the mouth of the bay, and marched north while the XVI Corps was shipped across the bay and landed near Donnelly Mills. As these two corps were moving to unite at Donnelly Mills another column was sent from Pensacola to Pollard, Alabama, to cut the railroad from Tensas Street, near Mobile Bay, to Montgomery. On 24 March Canby's two corps united and on the morning of the twenty-fifth they pushed north on parallel routes for Spanish Fort and Blakely. On the twenty-seventh Canby's force reached Spanish Fort and it was immediately invested by four divisions, two each from the XIII and XVI Corps. Opposite the Louisianians' position were the divisions of Brigadier General James Veatch and Brigadier General William Benton of Major General Gordon Granger's XIII Corps. Both divisions pushed their men to about 1,000 yards away from the Louisianian line and Fort McDermott on the night of 26 March with full plans to push and invest Spanish Fort the next day.[9]

Spanish Fort was still woefully underprepared, and to buy time Gibson decided to go on the offensive against the first push of the enemy. His goal was to show a force of strength and to catch the advancing horde off guard. On the night of the twenty-sixth Campbell was ordered to prepare the Louisiana Brigade for a sortie before daybreak the next day. Lieutenant Colonel Robert Lindsay, who was given command of the advance, arranged his small force of about 550 men. At 3:00 A.M. the Louisianians pushed forth from their works very quietly toward the enemy line about 1,000 yards away. They slammed into the skirmishers of Veatch's division, mainly on the 47th Indiana of Brigadier General James Slack's brigade. The Louisianians were able to push through the left flank of the 47th Indiana and force back the adjoining regiment on picket duty, the 11th Indiana of Brigadier

Sergeant Joseph H. Orillion, 30th Louisiana. The stay at Mobile in early 1865 allowed the Louisiana Brigade to recuperate from long months of hard fighting and marching during the Atlanta and Nashville campaigns. As seen from this photo of Orillion taken in Mobile in early 1865, the men of the brigade were able to replenish their clothing and accoutrements and went into combat in early 1865 well supplied (courtesy of Robert Gardner).

General Elias Dennis. With his regiment now flanked, Colonel John McLaughlin swung his regiment back and formed the 47th Indiana into line and then advanced on Lindsay. The Louisianians ran into two full brigades and were soon forced back into their works. The sortie that morning halted any progress in Campbell's front until about noon. A general push was made on Spanish Fort by Benton's and Veatch's divisions which resulted in their pushing into about 600 yards of Campbell's line and Fort McDermott with their skirmishers pushing to within 350 yards.[10]

Each day saw Canby strengthening his lines, digging parallels and getting closer to Confederate lines. Of considerable concern to Gibson was how close the trenches of Benton's division were to Redoubt 2, Fort Blair. Opposite of Fort Blair was Colonel Henry Day's brigade. It was Day's men that were digging relentlessly toward the 5th Company's position at Blair. When his brigade advanced and began building trenches on 27 March Day was 600 yards from the Confederate line. His line was pushed forward an additional 100 yards the next day and by the thirtieth his skirmish line was a scant 100 yards from Campbell's and Slocomb's trenches. One Louisianian said the Yanks "were in talking distance" and actually held conversations with their adversaries. In order to protect Fort Blair, Gibson ordered a small attack force organized, "designed to make a general attack on his part of the line." Gibson's inspector general, Captain Clement Watson, volunteered to lead the mission. He hand picked fifteen men, with the same amount volunteering to join and was assisted by Lieutenant A.C. Newton of Co. E of the 4th Louisiana Battalion. The unit digging toward the fort was the 7th Vermont. Prior to making his assault, Gibson had the

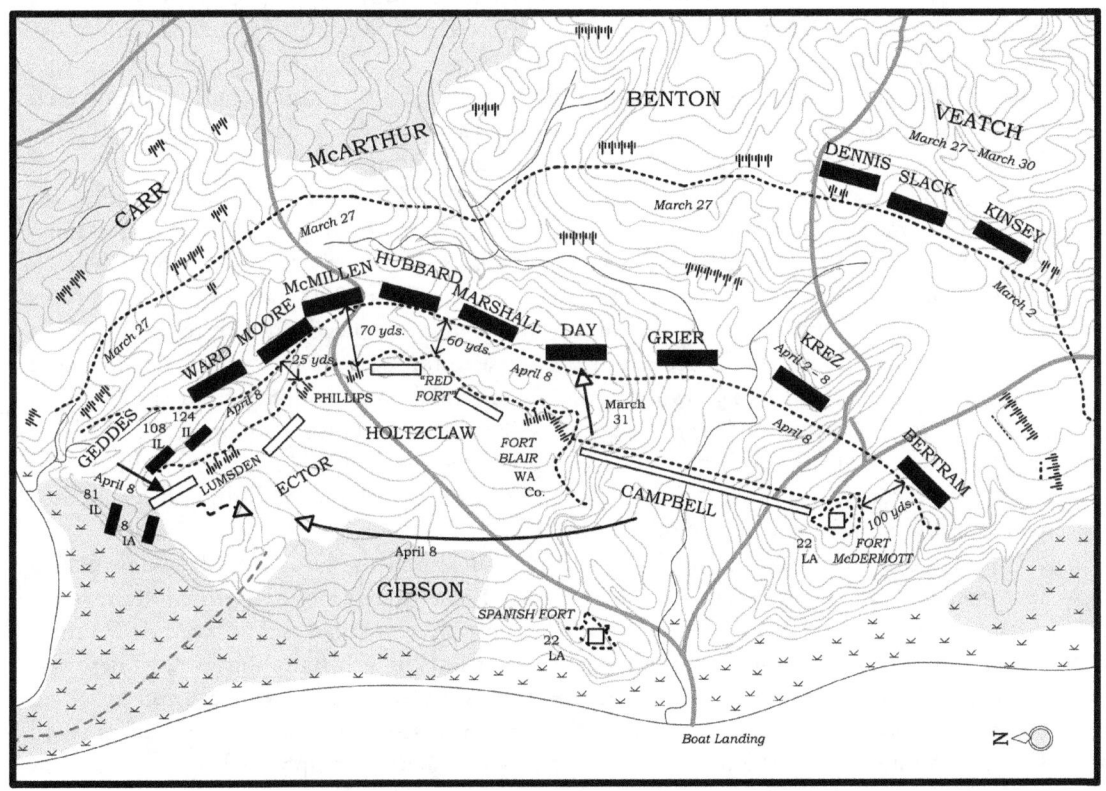

Siege of Spanish Fort, 27 March to 8 April 1865.

Louisianians fire on the felled trees and brush near the Vermont boys' trench. By doing so, the lead element of the regiment was cut off from the rest of the enemy line due to fire and heavy smoke. Captain Riley Sterns of the 7th Vermont said the fire made "so dense a smoke that our lines could not be seen." Camouflaged by the heavy smoke, Watson pushed his small group forward. From about 2:00 P.M., when the felled woods caught fire, to sunset Sterns and his party were lying as flat as possible under heavy Confederate fire. "At sunset the shelling suddenly ceased and the charge was made," said Sterns. Sterns described the charge as "so sudden and vigorous that we could offer but little resistance." In all, Sterns and 21 men were captured by Watson's and Newton's sortie, a small victory that brought encouragement to the brigade in face of hopeless odds.[11]

As Canby's line grew and strengthened, so did his amount of artillery. The first fire the Louisiana Brigade was subjected to was simply from the field batteries accompanying the XIII Corps' infantry. As of 4 April Canby had in place 37 field guns and 38 siege guns, of which six were 20-pounder rifles and 16 mortars. These 75 guns were unleashed for several hours but Canby was unable to maintain a rain of lead on Spanish Fort due to the poor conditions of the roads which retarded the movement of supplies to his guns. By 8 April the number of artillery had increased by an additional 15 siege guns, including an addition of four 20-pounder rifles. There was a total of 90 guns bearing down on Spanish Fort and, of that number, 10 of the siege guns were enfilading the right near Fort McDermott, and an additional five siege guns were enfilading the line from the left. Gibson said that, for the first ten days, he was able to hold Canby in check, but after that point, the weight of his numbers and artillery was too much. "While he was steadily digging up to our front and flanks," Gibson said, "his fleet kept up a well-directed and heavy fire in our rear, and mortars dropped over the entire surface shells of the largest size." Throughout the entire siege, from 27 March through 8 April Canby's artillery dropped 8,673 rounds on the beleaguered defenders. When Gibson issued an order to his troops saying, "You must dig, dig, dig. Nothing can save us here but the spade," he was not exaggerating.[12]

Gibson grew more desperate as each day wore on. He demanded more artillery and tools to dig more works to protect his lines. He varied his requests in hopes of ascertaining anything of use, including picks, axes and negroes for labor. Initially Gibson had 24 black laborers, some contracted and some slave. He asked for "200 good negroes with tools to work," and with no answer forthcoming from Maury, he pleaded down to "100 negroes with 50 axes and 50 picks." Three days later he asked for more tools, the next day for more "axes and negroes" and two days later for 200 more laborers. Judging from the flurry of messages from Gibson to Maury, it appears Gibson's requests went unanswered until the early hours of 8 April. Too little, too late as predicted by Gibson: "I must have the things I have asked for within the last three days, else disaster may happen. Think of our incomplete works and of the disparity of the forces."[13]

Outside from the sorties on 27 March and 31 March the Louisiana Brigade stuck to its trenches between Forts Blair and McDermott. Losses were a slow, continual drain as the siege pushed along. As of 6 April the brigade had lost 22 men killed and 64 wounded, almost 25 percent out of the 500 or so men. Austin Smith of the 4th Battalion said, "There was continual fighting around the fort from the time we arrived until we were compelled to evacuate." "My men are wider apart than they ever were under Johnston or Hood," moaned Gibson. With each day the men got wider and wider apart. Campbell's brigade was given recruits during the siege, from where, who and how many it is unclear. They apparently were an undesirable lot and could not be trusted. Gibson issued strict orders to the Louisianians that none of these men were to go beyond the main line of works for any reason. To arrest their desertion, and desertion among the regiments, Gibson offered furloughs for those that caught deserters, and he even encouraged the creation of secret police groups to secretly keep watch. Casualties and desertions added to the reducing size of the brigade as did the shuffling of units between Blakely and Spanish Fort. Thomas' Alabama Reserves were traded a few days in for two veteran, but very reduced, brigades: Brigadier General James Holtzclaw's and Brigadier General Matthew Ector's. The trade reduced Gibson's effective total to about 1,500 infantry. Out of desperation, Gibson shot a note to Maury on 5 April: "Have you any negro troops? I would be glad to get some." Gibson's request for black troops was fulfilled when on the last night of the siege, Gibson said, "The infirmary corps and several hundred negroes" had arrived "to be employed in the defense."[14]

Gibson realized that, unless drastic steps were taken to reinforce Spanish Fort, it would be lost. The men were worn and tired from almost two weeks of, as Gibson said, "constant work, night and day, with the musket and spade." The Louisianians' work was matched by their enemies who had more men, trenching tools, supplies and, more importantly, more artillery. Artillery superiority had been established by Canby's guns, which allowed his men to dig faster and closer to the Confederate lines. On 8 April Canby decided to unleash on Spanish Fort all 90 of his guns. It just so happened that Gibson planned to feel out the extent of the enemy's progress by a general firing of his artillery and skirmishers on the same day. The prescribed time for firing for Canby was 5:30 P.M. Unfortunately for Gibson, this was the about the same time he planned to test the resolve of enemy fire. When the Confederate guns opened, they were met by a massive avalanche of shells. "My artillery was soon disabled and silenced," observed Gibson. The Louisianians hugged the ground in their trenches tightly as enemy artillery pounded their lines. With Gibson's command pinned down part of Canby's right flank made a push on Spanish Fort. Throughout the bombardment Colonel James Geddes of Carr's division outflanked the left flank of the Spanish Fort defenses. Geddes, a former adversary of Gibson's from Shiloh's Hornets Nest, moved two of his regiments around the flank of Ector's brigade, and soon his entire brigade was pushed into action. Ector was forced to give up around 300 yards of trenches, and Lumsden's battery was captured and turned on the retreating Confederates.

It was the breakthrough Gibson feared. To mend the break Gibson turned to his Louisianians. Campbell was ordered out of line and toward Geddes. With part of the brigade posted to protect the only route of the fort along a footpath through the marshes, Campbell took the remainder of his brigade to check Geddes' breakthrough. Advancing in the darkness, Campbell approached to within 40 yards of Geddes' regiments and opened fire. Geddes had began converting Ector's line into works for his men and waited for the Louisianians to close. When the Louisiana regiments were a mere 25 yards from his line Geddes' ordered his men to open fire. Campbell's men "broke and fled" but were rallied and pushed forth again only to be stopped at 50 yards away. It was by far not the most intense fight the brigade had faced, but their show of force kept Geddes in place and bought Gibson precious time. Killed at the head of the attack was the brigade's tough provost officer, Lieutenant Alfred Clark. Recognized for his efficiency as an officer, Gibson had promoted him as commandant of the Spanish Fort post.[15]

The evacuation of Spanish Fort began immediately. "The moment had at length arrived when I could no longer hold the position without imminent risk of losing the garrison, " reported Gibson. To cover the withdrawal skirmishers were ordered to keep up a steady fire to deceive the enemy. In the meantime, all cannons were ordered spiked, and the "few remaining stores were issued" to the men as they fell back. The pathway taken was but an eighteen inch pathway from behind Ector's position on the left. The small pathway was 1,200 yards long and was covered with moss to help soften the men's walk on the planks laid down on the marsh. The men were ordered to take off their shoes so their movements could be made in a "noiseless manner." The pathway led from the left of the defenses to Batteries Huger and Tracey and was exposed to enemy artillery on the bluffs to the east. The high grass and moss concealed the pathway, and the quiet manner of the retreat, covered by heavy skirmishing, allowed the majority of the garrison to escape. Once at Battery Huger the brigade was met by boats, forwarded by Maury, to evacuate the garrison to Mobile.[16]

The evacuation of Spanish Fort on the eighth and the capture of Blakely with its garrison on the ninth meant Mobile could not be held. Maury's effective force, subtracting the casualties suffered at Spanish Fort and the capture of the garrison at Blakely, totaled less than 5,000 men. Maury spent the ninth through the eleventh removing all supplies he could from Mobile. Early on 12 April, Maury left Mobile with his main force. Left behind as the rear guard was Gibson and his Louisiana Brigade, numbering just 300 men. With the army safely away, Gibson notified the Federal fleet that Mobile had been evacuated and Federal forces could take possession of the city. From Mobile the brigade retreated to Citronelle. From there trains carried the men to Meridian where they arrived on 14 April.[17]

Gibson has reported the losses of the brigade at 86 on 6 April but there is no report for losses for the last two days of the siege. As with the late war campaigns of the Atlanta and Nashville Campaigns there are no reports issued showing total losses. The 1st Louisiana Regulars did report that they did not lose a man during the whole siege until the evacuation of the fort, but it did not state numbers lost. Brigade musters offer good insight. The brigade's first muster following Spanish Fort came on 20 April where the brigade's effective total numbers had swollen to 846 men but that was due to the addition of the Louisiana artillery units that were part of the Mobile garrison: the 1st Louisiana Heavy Artillery and the 22nd Louisiana Consolidated Regiment. Subtracting the two new units attached, Gibson's brigade numbered only 350 men, which was a 225 reduction in effective totals for the brigade before it left Mobile for Spanish Fort. During the period from 15 March to 20 April, the men reported as prisoners of war rose by 325, and the men listed as being absent without leave rose from 200 to 462. These numbers by no means establish an official number of losses but do provide insight to the large number of men who were captured and absent without permission. Desertion became such a problem that Gibson was forced to address it on 15 April with a general order stating that anyone "who shall detect and aid to convict any one in the act of desertion" would be rewarded with a furlough of 40 days. The issuing of full rations of bacon, beef and sugar while at Meridian was in no doubt to assist in rebuilding morale. To help build morale Gibson reorganized the brigade's band, even its leader, B. Moses, who had deserted when the brigade evacuated Mobile. Douglas Cater was summoned to Gibson's tent at Meridian where the general told him, "We must have some music." With orders in hand, the excited Cater was able to scrape together 16 men and immediately went to work. The desertion of an additional 55 men during late April and early May showed that the allure of furlough, full stomachs and good music was not enough to keep a sizeable percentage of the remaining men with the colors.[18]

Camp at Meridian was broken on 22 April and the Louisiana Brigade was ordered east toward Cuba Station where it arrived two days later. Maury received orders to refit his field batteries and equip his men to prepare to march east to join Joe Johnston's army in North

Carolina. Organizationally, the brigade went through two changes. First, the 19th Louisiana had been consolidated under Lindsay's command with the 1st, 16th and 20th regiments. At Cuba Station, the brigade underwent a total transformation with the root cause being the decrease in the multitude of men in the brigade. The units were divided into two regiments called the Pelican and Chalmette regiments.[19]

The Pelican Regiment was created by the consolidation of 4th Battalion 19th, 20th and 25th regiments with Frank Zacharie as its colonel. The regiment was created by the following means: The 19th Louisiana made up Companies A, D and E; the 25th Louisiana made up B and C; the 4th Louisiana Battalion broken into Companies F and G, and the 20th Louisiana became Company H. Private Austin Smith of the 4th Battalion was made ensign of the new regiment. In all the new Pelican Regiment fielded 220 men.[20]

The Chalmette Regiment, commanded by Colonel Francis Campbell, was formed by consolidating 1st Regulars, 4th, 13th and 16th regiments and the 30th Battalion and Austin's battalion. Limited records reveal that the Chalmette was divided as follows: 13th Louisiana made up Company A; 16th Louisiana made up Companies C, D, and F; Austin's battalion made up Company H, while the components of Companies E, G, I and K are unknown. Captain Chauncey Ford commanded Company C of the newly consolidated regiment. Ford, from the 16th Louisiana, commanded three reduced companies that once merged managed an effective strength of 36 men. That is only about 10 percent of the three companies' mustering total in 1861. Campbell mustered 186 men in his new command.[21]

All of the reorganization and preparation came of no use. Word reached the Louisianians, while at Cuba Station, of the surrender of the armies of Robert E. Lee and Joseph E. Johnston in the east. General Richard Taylor wrote Maury on 2 May saying, "Recent events make it due to the soldiers and citizens of this department, whose future welfare depends upon my action, that I shall make every effort to secure an honorable and speedy cessation of hostilities." Negotiations had already begun between Taylor and Canby a few days before at Citronelle. Taylor and Canby agreed to terms based on those of Lee's and Johnston's surrender in April: the men were to be paroled, and officers were to keep their side arms and horses. On 6 May it was announced to the men that they were to be surrendered, and Maury was given orders to move his command to Meridian "for the purpose of being paroled."[22]

The last muster roll of the Chalmette and Pelican regiments showed an effective total of 394 men. Captain Francis O. Trepagnier's 30th Louisiana symbolized the Louisiana regiments when mustered to surrender and sign their parole papers. Of the regiment's original 804 men there were only 60, including Trepagnier, that answered the call. The anemic scene was echoed throughout the brigade: Gibson's old immigrant-filled 13th Louisiana barely mustered 40 men out of its original 830 men; the 20th Louisiana had 39 of its 879, and the 1st Regulars mustered even less with close to 35. It was a common scene throughout all the regiments. Blurring the numbers of the men who were actually present with the colors in early May was the surfacing of paroled prisoners, sick and wounded from the hospitals and even deserters. As the brigade camped near Meridian and prepared for parole, Douglas Cater made note of the fact that, all of a sudden, men who "had never seen service and some who had quit on the change of commanders at Atlanta" showed themselves to receive their paroles. Naturally, the men who had served their time faithfully in the field were upset by the detached, absent and even deserters showing up for parole just like them. "Some of them," said Cater, "were handled roughly by our soldiers." Some of the soldiers who lined up for parole were men recently exchanged from capture at Spanish Fort. Men

George Provost, 19th Louisiana, survived four long years of campaigning to surrender with his regiment at Meridian (courtesy of Alabama Department of Archives and History, Montgomery).

25th Louisiana's flag carried home from the surrender at Meridian (courtesy of Confederate Memorial Hall Museum, New Orleans).

captured at Spanish Fort were forwarded to Ship Island, off the coast of Mississippi in the Gulf, and transported up the Mississippi to Vicksburg where they were then brought to a prisoner exchange camp known as Camp Townsend. From there, some of the more loyal and committed Louisianians made their way to Meridian to join back up with their units, only to be surrendered again.[23]

Also during this time came a filtering of prisoners from the east, not only from Lee's and Johnston's armies, but also Louisianians from the brigade that had begun to be exchanged in February and March. The United States government reopened the prisoner cartel again due to humanitarian reasons. These men, coming from camps all across the north, were transported to the east coast and down to Boulwares and Cox's Wharf below Richmond, where they were exchanged and then allowed to go home due to their conditions of parole and exchange. From the time of exchange it was almost a month before these men began filtering into the region. Take the case of William H. Duff of the 25th Louisiana, who was captured at Utoy Creek outside Atlanta. He stayed at Camp Chase, Ohio, until 13 February 1865 from which he was shipped via rail to Baltimore, Maryland. From there he was shipped to Boulwares and Cox's Wharf below Richmond for exchange. He left Richmond on 23 February and traveled by rail through Charlotte, North Carolina, then walked through South Carolina all the way past Atlanta, Georgia, where he was boarded on railroad cars again. Passing through Selma and Jackson by rail and boat, Huff walked the rest of the way home. Hundreds of men captured in 1863 and 1864 were granted these paroles and exchanges. Samuel Gustine, Company A of the 4th Louisiana Battalion, did not have as easy a time as Duff. Gustine was captured at Utoy Creek with Duff and also served his time at Camp Chase. He was paroled and exchanged in late February of 1865 at Boulwares and Cox's Wharf in Virginia and from there proceeded to make his way home to Madison Parish. As Gustine was making his way back home, he passed through Selma, Alabama, only to have the misfortune of being in that city when Major General James Wilson's cavalry attacked and captured the city. For ten days he stayed locked up as a prisoner of war, again. After two nights he was able to make an escape and made good his parole with the brigade at Meridian.[24]

One of the hardest things to swallow at the surrender was the giving up of the unit flags. As the Louisianians were stacking their arms during the surrender, Colonel Frank Zacharie approached the color bearer, Oscar Estell, from the 25th Louisiana. Refusing to surrender his regiment's flag, Estell was ordered by Zacharie to save the unit's flag. Having carried the colors since Perryville, Estell was more than happy to comply. Estell tore out the lining of his coat, slipped the flag inside the back of his jacket and resewed the lining back on. Years later, Estell passed the flag to Captain John Clayton, of Company C of the 25th Louisiana, who donated it to Confederate Memorial Hall in New Orleans, where the flag remains to this day. Then there was the flag of the 13th Louisiana, which was "concealed in an old sock" and brought home. Members of the 4th Battalion managed to sneak their flag out as well. It was a last act of defiance in the face of defeat.[25]

With men receiving their paroles and others making their own way home, the numbers of the brigade began to dwindle. Officers of the brigade and the brigade's band, "the only left in the army," marched to Maury's tent where it gave Maury "their farewell serenade." Gibson drew up a farewell address to the Louisianians that he issued on 8 May:

> FELLOW-SOLDIERS:
> For more than four years we have shared together the fortunes of war. Throughout all the scenes of this eventful revolution you have been fully tried, and now retire with the consciousness of having achieved a character for discipline, for valor, and for unselfish patriotism of which you may be justly proud. There is nothing in your career to look back upon with regret. You have always been in front of the enemy; you have never feasted in soft places at the rear, nor fought your battles at comfortable firesides. Your banners are garlanded with the emblems of every soldierly virtue. More than twenty battle-fields have seen them unfurled. They were never lowered save over the bier of a comrade. Forget not the good and true men who have fallen. No sculptured marble may perpetuate the memory of their services, but you will wear their names ever green in your hearts, and they will be enshrined forever in the affections of the Southern people, in whose cause they fell. Comrades, henceforth other duties will devolve upon you. Adversities can only strengthen the ties that bind you to your country and increase the obligations you owe to her interests and her honor. As soldiers, you have been among the bravest and most steadfast, and as citizens, be law abiding, peaceable, and industrious. You have not surrendered and will never surrender your self-respect and love of country. You separate not as friends, but brethren whom common hopes, mutual trials, and equal disasters have

made kinsmen. Hereafter you shall recount to your children, with conscious pride, the story of these rugged days, and you will always greet a comrade of the old brigade with open arms. Having commanded a company and regiment in the brigade, I have known many of you from the very beginning of the struggle, have been with you through all its varied fortunes, and offer to each one of you a grateful and affectionate farewell. May God bless you.[26]

The end of the war brought mixed feelings: Four years of terrible conflict was finally at an end, but the men of the brigade had served a defeated cause and must now return to a war devastated Louisiana. Writing from Mobile after his parole, in his last wartime letter, Douglas Cater told his cousin, "Whether or not I made a good solider is not for me to say, but I have done my duty in every capacity that I have been called up on to act as a soldier and now I believe that I can make a good citizen, at least I am willing to share the fate of my friends in the *seceded* states." Men were transported back to their homes mostly by being moved to Mobile then to New Orleans and dispersed across Louisiana from there.[27]

As the men returned home, they began picking up the pieces of their ravaged homes and returning to the lives of ordinary citizens. Peace and stability did not come soon due to Reconstruction, which lasted through 1877. Most returned to a peaceful life, while others fought Reconstruction, such as John McEnery of the 4th Louisiana Battalion. McEnery won the governor's race in 1872, and his acceptance speech was opened by remarks from E.J. Ellis. McEnery's reign was ended when he was forcibly removed from power by an order by President U.S. Grant. For Gibson, the end of the war meant a return to New Orleans. Gibson was very active in postwar Louisiana and fought Reconstruction through politics and diplomacy. In 1872, he was elected to the U.S. House of Representatives, but he refused the seat. In 1874, Gibson was elected to the same seat and accepted it. Gibson remained in his office until 1882, when he won election as a U.S. senator. He was re-elected in 1888. Major political events that Gibson was involved in include the Compromise Election of 1876 on the national

Postwar image of Senator Randall L. Gibson (courtesy of Confederate Memorial Hall Museum, New Orleans).

scene and the Lottery controversy in Louisiana politics. Gibson was also very active in creating Tulane University and served on its board of administration. The first president of Tulane, hired in 1884, was Gibson's long-time friend William P. Johnston. On 15 December 1892, at the age of 60, Randall Gibson died while on a visit to Hot Springs, Arkansas. Gibson was praised by many of his wartime and political contemporaries on the floor of the U.S. Congress following his death. Congress approved 8,000 copies of the eulogies given of Gibson to be printed and distributed. The strengths and talents that were observed in the 1850s in local political gatherings were carried to the battlefield. Gibson's trials and exploits at the head of his regiment and the brigade equipped him for the ruthless field of politics in postwar Louisiana.[28]

Gibson forever bore with him a burden for his 13th Louisiana Regiment and his Louisiana Brigade. He bitterly fought to restore the honor of his regiment when its character was slighted at the Battle of Jonesboro, and he was key in organizing the Gibson's Brigade Benevolent Society for indigent men from his old command. With that burden and pride he carried for his men Gibson also bore a long resentment toward Braxton Bragg and his rough treatment of him after Shiloh. Shiloh was an event that, as Gibson said, "has never ceased to engage the attention of the historian and military critic." Gibson and his brigade paid a dear price that day and were subjected to unfair criticism from Bragg for their part. Having undergone such a traumatic experience, it was an event that was "fresh and vivid in the recollections of the survivors." In 1876, Gibson, while speaking about Shiloh, said that after the death of Johnston the western army, or Army of Tennessee, "had such incompetency at the head of our operations—that the valor of troops, could not save us from shame & disgrace, even." Even as late as 1887, when Gibson spoke at a ceremony to commemorate a monument in Metairie Cemetery by the Veterans of the Army of Tennessee, the kindest word he could muster to describe Bragg, while talking of all the men and leaders associated with army at Shiloh, was only to call him "indefatigable." Whether this was meant as a compliment or not is reserved for Gibson.[29]

As the veterans died out in the late 1800s and early 1900s, their story did not. Anecdotal stories and events were recorded in journals, and diaries, with some even printed in the old *Confederate Veteran* publication. Their story became intertwined with the Lost Cause as it became the rallying call of a postwar South as it sought to find its identity and explain its failure and find hope in the future. Today, their graves scatter the country. Men moved west after the war and began new lives. One old soldier, Francis Cullen of the 13th Louisiana, made his way as far away as Australia, where he is buried today. Hundreds more filled shallow graves in northern states near old prisons, while others lay in graves along the campaign trails across the south. In 1900, members of the 16th Louisiana's old Company C held a ceremony at the Shreveport Courthouse to commemorate their going off to war in 1861. At the meeting, Lieutenant Thomas Pegues, who served with his regiment from Shiloh to the surrender at Meridian, gave a moving speech of his war experiences. Who better to articulate the sacrifices of the Louisiana Brigade than one of its seasoned veterans? Pegues said:

> Where are our comrades who stepped forth so gaily to battle for Southern rights? As the spirits that keep vigil over the gory fields of Shiloh, Perryville, Murfreesboro, Jackson, Chickamauga, Missionary Ridge, Dalton, Resaca, New Hope Church, Kennesaw Mountain, Atlanta, Jonesboro, Franklin, Nashville, and Spanish Fort.... They gave up their lives in defense of home and loved ones, to drive back the hirelings who sought to despoil our altars and devour our substance. Amid the roar of battle and the clash of arms their souls took flight. They were spared the ignominy and degradation of reconstruction. We are not called upon to prove they were

right; we know they were. They fought for a principle that is as eternal as the stars. Sacred ties bind us to their memory. Side by side we toiled with them on the weary march, and stood shoulder to shoulder with them where battle raged and death reveled in the slaughter. We can vouch for their valor as they faced and fought the foe, and can testify to their good names. In obedience to a sentiment of honor and a call of duty, they made the last human sacrifice; they gave up their lives for a grand and glorious cause. It was such courage as this, my comrades, that has made the "boys who wore the gray" the immortal heroes of our Southland, and as long as life lasts we will honor them in their grand achievements.[30]

Chapter Notes

Chapter 1

1. "Gen. Albert Sidney Johnson," *Confederate Veteran* 3 (1895): 85; William Preston Johnston, *The Life of Gen. Albert Sidney Johnston* (New York: Appleton, 1878), 582–83.
2. Ezra J. Warner, *Generals in Gray* (Baton Rouge: Louisiana State University Press, 1959), 3, 104.
3. Warner, *Generals in Gray*, 104; Dixon, "Gibson," 20–23.
4. Frank L. Richardson, "War as I Saw It," *The Louisiana Historical Quarterly* (VI 1923): 91; Frank L. Richardson to Father, 23 September 1861, Frank Liddell Richardson Papers, Southern Historical Collection, Wilson Library, The University of North Carolina at Chapel Hill, NC.
5. William Howard Russell, *The Civil War in America* (London: Trubner, 1861), 136–38.
6. *Richmond Daily Dispatch*, 30 April 1862; Warner, *Generals*, 104; Dixon, "Gibson," 24–25; Compiled Service Record of Randall L. Gibson, National Archives, Washington, DC (hereafter cited as CSR); Mary Gorton McBride and Ann Mathison McLaurin, *Randall Lee Gibson of Louisiana: Confederate General and New South Reformer* (Baton Rouge: Louisiana State University Press, 2007) 68.
7. John McGrath, "In a Louisiana Regiment," *Historical Society Papers* 31 (1979): 103–4, 106–7; *Mobile Register*, April 19, 1863; Frank L. Richardson to Father, 4 September 1861, Frank Liddell Richardson Papers.
8. *Ibid.*
9. Frank L. Richardson to Father, September 18, 1861, Frank Liddell Richardson Papers.
10. Frank L. Richardson to Father, September 23, 1861, Frank Liddell Richardson Papers.
11. Arthur W. Bergeron, *Guide to Louisiana Confederate Military Units, 1861–1865* (Baton Rouge: Louisiana State University Press, 1996), 104; Compiled Service Records of Confederate Soldiers Who Served in Organizations from the State of Louisiana, Microcopy M320, Rolls 245–252 (hereafter cited as CSR, 13th Louisiana Infantry, M320, Rolls 245–252. Similar muster roll work of whole regiments will follow the same format); McGrath, "In a Louisiana Regiment," 110–113. The author has been unable to confirm the death in the Compiled Service Records of the regiment; Charles James Johnson to Lou, 2 September 1861, LSU Special Collections, Hill Memorial Library John A. Harris Letters, Mss. 1881, 2548, 2549, 3008, Louisiana and Lower Mississippi Valley Collections (hereafter cited as LLMVC), LSU Libraries, Baton Rouge, LA; *The Daily Delta*, 29 October 1861.
12. Dixon, "Gibson," 24–25; McGrath, "In a Louisiana Regiment," 110–113; Richardson, "War as I Saw It," 92–93.
13. Benjamin Cooling, *Forts Henry and Donelson: The Key to the Confederate Heartland* (Knoxville: University of Tennessee Press, 1987), 231–34.
14. *The War of the Rebellion: A Compilation of the Official Records of the Union and Confederate Armies*, 128 vols. (Washington: GPO, 1880–1901), ser. 1, vol. 7, pt. 1, 900 (hereafter cited as *OR*, with all references to ser. 1, unless otherwise noted).
15. Richardson, "War as I Saw It," 9–97; *OR*, vol. 7, 893, 896.
16. McGrath, "War as I Saw It," 97–98; CSR, 20th Louisiana Infantry, M320, Rolls 308–315; 20th Louisiana scrapbook, Jackson Barracks. The 5th Louisiana Battalion and 12th Louisiana Regiment did not go from Columbus to Corinth. Instead they became part of the garrisons along the Mississippi River. The 5th Louisiana Battalion was soon organized into the 21st Louisiana.
17. *OR*, vol. 10, pt. 1, 382 and vol. 6, 824; F. Jay Tayler, ed., *Reluctant Rebel: The Secret Diary of Robert Patrick 1861–1865* (Baton Rouge: Louisiana State University Press, 1996), 37; Bergeron, *Guide*, 80, 121; Arthur W. Bergeron, ed., *The Civil War Reminiscences of Major Silas T. Grisamore* (Baton Rouge: Louisiana State University Press, 1993), 18–19.
18. McGrath, "In a Louisiana Regiment," 103.
19. *The Contemporary Review*. Vol. 3 (London: Strahan), 1868, 40–42.
20. Taylor, *Reluctant Rebel*: 31; *Bayou Sarah Ledger*, 8 June 1861, Camp Moore Museum.
21. Franklin Eady to Friend, 27 July 1861, 4th Louisiana Infantry File, Camp Moore Museum.
22. David C. Edmonds, *Yankee Autumn in Acadiana* (Lafayette, LA: Acadiana Press, 1979), 10–11; John S. Kendall, "Recollections of a Confederate Officer," *Louisiana Historical Quarterly* 29 (October 1946), 1053–55.
23. CSR, 4th Louisiana Infantry, M320, Rolls 134–142; Thomas H. Richey, *Tirailleurs: A History of The 4th Louisiana and The Acadians of Company H*

(New York: Writers Advantage, 2003), 28; *OR*, vol. 6, 832; Kendall, "Recollections," 1048–51; Taylor, *Reluctant Rebel*, 35.

24. Bergeron, *Guide*, 120–21; The 14th Louisiana was formed at Camp Pulaski in Amite, Louisiana, about 10 miles from Camp Moore. The 15th Louisiana was not formed at Camp Moore; it was created in Virginia.

25. William Terrell Lewis, *Genealogy of the Lewis Family in America, from the Middle of the Seventeenth Century Down to the Present Time* (Louisville, KY: Courier-Journal, 1893), 113–14; *OR*, vol. 3, 618; *OR*, vol. 4, 383; Richardson, "War as I Saw It," 92.

26. The National Cyclopedia of American Biography Being the History of the United States, Vol. 10 (New York: White, 1900), 495.

27. Ray Holder, "Col. Wesley Parker Winans, C.S.A.: A Character Profile," *Louisiana History* 30 (1989), 280–300.

28. Ralph Wooster, ed., "Four Years in the Confederate Infantry: The Civil War Letters of Private R.F. Eddins, 19th Louisiana," *The Texas Gulf Historical & Biographical Record* 7 (1971), 16.

29. Thomas Benjamin Davidson to Sister, 8 February 1862, Thomas Benjamin Davidson Papers, Southern Historical Collection, Wilson Library, The University of North Carolina at Chapel Hill, NC; Sergeant John Hunter, "As I Remember Now," Private Collection; *OR*, vol. 10, pt. 1, 493.

30. Joseph A. Harris to Wife, 7 March 1862, John A. Harris Letters, LLMVC; CSR of Isaac Stanley.

31. *OR*, vol. 1, 687–9.

32. *OR*, vol. 10, pt. 1, 382.

Chapter 2

1. Daniel L. Sutherland, ed., *Reminiscences of a Private: William E. Bevens of the First Arkansas Infantry, C. S. A.* (Fayetteville: University of Arkansas Press, 1992), 63.

2. Larry Daniel, *Shiloh: The Battle That Changed the Civil War* (New York: Simon & Schuster, 1997), 126–27; Donelson Caffery Jenkins Diary [Microfilm], #M-1932, Southern Historical Collection, Louis Round Wilson Special Collections Library, University of North Carolina at Chapel Hill (hereafter cited as Donelson Caffery Jenkins' Diary).

3. Stacy Allen, "Shiloh!" *Blue & Gray Magazine* 14 (Winter 1997): 19–21; Donelson Caffery Jenkins' Diary.

4. *OR*, vol. 10, pt. 1, 471, 480, 568.

5. *Ibid.*, 480, 483; Daniel, *Shiloh*, 151–152; McGrath, "War as I Saw It," 99; Sutherland, *Reminiscences of a Private*, 69.

6. Sutherland, *Reminiscences of a Private*, 67; Ken Durham, ed., "A Report on the Battle of Shiloh," *Louisiana History* 35 (Winter 1994), 86.

7. *OR*, vol. 10, pt. 1, 427, 430, 489; Kendall, "Recollections of a Confederate Officer," 1061–1062; Donelson Caffery Jenkins' Diary; McGrath, "War as I Saw It," 99; McBride and McLaruin, *Randall Lee Gibson*, 76.

8. *OR*, vol. 10, pt. 1, 466, 480.

9. Thomas Robertson to Mother, 9 April 1862, Robertson (Thomas Chinn) Papers, 1862–1912, Pearce Civil War Collection, Navarro College, Corsicana, Texas;

10. *OR*, vol. 10, pt. 1, 279; Daniel, *Shiloh*, 203–6.

11. Kendall, "Recollections of a Confederate Officer," 1064; *OR*, vol. 10, pt. 1, 480, 489; Sutherland, *Reminiscences of a* Private, 71; Donelson Caffery Jenkins' Diary; Brian Howerton's extensive research of the Compiled Service Records of Confederate Soldiers Who Served in Organizations from the State of Arkansas, Microcopy M317, Rolls 46–52 (hereafter cited as Howerton, CSR, 1st Arkansas Infantry, M317, Rolls 46–52).

12. *OR*, vol.10, pt. 1, 233–5, 281, 492–3; Sutherland, *Reminiscences of a Private*, 69.

13. Frank Richardson, "War as I Saw It," 100; *OR*, vol. 10, pt. 1, 235, 480, 483, 488, 493; Sarah A. Dorset, *Recollections of Henry Watkins Allen: Brigadier-General Confederate States Army, Ex-Governor of Louisiana* (New York: Doolady, and New Orleans: J.A. Gresham, 1866), 74–75

14. Frank Richardson, "War as I Saw It," 100; *OR*, vol. 10, pt. 1, 235, 480, 483, 488, 493; Sutherland, *Reminiscences of a Private*, 71.

15. Donelson Caffery Jenkins' Diary.

16. *OR*, vol. 10, pt. 1, 466, 486.

17. S.H. Lockett, "Surprise and Withdrawal at Shiloh," *Battles and Leaders*, vol. 1 (New York: Century, 1884–1887), 605; *OR*, vol. 10, pt. 1, 486.

18. *OR*, vol. 10, pt. 1, 483, 486; Kendall, "Recollections of a Confederate Officer," 1064; Richardson, "War as I Saw It," 100; Bergeron, *Major Grisamore*, 38.

19. Kendall, "Recollections of a Confederate Officer," 1065–66; Dorset, *Recollections of Henry Watkins Allen*, 74–75.

20. *OR*, vol. 10, pt. 1, 165–6, 183–4, 483.

21. *Ibid.*, 165–6, 183–4, 483; Johnson, John Lipscomb, *The University Memorial Biographical Sketches of Alumni of the University of Virginia Who Fell in the Confederate War*, Five Volumes in One (Baltimore: Turnball Brothers, 1871), 103–10; Howerton, CSR 1st Arkansas Infantry, M317, Rolls 46–52.

22. S.H. Lockett, "Surprise and Withdrawal at Shiloh," 605; Jeffrey J. Gudmens, *Staff Ride Handbook for the Battle of Shiloh, 6–7 April, 1862* (Fort Leavenworth, KS: Combat Studies Institute Press, 2005) 105; Taylor, *Reluctant Rebel*, 36; Richardson, "War as I Saw It," 102. In Gibson's report of the battle he reports four attacks on the Hornets Nest but the consensus with all other reports and personal accounts from soldiers confirm there were only three attacks. It is the interpretation of the author that only three attacks were made.

23. *OR*, vol. 10, pt. 1, 466, 482–87.

24. *Ibid.*, 466.

25. Braxton Bragg to Elise, 8 April 1862, Bixby Collection of Bragg Papers, Missouri Historical Society Archives.

26. *OR*, vol. 10, pt. 1, 493.

27. *Ibid.*, 472, 480, 484, 488; 493–494; Richardson "War as I Saw it," 103.

28. *OR*, vol. 10, pt. 1, 480, 493–494; Daniel, *Shiloh*, 255; Thomas Chinn Robertson to Mother, 9 April 1862, Robertson (Thomas Chinn) Papers.

29. *OR*, vol. 10, pt. 1, 473, 480, 518.

30. *Ibid.*, 170
31. *Ibid.*, 170–1, 190, 192, 480–1, 488, 491; Thomas Chinn Robertson to Mother, 9 April 1862, Robertson (Thomas Chinn) Papers.
32. *OR*, vol. 10, pt. 1, 489.
33. *Ibid.*, 440–1.
34. *OR*, vol. 10, pt. 1, 481; Thomas Chinn Robertson to Mother, 9 April 1862, Robertson (Thomas Chinn) Papers; Donelson Caffery Jenkins' Diary.
35. *OR*, vol. 10, pt. 1, 480–1, 488–91; *Richmond Daily Dispatch*, 30 April 1862.
36. *OR*, vol. 10, pt. 1, 480–1, 488–91; Dorset, *Recollections of Henry Watkins Allen*, 76.
37. *OR*. vol. 10, pt. 1, 494, 524, 534.
38. Sutherland, *Reminiscences of a Private*, 73; Kendall, "Recollections of a Confederate Officer," 1069–1070; *OR*, vol. 10, pt. 1, 482; Asa Morgan to Wife, 8 April 1862, Asa Stokely Morgan Letters (Arkansas History Commission, Little Rock).
39. *OR*, vol. 10, pt. 1, 395, 490, 493; CSR, 1st Arkansas Infantry, M317, Rolls 46–52.
40. Wesley Winans Journal, Winans Family Collection.

Chapter 3

1. *OR*, vol. 10, pt. 2, 408.
2. *OR*, vol. 10, pt. 1, 821, and pt. 2, 46, 303; William Arceneaux, *Acadian General: Alfred Mouton and the Civil War* (Lafayette: University of Southwestern Louisiana Press, 1981), 53.
3. CSR, 16th Louisiana Infantry, M320, Rolls 273–280.
4. Fannie Pittman to Brother and Sister, February 5, 1862, Wimberly Letters, Camp Moore Museum.
5. Louis Stagg to Wife, 6 October 1861, Louis Stagg Letters, Louisiana Room, Dupre Library, University of Louisiana at Lafayette, Lafayette, LA; E.J. Ellis to Father, October 12, 1861, E. John and Thomas C.W. Ellis Family Papers, Special Collections, Hill Memorial Library, Louisiana State University; J.S. Pittman to Alice, 12 November 1861, Wimberly Letters, Camp Moore Museum; Louis Stagg to Wife, 15 October 1861, Louis Stagg Letters; Cemetery List, Camp Moore Museum.
6. E.J. Lee to Brother, 15 November 1861, "A Collection of Louisiana Confederate Letters" edited by Frank E. Vandiver, *Louisiana Historical Quarterly* 4 (October 1943), 957–58; E.J. Ellis to Mother, 15 September 1861, E. John and Thomas C.W. Ellis Family Papers; Abraham Nesom to Father and Mother, 28 March 1862, Abraham Nesom Letters, Camp Moore Museum; CSR, 16th Louisiana Infantry, M320, Rolls 273–280. The 330 effective total for Shiloh does not count the men present in Company B which remained on guard duty in Corinth.
7. *OR*, vol. 10, pt. 1, 520; Abraham Nesom to Father and Mother, 28 March 1862, Abraham Nesom Letters.
8. CSR, 16th Louisiana Infantry, M320, Rolls 273–280; Michael F. Howell, *Feliciana Confederates: A Compilation of Soldiers of East & West Feliciana Parishes; 1861–1865* (St. Francisville, LA: 1989).
9. Family Bible, Daniel Gober, Jr. Photocopy of pages from Family Bible furnished by Edgar McDavitt Gober III of births, marriages and death of this family.
10. *OR*, vol. 10, pt. 2, 461, 468, 642.
11. "On the Stump: Arkansas Politics, 1819–1919," Old State House Museum, 2003, http://www.oldstatehouse.com/exhibits/arkansas-politics/default.asp.
12. CSR, 11th Louisiana Infantry, M320, Rolls 226–233; CSR, 18th Louisiana Infantry, M320, Rolls 290–296; *OR*, vol. 10, pt. 1, 519.
13. Wooster, ed., "Four Years in the Confederate Infantry," 23; Ken Durham, ed., "'Dear Rebecca': The Civil War Letters of William Edward Paxton, 1861–1863," *Louisiana History* 20 (Spring 1979): 185–88; Bergeron, *Major Grisamore*, 51; Daniel Blue to Wife, April 20, 1862, "Letter Collection," Camp Moore Confederate Museum, Tangipahoa, LA.
14. Kendall, "Recollections, " 1057; Frank L. Richardson to Father, 4 September 1861, Frank Liddell Richardson Papers.
15. Dorset, *Recollections of Henry Watkins Allen*, 74; Frank L. Richardson to Father, 4 September 1861, Frank Liddell Richardson Papers; William Kennedy to Wife, 14 March 1863, William Kennedy Letters, Camp Moore Museum; John A. Harris to Wife, 28 May 1862, John A. Harris Letters, LLMVC.
16. J.E. Carraway, "Reminiscences of the Civil War 1861–1865, Especially Company B, Nineteenth Louisiana Regiment: Truths Told After Fifty Years," Ron Brothers, Paris, Texas http://gen.1starnet.com/civilwar/carraway.htm.
17. *Mobile Register*, 19 April 1863.
18. *OR*, vol. 10, pt. 1, 805, 809.
19. *Ibid.*, 806, 809, 820
20. Major General Sam Jones in Special Order 41, 15 August 1862, announcing the appointment of Adams to command; CSR of Daniel Adams, National Archives; Reichard Family Papers; Ella Lonn, *Foreigners in the Confederacy* (Charlotte: University of North Carolina Press, 2002), 111, 133, and 142.
21. CSR, 20th Louisiana Infantry, M320, Rolls 308–315; Bruce S. Allardice, *Confederate Colonels: A Biographical Register* (Columbia and London: University of Missouri Press, 2008), 412.
22. CSR, 20th Louisiana Infantry, M320, Rolls 308–315; 20th Louisiana scrapbook, Jackson Barracks.
23. *OR*, vol. 10, pt. 1, p 496, 507; Bergeron, *Guide*, 123–124.
24. *OR*. vol. 10, pt. 1, 766–68; Wesley Winans Journal, Winans Family Collection.
25. CSR, 19th Louisiana Infantry, M320, Rolls 302–307; CSR, 20th Louisiana Infantry, M320, Rolls 308–315; Wesley Winans Journal, Winans Family Collection.
26. Louis Stagg to Wife, 22 July 1862, Louis Stagg Letters; J.A. Harris to Wife, 6 July 1862, John A. Harris Papers, LLMVC; Wesley Winans Journal, Winans Family Collection.
27. Thomas Davidson to Sister, 24 July1862, Thomas Benjamin Davidson Papers; T.H. Wimberly to Brother, 27 June 1862, Wimberly Letters.
28. Durham, "Dear Rebecca," 187; Wesley Winans Journal, Winans Family Collection; T.H. Wimberly to Brother, 27 June 1862, Wimberly Letters.
29. E.J. Ellis to Sister, 12 December 1862, E.P. Ellis

and Family Papers, Special Collections, Hill Memorial Library, Louisiana State University.

30. CSR, 4th Louisiana Infantry, M320, Rolls 134–142; Randall Shoemaker, ed., *The St. Helena Rifles* (Privately published, 1968), 3, 39.

31. CSR of Aristide Gerard; CSR of Stephen O'Leary; CSR, 13th Louisiana Infantry, M320, Rolls 245–252.

32. CSR, 13th Louisiana Infantry, M320, Rolls 245–252; John McGrath, "In a Louisiana Regiment," 119; Allardice, *Confederate Colonels*, 160; *OR*, vol. 22, pt. 2, 933–34; CSR of Aristide Gerard; CSR of M.O. Tracy; CSR of Stephen O'Leary.

33. William Terrell Lewis, *Genealogy of the Lewis Family in America: From the Middle of the Seventeenth Century Down to the Present Time* (Louisville, KY: Courier-Journal, 1893), 113–14; *The National Cyclopedia of American Biography Being the History of the United States*, Vol. 10 (New York: White, 1900), 495–96; Allardice, *Confederate Colonels*, 378; CSR, 19th Louisiana Infantry, M320, Rolls 302–307.

34. CSR, 19th Louisiana Infantry, M320, Rolls 302–307; Wooster, ed., "Four Years in the Confederate Infantry," 23; CSR of Camp Flournoy.

35. CSR William Walker; CSR Robert H. Lindsay; Bergeron, *Major Grisamore*, 50–51; CSR, 11th Louisiana Infantry, M320, Rolls 226–233; CSR, 18th Louisiana Infantry, M320, Rolls 290–296.

36. Douglas John Cater, *As It Was: Reminiscences of a Soldier of the Third Texas Cavalry and the Nineteenth Louisiana Infantry* (Austin, TX: State House Press, 1990), 136; T.H. Wimberly to Brother, 27 June 1862, Wimberly Letters; William Kennedy to Wife, 23 July 1862, William Kennedy Letters.

37. Miscellaneous Record Books of the Louisiana Brigade, Record Group 109; Bergeron, *Major Grisamore*, 72; E.J. Ellis to Mother, 10 August 1862, E. John and Thomas C.W. Ellis Family Papers; *OR*, vol. 16, pt. 2, 733; Bergeron, *Major Grisamore*, 72–73; John Harris to wife, 11 August 1862, John A. Harris Letters, LLMVC; Wesley Winans Journal, Winans Family Collection.

38. *OR*, vol. 16, pt. 2, 733; Wesley Winans Journal, Winans Family Collection.

39. Edwin Miles, "The Mississippi Press in the Jackson Era, 1824–1840," *Journal of Mississippi History* 19 (January 1957): 15–16; Warner, *Generals in Gray*, 3.

40. Warner, *Generals in Gray*, 3.

41. *OR*, vol. 10, pt. 1, 382, 787–88, 811 and pt. 2, 461, 528 and vol. 16, pt. 2, 733.

42. CSR, 25th Louisiana Infantry, M320, Rolls 330–335; Cater Johnson to Wife, March 22, 1862, Hubbard S. Bosley Papers, Mss. 963, Louisiana and Lower Mississippi Valley Collections, LSU Libraries, Baton Rouge, LA; Allardice, *Confederate Colonels*, 146; *OR*, vol. 2, 188; CSR of Stuart W. Fisk.

43. CSR of Francis C. Zacharie.

44. Carter Johnson to Wife, March 22, 1862, Bosley (Hubbard S.) Papers, Special Collections, Hill Memorial Library, LSU; Allardice, *Confederate Colonels*, 238; CSR of Joseph C. Lewis.

45. CSR, 25th Louisiana Infantry, M320, Rolls 330–335; *OR*, vol. 10, pt. 1, 814; Carter Johnston to Wife, 2 May 1862, Hubbard S. Bosley Papers, LLMVC; Kenneth W. Noe, *Perryville: This Grand Havoc of Battle* (Lexington: University Press of Kentucky, 2001), 371.

46. Samuel C. Scott to Dear Madam, 10 July, 1862. Courtesy of Captain Sam's Family; and CSR John F. Gibson.

47. Samuel C. Scott to Dear Madam, 10 July, 1862.

48. Miscellaneous Record Books of the Louisiana Brigade, Record Group 109.

49. *OR*, vol. 10, pt. 2, 396; CSR, 21st Louisiana Infantry, M320, Rolls 316–317; CSR of J.B.G. Kennedy.

50. CSR, 21st Louisiana Infantry, M320, 316–317.

51. Eleventh Louisiana Regimental Rosters, Civil War Rosters, Jackson Barracks Military History Library, New Orleans, Louisiana; Miscellaneous Record Books of the Louisiana Brigade, Record Group 109; CSR, 11th Louisiana Infantry, M320, Rolls 226–233; *OR*, vol. 110, pt. 2, 355, 386; Charles James Johnson to Lou, 27 August 1861, Charles James Johnson Papers, Mss. 1152, Louisiana and Lower Mississippi Valley Collections, LSU Libraries, Baton Rouge, LA.

52. Miscellaneous Record Books of the Louisiana Brigade, Record Group 109; CSR John Edward Austin.

53. 11th Louisiana Regimental File, Civil War Rosters, Jackson Barracks; CSR, 11th Louisiana Infantry, M320, Rolls 226–233. Austin's battalion is usually listed as the 14th Louisiana Battalion of Sharpshooters. This is a title given to the unit after the war; all contemporary accounts call the battalion Austin's. When reference to the 14th Louisiana Battalion is made by numerous secondary sources, they are referring to Austin's battalion.

54. 11th Louisiana Regimental File and 13th Louisiana Regimental File, Civil War Rosters, Jackson Barracks; Edward Baines to Sister, 14 January 1863, Henry Baines Papers, Mss. 1209, Louisiana and Lower Mississippi Valley Collections, LSU Libraries, Baton Rouge, LA.

55. Nathaniel C. Hughes, *The Pride of the Confederate Artillery: The Washington Artillery in the Army of Tennessee* (Baton Rouge: Louisiana State University Press, 1997), 4–5.

56. Ibid., 52–53.

57. Ibid., 9, 52–53.

Chapter 4

1. Kenneth W. Noe, *Perryville: This Grand Havoc of Battle*, 31–31, 36–37; *OR*, vol. 16, pt. 2, 759, 775, 777–78, 782.

2. W.L. Trask Journal, W.L. Trask Papers #380, 1861–1865, Special Collections Department, Robert W. Woodruff Library, Emory University (hereafter cited as Trask Journal); *Supplement to the Official Records of the Union and Confederate Armies* (Wilmington, NC: Broadfoot, 1996), part 1, vol. 24, 459 (hereafter cited as *Supplement*, with all references to part 1, unless otherwise noted).

3. Hafendorfer, *Perryville*, 15–16, 19; *OR*, vol. 16, pt. 2, 787, 789.

4. *OR*, vol. 16, pt. 2, 24, 31.

5. Trask Journal; *Supplement*, vol. 24, 459.

6. Hafendorfer, *Perryville*, 48; Trask Journal.

7. Hafendorfer, *Perryville*, 38, 45, 74

8. Daniel Adams to Wife, 23 September 1862, Louisiana Historical Association, Manuscripts Collection 55, Series 55-C, Louisiana Research Collection, Tulane University Libraries.

9. Hafendorfer, *Perryville*, 81, 97, 111–13, 175.

10. Ibid., 99.

11. Ibid., 178–79; *OR*, vol. 16, pt. 1, 1120–22.

12. Hafendorfer, *Perryville*, 209, 236, 239; Hughes, *The Pride of the Confederate Artillery*, 64–65.

13. *Supplement*, vol. 3, 279; *OR*, vol. 16, pt. 1, 1122, 1131, 1133.

14. *OR*, vol. 16, pt. 1, 1122–23; Hughes, *The Pride of the Confederate Artillery*, 64–65. Edward Scott's capture was confirmed by a letter from General Adams to his wife dated November 1, 1862. In that letter Adams' acknowledges he has received a dispatch from Edward from Jackson, Mississippi. Edward confirmed his and Lieutenant Philip Sayne's parole (Adams letter to wife, Adams' Letters, 11 November 1862, Louisiana Historical Association, Manuscripts Collection 55, Series 55-C, Louisiana Research Collection, Tulane University Libraries).

15. *OR*, vol. 16, pt. 1, 1122–23, 1133; Hughes, *The Pride of the Confederate Artillery*, 64–65.

16. Noe, *This Grand Havoc of a Battle*, 221; *OR*, vol. 16, pt. 1, 1044; James Maynard Shanklin, Kenneth P. McCutchan, ed., *Dearest Lizzie: The Civil War Letters of Lt. Col. James Maynard Shanklin* (Evansville, IN: Friends of Willard Library, 1988).

17. John W. Headly, *Confederate Operations in Canada and New York* (New York and Washington: Neale, 1908), 57; Trask Journal, Trask Papers.

18. Trask Journal, Trask Papers.

19. Ibid., *OR*, vol. 16, pt. 1, 1057–58;

20. *OR*, vol. 16, pt. 1, 1055–58

21. Ibid., 1123; Headly, *Confederate Operations*, 57; Douglas Cater to Fannie, 24 July 1863, Douglas Cater and Rufus W. Cater Papers, Manuscripts Division, Library of Congress, Washington, DC.

22. *OR*, vol. 16, pt. 1, 1058; Headly, *Confederate Operations*, 57. Beatty reports that he retreated after the Bottom Farm caught fire. Headly, fighting with Austin's battalion, wrote that after their brief attack and while they were aligning on Adams' right, in the ensuing time between the next advance, the Bottom Farm caught fire. Therefore this puts Austin's battalion attacking the 3rd Ohio and then the 15th Kentucky because that regiment came up after the barn caught fire.

23. *OR*, vol. 16, pt. 1, 1058; Ellis to Mother, 21 October 1862, E. John and Thomas C.W. Ellis Family Papers; Trask Journal.

24. Kirk C. Jenkins, *The Battle Rages Higher: The Union's 15th Kentucky Infantry* (Lexington: University Press of Kentucky, 2003), 74; *Supplement*, vol. 3, 281.

25. *OR*, vol. 16, pt. 1, 1058.

26. Headly, *Confederate Operations*, 58; *OR*, vol. 16, pt. 1, 1047, 1058, 1123–24; Ellis to Mother, 21 October 1862, E. John and Thomas C.W. Ellis Family Papers.

27. *OR*, vol. 16, pt. 1, 1125–26, 1055–56.

28. Ibid., 1050, 1056–57,

29. Ibid., 1047, 1123; Headly, *Confederate Operations*, 59.

30. *OR*, vol. 16, pt. 1, 1057, 1123, Trask Journal; Headly, *Confederate Operations*, 58–59; Noe, *Perryville: This Grand Havoc of a Battle*, 270–71; Spillard F. Horrall, *History of the Forty-Second Indiana Infantry* (Chicago: Donohue & Henneberry, 1892), 152–53; Miscellaneous Record Books of the Louisiana Brigade, Record Group 109.

31. *OR*, vol. 16, pt. 1, 1123

32. Ibid., 1127; Trask Journal.

33. Ibid.; Daniel W. Adams to Wife, 10 October 1862, Louisiana Historical Association, Manuscripts Collection 55, Series 55-C, Louisiana Research Collection, Tulane University Libraries; *OR*, vol. 16, pt. 1, 1045 and 1123.

34. *OR*, vol. 16, pt. 1, 94, 97 and 1123.

35. Ibid., 1123.

36. Ibid.; Trask Journal.

37. Ibid.

38. Hafendorfer, *Perryville*, 384; Daniel W. Adams to Wife, October 18, 1862, Louisiana Historical Association, Manuscripts Collection 55, Series 55-C, Louisiana Research Collection, Tulane University Libraries; Ellis to Mother, 21 October 1862, E. John and Thomas C.W. Ellis Family Papers; Randall Gibson to W.P. Johnston, 2 November 1862, Albert Sidney and William Preston Johnston Collection, Manuscript Collection 1, Louisiana Research Collection, Tulane University Libraries; Hughes, *The Pride of the Confederate Artillery*, 74; Trask Journal; CSR, 20th Louisiana Infantry, M320, Rolls 308–315.

39. Ellis to Mother, 21 October 21 1862, E. John and Thomas C.W. Ellis Family Papers; Hughes, *The Pride of the Confederate Artillery*, 74; Randal Gibson to W.P. Johnston, 2 November 1862, Johnston Collection.

Chapter 5

1. *OR*, vol. 16, pt. 2, 976; Daniel Adams to Wife, 11 November 1862, Louisiana Historical Association, Manuscripts Collection 55, Series 55-C, Louisiana Research Collection, Tulane University Libraries; Hughes, *The Pride of the Confederate Artillery*, 75–76.

2. *OR*, vol. 20, pt. 2, 412, 447–49, 456.

3. Miscellaneous Record Books of the Louisiana Brigade, Record Group 109; Bergeron, *Guide*, 104, 106, 113–14; *OR*, vol. 16, pt. 2, 577; *OR*, vol. 20, pt. 1, 230–31; Kurt Holman, "Perryville Order of Battle."

4. Bergeron, *Guide*, 105–6; Miscellaneous Record Books of the Louisiana Brigade, Record Group 109; CSR Stephen O'Leary.

5. Miscellaneous Record Books of the Louisiana Brigade, Record Group 109; E.J. Ellis to Father, 29 November 1862, E. John and Thomas C.W. Ellis Family Papers; CSR, William Walker; CSR, Robert H. Lindsay; CSR, Joseph C. Lewis.

6. Thomas McAdory Owen, and Marie Bankhead Owen, *History of Alabama and Dictionary of Alabama Biography* (Boston: Harvard University, 1921), 1125, 1179–80; *OR*, vol. 50, pt. 2, 22.

7. *OR*, vol. 20, pt. 2, 459; *OR*, vol. 16, pt. 2, 761–62; *Supplement*, vol. 3, 244; Stephen Burrell to Wife, 10 April 1862, Katharine (Morgan) McCarrier Collection.

8. *OR*, vol. 16, pt. 1, 888–91; *Supplement*, vol. 3, 245.

9. *OR*, vol. 16, pt. 2, 863; *Supplement*, vol. 3, 257.

10. *OR*, vol. 16, pt. 1, 761–62, 764, 887–91, 908, 938, 1020–21; *Supplement*, vol. 3, 372.

11. *OR*, vol. 16, pt. 1, 981; *OR*, vol. 30, pt. 2, 521; *OR*, vol. 31, pt. 3, 347; *OR*, vol. 6, pt. 336; *OR*, vol. 23, pt. 2, 860, 885;

12. Peter Cozzens, *No Better Place to Die: The Battle of Stones River* (Urbana: University of Illinois Press, 1990), 47; William C. Davis, *John C. Breckinridge* (Baton Rouge: Louisiana State University Press, 1974) 334–35.

13. John McGrath to Wife, 28 January 1863, John McGrath Family Papers, Mss. 3281, Louisiana and Lower Mississippi Valley Collections, LSU Libraries, Baton Rouge, LA.

14. *OR*, vol. 20, pt. 2, 659.

15. Davis, *Breckinridge*, 336–37; Cozzens, *No Better Place to Die*, 159–61.

16. *OR*, vol. 20, pt. 2, 350, 366, 461; Brigadier General Thomas Wood was wounded by the time of the Louisiana Brigade's attack; command of the division fell upon Hascall and Buell assumed command of Hascall's brigade.

17. *OR*, vol. 20, pt. 1, 468–470, 484, 493, 496–98, 544–45, 551–54, 556,

18. *Ibid.*

19. *Ibid.*, 455, 475–477; 522.

20. *Ibid.*, 543–44, 801; Wallace E. Edward Papers, Murfreesboro Battlefield Park Regimental Files, 15th Indiana; J. Morgan Smith to Katie, 17 January 1863, Murfreesboro Battlefield Regimental Files, 32nd Alabama.

21. *OR*, vol. 20, pt. 1, 793, 795, 800, 802–3; Ellis to Father, 12 January 1863, E. John and Thomas C.W. Ellis Family Papers.

22. *OR*, vol. 20, pt. 1, 793, 795, 800–801.

23. *Ibid.*, 712, 717.

24. *Ibid.*, 493, 793, 800.

25. William H. Newlin, D.H. Lawler, and J.W. Sherrick, *A History of the Seventy-Third Illinois Infantry Volunteers* (Springfield, IL: Regimental Reunion Association of the Survivors of the 73rd Illinois Infantry Volunteers, 1890), 132–133; John McGrath to Wife, 13, January 1863, John McGrath Papers, LLMVC; *OR*, vol. 30, pt. 1, 484, 553.

26. *OR*, vol. 20, pt. 1, 366, 793, 800; Morgan Smith to Katie, 17 January 1863, Murfreesboro Regimental Files, 32nd Alabama; S.T. Taylor to Wife, 22 August 1862, Special Collections, Auburn University; John W. Bell Journal, John W. Bell Papers, Mss. 771, Louisiana and Lower Mississippi Valley Collections, LSU Libraries, Baton Rouge, LA.

27. *OR*, vol. 20, pt. 1, 801; Ellis to Mother, 12 January 1863, E. John and Thomas C.W. Ellis Family Papers; Newlin, Lawler, and Sherrick, *A History of the Seventy-Third Illinois Infantry Volunteers*, 132–133.

28. *OR*, vol. 20, pt. 1, 795.

29. *Ibid.*, 484, 496; Asbury L. Kerwood, *Annals of the Fifty-Seventh Regiment Indiana Volunteers: Marches, Battles and Incidents of Army Life* (Dayton, OH: Shuey, 1868), 167; James Jones to Father and Mother, 8 January 1863, Murfreesboro Battlefield Regimental Files, 57th Indiana Infantry.

30. *OR*, vol. 20, pt. 1, 493, 496, 795; Kerwood, *Annals of the Fifty-Seventh Regiment*, 167; James Jones to Father and Mother, 8 January 1863, Murfreesboro Battlefield Regimental Files, 57th Indiana Infantry; John McGrath to Wife, 13 January 1863, John McGrath Family Papers, LLMVC.

31. *OR*, vol. 20, pt. 1, 493, 496, 551, 795–96; Kerwood, *Annals of the Fifty-Seventh Regiment*, 167; James Jones to Father and Mother, 8 January 1863, Murfreesboro Battlefield Regimental Files, 57th Indiana Infantry.

32. *OR*, vol. 20, pt. 1, 793, 802.

33. Daniel W. Adams to Wife, 19 January 1863, Louisiana Historical Association, Manuscripts Collection 55, Series 55-C, Louisiana Research Collection, Tulane University Libraries; *OR*, vol. 20, pt. 1, 794.

34. J. Morgan Smith to Katie, 17 January 1863, Murfreesboro Battlefield Regimental Files; *OR*, vol. 16, pt. 1, 800.

35. *OR*, vol. 16, pt. 1, 477, 793; Daniel W. Adams to Wife, 19 January 1863, Louisiana Historical Association, Manuscripts Collection 55, Series 55-C, Louisiana Research Collection, Tulane University Libraries; E.J. Ellis to Mother, January 12, 1863, E. John and Thomas C.W. Ellis Family Papers.

36. *OR*, vol. 20, pt. 1, 493, 803; James Jones to Father and Mother, 8 January 1863, Murfreesboro Battlefield Regimental Files, 57th Indiana Infantry.

37. *OR*, vol. 20, pt. 1, 484, 496, 674–75, 783, 801–3; Kerwood, *Annals of the Fifty-Seventh Regiment*, 170.

38. *OR*, vol. 20, pt. 1, 545.

39. *Ibid.*, 678, 794; Catherine Merrill, *The Soldier of Indiana in the War for the Union*, Vol. 2 (Merrill, 1889), 162; Daniel W. Adams to Wife, 19 January 1863, Louisiana Historical Association, Manuscripts Collection 55, Series 55-C, Louisiana Research Collection, Tulane University Libraries.

40. *OR*, vol. 20, pt. 1, 678, 794; Confederate Personnel; J. Morgan Smith to Katie, 17 January 1863, Murfreesboro Battlefield Regimental Files, 32nd Alabama; Adams to Wife, 19 January 1863, Louisiana Historical Association, Manuscripts Collection 55, Series 55-C, Louisiana Research Collection, Tulane University Libraries.

41. Ellis to Mother, 12 January 1863, E. John and Thomas C.W. Ellis Family Papers; John McGrath to Wife, 13 January 1863, John McGrath Family Papers, LLMVC.

42. *OR*, vol. 20, pt. 1, 667–78, 783–85.

43. Cozzens, *No Better Place to Die*, 181.

44. Stones River National Battlefield, Troop Movement Maps; *OR*, vol. 20, pt. 1, 796–98, 803.

45. *OR*, vol. 20, pt. 1, 575–77.

46. *Ibid.*, 798; William C. Davis, *The Orphan Brigade: The Kentucky Confederates Who Couldn't Go Home* (Baton Rouge: Louisiana State University Press, 1980), 157.

47. *OR*, vol. 20, pt. 1, 798, 833

48. *Ibid.*, 585–86, 595.

49. *Ibid.*, 798–99.

50. *Ibid.*, 786, 799, 802, 804; CSR Charles Guillet; CSR of Samuel L. Bishop.

51. *OR*, vol. 20, pt. 1, 833

52. *OR*, vol. 20, pt. 1, 312, 429, 518–19, 798–99.

53. *Ibid.*, 803.
54. *Ibid.*, 678, 675, 799, 792.
55. *Ibid.*, 230–31, 233. In the list of captured the Fortieth Louisiana is recorded as a unit and the 11th Louisiana is also listed. The total number of captured from these two units equaled four men. The only reasonable explanation is that these men were either from Austin's battalion or the 13th & 20th Louisiana in which the 11th Regiments' men were disbanded to.
56. *OR*, vol. 20, pt. 1, 788; 32nd Alabama Regimental File, Alabama State Archives, Birmingham, AL.
57. CSR of Roger Tammure.

Chapter 6

1. Thomas Connelly, *Autumn of Glory: The Army of Tennessee, 1862–1865* (Baton Rouge: Louisiana State University Press), 74; *OR*, vol. 20, pt. 1, 699.
2. *OR*, vol. 20 pt. 1, 699, 701.
3. *Ibid.*, 700.
4. *Ibid.*, 682–84.
5. *Ibid.*, 682.
6. *OR*, vol. 23, pt. 2, 613, 624, 632–33.
7. *OR*, vol. 20, pt. 1, 701 and vol. 23, pt. 2, 652.
8. Randall Gibson to James Seddon, 1 March 1863, Matt Collection, Hill Memorial Library, Louisiana State University; Dixon, "Gibson," 43.
9. Dixon, "Gibson," 44; *OR*, vol. 16, pt. 1, 1125; Daniel Adams to James Seddon, 22 January 1863, CSR of Randall L. Gibson.
10. *OR*, vol. 24, pt. 3, 623–24.
11. Adams to James Seddon, 22 January 1863, CSR of Randall L. Gibson; CSR of Leon von Zinken; *OR*, vol. 23, pt. 2, 619, 629, 757, 782.
12. *Ibid.*, 700, 778.
13. *Ibid.*, 619, 629, 757, 826, 847; vol. 24, pt. 3, 952; Miscellaneous Record Book of the Louisiana Brigade, Record Group 109; CSR, Edgar Martin Dubroca.
14. *OR*, vol. 23, pt. 2, 757.
15. *Ibid.*, 780, 813; Edward Baines to Sister, 2 May 1863, Henry Baines Papers, LLMVC; Rufus W. Cater to Fannie, 2 May 1863, Douglas Cater and Rufus W. Cater Papers.
16. J.A. Harris to Wife, 24 December 1862, John A. Harris Letters, LLMVC; Woodins, ed., "Four Years in the Confederate Infantry," 31; Rufus W. Cater to Fannie, 2 May 1863, Douglas Cater and Rufus W. Cater Papers.
17. Rufus Cater to Fannie, 23 May 1863, and Rufus Cater to Fannie, 13 May 1863, Douglas Cater and Rufus W. Cater Papers; Augustus Reichard Family Papers.
18. Rufus Cater to Fannie, 23 May 1863, and Rufus Cater to Fannie, 13 May 1863, Douglas Cater and Rufus W. Cater Papers; Davis, *The Orphan Brigade*, 172.
19. *OR*, vol. 23, pt. 2, 849; 32nd Alabama Record File; Davis, *The Orphan Brigade*, 172.
20. 32nd Alabama Record File; *OR*, vol. 24, pt. 3, 944, 950; Louis Stagg to Wife, 9 June 1863, Stagg Letters; Wooster, ed., "Four Years in the Confederate Infantry," 32.

21. *OR*, vol. 24, pt. 3, 978, 985; Douglas Cater to Fannie, 24 July 1863, Douglas Cater and Rufus W. Cater Papers; John Harris to Becky, 3 July 1863, John A. Harris Letters, LLMVC.
22. Hughes, *The Pride of the Confederate Artillery*, 107; *OR*, vol. 24, pt. 3, 988–89, 992–93.
23. *OR*, vol. 24, pt. 3, 461, 478, 993; Wooster, ed., "Four Years in the Confederate Infantry," 34; Hughes, *The Pride of the Confederate Artillery*, 107.
24. Hughes, *The Pride of the Confederate Artillery*, 107, 111; *OR*, vol. 24, pt. 2, 655–56.
25. Edwin C. Bearss and Warren Grabau, *The Battle of Jackson, May 14, 1863/The Siege of Jackson, July 10–17, 1863* (Baltimore: Gateway Press, 1981), 79–80; *OR*, vol. 24, pt. 2, 575, 603–4.
26. Hughes, *The Pride of the Confederate Artillery*, 112–13; Arthur Bergeron, "Fighting Erupts at Jackson, Mississippi," *Civil War: The Magazine of the Civil War Society* 49 (February 1995), 26–27; Carraway, "Reminiscences of the Civil War 1861–1865"; Douglas Cater to Fannie, 24 July 1863, Douglas Cater and Rufus W. Cater Papers.
27. *OR*, vol. 24, pt. 2, 604–5 655.
28. *Ibid.*, 604, 655, 656; CSR of Robert H. Lindsay; Douglas Cater to Fannie, 24 July 1863, Douglas Cater and Rufus W. Cater Papers.
29. Arthur E. Green, *Southern Boots and Saddles: The Fifteenth Confederate Cavalry C.S.A., First Regiment of Alabama and Florida Cavalry, 1863–1865* (Westminster, MD: Heritage Books, 2005), 5, 15; *OR*, vol. 49, pt. 2, 364; Owen and Owen, *History of Alabama and Dictionary of Alabama Biography*, 1179–80.
30. Sergeant John Hunter, "As I Remember Now," Private Collection.
31. Wooster, ed., "Four Years in the Confederate Infantry," 34; Hughes, *The Pride of the Confederate Artillery*, 119; Miscellaneous Record Books of the Louisiana Brigade Record Group 109; CSR, 13th Louisiana Infantry, M320, Rolls 245–252; CSR, 19th Louisiana Infantry, M320, Rolls 302–307; CSR, 20th Louisiana Infantry, M320, Rolls 308–315.
32. Wooster, ed., "Four Years in the Confederate Infantry," 34; Hughes, *The Pride of the Confederate Artillery*, 119; Miscellaneous Record Books of the Louisiana Brigade Record Group 109.
33. CSR of Daniel W. Adams, NA; *OR*, vol. 24, pt. 3, 1039; CSR of Augustus Reichard.
34. *OR*, vol. 10, pt. 1, 484–87.
35. *OR*, vol. 30, pt. 4, 529, 547.

Chapter 7

1. 32nd Alabama Regimental File; *OR*, vol. 30, pt. 1, 51–52 and pt. 3, 137; Miscellaneous Report Books of the Louisiana Brigade, Record Group 109.
2. *OR*, vol. 30, pt. 4, 600; Peter Cozzens, *This Terrible Sound: The Battle of Chickamauga* (Urbana: University of Illinois Press, 1992), 55.
3. *OR*, vol. 30, pt. 4, 610–11; 13th Louisiana Regimental Rosters, Jackson Barracks.
4. *OR*, vol. 20, pt. 1, 139, 518, 899, 904.
5. *OR*, vol. 30, pt. 1, 54 and pt. 2, 30–31.
6. *OR*, vol. 30, pt. 4, 657 and pt. 2, 139–40.
7. *OR*, vol. 30, pt. 2, 198, 229.

8. *Ibid.*, 198.
9. *Ibid.*, 198, 219–24, 227.
10. *Ibid.*, 227, 368.
11. *OR*, vol. 30, pt. 2, 236.
12. *OR*, vol. 30, pt. 1, 374 and pt. 2, 221, 229; Hughes, *The Pride of the Confederate Artillery*, 134–35.
13. *OR*, vol. 30, pt. 2, 233.
14. *Ibid.*, 199, 225, 229.
15. *OR*, vol. 30, pt. 1, 368–69, 378–79.
16. *Ibid.*, 430, 556 565, 781; *OR*, vol. 30, pt. 2, 231.
17. Charles E. Belknap, *History of the Michigan Organizations at Chickamauga, Chattanooga and Missionary Ridge, 1863* (Lansing, MI: Smith, 1899), 248; *OR*, vol. 30, pt. 2, 221.
18. *OR*, vol. 30, pt. 2, 217; Belknap, *History of the Michigan Organizations*, 248; *OR*, vol. 30, pt. 2, 224; CSR of George Walton.
19. *Ibid.*, 379; *OR*, vol. 30, pt. 2, 221, 225; Jack A. Overmyer, *A Stupendous Effort: The 87th Indiana in the War of the Rebellion* (Bloomington: Indiana University Press, 1997), 100; Carraway, "Reminiscences of the Civil War 1861–1865."
20. Winfrey Scott to Mrs. E.C. Scott, 3 October 1863, Winfrey Letters, courtesy Stephen Osman; Winfrey Scott to Mrs. E.C. Scott, 8 October 1863, Winfrey Letters; and CSR of John Bruton.
21. *OR*, vol. 30, pt. 1, 369, 379.
22. *OR*, vol. 30, pt. 2, 222; *OR*, vol. 30, pt. 1, 379.
23. Belknap, *Michigan*, 248; Cozzens, *This Terrible Sound*, 336.
24. *OR*, vol. 30, pt. 1, 565.
25. Albion W. Tourgee, *The Story of a Thousand: Being a History of the Service of the 105th Ohio Volunteer Infantry, in the War for the Union from August 21, 1862 to June 6, 1865* (Buffalo, NY: McGerald & Son, 1896), 227–228.
26. *OR*, vol. 30, pt. 2, 217, 227–8; Hughes, *The Pride of the Confederate Artillery*, 141.
27. *OR*, vol. 30, pt. 2, 228.
28. *Ibid.*, 222.
29. *Ibid.*, 34, 217, 220, 224, 226, 310; Cozzens, *This Terrible Sound*, 490.
30. *OR*, vol. 30, pt. 1, 288.
31. *Ibid.*, 279, 288.
32. *Ibid.*, 217, 201 and vol. 30, pt. 1, 171.
33. *OR*, vol. 30, pt. 2, 218–19, 223, 227.
34. *Ibid.*; R.L. Lafitte to Brother, 17 November 1863, Leonard Lafitte private collection; *Supplement*, pt. 2, vol. 24, 363.
35. Cozzens, *This Terrible Sound*, 336; *OR*, ser. 2, vol. 6, 326–27; Daniel W. Adams to Wife, 27 September 1863, Louisiana Historical Association, Manuscripts Collection 55, Series 55-C, Louisiana Research Collection, Tulane University Libraries; Warner, *Generals in Gray*, 1.
36. Richard DiNardo and James Furqueron, "The Day After: Braxton Bragg and the Aftermath of Chickamauga," *North & South* 1 (February 1998): 38.

Chapter 8

1. *OR*, vol. 30, pt. 2, 65–67. Of the twelve officers who signed the petition to Davis, two were lieutenant generals, two were major generals, seven were brigadier generals and one a colonel.
2. Gibson to John C. Breckinridge, 12 October 1863, CSR of Randall Gibson.
3. *OR*, vol. 31, pt. 3, 685; Hughes, *The Pride of the Confederate Artillery*, 150; Ellis to Sister, 16 November 1863, E. John and Thomas C.W. Ellis Family Papers.
4. *OR*, vol. 14, 931 and vol. 24, pt. 3, 1041 and vol. 31, pt. 3, 686.
5. John Howard Brown, ed., *The Twentieth Century Biographical Dictionary of Notable Americans* (Boston: Biographical Society, 1904).
6. Bergeron, *Guide*, 157–58.
7. *OR*, vol. 14, pt. 2, 487, 931, and vol. 24, pt. 3, 104.
8. Bergeron, *Guide*, 158; *OR*, vol. 30, pt. 2, 250.
9. Terry G. Scriber and Theresea Arnold-Scriber, *The Fourth Louisiana Battalion in the Civil War: A History and Roster* (Jefferson, NC: McFarland, 2008), 113; H.J. Lea, "With the Fourth Louisiana Battalion," *Confederate Veteran*, 27 (1919), p. 339; *Supplement*, pt. 2, vol. 6, 131.
10. Gibson to Cooper, 21 November 1863, Randall Lee Gibson Papers, Mss. 2422, Louisiana and Lower Mississippi Valley Collections, LSU Libraries, Baton Rouge, LA.
11. E.J. Ellis to Brother, 4 October 1863, and E.J. Ellis to Father, 2 November 1863, E. John and Thomas C.W. Ellis Family Papers; Louis Stagg to Wife, 27 October 1863, Stagg Letters; Lea, "With the Fourth Louisiana Battalion," 339.
12. Robert G. Athearn, ed., *Soldier in the West: The Civil War Letters of Alfred Lacey Hough* (Philadelphia: University of Pennsylvania Press, 1957), 129; John McGrath to Wife, 19 October 1863, John McGrath Family Papers, LLMVC; *OR*, vol. 31, pt. 3, p. 87.
13. *OR*, vol. 31, pt. 4, 722 and vol. 30, pt. 2, 219; Gibson to Cooper, November 21, 1863, Matt Collection; *Supplement*, vol. 6, 118.
14. Cozzens, *The Shipwreck of Their Hopes: The Battles of Chattanooga* (Urbana: University of Illinois Press, 1994), 15.
15. *Ibid.*, 142; *OR*, vol. 31, pt. 2, 676.
16. *Supplement*, vol. 6, 105–6, 123.
17. *Ibid.*, 105–6, 112, 123; *OR*, vol. 31, pt. 2, 743; Cozzens, *Shipwreck of Their Hopes*, 253.
18. *Supplement*, vol. 6, 120, 124–25, 129, 133, 110. It is not known what section of artillery this battery came from.
19. *OR*, vol. 31, pt. 2, 739–41.
20. *Supplement*, vol. 6, 136, 185.
21. *OR*, vol. 31, pt. 2, 14, 188; *Supplement*, vol. 6, 114.
22. *OR*, vol. 31, pt. 2, 195, 199, 244.
23. *Supplement*, vol. 6, 120, 124; W.M. Ives, "History of the Fourth Florida Regiment," *Confederate Veteran* 4 (1895), 102.
24. *Supplement*, vol. 6, 124; *OR*, vol. 31, pt. 1, 246.
25. *OR*, vol. 31, pt. 2, 229–30; *Supplement*, vol. 6, 105, 114–15.
26. *OR*, vol. 31, pt. 2, 202,
27. *Supplement*, vol. 6, 133; *OR*, vol. 31, pt. 2, 132; Glenn Longacre and John E. Haas, eds., *To Battle for God and the Right: The Civil War Letterbooks of*

Emerson Opdycke (Champaign: University of Illinois Press, 2003), 135.

28. *OR*, vol. 31, pt. 2, 132–3, 190, 208; John K. Shellenberger, "With Sheridan's Division at Missionary Ridge," *Sketches of War History, 1861–1865*, 4 (1896), 64; Longacre and Haas, *To Battle for God and the Right*, 135; James Marshall to Wife, December 7, 1863, James Marshall Christian Letters, Mss. 2432, Louisiana and Lower Mississippi Valley Collections, LSU Libraries, Baton Rouge, LA.

29. *Supplement*, vol. 6, 124–5.

30. *History of the Seventy-Fourth Illinois Infantry* (Adjutant General's Report); *OR*, vol. 31, pt. 2, 203.

31. *Supplement*, vol. 6, 114–6, 125–6.

32. *OR*, vol. 31, pt. 2, 480–1, 483–5, *Supplement*, vol. 6, 109, 124, 182–3.

33. *OR*, vol. 31, pt. 2, 195; *Supplement*, vol. 6, 125–6; James Christian to Wife, December 7, 1863, James Marshall Christian Letters, LLMVC.

34. E.J. Ellis to Mother, February 26, 1864, E.P. Ellis and Family Papers.

35. *OR*, vol. 31, pt. 1, 741; *Supplement*, vol. 6, 115.

36. *Ibid.*, 116–7; *OR*, vol. 31, pt. 2, 207; John Shellenberger, "With Sheridan's Division at Missionary Ridge," *Sketches of War History*, 64.

37. *Supplement*, vol. 6, 129–30, *OR*, vol. 31, pt. 2, 195.

38. *Supplement*, vol. 6, 131; Diary of Zachariah Smith, 20 November 1863, Louisiana Historical Association, Civil War Papers, 55-B, Tulane University Libraries.

39. *OR*, vol. 31, pt. 2, 742; Phil Sheridan, *Personal Memoirs of P.H. Sheridan, General United States Army* (New York: Webster, 1888), 312.

40. *Supplement*, pt. 2, vol. 6, 117, 127, 134; Hughes, *The Pride of the Confederate Artillery*, 150.

41. *OR*, vol. 31, pt. 2, 664; *Supplement*, vol. 6, 117, 121, 127, 130, 134; Hughes, *The Pride of the Confederate Artillery*, 167.

42. *Supplement*, vol. 6, 127; *OR*, vol. 31, pt. 2, 743.

43. *OR*, vol. 31, pt. 2, 191, 244.

44. *Supplement*, vol. 6, 127–8; *OR*, vol. 31, pt. 2, 212, 218, 234.

45. *Supplement*, pt. 2, vol. 6, 117–18.

46. *Ibid.*, 118.

47. *Ibid.*, 118, 122, 130–1, 134; CSR of Thomas Willbanks.

48. *Ibid.*, 110, 118–19.

49. *Ibid.*, 118–19; William P. Johnston to Randall Gibson, 14 September 1863, Randall Lee Gibson Papers, LLMVC; CSR of Randall L. Gibson.

Chapter 9

1. CSR of Randall Gibson; Dixon, "Gibson," 52.

2. *OR*, vol. 31, pt. 3, 775, 826, 858; *Mobile Advertiser*, February 23, 1864; *Daily Constitutional*, March 4, 1864; CSR of J.B. Lallande; CSR of Robert H. Lindsay.

3. Record Group 109; Wooster, ed., "Four Years in the Confederate Infantry," 35; John Harris to Friends, 25 April 1864, John A. Harris Letters, LLMVC; Douglas Cater to Fannie, 21 December 1863 and 19 January 1864, Douglas Cater and Rufus W. Cater Papers; John McGrath to Wife, 11 April 1864, John McGrath Family Papers, LLMVC.

4. *Charleston Mercury*, Charleston, South Carolina, 31 March 1864.

5. Oscar Penn Fitzgerald, *John B. Mcferrin: A Biography* (Nashville: Publishing House of the M.E. Church, South, 1888), 347; John McGrath to Wife, 27 June 1864, John McGrath Family Papers, LLMVC.

6. CSR, 1st (Strawbridge's) Infantry, M320, Rolls 82–89; Carraway, "Reminiscences of the Civil War, 1861–1865."

7. CSR, 1st (Strawbridge's) Infantry, M320, Rolls 82–89; 1st Louisiana Infantry Regulars File, Jackson Barracks; *OR*, vol. 32, pt. 2, 586 and pt. 3, 768; Dixon, "Gibson," 54; *OR*, vol. 32, pt. 3, 870.

8. *OR*, vol. 20, pt. 1, 658.

9. CSR, M320, for the following regiments: 13th Louisiana Infantry, Rolls 245–252; 16th Louisiana Infantry, Rolls 273–280; 19th Louisiana Infantry, Rolls 302–307; 20th Louisiana Infantry, Rolls 308–315; 25th Louisiana Regiment, Rolls 330–335; Austin's Battalion, Rolls 264–265.

10. Miscellaneous Report Books of the Louisiana Brigade, Record Group 109; *OR*, vol. 30, pt. 2, 218–19, 223, 227; CSR, M320, for the following regiments: 13th Louisiana Infantry, Rolls 245–252; 16th Louisiana Infantry, Rolls 273–280; 19th Louisiana Infantry, Rolls 302–307; 20th Louisiana Infantry, 308–315; 25th Louisiana Regiment, Rolls 330–335; Austin's Battalion, Rolls 264–265.

11. CSR of James C. Murphy; CSR of Daniel Gober; Gober Family Genealogical work by Peggy T.; CSR of Joseph C. Lewis.

12. Miscellaneous Report Books of the Louisiana Brigade, Record Group 109; John McGrath to Wife, 27 June 1862, John McGrath Papers, LLMVC; *OR*, vol. 38, pt. 3, 859, 868.

13. Allardice, *Confederate Colonels*, 88; CSR of Francis Campbell.

14. CSR of Edgar Martin Dubroca; CSR of M.O. Tracy.

15. CSR of Hyder A. Kennedy; Eighth Census of the United States, 1860 Population Schedules, National Archives, M653; "History of Kennedy Family," Givens-Hopkins Papers, Louisiana Room, University of Louisiana at Lafayette; *OR*, vol. 38, pt. 3, 865–66.

16. Howard Madaus and Robert Needham, *The Battle Flags of the Confederate Army of Tennessee* (Milwaukee: Milwaukee Public Museum, 1976), 23, 30, 37, 49, 63.

17. National Archives, RG 109, Ch. 2, Vol. 158 1/2, Page 205.

18. National Archives, RG 109, Ch. 2, Vol. 221, Page 10; Bergeron, ed., *Major Grisamore*, 31; Napier Bartlett, *Military Record of Louisiana* (Baton Rouge: Louisiana State University Press, 1964) 17; Inge, "Corinth, Miss., in War Times," 412.

19. *Ibid.*, 49–52.

20. National Archives, Confederate Papers Relating to Citizens or Business Firms, 1861–1865, M346, Roll 332.

21. Noe, *Perryville: This Grand Havoc of Battle*, 270; *OR*, vol. 30, pt. 1, 477.

22. *OR*, vol. 31, pt. 2, 190, 661 and pt. 3, 615–19 and vol. 30, pt. 2, 657–60.
23. Madaus and Needham, *The Battle Flags of the Confederate Army of Tennessee*, 71–72, 84–85; Natchez Rifles, Co. E, 4th Louisiana Battalion, Mississippi Department of Archives & History; and *Charleston Mercury*, 4 January, 1865.
24. *OR*, vol. 32, pt. 1, 478, 480.
25. *OR*, vol. 38, pt. 3, 855, 859, 861, 866.
26. *Ibid.*, 816, 854, 860.
27. *Ibid.*, 686, 862.
28. *Ibid.*, 818, 855, 867; Carraway, "Reminiscences of the Civil War 1861–1865."
29. *OR*, vol. 38, pt. 3, 646, 844 and vol. 38, pt. 2, 180.
30. *OR*, vol. 38, pt. 3, 863; Carraway, "Reminiscences of the Civil War 1861–1865."
31. *Ibid.*, 123, 166, 170–71, 180, 195–96; *OR*, vol. 38, pt. 3, 843–44, 863; Carraway, "Reminiscences of the Civil War 1861–1865."
32. *OR*, vol. 38, pt. 3, 843, 862–63; Carraway, "Reminiscences of the Civil War 1861–1865."
33. *OR*, vol. 38, pt. 2, 30, 196; *OR*, vol. 38, pt. 3, 844, 855, 863–64;
34. *Ibid.*, 863–64, 867; OR, vol. 38, pt. 2, 167, 180, 191.
35. *OR*, vol. 38, pt. 3, 818, 855, 860, 864, 867–68.
36. *Ibid.*, 686, 862–63.
37. *Ibid.*, 838.
38. *Ibid.*, 833, 846; Emmett Ross Diary, 1864, Emmett Ross Papers, Special Collections Department, Mitchell Memorial Library, Mississippi State University.
39. Emmett Ross Diary, Emmett Ross Papers.
40. Emmett Ross Diary, Emmett Ross Papers.
41. Carraway, "Reminiscences of the Civil War 1861–1865,"; Kendall, *Recollections*, 1164, 1189.
42. *OR*, vol. 38, pt. 3, 67; 617; McBride and McLaurin, *Randall Lee Gibson,*107.
43. Emmett Ross Diary, Emmett Ross Papers; Samuel Hunter to Wife, 24 July 1864, Hunter-Taylor Family Papers, Mss. 3024, Louisiana and Lower Mississippi Valley Collections, LSU Libraries, Baton Rouge, LA.
44. Bergeron, *Guide*, 79, 169; *OR*, vol. 32, pt. 3, 861 and vol. 38, pt. 4, 757; Patrick, *Reluctant Rebel*, 197; John S. Kendall, "The Diary of Surgeon Craig, Fourth Louisiana Regiment, 1864–1865," *Louisiana Historical Quarterly* 8 (January 1925): 55; John S. Kendall, "Recollections," 1045; Bergeron, *Guide*, 80.
45. Allardice, *Confederate Colonels*, 72.
46. Bergeron, *Guide*, 169, 181; Miscellaneous Record Books on the Louisiana Brigade, Record Group 109.

Chapter 10

1. *OR*, vol. 32, pt. 2, 699 and vol. 38, pt. 4, 787 and pt. 5, 885; Taylor, *Secret Diary*,197; Douglas John Cater, *As It Was,* 186; Carraway, "Reminiscences of the Civil War 1861–1865"; Emmett Ross Diary, Emmett Ross Papers.
2. Ronald Bailey, *The Civil War: Battles for Atlanta* (Alexandria, VA: Time-Life Books, 1985), 91–92, 96–97; Samuel Hunter to Wife, 24 July 1864, Hunter-Taylor Family Papers, LLMVC.
3. *OR*, vol. 38, pt. 3, 819–20.
4. *Ibid.*, 147, 156–57, 179–80.
5. *Ibid.*, 819–20; *Supplement*, vol. 7, 118–19, 125–27; Samuel Hunter to Wife, 24 July 1864, Hunter-Taylor Family Papers, LLMVC; Emmett Ross Diary, Emmett Ross Papers.
6. *OR*, vol. 38, pt. 3, 762.
7. *Ibid.*, 762, 856; Wooster, ed., "Four Years in the Confederate Infantry," 36–37. The 4th Louisiana Regiment is thought to have been deployed either on the right or the left of the 16th & 25th Regiment. The 1st Regulars' location is unknown.
8. *OR*, vol. 38, pt. 3, 821, 856–57.
9. *Ibid.*, 167, 343–44, 359; 856–57.
10. *Ibid.*, 167, 333–34, 359, 856.
11. *OR*, vol. 38, pt. 2, 343, 856.
12. William H. Knauss, *The Story of Camp Chase: A History of Confederate Prisons and Cemeteries* (Nashville and Dallas: Publishing House of the Methodist Episcopal Church, South, 1906) 91–92; *OR*, vol. 38, pt. 3, 344.
13. *OR*, vol. 38, pt. 2, 167, 856 and pt. 3, 856; Wooster, ed., "Four Years in the Confederate Infantry," 37.
14. *OR*, vol. 38, pt. 2, 167 and pt. 3, 338; Wooster, ed., "Four Years in the Confederate Infantry," 37; John H. Bass Diary, Mss. 3363, Louisiana and Lower Mississippi Valley Collections, LSU Libraries, Baton Rouge, LA; Kendall, "Recollections," 1177; Miscellaneous Report Books of the Louisiana Brigade, Record Group 109; AGO Vault, book #76, pg. 1, Jackson Barracks, 20th Louisiana; S.A. Hightower to Hyder Kennedy, August 15, 1864, Lewis Leigh Collection, U.S. Military History Institute, Carlisle Barracks.
15. Stacy Dale Allen, ed., *On the Skirmish Line Behind a Friendly Tree: The Civil War Memoirs of William Royal Oake, 26th Iowa Volunteers* (Helena, MT: Farcountry Press, 2006), 239; *OR*, vol. 38, pt. 3, 170.
16. Bergeron, *Guide*, 169.
17. *OR*, vol. 38, pt. 5, 1019; *OR*, vol. 49, pt. 2, 1193; Allardice, *Confederate Colonels*, 412.
18. *OR*, vol. 38, pt. 5, 937; W.H. Duff, *Six Months of Prison Life at Camp Chase, Ohio* (Clearwater, SC: Eastern Digital Resources, 2003), 18.
19. *OR*, vol. 38, pt. 1, 524
20. Duff, *Six Months*, 19–20.
21. *OR*, vol. 38, pt. 1, 745–46, 791; John H. Bass Diary, LLMVC.
22. Duff, *Six Months*, 19–20; Samuel Hunter to Wife, 18 August 1864, Hunter-Taylor Family Papers, LLMVC; CSR 13th Louisiana, M320, Rolls 245–252; CSR, 20th Louisiana Regiment, M320, Rolls 308–315.
23. Douglas Cater to Fannie, 4 August 1864, Douglas Cater and Rufus W. Cater Papers; Kendall, "Recollections," 1045, 1193; *OR*, vol. 38, pt. 3, 345, 687 and pt. 5, 494; Cater, *As It Was*, 188.
24. Samuel Hunter to Wife, 18 August 1864, Hunter-Taylor Family Papers, LLMVC.
25. *OR*, vol. 38, pt. 1, 747.
26. *OR*, vol. 38, pt. 5, 925.
27. Bailey, *Battles for Atlanta*, 140–43.
28. *OR*, vol. 38, pt. 3, 773, 821, 857; Randall L.

Gibson to Henry Clayton, July 25, 1879, Henry D. Clayton Collection, W.S. Hoole Special Collections Library, University of Alabama.

29. *OR*, vol. 38, pt. 3, 88, 149, 183, 199–200, 570, 773, 821, 857.

30. *Ibid.*, 149, 183, 199–200, 570.

31. *Ibid.*, 149, 183, 199–200, 265, 570, 821, 857.

32. *Ibid.*, 773–74, 835, 857; Committee of the 55th Illinois, *The Story of the 55th Regiment IL Volunteer Infantry in The Civil War, 1861–1865* (Clinton, MA: Coulter, 1887), 367.

33. *OR*, vol. 38, pt. 3, 764, 773; Gibson to Henry Clayton, November 30, 1877, Henry D. Clayton Collection.

34. *OR*, vol. 38, pt. 3, 822; Gibson to Henry Clayton, December 20, 1877, Henry D. Clayton Collection.

35. *OR*, vol. 38, pt. 2, 200, 218, 857–58; Gibson to Henry Clayton, December 20, 1877, Henry D. Clayton Collection; CSR of Robert Oliver; Committee of the 55th Illinois, *The Story of the 55th Regiment IL Volunteer Infantry*, 367.

36. *OR*, vol. 38, pt. 3, 199–200, 203, 774, 822, 857–58.

37. *OR*, vol. 38, pt. 3, 774; Randall Gibson to Henry Clayton, December 18, 1877, Henry D. Clayton Collection.

38. Kendall, "Recollections," 1200; Miscellaneous Record Books of the Louisiana Brigade, Record Group 109; Randall L. Gibson to Henry Clayton, July 25, 1879, Henry D. Clayton Collection; John H. Bass Diary, LLMVC; Samuel Hunter Report of on Losses at Jonesboro, 31 August 1864, Hunter-Taylor Family Papers, LLMVC.

39. *OR*, vol. 38, pt. 3, 768 and pt. 5, 104, 1016; Kendall, "The Diary of Surgeon Craig," 58.

Chapter 11

1. Miscellaneous Record Books of the Louisiana Brigade, Record Group 109; Samuel Hunter to Wife, 5 September 1864, Hunter-Taylor Family Papers, LLMVC; Samuel Hunter to Wife, September 25, 1864, Hunter-Taylor Papers.

2. CSR of John E. Austin; *OR*, vol. 39, pt. 2, 854.

3. CSR of Frank C. Zachary (labeled incorrectly as Francis M. Zachary).

4. J.B. Hood, *Advance and Retreat: Personal Experience in the United States and Confederate States Armies* (Philadelphia: Press of Burk A.M. Petridge, 1880), 253.

5. John H. Bass Diary, LLMVC; *OR*, vol. 39, pt. 2, 810.

6. John H. Bass Diary, LLMVC; *OR*, vol. 39, pt. 2, 811–12.

7. Miscellaneous Record Books of the Louisiana Brigade, Record Group 109; John H. Bass Diary, LLMVC; Kendall, "Recollections," 1208–09; Hunter to Wife, October 9, 1864, Hunter-Taylor Papers.

8. *OR*, vol. 9, pt. 2, 810; Cater, *As It Was*, 187; *OR*, vol. 38, pt. 3, 764.

9. Hood, *Advance and Retreat*, 263.

10. *OR*, vol. 38, pt. 3, 765 and vol. 39, pt. 1, 806, 808, 810–11; Kendall, "The Diary of Surgeon Craig," 60; Alfred Roman, *The Military Operations of General Beauregard in the War Between the States: 1861 to 1865* (New York: Harpers & Brothers, 1884), 286–87; John H. Bass Diary, LLMVC; Douglas Cater to Fannie, 22 October 1864, Douglas and Rufus W. Cater Papers.

11. *OR*, vol. 39, pt. 1, 580–84.

12. *Ibid.*, 811; R.H. Lindsay, "Capture of Florence, Ala., Under Hood," *Confederate Veteran* 5 (1897): 423; John A. Dicks, "More About the Capture of Florence, Ala.," *Confederate Veteran* 5 (1897): 214.

13. *OR*, vol. 39, pt. 1, 572; Lindsay, "Capture of Florence, Ala., Under Hood," 423; Dicks, "More About the Capture of Florence, Ala.," 214.

14. Lindsay, "Capture of Florence, Ala., Under Hood," 423; Dicks, "More About the Capture of Florence, Ala.," 214; John H. Bass Diary, LLMVC; *OR*, vol. 39, pt. 1, 811.

15. *OR*, vol. 45, pt. 1, 665, 702–4, 897; Miscellaneous Record Books of the Louisiana Brigade, Record Group 109.

16. Kendall, "The Diary of Surgeon Craig," 61; *OR*, vol. 45, pt. 1, 652.

17. *OR*, vol. 45, pt. 1, 697; R.H. Lindsay, "Seeing the Battle of Franklin," *Confederate Veteran* 9 (1901): 221.

18. Kendall, "Recollections," 1206–08; Samuel Hunter to Wife, November 18, 1864, Hunter-Taylor Family Papers, LLMVC; Douglas Cater to Fannie, 15 December 1864, Douglas Cater and Rufus W. Cater Papers.

19. *OR*, vol. 45, pt. 1, 698, 702; Miscellaneous Record Books on the Louisiana Brigade, Record Group 109.

20. *OR*, vol. 45, pt. 1, 290, 307, 698.

21. *Ibid.*, 235, 703.

22. *Ibid.*, 235, 243–44, 247, 261, 695; R.H. Lindsay, "The Retreat from Nashville," *Confederate Veteran* 7 (1899), 311.

23. Wiley Sword, *The Confederacy's Last Hurrah: Spring Hill, Franklin & Nashville* (New York: HarperCollins, 1992), 355; *OR*, vol. 45, pt. 1, 39–40, 132–33, 235, 243–44, 290, 305, 333, 703; L.G. Bennet and Wm. H. Haigh, *History of the Thirty Six Illinois* (Aurora, IL: Knickerbocker & Hodder, 1876), 690.

24. *OR*, vol. 45, pt. 1, 703.

25. Charles T. Clark, *Opdycke Tigers, 125th O.V.I.: A History of the Regiment and of the Campaigns and Battles of the Army of the Cumberland* (Columbus, OH: Spahr & Glenn, 1895), 367; Douglas Cater to Fannie, 15 December 1864, Douglas Cater and Rufus W. Cater Papers.

26. *OR*, vol. 45, pt. 1, 702; "Letter from General R.L. Gibson," *Southern Historical Society Papers* 5 (1878): 133.

27. *OR*, vol. 45, pt. 1, 565, 607, 689–90, 699–700, 703; Miscellaneous Record Books on the Louisiana Brigade, Record Group 109; Kendall, "Recollections," 1211–12.

28. *OR*, vol. 45, pt. 1, 703, 706.

29. *Ibid.*, 607, 689, 703, 766.

30. *Ibid.*, 699; R.R. Hancock, *Hancock's Diary: A History of the Second Tennessee Cavalry with Sketches of First and Seventh Battalions; Also Portraits and Biographical Sketches* (Nashville, TN: Brandon, 1887) 534.

31. *OR*, vol. 45, pt. 1, 696, 703 and vol. 45, pt. 2, 237.
32. Kendal, "The Diary of Surgeon Craig," 62; Douglas Cater to Fannie, 12 January 1865, Douglas Cater and Rufus W. Cater Papers; *Supplement*, vol. 23, 783.
33. Kendall, "Recollections," 1207; Douglas Cater to Fannie, 12 January 1865, Douglas Cater and Rufus W. Cater Papers.
34. Miscellaneous Report Books of the Louisiana Brigade, Record Group 109; *OR*, vol. 45, pt. 2, 795–96; Douglas Cater to Fannie, 3 February 1865, Douglas Cater and Rufus W. Cater Papers.

Chapter 12

1. *OR*, vol. 45, pt. 2, 794 and vol. 49, pt. 1, 1045; Kendall, "The Diary of Surgeon Craig," 63–64; Douglas Cater to Fannie, February 3, 1865, Cater Papers, LOC; *Supplement*, vol. 24, 456.
2. Miscellaneous Report Books of the Louisiana Brigade, Record Group 109.
3. CSR of Michael O. Tracy; CSR of Francis L. Campbell; CSR of Leon von Zinken.
4. *OR*, vol. 49, pt. 1, 91–93. *OR*, vol. 49, pt. 1, 91–92, 314; *Supplement*, vol. 7, 950.
5. *Supplement*, vol. 7, 90–91; *OR*, vol. 49, pt. 1, 314–15.
6. Hughes, *The Pride of the Confederate Artillery*, 266; *OR*, vol. 49, pt. 1, 91–92, 314; *Supplement*, vol. 7, 950–51.
7. *Ibid.*, 1046; *Supplement*, vol. 7, 951.
8. *OR*, vol. 49, pt. 1, 142, 314–15 and vol. 49, pt. 2, 1163–65.
9. *OR*, vol. 49, pt. 1, 94–95.
10. *Ibid.*, 156, 161, 166, 315.
11. Cater, *As It Was*, 208–09; *OR*, vol. 49, pt. 1, 226.
12. *Ibid.*, 95–96, 153, 316.
13. *OR*, vol. 49, pt. 2, 1194, 1200, 1211, 1214–16.
14. *Ibid.*, 1201, 1204–05, 1211; "A Short Record of the Part Taken by Austin Williams Smith of Natchez, Mississippi in the War Between the States from 1861 to 1865," Routh-Williams-Smith Family Papers, Mississippi State Archives.
15. *OR*, vol. 49, pt. 1, 317.
16. *OR*, vol. 49, pt. 1, 316–17; Cater, *As It Was*, 209; Vincent Cortright, "Last-Ditch Defenders at Mobile," *America's Civil War* 9 (January 1997): 63; *Supplement*, vol. 7, 951.
17. *Supplement*, vol. 7, 952–53.
18. Miscellaneous Report Books of the Louisiana Brigade, Record Group 109; *OR*, vol. 49, pt. 2, 1240, 1250; Cater, *As It Was*, 211.
19. Miscellaneous Report Books of the Louisiana Brigade, Record Group 109.
20. Natchez Rifles, Co. E, 4th Louisiana Battalion, Mississippi Department of Archives & History.
21. Miscellaneous Report Books of the Louisiana Brigade, Record Group 109.
22. *OR*, vol. 49, pt. 2, 448, 599, 1283–85.
23. Napier Bartlett, *Military Record of Louisiana*, 24; CSR, 13th Louisiana Infantry, M320, Rolls 245–252; CSR, 20th Louisiana Infantry, M320, Rolls 308–315; CRS, 1st (Strawbridge's) Infantry, M320, Rolls 82–89; Cater, *As It Was*, 211.
24. W.H. Duff, *Six Months*, 48–51; CSR, Samuel Gustine; "Samuel Gustine," *Confederate Veteran* 1 (1916), 467.
25. Flags Archives, Confederate Memorial Hall, New Orleans. The flag that Estell saved was presented to the regiment in 1862 by the niece of Colonel Stuart W. Fisk. The flag had a white field, blue St. Andrew's Cross, and gold fringe and gold lettering that said: "Trust and Go Forward"; Natchez Rifles, Co. E, 4th Louisiana Battalion, Mississippi Department of Archives & History; Retail Clerks International Association, Retail Clerks International Union, *Retail Clerks Advocate* 8 (1953), 23.
26. Dabney Herndon Maury, *Recollections of a Virginian in the Mexican, Indian, and Civil Wars* (New York: Scribner's, 1894), 231; Cater, *As It Was*, 211; *OR*, vol. 49, pt. 1, 319.
27. Douglas Cater to Lawerance, 16 May 1865, Douglas Cater and Rufus W. Cater Papers.
28. Warner, *Generals in Gray*, 104; Charles Roland, *Albert Sidney Johnston: Soldier of Three Republics* (Austin: University of Texas Press, 1964), 262; Memorial Addresses on the Life and Character of Randall Lee Gibson, A Senator from Louisiana (Washington: Government Printing Office, 1894), 2.
29. Randall Gibson to W.P. Johnston, 1 February 1876, Albert Sidney and William Preston Johnston Collection; *New Orleans Picayune*, 7 April 1887.
30. "Reunion of Company C," *Confederate Veteran* 8 (1900), 405.

Bibliography

Manuscripts

Alabama Department of Archives and History, Montgomery, AL
    32d Alabama Regimental File

University of Alabama, W.S. Hoole Special Collections Library, Tuscaloosa, AL
    Henry D. Clayton Collection

Arkansas History Commission, Little Rock, AR
    Asa Stokely Morgan Letters

Camp Moore Museum, Tangipahoe, LA
    Wimberly Letters
    Abraham Nesom Letters
    Kennedy Letters

Captain Samuel Scott's Family
    Samuel Scott Letter

Jackson Barracks Military History Library, New Orleans, LA
    Civil War Rosters

Emory University, Special Collections, Robert W. Woodruff Library, Atlanta, GA
    W.L. Trask Papers

Library of Congress, Washington, DC
    Douglas Cater and Rufus W. Cater Papers

Louisiana State University Libraries, Hill Memorial Special Collections, Baton Rouge, LA
    E.J. Ellis Collection
    John A. Harris Collection
    Matt Collection
    Charles J. Johnson Papers
    Bosley (Hubbard S.) Papers
    Henry Baines Papers
    James Marshall Christian Letters
    Hunter-Taylor Papers
    John H. Bass Diary

Mississippi Department of Archives and History, Jackson
    "Trust And Go Forward"; Natchez Rifles, Co. E, 4th Louisiana Battalion, Mississippi Department of Archives & History

Mississippi State University, Special Collections, Mitchell Memorial Library
    Emmett Ross Papers

Missouri Historical Society
    Bixby Collection of Bragg Papers

Murfreesboro Battlefield Park Regimental Files
    15th Indiana, Wallace E. Edward Papers
    32nd Alabama, J. Morgan Smith Letters
    57th Indiana, James Jones Letter

National Archives and Record Service, Washington, DC
    Compiled Service Records of Generals and Staff Officers. Record Group 109.
    Compiled Service Records of Confederate Soldiers Who Served in the Organizations from the State of Louisiana. Record Group 109.

Stephen Osman
    Winfrey Scott Letters

Tulane University, Special Collections, Howard Tilton Library, New Orleans, LA
    Albert Sidney and William Preston Johnston Papers, Louisiana Historical Society
    Daniel W. Adams, Confederate Personnel, 1861–1865, Louisiana Historical Society
    University of Notre Dame Rare Books and Special Collections
    Caley Family Correspondence

U.S. Military History Institute, Carlisle Barracks
    Lewis Leigh Collection

Miscellaneous Record Books of the Louisiana Brigade Commanded by Brigadier Generals
    Daniel W. Adams and Randall L. Gibson, 1862–1865. Record Group 109. National Archives and Record Service, Washington, DC

University of Louisiana at Lafayette, Louisiana Room, Dupre Library, Lafayette, LA
    Louis Stagg Letters
    Givens-Hopkins Papers

University of North Carolina, Southern Historical Collection, Wilson Library, Chapel Hill, NC
    Frank L. Richardson Papers

Thomas Benjamin Davidson Papers
Donelson Caffery Jenkins' Diary
Pearce Museum at Navarro College
Thomas Chinn Robertson Collection
Wesley Winans Journal, Winans Family Collection
Stephen Burell Letters, Katharine (Morgan) McCarrier Collection

Newspapers

Bayou Sara (Louisiana) *Ledger*
Charleston (South Carolina) *Mercury*
Daily Constitutionalist (Augusta, Georgia)
The Daily Delta (Mobile, Alabama)
Daily Evansville (Indiana) *Journal*
Mobile (Alabama) *Advertiser*
Richmond (Virginia) *Daily Dispatch*

Government Documents

The War of the Rebellion: A Compilation of the Official Records of the Union and Confederate Armies, 128 vols. Washington: GPO, 1880–1901.
Atlas to Accompany the Official Records of the Union and Confederate Armies. Washington: GPO, 1891–1895.
Memorial Addresses on the Life and Character of Randall Lee Gibson, a Senator from Louisiana. Washington: GPO, 1894.

Printed Primary Sources

Belknap, Charles E. *History of the Michigan Organizations at Chickamauga, Chattanooga and Missionary Ridge, 1863.* Lansing, MI: Smith, 1899.
Bennet, L.G., and Wm. H. Haigh. *History of the Thirty Six Illinois.* Aurora, IL: Knickerbocker & Hodder, 1876.
Cater, Douglas John. *As It Was: Reminiscences of a Soldier of the Third Texas Cavalry and the Nineteenth Louisiana Infantry.* Austin, TX: State House Press, 1990.
Clark, Charles T. *Opdycke Tigers, 125th O.V.I.: A History of the Regiment and of the Campaigns and Battles of the Army of the Cumberland.* Columbus, OH: Spahr & Glenn, 1895.
Committee of the 55th Illinois. *The Story of the 55th Regiment IL Volunteer Infantry in the Civil War, 1861–1865.* Clinton, MA: Coulter, 1887.
The Contemporary Review. Vol. 3. London: Strahan, 1868.
Dicks, John A. "More About the Capture of Florence, Ala." *Confederate Veteran* 5 (1897): 214.
Dorset, Sarah A. *Recollections of Henry Watkins Allen, Brigadier-General Confederate States Army, Ex-Governor of Louisiana.* New York: Doolady, and New Orleans: J.A. Gresham, 1866.
Duff, W.H. *Six Months of Prison Life at Camp Chase, Ohio.* Clearwater, SC: Eastern Digital Resources, 2003.
Durham, Ken, ed. "'Dear Rebecca': The Civil War Letters of William Edward Paxton, 1861–1863." *Louisiana History* 20 (Spring 1979): 169–96.
Fitzgerald, Oscar Penn. *John B. Mcferrin: A Biography.* Nashville: Publishing House of the M.E. Church, South, 1888.
"Gen. Albert Sidney Johnston." *Confederate Veteran* 3 (1895): 85.
Gibson, Randall L. "Letter from General R.L. Gibson." *Southern Historical Society Papers* 5 (1878):132–33.
Gustine, Samuel. "Samuel Gustine." *Confederate Veteran* 1 (1916), 467.
Hancock, R.R. *Hancock's Diary: A History of the Second Tennessee Cavalry with Sketches of First and Seventh Battalions; Also Portraits and Biographical Sketches.* Nashville: Brandon, 1887.
Hood, J.B. *Advance and Retreat: Personal Experience in the United States and Confederate States Armies.* Philadelphia: Petridge, 1880.
Inge, F.A. "Corinth, Miss., in War Times." *Confederate Veteran* 9 (1915): 412.
Ives, W.M. "History of the Fourth Florida Regiment." *Confederate Veteran* 4 (1895), 102–103.
Johnston, William Preston. *The Life of Gen. Albert Sidney Johnston.* New York: Appleton, 1878.
Kendall, John S. "The Diary of Surgeon Craig, Fourth Louisiana Regiment, 1864–1865." *Louisiana Historical Quarterly* 8 (January 1925): 53–70.
———. "Recollections of a Confederate Officer." *Louisiana Historical Quarterly* 29 (October 1946): 1041–1228.
Kerwood, Asbury L. *Annals of the Fifty-Seventh Regiment Indiana Volunteers: Marches, Battles and Incidents of Army Life.* Dayton, OH: Shuey, 1868.
Lea, H.J. "With the Fourth Louisiana Battalion." *Confederate Veteran* 27 (1919): 339–340.
Lindsay, R.H. "Capture of Florence, Ala., Under Hood." *Confederate Veteran* 5 (1897): 423.
———. "Seeing the Battle of Franklin." *Confederate Veteran* 9 (1901): 221.
Lockett, S.H. "Surprise and Withdrawal at Shiloh." *Battles and Leaders.* Vol. 1. New York: Century, 1884–1887, 604–606.
Maury, Dabney Herndon. *Recollections of a Virginian in the Mexican, Indian, and Civil Wars.* New York: Scribner's, 1894.
McGrath, John. "In a Louisiana Regiment." *Southern Historical Society Papers* 31 (1903): 103–20.
Newlin, William H., D.H. Lawler, and J.W.

Sherrick. *A History of the Seventy-Third Illinois Infantry Volunteers.* Springfield, IL: Regimental Reunion Association of the Survivors of the 73rd Illinois Infantry Volunteers, 1890.

Richardson, Frank L. "War as I Saw It." *Louisiana Historical Quarterly* 6 (January 1923): 89–106, 223–54.

Russell, William Howard. *The Civil War in America.* London: Trubner, 1861.

Shanklin, James Maynard, and Kenneth P. McCutchan, eds. *Dearest Lizzie: The Civil War Letters of Lt. Col. James Maynard Shanklin.* Evansville, IN: Friends of Willard Library, 1988.

Shellenberger, John K. "With Sheridan's Division at Missionary Ridge." *Sketches of War History, 1861–1865* 4 (1896), 51–67.

Sheridan, Phil. *Personal Memoirs of P.H. Sheridan, General United States Army.* New York: Webster, 1888.

Shoemaker, Randall, ed., *The St. Helena Rifles.* Privately published, 1968.

Supplement to the Official Records of the Union and Confederate Armies. Wilmington, NC: Broadfoot, 1996.

Sutherland, Daniel L., ed. *Reminiscences of a Private: William E. Bevens of the First Arkansas Infantry, C. S.A.* Fayetteville: University of Arkansas Press, 1992.

Tourgee, Albion W. *The Story of a Thousand: Being a History of the Service of the 105th Ohio Volunteer Infantry, in the War for the Union from August 21, 1862, to June 6, 1865.* Buffalo, NY: McGerald & Son, 1896.

Vandiver, Frank E., ed. "A Collection of Louisiana Confederate Letters." *Louisiana Historical Quarterly* 26 (October 1943), 937–974.

Wooster, Ralph, ed. "Four Years in the Confederate Infantry: The Civil War Letters of Private R.F. Eddins, 19th Louisiana." *The Texas Gulf Historical & Biographical Record* 7 (1971), 11–37.

Secondary Books

Allardice, Bruce S. *Confederate Colonels: A Biographical Register.* Columbia and London: University of Missouri Press, 2008.

Arcenaux, William. *Acadian General: Alfred Mouton and the Civil War.* Lafayette: University of Southwestern Louisiana Press, 1981.

Athearn, Robert G., ed., *Soldier in the West: The Civil War Letters of Alfred Lacey Hough.* Philadelphia: University of Pennsylvania Press, 1957.

Bailey, Ronald. *The Civil War: Battles for Atlanta.* Alexandria, VA: Time-Life Books. 1985.

Bartlett, Napier. *Military Record of Louisiana.* Baton Rouge: Louisiana State University Press, 1964.

Bearss, Edwin, and Warren Grabau. *The Battle of Jackson, May 14, 1863/The Siege of Jackson, July 10–17, 1863.* Baltimore: Gateway Press, 1981.

Bergeron, Arthur, Jr. *The Civil War Reminiscences of Major Silas T. Grisamore.* Baton Rouge: Louisiana State University Press, 1993.

_____. *Confederate Mobile.* Oxford: University of Mississippi Press, 1991.

_____. *Guide to Louisiana Confederate Military Units.* Baton Rouge: Louisiana State University Press, 1989.

Connelly, Thomas. *Army of the Heartland.* Baton Rouge: Louisiana State University Press, 1967.

_____. *Autumn of Glory: The Army of Tennessee, 1862–1865.* Baton Rouge: Louisiana State University Press, 1971.

Cooling, Benjamin. *Forts Henry and Donelson: The Key to the Confederate Heartland.* Knoxville: University of Tennessee Press, 1987.

Cozzens, Peter. *No Better Place to Die: The Battle of Stones River.* Urbana: University of Illinois Press, 1990.

_____. *This Terrible Sound: The Battle of Chickamauga.* Urbana: University of Illinois Press, 1992.

_____. *The Shipwreck of Their Hopes: The Battles for Chattanooga.* Urbana: University of Illinois Press, 1994.

Daniel, Larry. *Soldiering in the Army of Tennessee.* Chapel Hill: University of North Carolina Press, 1992.

_____. *Shiloh: The Battle That Changed the War.* New York: Simon & Schuster, 1997.

Davis, William. *Braxton Bragg and Confederate Defeat.* New York: Columbia University Press, 1969.

_____. *John C. Breckinridge: Statesman, Soldier, Symbol.* Baton Rouge: Louisiana State University Press, 1974.

_____. *The Orphan Brigade: The Kentucky Confederates Who Couldn't Go Home.* Baton Rouge: Louisiana State University Press, 1980.

Edmonds, David C. *Yankee Autumn in Acadiana.* Lafayette, LA: Acadiana Press, 1979.

Green, Arthur E. *Southern Boots and Saddles: The Fifteenth Confederate Cavalry C.S.A., First Regiment of Alabama and Florida Cavalry, 1863–1865.* Westminster, MD: Heritage Books, 2005.

Hafendorfer, Kenneth. *Perryville: Battle for Kentucky.* Utica, KY: McDowell, 1981.

Headly, John W. *Confederate Operations in Canada and New York.* New York and Washington: Neale, 1908.

Hearn, Chester G. *Mobile Bay and the Mobile Campaign: The Last Great Battle in the Civil War.* Jefferson, NC: McFarland, 1993.

Howell, Michael F. *Feliciana Confederates: A Compilation of Soldiers of East & West Feliciana*

Parishes; 1861–1865. St. Francisville, LA: Feliciana Confederates, 1989.
Hughes, Nathaniel C. *The Pride of the Confederate Artillery: The Washington Artillery in the Army of Tennessee.* Baton Rouge: Louisiana State University Press, 1997.
Jamie, Perry D., and Grady McWhiney. *Attack and Die: Civil War Military Tactics and the Southern Heritage.* University: University of Alabama Press, 1982.
Jenkins, Kirk C. *The Battle Rages Higher: The Union's 15th Kentucky Infantry.* Lexington: University Press of Kentucky, 2003.
Johnson, John Lipscomb. *The University Memorial Biographical Sketches of Alumni of the University of Virginia Who Fell in the Confederate War,* Five Volumes in One. Baltimore: Turnball Brothers, 1871.
Knauss, William H. *The Story of Camp Chase: A History of Confederate Prisons and Cemeteries.* Nashville and Dallas: Publishing House of the Methodist Episcopal Church, South, 1906.
Lewis, William Terrell. *Genealogy of the Lewis Family in America, from the Middle of the Seventeenth Century Down to the Present Time.* Louisville, KY: Courier-Journal, 1893.
Longacre, Glenn, and John E. Haas, eds., *To Battle for God and the Right: The Civil War Letterbooks of Emerson Opdycke.* Champaign: University of Illinois Press, 2003.
Lonn, Ella. *Foreigners in the Confederacy.* Charlotte: University of North Carolina Press, 2002.
Madaus, Howard, and Robert Needham. *The Battle Flags of the Confederate Army of Tennessee.* Milwaukee: Milwaukee Public Museum, 1976.
McBride, Mary Gorton, and Ann Mathison McLaurin. *Randall Lee Gibson of Louisiana: Confederate General and New South Reformer.* Baton Rouge: Louisiana State University Press, 2007.
McDonough, James Lee. *Shiloh: In Hell Before Night.* Knoxville: University of Tennessee Press, 1977.
_____. *Stones River: Bloody Winter in Tennessee.* Knoxville: University of Tennessee Press, 1980.
_____. *Chattanooga: Death Grip on the Confederacy.* Knoxville: University of Tennessee Press, 1984.
McWhiney, Grady. *Braxton Bragg and Confederate Defeat.* New York: Columbia University Press, 1969.
Merrill, Catherine. *The Soldier of Indiana in the War for the Union.* Vol. 2. New York: Merrill, 1889, 162.
The National Cyclopedia of American Biography Being the History of the United States. Vol. 10. New York: White, 1900.
Noe, Kenneth W. *Perryville: This Grand Havoc of Battle.* Lexington: University Press of Kentucky, 2001.
Overmyer, Jack A. *A Stupendous Effort: The 87th Indiana in the War of the Rebellion.* Bloomington: Indiana University Press, 1997, 100.
Owen, Thomas McAdory, and Marie Bankhead Owen. *History of Alabama and Dictionary of Alabama Biography.* Boston: Harvard University, 1921.
Patrick, Robert. *Reluctant Rebel: The Secret Diary of Robert Patrick, 1861–1865.* Baton Rouge: Louisiana State University Press, 1959.
Retail Clerks International Association, Retail Clerks International Union. *Retail Clerks Advocate* 8 (1953).
Richey, Thomas H. *Tirailleurs: A History of the 4th Louisiana and the Acadians of Company H.* New York: Writers Advantage, 2003.
Roland, Charles. *Albert Sidney Johnston: Soldier of Three Republics.* Austin: University of Texas Press, 1964.
Roman, Alfred. *The Military Operations of General Beauregard in the War Between the States: 1861 to 1865.* New York: Harpers & Brothers, Franklin Square, 1884.
Scriber, Terry G., and Theresea Arnold-Scriber. *The Fourth Louisiana Battalion in the Civil War: A History and Roster.* Jefferson, NC: McFarland, 2008.
Sword, Wiley. *The Confederacy's Last Hurrah: Spring Hill, Franklin & Nashville.* New York: HarperCollins, 1992.
_____. *Mountains Touched with Fire.* New York: St. Martin's Press, 1995.
_____. *Shiloh: Bloody April.* New York: Morrow, 1974.
Warner, Ezra. *Generals in Gray.* Baton Rouge: Louisiana State University Press, 1959.
Woodhead, Henry, ed. *Echoes of Glory: Illustrated Atlas of the Civil War.* Alexandria, VA: Time-Life Books, 1996.

Secondary Articles

Allen, Stacy. "Shiloh!" *Blue & Gray Magazine* 14 (Winter 1997): 7–64.
Bergeron, Arthur, Jr. "Fighting Erupts at Jackson, Mississippi." *Civil War: The Magazine of the Civil War Society* 49 (February 1995): 28–29.
_____. "Tenacity of Soldiers of the Deep South at Murfreesborough." *Civil War: The Magazine of the Civil War Society* 52 (August 1995): 28–29.
_____. "The Twenty-Second Louisiana Consolidated Infantry in the Defense of Mobile, 1864–1865." *Alabama Historical Society* (Fall 1976): 204–13.

———. "Yankee Invaders Caught Unprepared." *Civil War: The Magazine of the Civil War Society*, 53 (October 1995): 36.

Cortright, Vincent. "Last-Ditch Defenders at Mobile." *America's Civil War* 9 (January 1997): 58–64.

DiNardo, Richard, and James Furqueron. "The Day After: Braxton Bragg and the Aftermath of Chickamauga." *North & South* 1 (February 1998): 30–39.

Holder, Ray. "Col. Wesley Parker Winans, C.S.A.: A Character Profile." *Louisiana History* 30 (1989), 280–300.

Miles, Edwin. "The Mississippi Press in the Jackson Era, 1824–1840." *Journal of Mississippi History* 19 (January 1957): 1–20.

Tucker, Glenn. "Chattanooga." *Great Battles of the Civil War*, 390–426. New York: Gallery Books, 1984.

Secondary Unpublished Work

Donald Dixon. "Randall Lee Gibson of Louisiana." Master's thesis, Louisiana State University, 1971.

Index

Numbers in ***bold italics*** indicate pages with photographs.

Adams, Daniel Weisiger 10, 54, 60–62, 65–67, 69–70, 73–76, 79, 82–85, 87–95, 101, 104, 107, 109–115, 119–120, 122, 124, 125, 127–131, 134–135, 154–155, 158, 160, 165, 201
Adams, Samuel 16
Adams, Wirt 54
Airey, Fred 77
Alabama Reservists 223, 227
Allen, Henry Watkins ***11***, 11–13, 22–23, 25, 27, 33, 42, 49–50, ***115***, 116, 176
Anderson, James P. 142, 194, 198
Anderson, John 15
Anderson, Patton 29, 40, 43–44, 54, 56, 65–66, 79, 81, 104, 160, 201
Anderson, Samuel R. 83
Army of Tennessee 79, 84, 100, 102–103, 105, 116, 119, 135, 155–157, 167, 169, 178–179, 183, 203, 205, 214, 219, 223, 234
Army of the Mississippi 10–11, 16, 29, 33, 37, 41, 43, 45, 52, 57, 60–62, 82
Assenheimer, Charles 44
Atlanta, Battle of 181–182, ***182***, ***183***; siege of 190–193; evacuation of 199
Atlanta, Georgia 52, 175
Auguste, Lufoy 42
Austen, John 12
Austin, John E. "Ned" 59–60, 67, ***69***, 92, 95, 130–131, 145–146, 149, 152, 166, 169, 170–171, 200
Austin, Dr. William 59
Austin's Sharpshooters Battalion 59, 61, 62, 67, 69, 73–75, 77, 84, 92–93, 100, 111, 120, 122, 124, 131, 134, 139, 142–143, 145, 151, 153, 159, 166, 169, 172–173, 178, 184, 194, 207–208, 211, 219–220, 223, 229
Avegno, Anatole 6, 27, 33, 50

Baines, Edward 60
Baird, Absalom 132, 134, 192–193

Banner 51
Barnes, Sidney 132
Barrow, Robert H. 11, 13, 59
Bass, John 188, 198, 204
Batchelor, S.S. 158, 166
Bate, William 142, 150, 152, 156, 205
Beatty, John 69–70, 73, 120, 122, 124–125
Beatty, Samuel 211–212
Beauregard, P.G.T. 29, 32, 35, 43, 52, 55, 164, 205
Bein, Hugh 115
Bell, Charles 177, 187, 189
Bell, John 89
Belmont, Battle of 8, 41, 59
Benjamin, Judah 44, 54
Benton, William 224–225
Bevens, William 18, 20, ***20***
Bickham, Thomas ***217***
Big Cane Rifles 38, 40
Biloxi, Mississippi 12
Bishop, Samuel 139, 150, ***159***, 162, 166, 173
Bisland, T. Alexander 200, 208
Blair, Thomas 76, ***130***
Blake, William 89
Blakely, Alabama 222, 228
Blasco, Eugene 149
Bledsoe's Missouri Battery 217–218
Blue, Daniel 41, ***41***
Boulwares and Cox's Wharf 231–232
Boyd, Samuel 51
Bragg, Braxton 3, 10, 18, 21–22, 25, 27–29, 37, 40, 42, 47, 52, 54, 57–60, 63, 65, 75–77, 79, 84–85, 94–95, 101–103, 105–107, 115–117, 119, 131, 135–136, 139–140, 142–143, 150, 152, 155, 164, 222, 234
Brashear City 12
Breaux, Gustavus 177
Breckinridge, John C. 17, 79, 83–85, 88, 95, 98, 101, 103–104, 107, 109, 110, 114, 116, 117, 119–120, 124, 131–132, 136–137, 141–142, 155, 160, 162, 189
Brenigan, Mike 6, 10
Bridge's Illinois Battery 122
Brooks-Baxter War 40
Brown, John C. 65, 181, 183–185
Buckner, Simon 66, 69, 76, 136
Buell, Don 63, 65
Buford, "Abe" 217
Buie, Duncan F. 169
Burnside, Ambrose 117
Burrell, Stephen 82
Butler, E.G.W. 59
Butler, Loudon 127, 162

Caddo Guards 55
Caddo 10th 15
Camp Benjamin 39, 44
Camp Chalmette 7, 15, 39
Camp Chase 232
Camp Dick Robinson 77
Camp Hurricane 114
Camp Moore 4, 6–8, 12–13, 15, 33, 38–39, 49–50, 115, 163
Camp Townsend 231
Camp Walker 4, 11–12
Campbell, Archibald P. 119
Campbell, Eloy ***184***
Campbell, Francis L. 104, 145–146, 149–153, ***161***–162, 166, 173, 200, 208, 218, 220, 222–227, 229
Campbell, Leon ***48***
Canby, R.S. 222–226, 227, 229
Candy, Charles 170–172
Carraway, J.E. 158, 169–171, 175
Castor Guards 38
Cater, Douglas ***15***, 52, 112, 179, 188, 193, 204–205, 214, 219, 228–229, 233
Cater, Rufus ***15***, ***127***
Chalaron, Adolphe 130
Chalmers, James 35, 88, 94, 104, 217
Chalmette Regiment 229
Chattanooga, Siege of 139–154; defense of Missionary Ridge 141–152; brigade losses at 153

255

Index

Chattanooga, Tennessee 52, 54, 62, 79, 82, 106, 109, 116–117, 119, 134–135, 203
Chattanooga Rebel 102
Cheatham, Benjamin Franklin 32–33, 102–103, 132, 179, 181–182
Chicago Times 119
Chickamauga, Battle of 120–*121*, 122–134; brigade losses at 134
Christian, James 147
Cincinnati Commercial 189
Citronelle, Alabama 113, 228
Claiborne Volunteers 163
Clark, Alfred 209, 227
Clayton, Henry 137, 167, 169, 173, 179, 181, 183, 188, 190–194, 196, 198, 205–206, 208–209, 211–212, 214, 216–218
Clayton, John 232
Cleburne, Patrick 40, 70, 73, 83, 103, 107, 120, 165, 205
Cobb, Howell 189
Cobb's Kentucky Battery 112, 120, 142, 151–152
Columbus, Kentucky 8, 10, 41, 48
Confederate Veteran 234
Conscription Act of 1862 40, 46–47, 49
Cooper, Samuel 58–59, 115–116, 139, 158
Coppen's Zouave Battalion 55
Corinth, Mississippi 8, 10, 13, 15, 16, 20, 33, 35–37, 40–41, 44–46, 54, 56, 58, 158, 219
Cox's Tenth Indiana Battery 86–90, 92, 165
Crescent Regiment (Twenty-Fourth Louisiana Infantry) 10, 35, 39
Croxton, John 206
Cruft, Charles 23, 35, 98, 100
Cuba Station, Alabama 228–229
Cullen, Francis 234
Cumberland Gap 77
Cunningham, E.H. 169, 184–185

Daily Constitutional 155
Daily Evansville Journal 165
Daily Herald 189
Dalton, Georgia 119, 155, 166
Davidson, Thomas 15, 46
Davis, Jefferson 79, 103, 106, 107, 136–138, 155, 179, 203
Deas, James *137*
Deas, Zachariah 194, 196
Delta Rifles 12
Dennis, Elias 225
Devilbiss, Andrew 207, *207*
Dicks, John 208
Dilworth, W.S. 124
disease 7, 13–15, 41, 46, 56
Dixon, William *186*
Dodge, Joseph 125
Donelson, Daniel 88, 91
Dreaux's First Louisiana Battalion 13, 54, 59, 156
Dresel, Alexander 57, 200, 208, 219
Dubroca, Edgar Martin 31, 33, 106, 115, 128, 161–162, *162*

Duff, William H. 192, 231
Dunlap, Henry 152
Dunn, John 60
Dupre, Lucius J. 160

Ector, Matthew 227
Eddins, R.F. 15, 51, 188
Eighteenth Alabama Infantry 216–218
Eighteenth Louisiana Infantry 10–11, 37, 39, 41, 43, 45, 52, 54, 160
Eighteenth Missouri Infantry 22
Eighteenth Ohio Infantry 100, 125, 127
Eighteenth Wisconsin Infantry 22
Eighth Arkansas Infantry 158
Eighth Iowa Infantry 27
Eighth Kentucky Mounted Infantry 218
Eighty-Eighth Illinois Infantry 150
Eighty-Eighth Indiana Infantry 74, 122, 125, 127
Eleventh Indiana Infantry 32, 224
Eleventh Kentucky Infantry (U.S.) 97
Eleventh Louisiana Infantry 10, 41, 43, 52, 57–60, 159, 200
Eleventh Michigan Infantry 125, 127, 129, 147
Elliott, Washington 211–212
Ellis, E. John 49, 75, 78, 95, 137, *148*, 149, 233
Emmett, Ross 181
Estell, Oscar 232
Estep's Eighth Indiana Battery 86
Eustis, Cartwright 213
Ezra Church, Battle of 183–*185*, 186–189, *190*; brigade losses at 188–189

Fagan, James F. 15, *16*, 22–23, 27, 32, 40
Farmington, Battle of 43–44, 56
Favrot, H.M. 27
Fenner's Louisiana Battery 156
Fifteenth Confederate Cavalry 113
Fifteenth Indiana Infantry 86, 91, 93, 94, 151, 153
Fifteenth Kentucky Infantry 67, 70, 73, 122, 125
Fifteenth Missouri Infantry 86, 89, 146
Fifth Kentucky Infantry (U.S.) 129
Fifth Louisiana Battalion 58
Fifth Ohio Infantry 170–171
Fifty-Eighth Alabama Infantry 137, 169
Fifty-Eighth Indiana Infantry 86, 94
Fifty-Fifth Illinois Infantry 194, 196–197
Fifty-First Tennessee Infantry 88
Fifty-Seventh Indiana Infantry 86, 91, 93–94
Fifty-Seventh Ohio Infantry 194, 196–197
Finley, Jesse 142–143, 145, 149–150

First Arkansas Infantry 11, 15–17, 20, 22–23, 27, 31, 35, 40
First Florida Infantry 124, 142, 149, 150
First Illinois Light Artillery 195
First Louisiana Artillery 4
First Louisiana Heavy Artillery 228
First Louisiana Regulars 10, 13, 54, 57, 59, 61, 158, 162, 166, 176, 178, 183, 194, 200, 208, 220, 223, 228, 229
First Ohio Artillery, Battery G 212
Fisk, Stuart W. 54, *55*, 56, 81, 88, 90, 161, 201
flags 162–166, 188–189, 196, 214, 232
Florence, Alabama 206–207, 209
Flourney, Thomas B. 15
Flournoy, Camp 51, 200, 201, 208, 220, 222–223
Ford, Chauncy 229
Forrest, Nathan Bedford 83, 131, 205, 208
Fort Blair 222, 225–226
Fort DeRussy 50
Fort Donelson 8, 10, 60, 177
Fort Gaines 82
Fort Henry 8
Fort McDermott 222–226
Fort Morgan 82, 223
Fort Pillow 41, 82
Fort St. John Phillip 44
Fortieth Indiana Infantry 94, 152
Fortin, Louis 177, *192*, 193
Forty-First Alabama Infantry 97
Forty-Fourth Illinois Infantry 86, 89, 143
Forty-Fourth Tennessee Infantry 66, 75
Forty-Second Illinois Infantry 143
Forty-Second Indiana Infantry 67, 69, 74–75, 122, 125, 165
Forty-Seventh Indiana Infantry 224–225
Forty-Sixth Ohio Infantry 187–188
Fourteenth Iowa Infantry 27
Fourth Florida Infantry 142, 145
Fourth Kentucky Infantry 97, 107
Fourth Louisiana Battalion 137–139, 142, 150, 153, 162, 166, 169, 178, 183, 188, 208–209, 220, 223, 225, 226, 229, 232, 233
Fourth Louisiana Infantry 10–11, 18, 20–22, 25, 28, 33, 35, 40, 42, 49, 116, 166, *167*, 175–176, 178, 188, 190, 192, 194, 196, 198, 200, 203–204, 208, 216, 219–220, 223, 229
Fourth Ohio Cavalry 82
Fourth Tennessee Cavalry (U.S.) 217
Fourth Tennessee Infantry 21
French, Samuel 110
Fulton, John 66

Gadsden, Alabama 205, 219
Gall, Jacob 165
Garibaldi, Giuseppe 11
Gauthier, Anatole *177*

Index

Geary, John 169, 171–172
Geddes, James L. 27, 227
Gerard, Aristide 6, 50, 161–162
Gibson, John F. 56
Gibson, Randall L. 3, *5*, 10–11, 17–18, 20–23, 25, 27–29, 31–32, 35, 37–38, 40, 78–81, 88, 90–32, 95, 97, 102–106, 115, 124, 127–128, 130, 132, 134–137, 139–143, 145–147, 149–153, 155–156, *157*, 158, 161–163, 167, 169, 171–173, 174–175, 178, 182, 185–186, 188, 192–193, 195–196, 198–201, 203, 205–206, 208–209, 211–212, 214, 216–218, 220, 222–*223*, 224–229, 232, *233*, 234
Gibson, W.H. 100
Gilbert, Charles C. 75–76
Gist, States R. 132
Gladden, Adley 54
Gladden, Henry 158
Gladden Rifles 7
Gleason, Newell 192
Gober, Daniel 38, *39*, 40–41, 43–44, 51, 122, 127–128, 143, 145–147, 152–153, 160–161, 201
Governor's Guards (Avegno's Zouaves) 6, 7, 161
Grand Junction, Tennessee 13
Granger, Gordon 146, 224
Grant, Ulysses S. 8, 29, 39, 44, 55, 109, 138, 140, 142, 169, 233
Graves, Rice 111
Grider, Benjamin 97, 98
Grisamore, Silas 41, 45
Grose, William 125
Guillet, Charles 51, 80, 95, 97–98, 105
Gustine, Samuel 232

Hagen, James 54
Hammond, John H. 216
Hanson, Roger 95, 97
Hardee, William 17, 18, 20, 54, 62, 65–66, 79, 81, 102–104, 106–107, 109, 117, 154–155, 165, 181, 191, 194, 196, 199
Hargrove, A.C. 223
Harker, Charles G. 143, 145, 147, 149–152
Harper's Weekly 189
Harrar, F.H. Jr. 158
Harris, John 42, 46
Harris, Leonard 67, 73–74, 76, 82
Hascall, Milo 86
Hays, Harry 169
Hazen, William 86, 88, 94, 98, 194–195
Headly, John 69, 74
Helm, Benjamin 107, 109, 120, 124, 132
Henderson, Thomas 138
Henry Marshall Guards 13
Hickenlooper's Fifth Ohio Battery 27–28, 112–113
Hicks, Borden 129
Hightower, S.A. 188
Hill, Daniel H. 117, 119, 136, 155

Hindman, Thomas 28, 120, 142, 166
Hodge, Benjamin L. 13, 14, *14*, 23, 25, 29, 33, 35, 51
Hodgson, Washington I. 35, 60
Hollingsworth, James M. 13, 15, 33, 51
Hollow Tree Gap 214, *215*, 216–217
Holtzclaw, James 181, 183–184, 211–212, 216, 218, 227
Hood, John Bell 169, 178–179, 181–182, 190, 193, 199, 200, 203–206, 208–209, 213, 219, 220
Hooker, Joseph 167, 169, 171–173
Hotchkiss' Second Minnesota Artillery 74
Hovey, Alvin 32
Hulbert, Stephen 22
Hunter, Samuel 33
Hunter, Samuel E. *170*, 176, 179, 196, 198, 200, 204, 208–209, 216, 219

Island No. 10 41, 43, 58

Jackson, John K. 84, 86, 132, 134, 140
Jackson, William *214*
Jackson, Mississippi 107, 109, 138
Jackson Campaign 109–114; brigade losses at 114
Jackson Regiment 58
Jacques, John 158
Jameson Light Guards 162
Jenkins, Donelson 17, 22, 25, 33
Johnson, Bushrod 66, 67, 69, 75, 211
Johnson, Carter 55
Johnson, Charles 8, 59
Johnson, Richard 217–218
Johnson, Richard W. 143
Johnston, Albert Sidney 3, 8, 10, 17–18, 29, 39
Johnston, Joseph E. 103, 107, 109–110, 114, 116, 154–155, 163, 164, 165, *167*, 167, 189, 228–229, 231
Johnston, William Preston 3, 104, 106, 154, 234
Jones, Bush 169, 171–173, 181, 194
Jones, Dudley W. 169
Jones, H.P. 200
Jones, James 67
Jones, Sam 83
Jones, Theodore 194–196
Jones, Tom 65
Jones, Wells 194, 197
Jonesboro, Battle of 194–*195*, 196, *197*, 198; brigade losses at 198

Keachi Warriors 15
Kearney, Thomas 139
Keen, Robert 173
Kendall, John 33, 175, 204, 219
Kennedy, Hyder 127, 162, 163, 166, 173, 188, 189
Kennedy, J.B.G. 57–58
Kennedy, William 42, 52

Kimball, John 113, 130
Kimball, Nathan 211
King, H. 125, 134
Knefler, Frederick 213
Knipe, Joseph 216–218

Labouisse, John 130, *131*
Lafayette, Georgia 119
Lafitte, R.L. 134
Laibolt, Bernard 89–90
Landry, Trasimond *216*
Lane, John 152, 212
Lauman, Jacob 22, 110, 112
La Vergne, Battle of 83
Lea, H.J. 138
Lee, Robert E. 229, 231
Lee, Stephen D. 183, 186, 190, 193–194, 196, 198–199, 204, 206, 208, 211, 216
Lee & Gordon's Mill 119–120
Lewis, Joseph (Sixth Kentucky) 97, 100
Lewis, Joseph C. 54–55, 81, 161, 166, 173, 196–197, 201
Liddell, St. John 132, 223
Lightburn, Joseph 181
Lindsay, Robert H. 51, 81, 90, 113, 206, 208–209, 213, 220, 223–225, 229
Lingan, James 59, *160*
Lipscomb, A.A. 97
Lipscomb, Albert 60
Little Rock, Arkansas 15–16
Lockett, Samuel H. 25
London Times 6
Longstreet, James 136, 179
Loomis, John 43
Loomis' First Michigan Light Battery 66, 69, 74
Louisiana Volunteers 44
Louisville, Kentucky 15
Love, Louis 186–188
Lovejoy Station, Georgia 199, 203
Lovell, Mansfield 10, 55
Lowd, W.Q. 124, 208
Lytle, William H. 66, 67, 69–70, 73, 76, 175

Magruder, John 50
Maney, George 132
Manigault, Arthur 181
Marks, Samuel F. 58–59
Marler, John 13
Martin, A.T. 200, 211, 219
Mason, Enoch 38, 51
Maury, Dabney 222–223, 226, 228, 232
Maury, Henry 81–82, 88–90, 92, 107, 113, *113*
Maxey, Samuel 82, 178
McAuley, John R. *50*
McCall's Battery 143
McCook, George 119
McCown, John 102
McEnery, John 138, 166, 169, 233
McFerrin, John B. 157
McGrath, John 6, 10, 22, 83, 89, 91, 95, 139, 156–157

McKenzie's Eufaula Battery 143, 147, 211, 214
McKinstry, Alexander **81**–83
McLaughlin, John 225
McMahan, Jesse 23
McNeil, John 138
McPherson, James 181
Mellon, W.F. 201
Memphis, Tennessee 10, 16, 55
Meridian, Mississippi 209, 228–229, 231–232
Mexican-American War 16, 56
Miller, C.C. 58
Miller, John 83
Miller, Madison 22
Mire, E. Camille 41
Mobile, Alabama 52, 54, 82, 107, 109, 113, 200, 219, 223, 228
Mobile Advertiser 155
Mobile Register 42
Moore, Calvin H. 201
Moore, J.C. 40
Moore, Marshall 147, 149–150
Moore, Thomas O. 4, 54, 59
Morgan, Asa 35
Morton, Mississippi 114–155
Morton, Quin 23
Moses, B. 228
Mouton, Alfred 37, 41, 52
Munch's Battery 20, 23
Munfordville, Kentucky 63
Murfreesboro, Battle of 84, **85**, 86–100; brigade losses at 94, 100–101
Murphy, Elias **149**
Murphy, James 7, 160

Nashville, Battle of 209–**210**, 211–**213**, 214; brigade losses at 216
Negley, James 83
Nesom, Abraham 39
New Hope Church, Battle of 169–173; brigade losses at 216
New Orleans, Louisiana 4, 6–8, 33, 37, 39, 42, 44, 49, 54–55, 57–58, 60, 11–13, 177
Newton, A.C. 225–226
Nineteenth Illinois Infantry 125, 127, 129, 147, 156
Nineteenth Louisiana Infantry 10–11, 13, 15, 18, 20, 22–23, 28–29, 31, 33, 35, 40, 42–43, 45–46, 51–52, 54, 106–107, 110, 112, 114, 117, 120, 124, 127–128, 130, 137, 139, 142, 145, 150, 153, 158–159, 161–163, 166, **167**, 169, 172–173, 175, 178–179, 183, 188, 191, 194, 200, 204–205, 208, 214, 220, 223, 229
Nineteenth Ohio Infantry 97–98
Nineteenth Pennsylvania Cavalry 216
Nineteenth Tennessee Infantry 142–143, 147
Ninetieth Ohio Infantry 100
Ninety-Seventh Ohio Infantry 152
Ninth Indiana Cavalry 217–218
Ninth Indiana Infantry 86, 89

Ninth Kentucky Infantry 107
Ninth Kentucky Infantry (U.S.) 97
Ninth Louisiana Battalion 51
Ninth Pennsylvania Cavalry 119
Noel Guards 44
Norton Guards 7

O'Leary, Stephen 10, 27, 33, 50, 81, 161
Oliver, John 185–186, 188
One Hundred Fifth Ohio Infantry 129
One Hundred Forty-Eighth Infantry 170
One Hundred Fourth Illinois Infantry 122, 125
One Hundred Sixteenth Illinois Infantry 194
One Hundred Tenth Illinois Infantry 86, 91, 93
One Hundred Third Illinois Infantry 187–188
One Hundred Twenty-Fifth Ohio Infantry 146, 150–151, 214
One Hundred Twenty-Seventh Illinois Infantry 194, 196
One Hundredth Illinois Infantry 86, 91, 93
Opdycke, Emerson 146, 152, 211–214
Orillion, Joseph H. **224**
Orleans Cadets 59
Orleans Guards Battalion 10, 177
Osburn's First Ohio Artillery 86, 94
Ouachita Blues 138

Packwood, George H. 49
Packwood Rifles 49
Palmer, John 43, 83, 190
Patrick, Robert 12, 13, 176
Paxton, William 20, 41, 46
Peabody, Everett 18, 22
Pegues, Thomas 207, 233–234
Pelican Regiment 229
Pemberton, John C. 104
Pennington, William 49, 219
Perryville, Battle of 65–**68**, 69–76; brigade losses at 76
Person, Michael 145
Pettus, Edmund 211–214, 216
Peyton, Thomas W. 59
Phillips, J.W. 223
Pickett Cadets 177
Picolet, Arthur 189, 208, 219
Pillow, Gideon 95, 98
Pittman, James 38
Plummer, J.B. 43
Polk, Leonidas 8, 13, 17, 43, 54–55, 58, 62–63, 65, 79–80, 85–87, 102–103, 131, 158, 160, 175
Pollard, Alabama 54, 106, 224
Pond, Preston 29, 31, 37–**38**, 39–41
Pope, Curran 70
Pope, John 43
Post, Sidney 211–212
Powell, Samuel 65–66, 76
Prentiss, Benjamin 18, 22, 29
Preston, William 95, 98, 104
prisoner exchange 158–159, 229, 231

Provost, George **230**
Pugh, Isaac 110–113
Pugh, Robert 115

Quarles, William 176
Quirk, William 200

Randolph, George 80
Raxsdale, Frank 201, **201**
Rector, Henry 15–16
Reichard, Augustus 10, 44–45, **45**, 52, 54, 106–107, 115
Reichard Rifles 44
religious revival 157
Resaca, Battle of 167, 169
Rheams, Lawson **187**
Richard Musketeers 177
Richardson, Frank 6–8
Rogers, J.S. 114
Rosecrans, William 83, 116–117, 119–120, 131, 135
Rosedale Guards 60
Ross, Emmett 169, 174
Rousseau, Lovell 67, 73074, 76
Ruggles, Daniel 10–11, 15, 29, 31–32, 39, 41, 43–44, 201
Russell, Robert 41
Russell, William H. 6

St. Mary Volunteers 7
Savage, John 88
Sayne, Philip 76
Schaefer, Frederick 86, 89
Schofield, John 190–192
Scott, E.M. 66
Scott, Samuel 56, **77**
Scott, Winfrey 128, 145, 150
Scribner, Benjamin 125, 132
Second Kentucky Infantry 97, 100, 107
Second Missouri Infantry 86, 89–90
Seddon, James 104, 155
Seventeenth Louisiana Infantry 10–11, 39
Seventeenth Missouri Infantry 185–186
Seventeenth Tennessee Infantry 107
Seventh Florida Infantry 142
Seventh Ohio Infantry 170–171
Seventh Vermont Infantry 225
Seventieth Ohio Infantry 186–187
Seventy-Fourth Illinois Infantry 146, 150
Seventy-Third Illinois Infantry 86, 89–90, 143
Shaver, R.G. 18
Sheridan, Phillip 76, 86, 143, 146, 150, 152, 165
Sherman, Francis T. 143, 145–147, 150–152
Sherman, William T. 18, 32, 44, 109–110, 167, 174, 179, 183, 190, 193, 204–205, 219
Shields, Thomas **176**, 177–178, 187, 189
Shiloh, Battle of 17–**19**, 20–36; brigade losses at 35
Ship Island, Mississippi 231

Index

Shreveport, Louisiana 15, 55
Shreveport Greys 13
Simonson's Fifth Indiana Battery 67, 69, 74
Sixteenth Louisiana Infantry 10–11, 37–40, 42–43, 46, 49, 61, 70, 73, 75, 76, 78, 80–81, 84, 88–90, 92, 94–95, 97–98, 100–101, 105, 107, 109–111, 113–114, 120, 122, 125, 127–129, 132, 134, 137, 139–140, 142–143, 145, 147, 149, 153, 156, 159, 161, **163**, 164, 166, 172–173, 178, 183, 192, 194, 196–198, 201, 204, 207–209, 213, 217, 218, 220, 223, 229, 234
Sixteenth Tennessee Infantry 88
Sixth Kentucky Infantry 97, 100, 107
Sixth Louisiana Battalion 44
Sixtieth North Carolina Infantry 149
Sixty-Fourth Ohio Infantry 146, 150–151
Sixty-Ninth Ohio Infantry 147
Sixty-Sixth Ohio Infantry 170
Slack, James 224
slavery 14–15, 41–43, 189, 226–227
Slocomb, Cuthbert H. 60, 66–67, 70, **71**, 73, 75, 79, 111–114, 120, 124, 128, 131, 152, 223
Smith, Andrew 211
Smith, Austin 226, 229
Smith, Edmund Kirby 62, 65, 77, 102
Smith, Milo 181
Smith, Morgan 92
Smith, Morgan L. 31–32, 181
Smith, Thomas 156
Smith, Zachariah 150
Southern Celts 7
Spanish Fort, Siege of 222–229; brigade losses at 226, 228
Stagg, Louis 38–39, 46
Standford's Battery 211–212
Stanley, Timothy 98, 125, 128–129, 131
Steedman, James 212
Stengel, Henry **47**
Sterns, Riley 226
Steuben Guards 44
Stevenson, Carter 140, 167, 209, 211, 213, 218
Stewart, Alexander P. 18, 20–21, 137, 140–141, 143, 145, 147, 153, 155, 157, 165, 167, 170, 173–174, 179, 203
Stoughton, William 125, 143, 147
Stovall, Marcellus 113, 120, 124–125, 130–132, 155, 165, 169, 173–174, 181, 214, 216, 218
Strahl, Otho F. 142–143, 145–146, 165
Strawbridge, James 158
Streight, Abel 212
Stuart, A.L. 151
Sumter Regiment 176
Sutter, Samuel 162, 208
Swain, Andy 111, **112**

Tammure, Roger 101
Taylor, Richard 50, 200, 229
Tenth Indiana Cavalry 216–217
Tenth Ohio Infantry 67, 70, 73, 175
Tenth Tennessee Cavalry (U.S.) 206
Third Dismounted Florida Cavalry 124, 142, 149, 150
Third Iowa Infantry 112
Third Kentucky Infantry (U.S.) 152
Third Missouri Infantry 185
Third Ohio Infantry 66–67, 69, 70, 73
Thirteenth Arkansas Infantry 21
Thirteenth Louisiana Infantry 6–8, 10, 12, 18, 20, 22–23, 25, 27, 29, 31, 33, 35, 37, 40, 42, 45, 50, 54, 60–61, 63, 75, 80, 83–84, 88–91, 94–95, 97–98, 100–101, 104–107, 114–115, 117, 120, 122, 125, 127–128, 132, 134, 139–140, 142–143, 145–146, 149, **151**–153, 156, 159–162, 166, **167**, 173, 178, 183, 186–187, **190**, 194, 198, 201, 208, 214, 220, 222–223, 229, 232, 234
Thirtieth Louisiana Battalion 166, 176–178, 183, 186–189, 194, 200, 205, 208, 216, 219, 223, 229
Thirtieth Ohio Infantry 198
Thirty-Eighth Illinois Infantry 76
Thirty-Eighth Tennessee Infantry 39
Thirty-First Indiana Infantry 25, 100
Thirty-First Missouri Infantry 185
Thirty-Fourth Kentucky Infantry 160
Thirty-Ninth Georgia Infantry 214
Thirty-Ninth North Carolina Infantry 88, 91
Thirty-Second Alabama Infantry 81–83, 88–90, 92, 94–95, 100, 107, 110, 112–113, 117, 120, 122, 124, 130, 132, 134, 137, 139, 166, 169
Thirty-Second Indiana Infantry 100, 160
Thirty-Second Missouri Infantry 189
Thirty-Sixth Alabama Infantry 173
Thirty-Sixth Illinois Infantry 143, 150, 151
Thirty-Third Missouri Infantry 185
Thomas, Bryan 223, 227
Thomas, George 132, 154, 166, 205
Thompson, James 27–28
Thompson's Ninth Indiana Battery 31
Thurber's First Missouri Battery 31–32
Tidwell, David **116**
Tourgee, Albion 129–130
Tracy, Michael O. 162, 222
Trask, W.L. 62, 70, 74–76
Trepagnier, Francis O. 187, 229
Tulane University, New Orleans 234

Tullahoma, Tennessee 79, 82, 101, 104, 106, 116
Tupelo, Mississippi 45–46, 52, 106, 219–220
Turner, Richard W. 51, 124, 162, 188
Turner Guards 44
Tuttle, James 22–23
Twelfth Michigan Battalion 160
Twelfth Michigan Infantry 22
Twelfth Missouri Infantry 185–186
Twelfth Tennessee Cavalry (U.S.) 206
Twentieth Louisiana Infantry 10, 44–45, 51, 57–58, 60–62, 75, 77, 80, 84, 88–91, 94–95, 97–98, 100, 104–107, 110, 114–115, 117, 120, 122, 125, 127–128, 132, 134, 139–140, 142–143, 145, 149, 151–153, 156, 159–162, 166, 173–174, 178–179, 183, 188, 194, 200–201, 203, 208–09, 219, 220, 222–223, 229
Twenty-Eighth Pennsylvania Infantry 170–171
Twenty-Fifth Louisiana Infantry 54–56, 61, 75, 80–81, 84, 88–90, 92, 94–95, 97–98, 100–101, 105, 107, 110–111, 113–114, 120, 122, 125, 127–129, 132, 134, 139–140, 142–143, 145, 147, 149, 153, 156, 159, 161, **163**, 166, 172–173, 178, 183, 192, 194, 196, 197–198, 201, 204, 208–209, 220, 223, 229, **231**
Twenty-Fifth Tennessee Infantry 66, 75
Twenty-First Louisiana Infantry 44, 57–59
Twenty-First Missouri Infantry 22
Twenty-Fourth Indiana Infantry 32
Twenty-Fourth Tennessee Infantry 142
Twenty-Ninth Missouri Infantry 185–186
Twenty-Second Consolidated Louisiana Infantry 222, 228
Twenty-Second Illinois Infantry 150
Twenty-Sixth Illinois Infantry 43
Twenty-Sixth Ohio Infantry 153
Twenty-Third Missouri Infantry 23
Tyner's Station, Tennessee 117, 119

U.S. Frontier Regiments 160
United States Military Academy, Maryland 161
Utoy Creek, Battle of 191–193

Vance Guards 51
Van Cleve, Horatio 97–98, 100
Van Derveer, Ferdinand 125
Van Dorn, Earl 20
Vass, R.C. 60
Vaught, W.C.D. 88, 93, **93**, 95, 100
Veatch, James 224–225
Vertner, Aaron 20
Vick, Thomas 49

Vickers, John 42
Ville Platte, Louisiana 40

Wagner, George 86–87, 91, 93, 149, 151–153, 186, 188
Walcutt, Charles 186, 188
Walker, Lucius M. 37, 40–41, 43–44, 54
Walker, W.H.T. 116, 131, 138, 140
Walker, William 51, 81
Wallace, Lew 31
Walton, George 127
Wangelin, Hugo 185–189
Wartrace, Tennessee 106–107, 109
Washington Artillery, 5th Company 10, 35, 60–61, 66–67, 70, *73*, 74, 76, 78, *84*, 93, 109–110, 112–114, 131–132, 134, 137, 152, 165–166, 223, 225
Waterhouse's First Illinois Light Artillery 18
Watson, Clement 225–226
West, Douglas 200
Western Military Institute 6, 15
Willbanks, Thomas 153
Williams, Alpheus 172
Willich, August 125
Wilson, C.C. 138
Wilson, James 232
Wimberly, T.H. 49, 52
Winans, Wesley P. 13, 15, 35, 46–47, 51, 137, 145, 153, ***153***, 162
Wingfield, James 49

Withers, Jones 33, 82, 102–103, 158
Wolf, Gustave 209
Womack, J.K. 49
Wood, Gustavus 91
Wood, S.A.M. 18, 31–32
Wood, Thomas J. 86, 93
Woods, Charles 181
Woods, Thomas 211, 213
Wright, Marcus 132

Zacharie, Frank C. 55, 90, ***90***, 92, 95, 97, 100, 210, 203, 208–209, 220, 223, 229, 232
Zinken, Leon von 44, 51, 80, 104–***105***, 106, 132, 134, 136, 161–162, 184–185, 189, 222

www.ingramcontent.com/pod-product-compliance
Lightning Source LLC
Chambersburg PA
CBHW060258240426
43661CB00060B/2828